IARIA

AA004345

ICN 2017

The Sixteenth International Conference on Networks

SOFTNETWORKING 2017

The International Symposium on Advances in Software Defined Networking and Network Functions Virtualization

April 23 - 27, 2017

Venice, Italy

ICN 2017 Editors

Carlos Becker Westphall, University of Santa Catarina, Brazil

Eugen Borcoci, University "Politehnica" of Bucharest (UPB), Romania

Wouter Tavernier, Ghent University - imec, IDLab - Department of Information Technology, Belgium

Paolo Secondo Crosta, Head of Collaborative Research Projects, Italtel S.p.A. - Milan, Italy

Nivia Cruz Quental, Universidade Federal de Pernambuco, Brazil

Cristian Anghel, Telecommunications Department, University Politehnica of Bucharest, Romania

Printed from e-media with permission by:

Curran Associates, Inc.
57 Morehouse Lane
Red Hook, NY 12571

Some format issues inherent in the e-media version may also appear in this print version.

Printed by Curran Associates, Inc. (2017)

International Academy, Research, and Industry Association (IARIA)
412 Derby Way
Wilmington, DE 19810

Phone: (408) 893-6407
Fax: (408) 527-6351

petre@iaria.org

Additional copies of this publication are available from:

Curran Associates, Inc.
57 Morehouse Lane
Red Hook, NY 12571 USA
Phone: 845-758-0400
Fax: 845-758-2633
Email: curran@proceedings.com
Web: www.proceedings.com

TABLE OF CONTENTS

ICN 1: NETWORKING I

ICN 2: COMPUTATION AND NETWORKING

ICN 3: COMMUNICATION

ICN 4: NETWORKING II

ICN 5: NGN AND NETWORK MANAGEMENT

ICN 6 / AAFAA: ADVANCES IN ADAPTIVE FILTERING FOR ACOUSTIC APPLICATIONS

ICN 7 / DMM: DISTRIBUTED MOBILITY MANAGEMENT – TOWARDS EFFICIENT AND SCALABLE MOBILE NETWORKS

SOFTNETWORKING 1: SOFTWARE DEFINED NETWORKING

SOFTNETWORKING 2 / SDNNFV: CONTROL, SCALABILITY AND PERFORMANCE

ICN 2017

Forward

The Sixteenth International Conference on Networks (ICN 2017), held between April 23-27, 2017 in Venice, Italy, continued a series of events targeting general networking and services aspects in multi-technologies environments. The conference covered fundamentals on networking and services, and highlighted new challenging industrial and research topics. Network control and management, multi-technology service deployment and assurance, next generation networks and ubiquitous services, emergency services and disaster recovery and emerging network communications and technologies were considered.

IPv6, the Next Generation of the Internet Protocol, has seen over the past three years tremendous activity related to its development, implementation and deployment. Its importance is unequivocally recognized by research organizations, businesses and governments worldwide. To maintain global competitiveness, governments are mandating, encouraging or actively supporting the adoption of IPv6 to prepare their respective economies for the future communication infrastructures. In the United States, government's plans to migrate to IPv6 has stimulated significant interest in the technology and accelerated the adoption process. Business organizations are also increasingly mindful of the IPv4 address space depletion and see within IPv6 a way to solve pressing technical problems. At the same time IPv6 technology continues to evolve beyond IPv4 capabilities. Communications equipment manufacturers and applications developers are actively integrating IPv6 in their products based on market demands.

IPv6 creates opportunities for new and more scalable IP based services while representing a fertile and growing area of research and technology innovation. The efforts of successful research projects, progressive service providers deploying IPv6 services and enterprises led to a significant body of knowledge and expertise. It is the goal of this workshop to facilitate the dissemination and exchange of technology and deployment related information, to provide a forum where academia and industry can share ideas and experiences in this field that could accelerate the adoption of IPv6. The workshop brings together IPv6 research and deployment experts that will share their work. The audience will hear the latest technological updates and will be provided with examples of successful IPv6 deployments; it will be offered an opportunity to learn what to expect from IPv6 and how to prepare for it.

Packet Dynamics refers broadly to measurements, theory and/or models that describe the time evolution and the associated attributes of packets, flows or streams of packets in a network. Factors impacting packet dynamics include cross traffic, architectures of intermediate nodes (e.g., routers, gateways, and firewalls), complex interaction of hardware resources and protocols at various levels, as well as implementations that often involve competing and conflicting requirements.

Parameters such as packet reordering, delay, jitter and loss that characterize the delivery of packet streams are at times highly correlated. Load-balancing at an intermediate node may, for example, result in out-of-order arrivals and excessive jitter, and network congestion may manifest as packet losses or large jitter. Out-of-order arrivals, losses, and jitter in turn may lead to unnecessary retransmissions in TCP or loss of voice quality in VoIP.

With the growth of the Internet in size, speed and traffic volume, understanding the impact of underlying network resources and protocols on packet delivery and application performance has assumed a critical importance. Measurements and models explaining the variation and interdependence of delivery characteristics are crucial not only for efficient operation of networks and network diagnosis, but also for developing solutions for future networks.

Local and global scheduling and heavy resource sharing are main features carried by Grid networks. Grids offer a uniform interface to a distributed collection of heterogeneous computational, storage and network resources. Most current operational Grids are dedicated to a limited set of computationally and/or data intensive scientific problems.

Optical burst switching enables these features while offering the necessary network flexibility demanded by future Grid applications. Currently ongoing research and achievements refers to high performance and computability in Grid networks. However, the communication and computation mechanisms for Grid applications require further development, deployment and validation.

The conference had the following tracks:

- Networking
- Computation and Networking
- Communication
- Next generation networks (NGN) and network management
- Advances in Adaptive Filtering for Acoustic Applications
- DMM: Distributed Mobility Management - Towards Efficient and Scalable Mobile Networks

The conference also featured the following symposiun:

- **SOFTNETWORKING 2017, The International Symposium on Advances in Software Defined Networking and Network Functions Virtualization**

We take here the opportunity to warmly thank all the members of the ICN 2017 technical program committee, as well as all the reviewers. The creation of such a high quality conference program would not have been possible without their involvement. We also kindly thank all the authors that dedicated much of their time and effort to contribute to ICN 2017. We truly believe that, thanks to all these efforts, the final conference program consisted of top quality contributions.

We also gratefully thank the members of the ICN 2017 organizing committee for their help in handling the logistics and for their work that made this professional meeting a success.

We hope that ICN 2017 was a successful international forum for the exchange of ideas and results between academia and industry and to promote further progress in the area of networks. We also hope that Venice, Italy provided a pleasant environment during the conference and everyone saved some time to enjoy the unique charm of the city.

ICN 2017 Committee

ICN Steering Committee
Pascal Lorenz, University of Haute Alsace, France
Carlos Becker Westphall, University of Santa Catarina, Brazil
Tibor Gyires, Illinois State University, USA
Iwona Pozniak-Koszalka, Wroclaw University of Technology, Poland
Carlos T. Calafate, Technical University of Valencia, Spain
Calin Vladeanu, University Politehnica of Bucharest, Romania
Gary Weckman, Ohio University, USA
Yenumula B. Reddy, Grambling State University, USA
Eric Renault, Institut Mines-Télécom - Télécom SudParis, France
Sherali Zeadally, University of Kentucky, USA

ICN Industry/Research Advisory Committee
Marc Cheboldaeff, T-Systems International GmbH, Germany
Megumi Shibuya, KDDI Research, Inc., Japan
Arslan Brömme, Vattenfall GmbH, Berlin, Germany
Abdelmajid Khelil, Landshut University of Applied Sciences, Germany

ICN 2017
Committee

ICN Steering Committee

Pascal Lorenz, University of Haute Alsace, France
Carlos Becker Westphall, University of Santa Catarina, Brazil
Tibor Gyires, Illinois State University, USA
Iwona Pozniak-Koszalka, Wroclaw University of Technology, Poland
Carlos T. Calafate, Technical University of Valencia, Spain
Calin Vladeanu, University Politehnica of Bucharest, Romania
Gary Weckman, Ohio University, USA
Yenumula B. Reddy, Grambling State University, USA
Eric Renault, Institut Mines-Télécom - Télécom SudParis, France
Sherali Zeadally, University of Kentucky, USA

ICN Industry/Research Advisory Committee

Marc Cheboldaeff, T-Systems International GmbH, Germany
Megumi Shibuya, KDDI Research, Inc., Japan
Arslan Brömme, Vattenfall GmbH, Berlin, Germany
Abdelmajid Khelil, Landshut University of Applied Sciences, Germany

ICN 2017 Technical Program Committee

Alireza Abdollahpouri, University of Kurdistan, Sanandaj, Iran
Hussein Al-Zubaidy, KTH Royal Institute of Technology, Sweden
Cristian Anghel, Politehnica University of Bucharest, Romania / Pentalog, France
Jocelyn Aubert, Luxembourg Institute of Science and Technology (LIST), Luxembourg
Harald Baier, Hochschule Darmstadt / CRISP, Germany
Katherine Barabash, IBM, Israel
Alvaro Barradas, University of Algarve, Portugal
Carlos Becker Westphall, University of Santa Catarina, Brazil
Djamel Benferhat, University of South Brittany, France
Erika R. Bérczi-Kovács, Eötvös Loránd University, Budapest, Hungary
Robert Bestak, Czech Technical University in Prague, Czech Republic
Patrick-Benjamin Bök, Weidmüller Group, Germany
Fernando Boronat Seguí, Universitat Politecnica de Valencia, Spain
Radoslav Bortel, Czech Technical University in Prague, Czech Republic
Christos Bouras, University of Patras / Computer Technology Institute & Press "Diophantus", Greece
Arslan Broemme, GI BIOSIG - GI e.V., Germany

Carlos T. Calafate, Technical University of Valencia, Spain
Otavio Augusto S. Carpinteiro, Federal University of Itajuba, Brazil
Marc Cheboldaeff, T-Systems International GmbH, Germany
Luiz H. A. Correia, Federal University of Lavras, Brazil
Nivia Cruz Quental, Federal University of Pernambuco (UFPE), Brazil
Fábio Diniz Rossi, Farroupilha Federal Institute of Science, Education and Technology, Brazil
Ali Ebnenasir, Michigan Technological University, USA
Gledson Elias, Federal University of Paraíba (UFPB), Brazil
Pedro Felipe do Prado, Universidade de São Paulo (USP), Brazil
Mário F. S. Ferreira, University of Aveiro, Portugal
Alexander Ferworn, Ryerson University, Canada
Edelberto Franco Silva, Universidade Federal Fluminense, Brazil
Eva Gescheidtova, Brno University of Technology, Czech Republic
Markus Goldstein, Kyushu University, Japan
Róza Goscien, Wroclaw University of Technology, Poland
Tibor Gyires, Illinois State University, USA
Hiroyuki Hatano, Utsunomiya University, Japan
Tuong Hoang Duc, INRS-EMT | University of Quebec, Canada
Markus Hofmann, Nokia Bell Labs, USA
Dragos Ilie, Blekinge Institute of Technology (BTH), Sweden
Ali Kadhum Idrees, University of Babylon, Iraq
Kyungtae Kang, Hanyang University, Korea
Andrzej Kasprzak, Wroclaw University of Technology, Poland
Toshihiko Kato, University of Electro-Communications, Japan
Sokratis K. Katsikas, Norwegian University of Science & Technology (NTNU), Norway
Abdelmajid Khelil, Bosch Software Innovations, Germany
Sun-il Kim, North Central College, USA
Pinar Kirci, Istanbul University, Turkey
Wojciech Kmiecik, Wroclaw University of Technology, Poland
Leszek Koszalka, Wroclaw University of Science and Technology, Poland
Tomas Koutny, University of West Bohemia, Pilsen, Czech Republic
Francine Krief, Bordeaux INP, France
Feng Lin, University at Buffalo, SUNY, USA
Pascal Lorenz, University of Haute Alsace, France
Ahmed Mahdy, Texas A&M University - Corpus Christi, USA
Zoubir Mammeri, IRIT - Paul Sabatier University, France
Antonio Martín-Montes, Sevilla University, Spain
Mario Montagud Climent, Universitat Politècnica de València (UPV), Spain
Shintaro Mori, Fukuoka University, Japan
Masayuki Murata, Osaka University, Japan
Mahshid R. Naeini, Texas Tech University, USA
Constantin Paleologu, University Politehnica of Bucharest, Romania
Agnieszka Piotrowska, Silesian University of Technology - Gliwice, Poland
Marcial Porto Fernandez, Universidade Estadual do Ceara (UECE), Brazil

Iwona Pozniak-Koszalka, Wroclaw University of Science and Technology, Poland
M. J. Shankar Raman, Indian Institute of Technology Madras, India
Yenumula B. Reddy, Grambling State University, USA
Eric Renault, Institut Mines-Télécom - Télécom SudParis, France
Karim Mohammed Rezaul, Glyndwr University, Wrexham, UK
Panagiotis Sarigiannidis, University of Western Macedonia, Greece
Masahiro Sasabe, Nara Institute of Science and Technology, Japan
Narasimha K. Shashidhar, Sam Houston State University, USA
Megumi Shibuya, KDDI Research, Inc., Japan
Andrew Snow, Ohio University, USA
Kostas Stamos, University of Patras, Greece
Cristian Stanciu, University Politehnica of Bucharest, Romania
Aaron Striegel, University of Notre Dame, USA
Bruno Tardiole Kuehne, Federal University of Itajuba, Brazil
Muhammad Mahboob Ur Rahman, Information Technology University (ITU), Lahore, Pakistan
Muhammad Usman, University of Trento, Italy
Robert van der Mei, VU University, Netherlands
Calin Vladeanu, University Politehnica of Bucharest, Romania
Lukas Vojtech, CTU in Prague, Czech Republic
Gary Weckman, Ohio University, USA
Alexander L. Wijesinha, Towson University, USA
Maarten Wijnants, iMinds-EDM-UHasselt, Belgium
Bernd E. Wolfinger, University of Hamburg, Germany
Qimin Yang, Harvey Mudd College, USA
Sherali Zeadally, University of Kentucky, USA

SOFTNETWORKING 2017 Advisory Committee

Eugen Borcoci, University Politehnica of Bucharest, Romania (Chair)
Pedro A. Aranda Gutiérrez, Telefónica, Spain
Nicola Ciulli, Nextworks, Italy
Wolfgang John, Ericsson Research, Sweden

SOFTNETWORKING 2017 Program Committee Members

Robert Bestak, Czech Technical University in Prague, Czech Republic
Eugen Borcoci, University "Politehnica" of Bucharest (UPB), Romania
Cristina Cervelló-Pastor, Universitat Politècnica de Catalunya (UPC), Spain
Nicola Ciulli, Nextworks, Italy
Didier Colle, iMinds - Ghent University, Belgium
Paolo Comi, Italtel S.p.A. - Lecco, Italy
Christian Esteve Rothenberg, University of Campinas (UNICAMP), Brazil
Rung-Hung Gau, National Chiao Tung University, Taiwan
Xavier Hesselbach, Universitat Politecnica de Catalunya (UPC), Spain

Zhen Jiang, West Chester University, USA
Wolfgang John, Ericsson Research, Sweden
Wolfgang Kiess, DOCOMO Euro-Labs, Germany
Diego Kreutz, University of Luxembourg, Luxembourg
Francesco Longo, University of Messina, Italy
Farnaz Moradi, Ericsson Research, Sweden
Ioannis Moscholios, University of Peloponnese, Greece
Bertrand Pechenot, Acreo Swedish ICT, Sweden
Nicholas Race, Lancaster University, UK
David Rincón, Universitat Politecnica de Catalunya (UPC), Barcelona, Spain
Paolo Secondo Crosta, ITALTEL SPA, Italy
Kazem Sohraby, South Dakota School of Mines and Technology, USA
Yuzo Taenaka, University of Tokyo, Japan
Yutaka Takahashi, Kyoto University, Japan
Ricard Vilalta, CTTC, Spain

Copyright Information

A Congestion Control Approach for M2M Networks

David Aragão
Universidade Federal do Ceará
Fortaleza, Ceará
Email: davidbpa@great.ufc.br

Dario Vieira
Ecole d'Ingénieur Généraliste en Informatique
et Technologies du Numérique (EFREI)
Paris, France
Email: dario.vieira@efrei.fr

Miguel Franklin de Castro
Universidade Federal do Ceará
Fortaleza, Ceará
Email: miguel@great.ufc.br

Abstract—**Machine-to-Machine (M2M) is a communication model used by devices where data can be exchanged with little or no human intervention. The M2M communication, when applied in the context of LTE networks, can lead to overload and congestion problems due to its intrinsic particularities. Accordingly, in this paper we propose a congestion control approach for Long-Term Evolution (LTE) that reduces the impact over the Human-to-Human (H2H) devices and establishes priority amongst M2M devices through the use of classes. The results obtained through extensive simulations in Network Simulator (NS-3) show that the proposed approach can control the impact over H2H devices, establishes intra and inter-class priority for the devices, reduces the access delay and it is compatible with the LTE network standard.**

Keywords–LTE; M2M; Congestion Control

I. Introduction

M2M communication is a technology that enables information exchange between autonomous devices with few or no human intervention [1]. Device types can be of common (e.g., home appliance, cars, cell phones, etc.) or specific purpose (e.g., sensors, actuators, etc.). The M2M communication is expected to play an important role to leverage the Internet of Things (IoT). The goal of the IoT paradigm is to facilitate daily tasks, generating a huge impact on society behavior [2].

The Long-Term Evolution (LTE) [3] is a networking standard that presents advantages like mobility, accessibility, good coverage area, security, and other relevant key features for M2M services and applications. Since LTE networking was mainly designed for H2H communication, some adaptations need to be done to cope with M2M communication requirements. The Third Generation Partnership Project (3GPP) [4], organization that is responsible for the LTE specification, works to identify and propose solutions for the problems and requirements that may arise with the integration of M2M devices into the LTE network.

The overload and congestion control in the LTE Radio Access Network (RAN) is considered by 3GPP as a high priority issue that needs to be treated to enable the M2M communication over the LTE networks. Overload and congestion on LTE network normally occur when a huge number of access requests are sent by devices to a single base station during the Random Access CHannel Procedure (RACH procedure). The RACH procedure presents a very low efficiency as the number of devices increases [5]. In Section II, we present an overview of the LTE networks and the RACH procedure.

The 3GPP presents six alternatives to mitigate the overload and congestion problems on the LTE network: (i) Access Class Barring (ACB), (ii) Backoff, (iii) Separated RACH, (iv) Dynamic Resource Allocation for RACH, (v) Slotted-Aloha and (vi) Pull Schema. Some approaches in the literature (e.g., [6], [7], [8]) combine two or more of these mechanisms to achieve better results. However, the solutions to mitigate the overload and congestion problems normally consider only the M2M traffic in their approaches [5]. Another drawback in these proposals is the lack of compatibility with the LTE standard. The related works are presented and discussed in Section III. These problems have motivated the development of our proposal. In this paper, we propose a mechanism, presented and discussed in Section IV, to mitigate the congestion in the RAN of LTE networks that presents low implementation complexity. In addition, in our solution, we propose mechanisms to control the impact of M2M over H2H devices and we create priorities among M2M devices. To accomplish these objectives, we split the M2M devices into high and low priority classes and we define a third class for H2H devices.

The results obtained through exhaustive simulations using NS-3, presented and discussed in Section V, show that our approach presents good results for inter and intra-class priority for M2M and H2H devices. Moreover, our approach is highly compatible with the LTE networks, easily implemented and mitigates the congestion problems during the RACH Procedure. In Section VI, we present our conclusion and future works.

II. Overview

A. Machine-to-Machine Communication

The M2M communication, also called Machine-Type Communication (MTC) by 3GPP, is a technology where devices can exchange information with little or no human intervention. In addition to the applications diversity and number of devices, other common features of M2M communication are [9]: (i) traffic in the uplink is higher than in the downlink, (ii) sporadic data transmission, (iii) usual transmission of small portion of data. Thus, due to these intrinsic features new approaches are needed to adapt the LTE network to the M2M environment.

B. RACH Procedure

In LTE networks, the random access can be contention-based or contention-free. In the former, the random access request is initialized by the device. In the latter, requests are started by the base station (evolved Node B - eNodeB).

The contention-based RACH procedure is divided into four signal messages (represented in Figure 1, mgs1, msg2, msg3, msg4) managed by the Radio Network Controller (RNC) [10]. Figure 1 illustrates the message exchange during the contention-based procedure. Information related to the

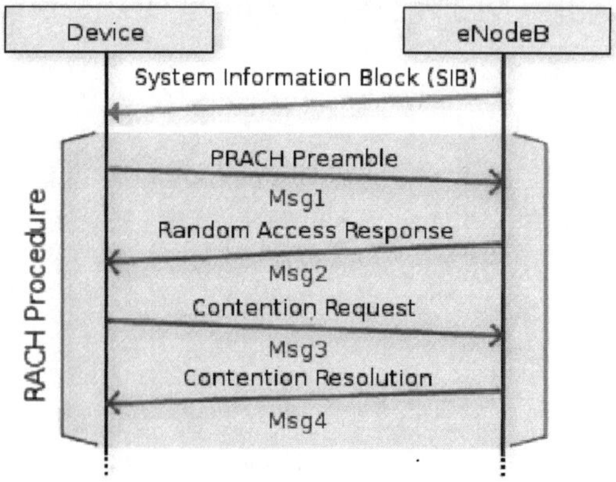

Figure 1. Random access procedure based on contention.

RACH procedure, as preamble code available and random-access slots (RA-Slots) opportunities, is periodically sent through the System Information Block (SIB) to devices. The following activities are done in each stage of the RACH message exchange procedure:

1) PRACH Preamble (Msg1): The device randomly selects and transmits a preamble code to eNodeB on Physical Random Access CHannel (PRACH).
2) Random Access Response - RAR (Msg2): In this stage, the following occur: (i) detection of access requests sent by devices to eNodeB, (ii) assignment of a Temporary Cell Radio Network Temporary Identifier (TC-RNTI) to devices and (iii) a resource is granted on the uplink channel for subsequent messages exchanges between the devices and the base station.
3) Contention Request (Msg3): Devices send the TC-RNTI, the one assigned in the previous message. This exchange is done over the uplink shared channel (PUSCH), also configured in previous stage.
4) Contention Resolution (Msg4): Devices wait for the contention resolution message from the eNodeB, which is sent by the eNodeB through the Downlink Shared Channel (DL-SCH). If the device identifier is present in the contention message, an ACK message is sent to the eNodeB, otherwise the device randomly select a backoff time before retry transmission.

Collisions during the RACH procedure occur when two or more devices send the same preamble code to the eNB. In this case, devices do not receive the Random Access Response (msg2) and the waiting time window is reached.

III. Related Work

In [11], devices are classified into classes. Class priorities are based on the backoff time. When a collision occurs, the device waits for the backoff time, which is randomly selected from the interval ($X \sim Unif(0, T)$), where X is a random variable and $Unif$ an uniform distribution. The interval (T) is divided by the number of classes (C) with the interval size based on the congestion level (p_0) broadcasted by the base station. The interval range for M2M devices is given by the following equation: $T_{bf}^{MTC}(i) = p_0 T + Unif(i\frac{(1-p_0)T}{C}, (i+1)\frac{(1-p_0)T}{C})$. To prevent that the M2M interval becomes equal to zero when the networks is congested, the authors propose the following equation for the backoff calculus: $T_{bf}^{MTC}(i) = T + Unif(i\frac{kT}{C}, (i+1)\frac{kT}{C})$. Another strategy presented by the authors is to change the backoff range based on the M2M device class. Using this second approach the backoff calculus is done by the following equation: $T_{bf}^{MTC}(i) = Unif(0, k_i T)$, where k_i represents the multiplier of the ith type of MTC user. The second strategy can be seen as an enhancement of the specific backoff schema with the adoption of more than one type of M2M devices. The third approach combines the ACB with the backoff class. Since our main priority is to analyze the performance of backoff strategies with our approach, we choose to implement the first approach. Classifying devices into classes with different backoff interval represents an upgrade when compared with the conventional backoff and the Slotted Aloha approaches. However, this approach is not optimized. The interval class does not consider the number of devices in each class. Thus, classes with a few hundreds of devices have the same interval size as classes with thousands of devices. Moreover, there are no intra-class priorities among the types of M2M devices.

In [7], the authors propose a static and a dynamic approach to split the RACH resources between M2M and H2H devices. Before the resource allocation, the devices pass through the ACB selection. The implementation complexity and no prioritization between devices are some of the drawbacks of this approach. In [12], an algorithm is proposed that helps devices to select the base station (eNodeB) which they should be connected to. The algorithm uses a Q-Learning technique and considers the application Quality of Service (QoS) during the selection. In this proposal, no priority is defined among M2M devices and it is applied only to scenarios where the devices are covered by more than one eNodeB.

In [13], the idea is an overload control mechanism that uses the dynamic resource allocation for RACH technique. To identify the overload level at the RAN in the LTE networks, the authors consider the average number of preambles sent by devices to get access to the network. The algorithm considers the number of retries made by the devices before successfully accessing the network to infer the congestion level into the network. The authors also combine other 3GPP proposal techniques (Slotted-Access, Backoff and ACB) to mitigate the M2M impact over the H2H devices and define priority between M2M devices. This approach has a high complexity level of implementation and was not evaluated by simulation or by analytical approach.

In [14], the authors present a testbed framework to analyze the congestion control strategies of LTE networks. The congestion caused by M2M devices can impact other domains of the network (e.g., core network). However, better results are achieved by the strategies applied in the RAN [12].

IV. Control Congestion Proposal

In this section, we present our proposal to control the congestion in LTE networks. Our goal is: (i) to reduce the impact on H2H devices, (ii) to define inter and intra-class priorities among the devices and (iii) to increase the success access rate. The inter-class behavior presented in our approach is defined between the H2H, M2M with high priority and M2M with low priority. The intra-class priority is among the same type of M2M devices, with higher priority given for those devices that are more likely to reach the maximum number of connection tries. Furthermore, in Section IV-A, we describe the congestion problem during the RACH procedure in LTE networks.

A. Problem

The RACH procedure in LTE networks follows the Slotted Aloha principle [15]. Based on this relation, it is possible to use the following equation to estimate the collision probability (P_c) during the RACH procedure [16], [17]: $P_c = 1 - e^{(-\lambda/L)}$, where L is the total number of Random Access Slots (RA-Slots) available per second and λ is the average number of requests per second targeting a single eNodeB. For a bandwidth (B) in MHz, such that $B \in \{1.4, 2.5, 5, 10, 15, 20\}$ the number of Physical Resource Blocks (PRBs) available per frame is given by: $PRB_{TotalFrame} = {}^{B}/_{F_{subframe}} \times T_{frame} \times 2$, where T_{frame} is the frame timing in milliseconds and $F_{subframe}$ is the frame frequency in kHz. Since an RA-Slots can be configured to occurs n times within a T_{frame} interval, where $n \in \{0.5, 1, 2, 3, 5, 10\}$, the number of PRB available per second for the RACH procedure is given by: $PRB_{Total} = {}^{PRB_{TotalFrame}}/_{2} \times {}^{1000}/_{T_{frame}} \times n$. Thus, the base station can support T_{RAR} request per second, where T_{RAR} is given by the following equation: $T_{RAR} = {}^{PRB_{Total}}/_{PRB_{RACH}}$ Where PRB_{RACH} is the number of Physical Resource Blocks per RACH request. In LTE networks, the number of PRB_{RACH} is equal to six. For a given collision probability (P_c), the number of RA-slots per second (L) to support the random access intensity (λ) is given by [17]: $\lambda = -L \times ln(1 - P_c)$. Thus, more collisions will occur as the number of devices increases.

B. Proposal

Mechanisms to control the overload and congestion problems presented in Section I and III may be considered as good approaches to mitigate the problem. However, except for [11], these mechanisms present a high implementation complexity, with changes on the physical layer of LTE network. In [11], the implementation is based on how devices calculate the backoff interval and how the base station infers the congestion level in the RAN. However, this approach does not consider the number of devices during the class division. Accordingly, the algorithm defines the network resources for classes with the same interval range regardless of the number of devices in each class. In addition, this approach does not consider priority among M2M devices.

1) Congestion Level Identification: In our approach, the base station classifies and reports as low, medium, and high the congestion level in the RAN of LTE network. This classification is based on the results obtained in [18] that show the relation between the average number of access attempts, the collision probability and the RACH procedure ratio utilization. These results show that for a maximum resource utilization, which is approximately 50%, the collision ratio is around 20% and the proportion of successful requests is about 50%. Thus, when more than 50 requests are done per RA-Slot we consider the congestion level as high (P_{cong} = 1). However, we consider the congestion level as low ($P_{cong} = 0$) when there are less than 25 request per RA-Slot. The relation between the number of requests and the congestion level adopted in our approach is presented in Table I.

TABLE I. CONGESTION LEVEL

Level	Request per RA-Slot	P_{cong}
Low	< 25	P_{cong} = 0.0
Medium	> 25 and ≤ 50	P_{cong} = 0.5
High	> 50	P_{cong} = 1.0

2) Devices Priority: We classify the devices into H2H, M2M with high priority and M2M with low priority [6]. To guaranty priority in accordance with the device type, we use a class-based approach. The priorities between classes are based on the preamble transmission probability and backoff interval. The preamble transmission probability indicates when the device can send an access request. Based on the ACB approach, to get access to the network the device has to calculate a random number $X \sim Unif(0, P_s)$ within the interval (0,P_s), where P_s is giving by:

$$P_s(i,t,L) = \begin{cases} p_{ac} & P_{cong} = 0.0; \\ p_{ac} \times (((\frac{L}{t}) \times i) \times \alpha) & P_{cong} = 0.5; \\ p_{ac} \times (((\frac{L}{t}) \times i) \times \alpha) & P_{cong} = 1.0; \end{cases} . \quad (1)$$

where i is the device type (H2H, M2M low priority, M2M high priority), p_{ac} is the blocking parameter broadcasted by the base station (eNodeB), L is the maximum number of preamble retransmissions and t is the number of requests sent to access the network. The α parameter is related to the congestion level on RAN and defines the dispersion between the classes of devices. The results show that an optimized value for α is 1.0 when P_{cong} = 0.5 and 1.5 when P_{cong} = 1.0. The calculus of the expected transmission probability of a device k from a class i is given by:

$$E[X] = \frac{1}{2} \times (0 + P_s(i_k, t_k, L)) \quad (2)$$

Following the ACB behavior, the device can transmit an access preamble request during the RACH procedure when $X \leq p_{ac}$, i.e., with the probability given by $P_{access}(X \leq p_{ac})$. To conclude, the cumulative density function (CDF) F_X of a device k from a class i after t access attempts is given by:

$$F_X(x) = P(X \leq p_{ac}) = \frac{p_{ac}}{P_s} \quad (3)$$

Based on (2) and (3) the preamble transmission probability increases with the class index and the number of access attempts made by the device, as illustrated in Figures 2 and 3. These figures also show that as the number of classes increases the preamble transmission probability for classes with low priority decreases. However, for the number of classes considered in our algorithm, the probability of a preamble transmission can be around 50% for the class with low priority.

When X is greater than p_{ac} ($X > p_{ac}$) the backoff $T_{backoff}$ is individually calculated by each device through the equation:

$$T_{backoff}(i) = \begin{cases} 20\ ms & \text{for i} = 0; \\ 50\ ms \times i & \text{for i} \geq 1; \end{cases} \quad (4)$$

The backoff technique avoids successive requests from devices to the base station (eNodeB) after a collision.

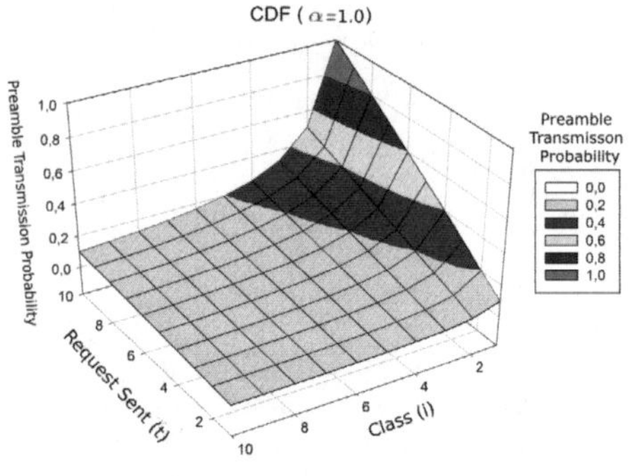

Figure 2. Cumulative Density Functions (cf. Eq. 3)

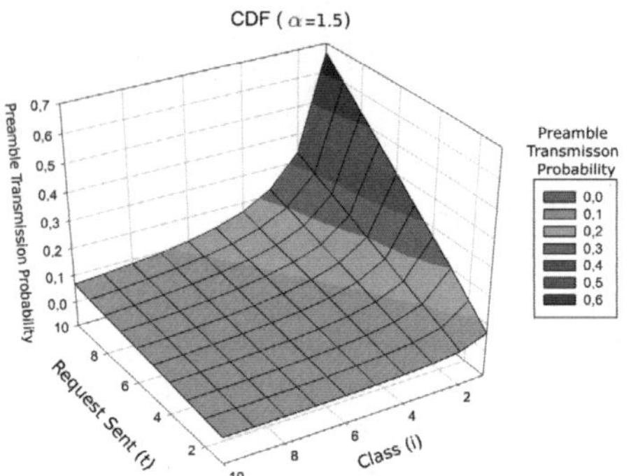

Figure 3. Cumulative Density Functions (cf. Eq. 3)

V. SIMULATION ENVIRONMENT AND NUMERICAL RESULTS

In this section, we present and analyze our simulation results. In Section V-A, we present the Performance Key Indicators (PKIs) selected to evaluate the implemented approach. In Section V-B, we describe the simulation environment and the configuration parameters.

A. Key Performance Indicators

In this paper, the performance indicators to analyze the approaches are the access delay, the blocking probability, the number of accesses, and the number of transmitted preambles. We define the access delay as the time interval between the instant when the device sends the first access request to the base station, and the time when the device successfully receives the contention resolution message from the base station. The blocking probability is the ratio between non-successful accesses and the total number of access requests received by the base station. The number of transmitted preambles indicates the access retries sent by the device to access the network. Such indicators will be useful during the analysis of the following aspect of each strategy: (i) impact control of M2M devices over H2H devices, (ii) priority between M2M devices and (iii) energy efficiency during the RACH procedure.

B. Simulation Environment

To evaluate our approach, we choose the simulator NS-3 [19]. The official version of NS-3 has a LTE module, but some key features of the RACH procedure were not

TABLE II. PARAMETERS OF THE SIMULATIONS

General Parameters	
Bandwidth	5 MHz (25 RBs)
Runs	15
Number of base stations(eNodeB)	1
PRACH Configuration Index	6
Preamble Retransmissions (L)	10
Preamble Codes	54
Random Access Response Timeout Window	5 ms
H2H Devices	{ 100,100,100,...,100 }
M2M Devices With High Priority	{ 10,500,1000,...,4000}
M2M Devices With Low Priority	{ 2,125,250,...,1000 }
Arrival Rate (H2H)	Poisson(λ), λ = 1/300
Arrival Rate (M2M)	Poisson(λ), λ = 1/900
Arrival Interval	[0,...,1] s
Simulation Time	5 s
Other Parameters	
i = 0 for H2H devices, i = 1 for M2M devices w/ high priority, i = 2 for M2M devices w/ low priority.	
α = 1 for Low Congestion Level, α = 1.5 for High Congestion Level (cf. Table I).	

implemented at the time this paper was written. Moreover, for the number of M2M devices simulated in this paper the simulator performance can become extremely low. Thus, we have extended the LTE module to implement other functionalities for the RACH on NS-3 for this paper.

We have also implemented three algorithms found in the literature that are compatibles with the LTE network. The first ones is the Slotted Aloha, which is the most naive solution implemented and which gives a good understanding of the congestion problem during RACH procedure. The Backoff Specific, which defines different backoff interval for M2M and H2H devices, is the second implemented approach [20]. The third approach is presented in [11] and differs from the Slotted Aloha and Backoff Specific by setting priority among M2M devices. In [11], the devices are classified into classes with different levels of priority. The priority among classes considers the backoff interval such that access requests can be more or less spread over the time.

In our scenarios, we simulate H2H and M2M devices, where the number of H2H devices is constant and equal to 100. The M2M devices priorities are classified into high and low as presented in Section IV-B2. The number of M2M devices with low priority are: {10, 500, 1000, 1500, ... ,4000}, and the number of M2M devices with high priority are: {2, 125, 250, ... , 1000}, i.e., $\frac{1}{4}$ of the number of M2M devices with low priority. The arrival rate considered for the H2H and M2M devices follows the Poisson distribution with arrival parameters $\lambda_{H2H} = \frac{1}{300}$ and $\lambda_{M2M} = \frac{1}{900}$. The number of preamble codes available for RACH procedures is 64 - N, where N is the number of codes dedicated for the contention-free random access method and equal to 10. For the PRACH Configuration Index 6, we have two RA-Slots available per LTE frame (10 ms), and so we have 200 RACH/s (1000 ms / 10 ms $\times$ 2). For a bandwidth of 5 MHz, there are 25 PRBs available for each 0,5 ms, and knowing that each RA-Slots occupies six PRBs in the frequency domain and one subframe on the time domain, the base station (eNodeB) can handle four requests per PRACH procedure. Thereby, in an ideal scenario, i.e., without collision, 800 (200 RA-slots/s $\times$ 4) devices can get access to the network within the interval of one second. The above configurations are presented in Table II.

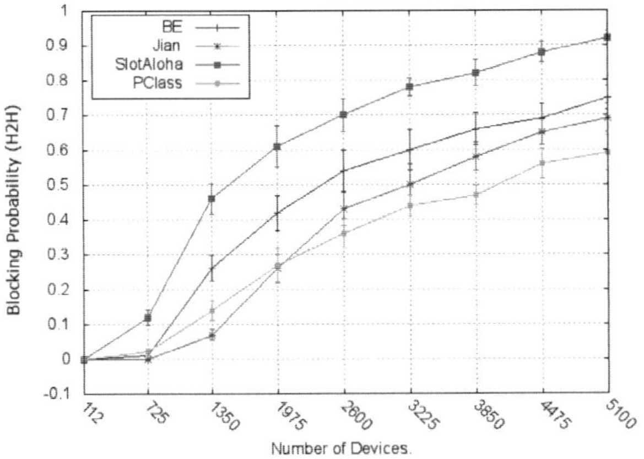

Figure 4. Impact Control Over H2H Devices - Blocking Probability.

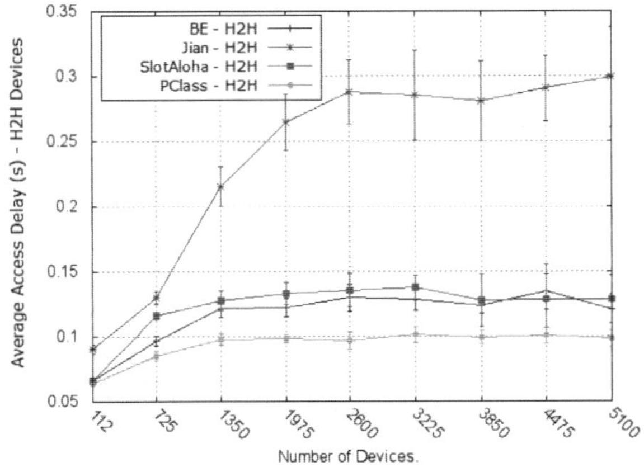

Figure 5. Impact Control Over H2H Devices - Average Access Delay.

C. Simulated Congestion Control Mechanisms

The approaches [11], [17] have in common with our approach the implementation viability in a practical context of the LTE networks. In [11], three techniques to split the classes are presented. However, for the reasons already presented (cf. Section III), only the first technique is implemented in this paper. Since there is no information in [11] on how the authors identify the congestion level in the RAN, we choose to apply the approach presented in Section IV-B1. The default backoff time configured to the network is set to 20 ms [17]. In [17] an Specific backoff approach is presented, in this approach H2H and M2M devices receives different backoff interval value. The maximum backoff value for M2M devices of 920 ms is within the defined arrival interval presented in [17]. To keep this behavior for scenario used in this paper, we define the maximum backoff time for M2M devices limited to 100 ms (Arrival Interval / Number of possible retransmission attempts).

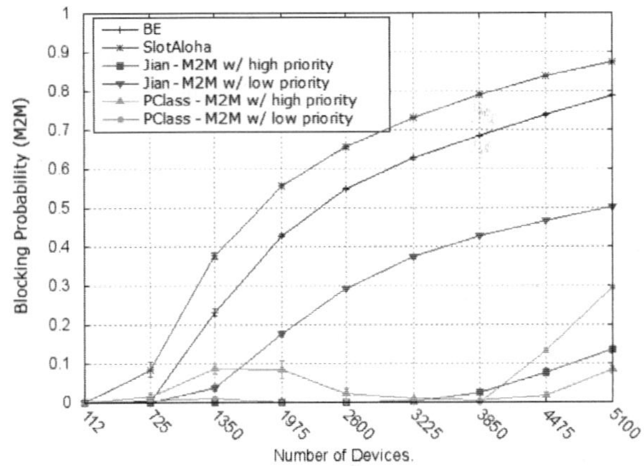

Figure 6. Impact Control Over M2M Devices - Blocking Probability.

D. Results

In the next sections, the approaches presented in [11], [17] will be respectively referenced by "Jian" and "BE". The scenario where no congestion control is applied will be referenced as "SlotAloha". As presented in Section V-A, the performance indicator will be useful to analyze the following features: (i) impact control of M2M devices over H2H devices, (ii) priority between M2M devices and (iii) energy efficiency during the RACH procedure. Besides, our approach is referred by PClass.

1) Impact over H2H Devices: The relation between the blocking probability and the number of devices illustrated in Figure 4 shows that PClass has a performance improvement of 19% when compared to Jian and 40% when compared to SlotAloha. For around 1350 devices, the performance of Jian is about 10% better than PClass. However, between 1900 and 2000 devices, occurs an inversion on the blocking probability, i.e., PClass approach is able to handle congested scenarios better than Jian algorithm.

The priority inversion around 1975 devices is related to the congestion level (P_{cong}), explained in Section IV-B1. Scenarios with moderate level of congestion (P_{cong}) are less restrictive. In this case, more M2M devices try to access the network. Thus, more collisions may occur and emphasize the impact over H2H devices.

As illustrated in Figure 5, the access delay is almost constant for all implemented techniques. However, it is important to notice that the average access time considers only devices that accessed the network with success. Thereby, even if the average access time of the H2H devices is considered constant, it can be observed in Figure 4 that the number of successful accesses decreases. The algorithm Jian considers a big backoff interval for the H2H devices. Accordingly, the access delay of H2H devices increases, since the access requests are more spread over the time.

2) Priority Between M2M Devices: As illustrated in Figure 6, the blocking probability increases with the number of devices in all implemented approach. Once the algorithms SlotAloha and BE do not define priority between devices, both types of devices (H2H and M2M) are equally penalized.

In the SlotAloha and BE algorithms the requests sent by M2M devices are spread into the interval of 20 ms and 100 ms, respectively. As the interval increases, the number of collisions decreases and more devices has access to the

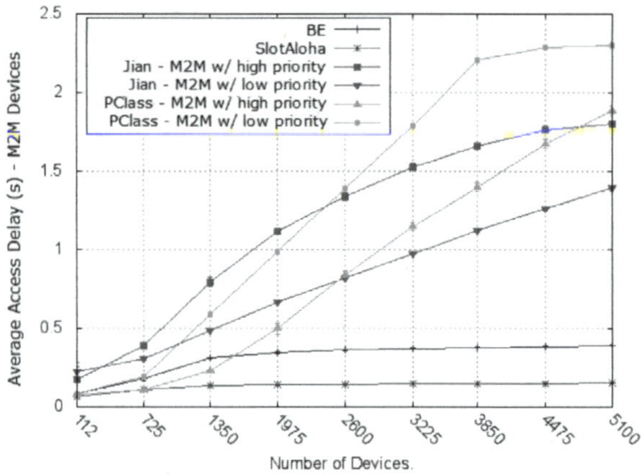

Figure 7. Impact Control Over M2M Devices - Average Access Delay.

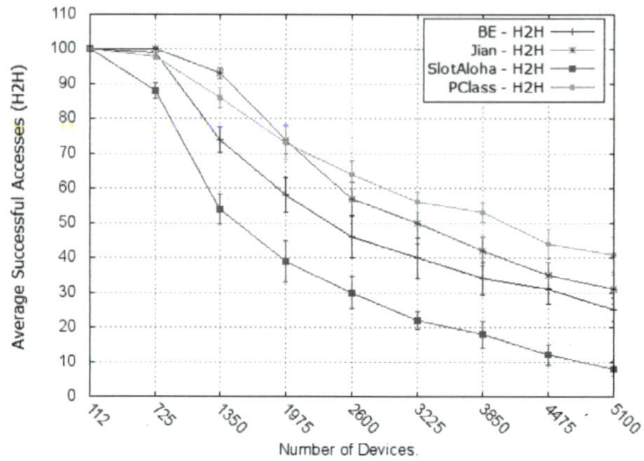

Figure 8. Average Succesful Access - H2H Devices.

network with success. The results presented by Jian are better than SlotAloha and BE since they define priority between M2M devices. In relation to PClass, the Jian algorithm presents a performance around 12% better for the blocking probability between M2M devices with high priority for scenarios with around 725 to 3530 devices. However, the PClass presents a better performance in scenarios with more than 3530 devices. In relation to M2M devices with low priority, the technique applied by the algorithm Jian behaves like SlotAloha and BE, i.e., the access time increases with the number of devices. The PClass algorithm presents the same performance as Jain, when compared with SlotAloha and BE in relation to the priority between M2M devices. Notice that PClass exceed the number of retries within scenarios less congested, i.e., those with fewer devices (around 1350), see Figure 6. However, for more congested scenarios, the algorithm PClass shows better results amongst the implemented approaches. The behavior presented by the PClass algorithm for scenarios within the interval of 1350 and 3850 devices is consequence of the parameter P_{cong}, which affects the devices transmission probability (cf., Equations 1 and 3).

3) Successful Access: As illustrated in Figures 8 and 9, the impact over the H2H devices increases with the number of M2M devices. The algorithms Jian and PClass have a similar behavior, however, the PClass algorithm converges to higher values than Jian. For scenarios where the number of device is above 1800, the PClass offers better access performance than Jian (cf. Figure 5).

For the M2M devices with high priority, the PClass algorithm presents advantage in relation to the number and average access delay for scenarios with about 1350 devices when compared with Jian (cf., Figure 9 and 7). However, for scenarios with more than 1350 devices, the average access delay of the PClass algorithm is higher than Jian algorithm, but PClass presents a better access performance of H2H devices than Jian algorithm.

4) Preamble Transmission: The average number of preamble transmission retries shown in Figures 11 and 10 is directly related with the power consuming. Once radio transition activity demands a significant amount of power, when more preambles are transmitted more energy is consumed. The decreases shown in Figure 10 in the number of preambles at 2600 to 5100

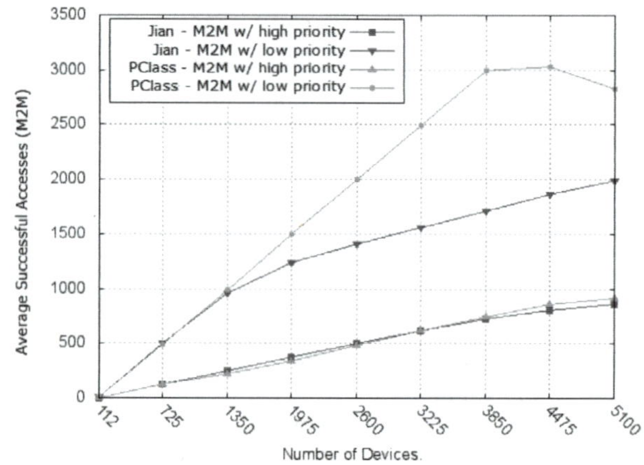

Figure 9. Average Succesful Access - M2M Devices of High and Low Priority.

devices is related with the network congestion. Since more devices are trying to access, less preambles will be transmitted by the PClass. Depending on the application type, devices can use batteries as their primary energy source. However, as the number of devices and the type of application grow, it becomes clearer that the management of energy resources is an important aspect for feasibility of some applications (e.g., environment monitoring, smart cities, etc). Thereby, energy awareness strategies play an important role in this process. Our proposal considers the energy aspect to keep the number of preamble transmission lower than other proposed approaches, see Figure 10.

In our proposal, the preamble transmission is controlled by blocking the access request of devices. As illustrated in Figure 11, in our approach the H2H devices show a lower performance when compared to Jian algorithm. However, since the expected number of M2M devices is higher than H2H devices, our proposal causes less impact over the network than Jian algorithm. Furthermore, energy consumption is a more important issue when related to autonomous devices (M2M) than non-autonomous ones (H2H).

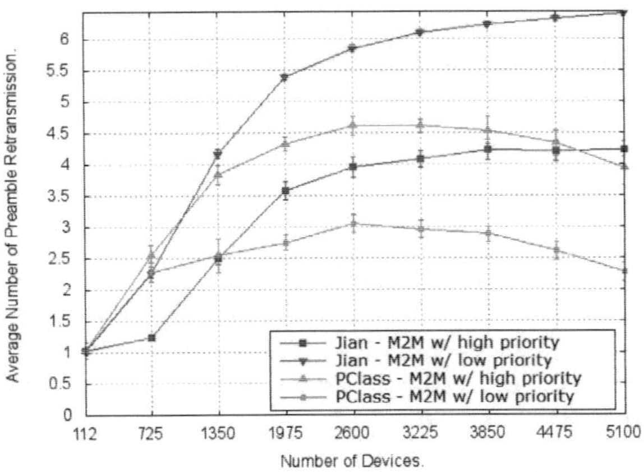

Figure 10. Average Preamble Transmission - M2M Devices.

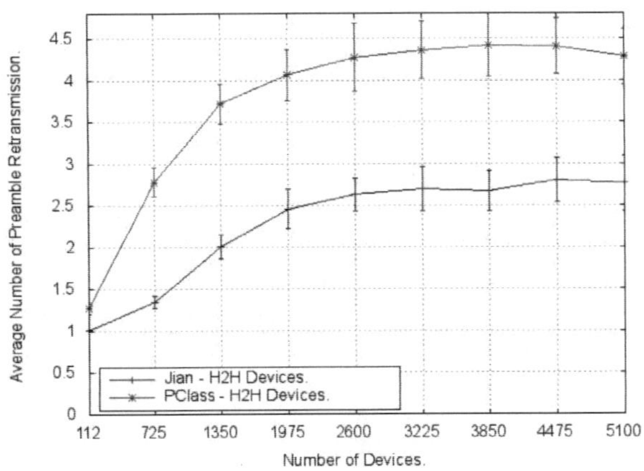

Figure 11. Average Preamble Transmission - H2H Devices.

VI. Conclusion and Future Works

In this paper, we have presented a new congestion control approach for LTE that can reduce the impact over the H2H devices and establishes priorities amongst M2M devices using classes of priorities. Besides, the proposed mechanism can mitigate the impact of M2M devices in the LTE networks and presents a low implementation complexity. In this context, our approach shows a good result when compared with the others in the literature. From the analysis of the results obtained by simulations, we observe that our approach to change the probability of both access and backoff time (as a strategy to differentiate the priorities between M2M and H2H classes and amongst M2M classes) can mitigate the impact of congestion caused by excessive M2M devices on LTE network. We have observed also that our approach to identify the congestion level (as low, medium, and high in the RAN of LTE network), in the base station constraints the amount of devices that can successfully access the base station.

References

[1] A. M. Maia, M. F. d. Castro, D. Vieira, and Y. Ghamri-Doudane, "Toward a new lte uplink packet scheduler for machine-to-machine communication," in 2014 Brazilian Symposium on Computer Networks and Distributed Systems, May 2014, pp. 122–129.

[2] Y. Chang, C. Zhou, and O. Bulakci, "Coordinated random access management for network overload avoidance in cellular machine-to-machine communications," in European Wireless 2014; 20th European Wireless Conference; Proceedings of. VDE, 2014, pp. 1–6.

[3] E. Dahlman, S. Parkvall, and J. Skold, 4G: LTE/LTE-advanced for mobile broadband. Academic press, 2013.

[4] 3GPP. http://www.3gpp.org/about-3gpp/about-3gpp. [Online; retrived March 19, 2017].

[5] K. Zheng, S. Ou, J. Alonso-Zarate, M. Dohler, F. Liu, and H. Zhu, "Challenges of massive access in highly dense lte-advanced networks with machine-to-machine communications," Wireless Communications, IEEE, vol. 21, no. 3, 2014, pp. 12–18.

[6] T.-M. Lin, C.-H. Lee, J.-P. Cheng, and W.-T. Chen, "Prada: Prioritized random access with dynamic access barring for mtc in 3gpp lte-a networks," Vehicular Technology, IEEE Transactions on, vol. 63, no. 5, Jun 2014, pp. 2467–2472.

[7] K.-D. Lee, S. Kim, and B. Yi, "Throughput comparison of random access methods for m2m service over lte networks," in GLOBECOM Workshops (GC Wkshps), 2011 IEEE. IEEE, 2011, pp. 373–377.

[8] S.-Y. Lien, T.-H. Liau, C.-Y. Kao, and K.-C. Chen, "Cooperative access class barring for machine-to-machine communications," Wireless Communications, IEEE Transactions on, vol. 11, no. 1, January 2012, pp. 27–32.

[9] 3GPP, "Service requirements for machine-type communications (mtc)," 3GPP, Tech. Rep., 2013.

[10] B. Yang, G. Zhu, W. Wu, and Y. Gao, "M2m access performance in lte-a system," Transactions on Emerging Telecommunications Technologies, vol. 25, no. 1, 2014, pp. 3–10.

[11] X. Jian, Y. Jia, X. Zeng, and J. Yang, "A novel class-dependent back-off scheme for machine type communication in lte systems," in Wireless and Optical Communication Conference (WOCC), 2013 22nd. IEEE, 2013, pp. 135–140.

[12] M. Hasan, E. Hossain, and D. Niyato, "Random access for machine-to-machine communication in lte-advanced networks: issues and approaches," Communications Magazine, IEEE, vol. 51, no. 6, 2013.

[13] A. Lo, Y. W. Law, M. Jacobsson, and M. Kucharzak, "Enhanced lte-advanced random-access mechanism for massive machine-to-machine (m2m) communications," in 27th World Wireless Research Forum (WWRF) Meeting, 2011, pp. 1–5.

[14] J.-L. Chen, H.-C. Hsieh, and Y. Larosa, "Congestion control optimization of m2m in lte networks," in Advanced Communication Technology (ICACT), 2013 15th International Conference on, Jan 2013, pp. 823–827.

[15] A. Laya, L. Alonso, and J. Alonso-Zarate, "Is the random access channel of lte and lte-a suitable for m2m communications? a survey of alternatives," Communications Surveys Tutorials, IEEE, vol. 16, no. 1, First 2014, pp. 4–16.

[16] U. Phuyal, A. T. Koc, M.-H. Fong, and R. Vannithamby, "Controlling access overload and signaling congestion in m2m networks," in Signals, Systems and Computers (ASILOMAR), 2012 Conference Record of the Forty Sixth Asilomar Conference on. IEEE, 2012, pp. 591–595.

[17] 3GPP, "Study on ran improvements for machine-type communication," 3GPP, Tech. Rep., 2014.

[18] M.-Y. Cheng, G.-Y. Lin, H.-Y. Wei, and C.-C. Hsu, "Performance evaluation of radio access network overloading from machine type communications in lte-a networks," in Wireless Communications and Networking Conference Workshops (WCNCW), 2012 IEEE. IEEE, 2012, pp. 248–252.

[19] The network simulator - NS-3. http://www.nsnam.org. [Online; retrived April 10, 2017].

[20] ZTE, "Backoff enhancements for ran overload control," 3GPP, Tech. Rep., 2011.

Offline Routing and Spectrum Allocation Algorithms for Elastic Optical Networks with Survivability

Rana Alaskar, Anwar Alyatama, Imtiaz Ahmad
Computer Engineering Department, Kuwait University, Kuwait
Email: rana.alaskar@hotmail.com, a.yatama@ku.edu.kw, imtiaz.ahmad@ku.edu.kw

Abstract—**Elastic optical networks (EONs) are a promising solution for future high-speed networks, because of their ability to efficiently manage network resources and provide better spectrum utilization. The intractable routing and spectrum allocation (RSA) problem and the eventually imposed survivability constraints play key roles in the effective design and control of EONs. In this work, we investigate priority allocation algorithms designed to solve the offline RSA problem in protection-based EONs. These algorithms are analyzed from the point of view of their main objective (minimizing the total amount of spectrum needed to serve the traffic demand), when the demand includes unicast unprotected and unicast protected requests. Unicast protected requests utilize a 1+1 dedicated path protection, with the same channel. The proposed priority allocation algorithms are based on the compact scheduling algorithm and the ordering obtained with two different metrics, both of which consider the bandwidth and required number of links of the requests presented to the network. We evaluate the performance and efficiency of the proposed algorithms across a range of demand frequency slots distributions in a mesh network. A comparative analysis of the obtained experimental results reveals that the proposed algorithms outperform existing reference algorithms in terms of spectrum utilization.**

Keywords-elastic optical networks; spectrum allocation; survivability; spectrum utilization.

I. INTRODUCTION

The increasing demand of multimedia streaming services, such as audio and video conferences, and cloud computing applications, requires increasingly higher data rates, flexible network resource management, and efficient spectral utilization. Traditional optical networks are unable to keep pace with the high data rate demands, because they are based on wavelength division multiplexing (WDM) technology, which wastes a large portion of the spectrum [1]. A different type of optical network—elastic optical network (EON)—has been recently presented in [2][3]. It can efficiently manage network resources and provide better spectrum utilization, because it is based on orthogonal frequency-division multiplexing (OFDM) technology [4]. OFDM is a multi-carrier modulation scheme that transmits a high-speed data stream by splitting it into several parallel data streams, each carrying a relatively low data rate.

Many challenges have been faced by EON researchers concerning hardware development, network control and management, and spectrum management. Routing and spectrum allocation (RSA) [5][6] is one of the key challenges to be faced, and has received much attention from researchers in recent years, because it lies at the core of the design and control of EONs. RSA includes two main functions: assigning a suitable physical path between the source and destination(s), and allocating contiguous, continuous, and non-overlapping parts of the spectrum to meet traffic demand, while minimizing the total amount of spectrum needed to serve it. RSA is an NP-hard problem, because of the continuity constraint [5]. It can be divided into offline and online RSA. The former is used when traffic demand is known in advance, and traffic variations occur over a long period of time, whereas the latter is used when traffic arrives in a random manner.

Many research has been conducted addressing the offline RSA problem. This problem was introduced by Jinno et al. [7]. Talebi et al. [8] mapped the offline RSA problem to a scheduling problem in multiprocessor systems. Genetic algorithms [9] and the tabu search algorithm [10] have also been proposed to solve the offline RSA problem and enhance spectrum utilization. We have recently proposed priority allocation algorithms [11] to handle offline RSA problem in unicast unprotected EONs. For more details about the spectrum management techniques in EONs, readers are referred to the recent excellent surveys in [1][12].

Data transmitted through the network can be of critical nature (e.g., military, medical, or financial information). Protecting the paths followed by those data is crucial, to ensure a continuous transfer of data. Survivability is an important design criterion for traditional networks in general and optical networks in particular, including EONs [13][14]; it describes the ability to continue providing services in the presence of a single failure, which could be caused by fiber cuts, active component failure inside the network equipment, or node failure [15]. Given that EONs have the capability of transmitting huge amounts of data, data transfer interruption due to node or link failures should be minimized or—if possible—completely avoided. Networks serve two types of request: protected and unprotected. Protected requests are designed to overcome a single network failure, most commonly by assigning a disjoint backup path (optical path, in the context) for each working path. The commonly used protection techniques can be divided into dedicated path protection (DPP) and shared path protection (SPP) techniques. Dedicated path protection means that each working path is assigned its own dedicated backup path, to which it can switch in case of a failure. On the other hand, shared path protection means that backup spectrum subcarriers can be shared on some links, as long as their protected segments (links, subpaths, paths) are mutually disjoint. Dedicated path protection can be either 1+1 or 1:1. In 1+1 dedicated path protection, traffic is simultaneously transmitted on both the working and backup paths. On the contrary, in 1:1 dedicated path protection, the backup path is idle and can be used to transmit low-priority traffic during normal operation. Two different channel allocation policies can be applied with the aforementioned protection schemes. The first one is a same channel (SC) policy, where the working path and the backup path share the same central frequency. The second is the different channel (DC) policy, where both the working path and the backup path can utilize any available central frequency. The different channel policy is considered to be a resource-consuming solution, in contrast with the same channel policy, which is a much more cost-effective solution [16]. In this paper, we the address offline routing and spectrum allocation problem with dedicated path protection in EONs with same channel (RSA/DPP/SC). It is worth mentioning that DPP is considered an expensive scheme, but has a quick recovery time. On the other hand, SPP saves network resources, but it needs much more time than DPP to recover from failure.

A significant amount of research has been carried out to study the issue of survivability of EONs. Some of these research efforts have been directed to the online (i.e., dynamic) RSA problem [17][18], whereas others considered the offline (i.e., static) RSA problem in survivable EONs, considering the different protection techniques mentioned above. (This later problem is the focus of this work.) In particular, the use of DPP in EONs has been addressed in [16][19]-[21]. Recently, Ruan et al. [15] studied the offline survivable multi-path RSA problem with DPP in EONs. They formulated the problem as an integer linear programming (ILP) problem. In the same context, Klinkowski [9] addressed RSA problem in EONs with DPP with static traffic demand, and he used genetic algorithms to develop an efficient algorithm, which performs better than other reference algorithms. Concurrently, the use of SPP in EONs has also been studied by many researchers [22]-[24]. Walkowiak et al. [23] addressed the offline RSA problem in EONs with SPP, formulating it also as an ILP problem. More details about the use of protection techniques in EONs can be found in [25], a recent survey of the topic.

In a recent paper [11], we addressed the offline RSA problem in EONs by introducing priority allocation algorithms for unicast unprotected networks. These algorithms are based on both the compact scheduling algorithm [8] and a combination of the request bandwidth and the number of links used by that request. Simulation results show that our proposed priority allocation algorithms, when applied to different network topologies (e.g., a chain network and the National Science Foundation network (NSFNET)) with diverse bandwidth distributions outperform the existing algorithms, and produce close to optimal solutions in a unicast unprotected network. In this paper, we extend our priority allocation algorithms to handle survivability in EONs with the goal of minimizing the amount of spectrum needed to serve the traffic demand. In particular, we study the behavior of the proposed algorithms when the traffic demand includes unicast unprotected, and unicast protected requests. We consider spectrum usage as a performance metric, to show the effectiveness of the proposed algorithms.

The rest of the paper is structured as follows. Section II formulates the problem. Section III reviews priority allocation algorithms, with working examples. Section IV discusses the experimental results. We present our conclusion in the last section.

II. PROBLEM FORMULATION

In this section, we present and explain the offline RSA problem in protection-based EONs, with an example that will be used in the priority allocation algorithms section.

A. Problem Statement

The problem to be addressed can be formulated as follows: Given: a) A directed graph $G(V, E)$, where G denotes the physical topology of an EON, V denotes the set of nodes, and E denotes the set of bidirectional optical links. b) A set of frequency slices (i.e., subcarriers) in each optical link, of cardinality sc. c) A set of requests between source-destination pairs $(s, d)_i$ of request size sz (i.e., the number of frequency slices needed to serve a request), where $i \in I$ represents the request type. Our aim is to minimize the amount of spectrum needed to serve the traffic demand—which includes different types of request to the mesh network—under the following constraints:

1) Spectrum contiguity constraint: Each request should be assigned to a contiguous portion of the spectrum.

2) Spectrum continuity constraint: Each request should be assigned to a similar portion of spectrum for all the corresponding links.

3) Non-overlapping spectrum constraint: Requests that need to use similar links should be assigned to non-overlapping portions of the spectrum.

4) Same channel (applies only to RSA/DPP/SC): For each unicast protected request, the working and backup paths should be assigned to similar portions of the spectrum.

In this paper, we consider two types of request, $I = \{1, 2\}$. A request can be unicast unprotected ($i = 1$), or unicast protected ($i = 2$). When the demand includes a unicast unprotected request $(s, d)_1$ from source s to destination d, the request will be served by contiguous subcarriers on all optical links belonging to the predetermined fixed working path from s to d. However, when the demand includes a unicast protected request $(s, d)_2$, the request will be served by contiguous subcarriers on all optical links belonging to both the predetermined fixed working path and the predetermined fixed backup path from s to d.

B. RSA/DPP/SC Example

To exemplify the problem, consider the mesh network illustrated in Figure 1, with four nodes and five bidirectional links, and the corresponding spectrum demand matrix $\boldsymbol{D}$ shown below. The demand matrix includes the requests from each source to each destination in the mesh network; the total number of requests in this example is therefore equals to 12.

In the case of a unicast unprotected request, the routing algorithm chooses an arbitrary fixed path (the working path) selected from the set of shortest paths computed with Dijkstra's algorithm. Unicast protected requests with DPP utilize both a working path and a backup path. The working path is fixed and arbitrarily selected from the set of shortest paths computed with Dijkstra's algorithm; likewise, the backup path is fixed and arbitrarily selected from the set of shortest paths computed by Dijkstra's algorithm, after removing all edges belonging to the working path.

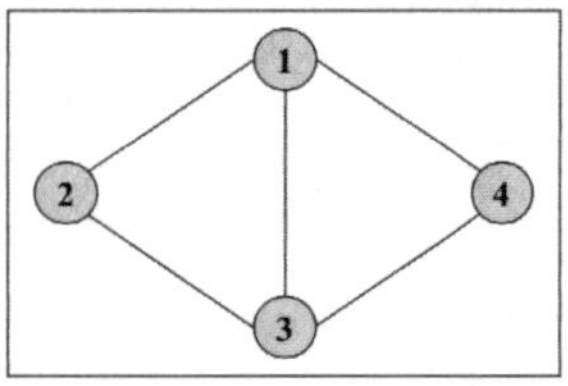

Figure 1. Mesh network with four nodes.

$$\mathbf{D} = \begin{bmatrix} 0 & 1 & 10 & 100 \\ 100 & 0 & 100 & 1 \\ 1 & 10 & 0 & 4 \\ 10 & 100 & 10 & 0 \end{bmatrix}$$

TABLE I. REQUESTS MADE TO THE MESH NETWORK

Requests $(s, d)_i$	Type of request	Size (sz)	Working path	Backup path
τ_1 $(1, 3)_2$	Unicast protected	10	1-3	1-4-3
τ_2 $(4, 3)_2$	Unicast protected	10	4-3	4-1-3
τ_3 $(2, 4)_2$	Unicast protected	1	2-1-4	2-3-4
τ_4 $(2, 1)_1$	Unicast unprotected	100	2-1	____
τ_5 $(2, 3)_2$	Unicast protected	100	2-3	2-1-3
τ_6 $(1, 2)_1$	Unicast unprotected	1	1-2	____
τ_7 $(3, 1)_2$	Unicast protected	1	3-1	3-2-1
τ_8 $(3, 2)_1$	Unicast unprotected	10	3-2	____
τ_9 $(3, 4)_2$	Unicast protected	4	3-4	3-1-4
τ_{10} $(4, 1)_1$	Unicast unprotected	10	4-1	____
τ_{11} $(1, 4)_1$	Unicast unprotected	100	1-4	____
τ_{12} $(4, 2)_1$	Unicast unprotected	100	4-1-2	____

Table I shows the requests made to the mesh network, type (unicast unprotected or protected), size (1, 4, 10, 40, or 100), and the nodes traversed by the working and backup paths. Those requests will be sorted based on the selected sorting mechanism, and the sorted list of requests will be used as an input to the compact scheduling algorithm [8].

III. PRIORITY ALLOCATION ALGORITHMS

In this section, we evaluate the extended version of the proposed algorithms [11] as a solution to the offline RSA problem in survivable OFDM optical networks; the objective is to minimize the amount of spectrum needed to serve traffic demand when it includes unicast unprotected, and unicast protected requests. The RSA problem has two different dimensions: the spectrum (or bandwidth) and the links. The combination of these two dimensions plays a key role in improving the process of spectrum allocation. Therefore, the proposed solution is based on combining them in multiple ways. First, we introduce the compact scheduling algorithm [8], which has been used to show the effectiveness of the proposed algorithms. We then review our priority allocation algorithms; specifically, the sorting mechanisms. Finally, we show a working example, to demonstrate the performance of the algorithms when compared with the existing algorithms.

A. Compact Scheduling Algorithm

The priority allocation algorithms proposed in [11] are based on an existing algorithm, the compact scheduling algorithm, proposed by Talebi et al. [8]. The compact scheduling algorithm is a typical list scheduling algorithm, where the quality of the solution is very sensitive to the order of requests in the list. It has a complexity of $O(n^2)$, where n is the number of requests in the list. The input to the compact scheduling algorithm is a sorted list of requests to the mesh network. The algorithm is constituted by the following steps:

1) Select the first request in the list and assign it to a set of consecutive links.
2) Delete the executed request from the list, and update the status (idle or busy) of the corresponding links.
3) Scan the list at the same scheduling instant to select requests that can be executed simultaneously with the currently executed requests.
4) Continue scanning the list until there are no other requests that can be executed at that scheduling instant or no available links.
5) Advance the scheduling time based on the earliest finishing request, and add the available links to the set of free links.
6) Repeat the aforementioned steps until all the requests have been satisfied.

B. Sorting Mechanisms

In [11], we proposed two priority allocation algorithms that consider both dimensions of the problem: the links and the spectrum (or bandwidth). It is worth mentioning that in the present paper the link dimension is represented by the number of links used by the working path in the case of unicast unprotected requests, and by the number of links used by both the working and backup paths in the case of unicast protected requests. On the other hand, in our previous work [11], the link dimension was represented by the number of links used by only the working path, because only unicast unprotected requests were being considered there. The sorting mechanisms, the longest then widest compact algorithm (LWC) and the area compact algorithm (AC), are described below.

1) Longest then Widest Compact Algorithm (LWC): In the first proposed algorithm, we consider both dimensions of the problem, the links and spectrum (or bandwidth), using two levels (a primary and a secondary sorting mechanisms) to sort the requests in the demand. In the primary sorting mechanism, requests are sorted based on the amount of needed spectrum or bandwidth (BW_i), from higher to lower. Then, in the secondary sorting mechanism, requests with equal bandwidth are sorted based on the required number of links (LK_i)—obtained in the terms described before—from higher to lower.

2) Area Compact Algorithm (AC): In the second proposed algorithm, we also consider both dimensions of the problem, but in a different way. The amount of spectrum needed for a request and the required number of links (in the working path, or the working and backup paths, depending on the type of request) are multiplied ($LK_i \times BW_i$), thus providing a shape area. This area captures both dimensions of the problem and constitutes a better ordering metric. In this mechanism, the areas are used to sort the requests in the list, from higher to lower.

C. Working Example

In this subsection, we discuss the behavior of the above-mentioned algorithms, and show how different sorting mechanisms can affect the amount of spectrum needed to satisfy the demand, when it includes both unicast unprotected and unicast protected requests. The requests lists presented below are based on the spectrum demand described in the problem formulation section.

1) Existing Algorithms:

The longest first compact algorithm (LFC), which was proposed in [8], sorts the requests based on the required amount of spectrum, from higher to lower. The sorted list of requests that will be used as input to the compact scheduling algorithm after applying the LFC algorithm is shown below:

$$\{\tau_4, \tau_5, \tau_{11}, \tau_{12}, \tau_8, \tau_{10}, \tau_1, \tau_2, \tau_9, \tau_6, \tau_7, \tau_3\}$$

Running the compact scheduling algorithm with LFC shows that 224 subcarriers are needed to serve the considered demand (which includes both unicast unprotected and unicast protected requests).

The widest first compact algorithm (WFC), also proposed in [8], sorts the requests based on the required number of links used by the working and/or backup paths, from higher to lower. The sorted list of requests that will be used as input to the compact scheduling algorithm after applying the WFC algorithm is shown below:

$$\{\tau_3, \tau_2, \tau_5, \tau_7, \tau_9, \tau_1, \tau_{12}, \tau_4, \tau_6, \tau_8, \tau_{10}, \tau_{11}\}$$

Running the compact scheduling algorithm with WFC shows that 215 subcarriers are needed to serve the considered demand.

2) LWC:

The sorted list of requests that will be used as input to the compact scheduling algorithm after applying the LWC algorithm is shown below:

$$\{\tau_5, \tau_{12}, \tau_{11}, \tau_4, \tau_1, \tau_2, \tau_8, \tau_{10}, \tau_9, \tau_3, \tau_7, \tau_6\}$$

Running the compact scheduling algorithm with LWC shows that only 202 subcarriers are needed to serve the same demand. The number of subcarriers needed with LWC is therefore lower than if either LFC or WFC are used (224 and 215, respectively).

3) AC:

The sorted list of requests that will be used as input to the compact scheduling algorithm after applying the AC algorithm is shown below:

$$\{\tau_5, \tau_{12}, \tau_4, \tau_{11}, \tau_1, \tau_2, \tau_9, \tau_{10}, \tau_8, \tau_3, \tau_7, \tau_6\}$$

In Figure 2 (a), request 5 is assigned at t = 0, and it occupies 100 subcarriers from the following links: 2-3, 2-1, and 1-3. Then, request 12 is assigned, and it occupies 100 subcarriers from the following links: 4-1, and 1-2. After that, request 11 is assigned, and it occupies 100 subcarriers from link 1-4. Last request that will be assigned at t = 0 is request 8, and it occupies 10 subcarriers from link 3-2. Figure 2 shows the spectrum utilization as time proceeds, using the AC algorithm. Running the compact scheduling algorithm with AC shows that 202 subcarriers are required for the considered demand. The number of subcarriers needed for AC is equal to the number of subcarriers needed for LWC, and lower than the numbers needed for both LFC and WFC (224 and 215, respectively).

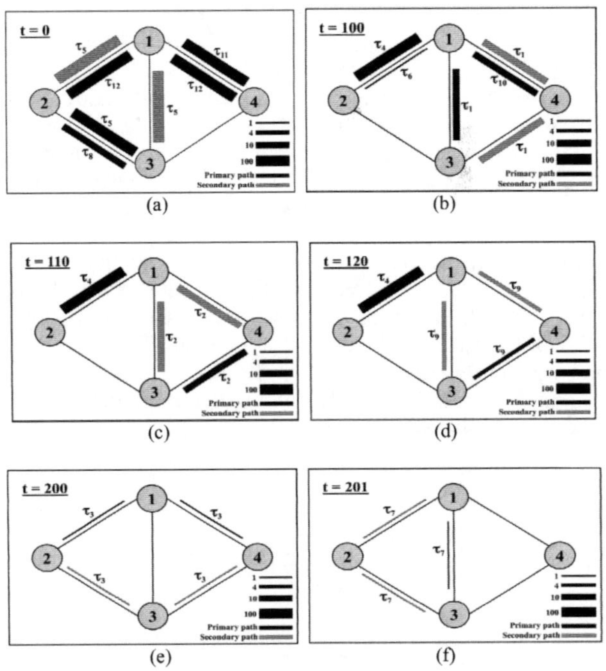

Figure 2. Area compact algorithm progression. (a) Step 1. (b) Step 2. (c) Step 3. (d) Step 4. (e) Step 5. (f) Step 6.

Although in the example both LWC and AC require the same number of subcarriers (i.e., 202 subcarriers) to serve the demand, their behaviors are quite different. They have different request ordering mechanisms and different request allocation orders. The performance difference between them will be discussed in the experimental results and analysis section.

IV. Eperimental Results and Analysis

In this section, we present a comparative evaluation between our algorithms and the heuristics recently proposed in [8] (i.e., LFC and WFC). We start by presenting the comparison metric used for performance evaluation, along with the simulation environment. We use three traffic frequency slot distributions (discrete uniform, discrete high, and discrete low) to measure and compare the performances of our algorithms. Finally, we present the performance and analysis results. It is worth mentioning that both LFC and WFC were developed in the context of an RSA problem without additional survivability constraints in the mesh network. Therefore, we modified the aforementioned existing algorithms to address the new constraints resulting from the use of protection.

A. Comparison Metric

We consider spectrum usage as the goal metric to evaluate the performance of our proposed algorithms. Spectrum usage is defined here as the number of subcarriers needed to serve a traffic demand including the three different types of request (i.e., unicast unprotected and unicast protected requests).

B. Simulation Setup

To test the proposed algorithms in terms of survivability EONs, we use the NSFNET like topology as in [11]. The mesh network is composed of 14 nodes and 20 bidirectional links, as shown in Figure 3. In the case of unicast unprotected requests, the routing algorithm assumes an arbitrary fixed path, selected from the set of shortest paths computed with Dijkstra's algorithm. Unicast protected requests with dedicated path protection utilize both a working path and a backup path. As with the unicast unprotected requests, the working path is fixed and arbitrarily selected from the set of shortest paths computed with Dijkstra's algorithm; likewise, the backup path is fixed and arbitrarily selected from the set of shortest paths computed with Dijkstra's algorithm, after removing all edges belonging to the working path.

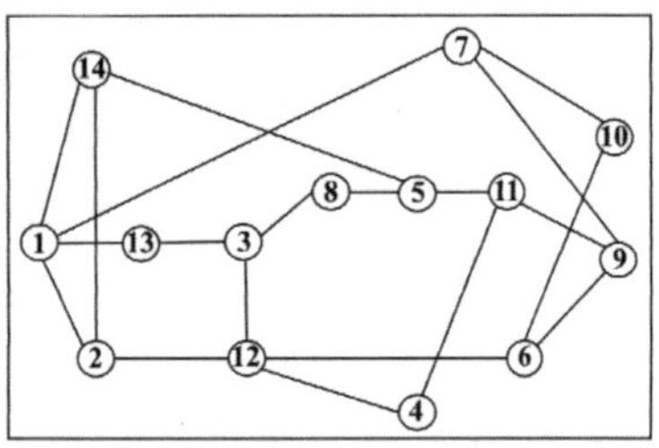

Figure 3. NSFNET-like topology.

We use a distance-adaptive spectrum allocation strategy to allocate the spectrum for each traffic demand based on its needed frequency slots and the length of its path as reported in [7][8][26]. We assume an elastic optical network with five different types of request sizes. Each demand requests 1, 4, 10, 40, and 100 frequency units. The size of the traffic demand is generated using three different types of frequency slot distributions (discrete uniform, discrete high, and discrete low). In the discrete uniform distribution case, all frequency slots have the same probability, whereas in the discrete high distribution higher frequency slots have higher probabilities, and in the discrete low distribution higher frequency slots have lower probabilities. The details of these three distributions and their frequency slot selection probabilities are listed in Table II.

TABLE II. Details of the Used Traffic Frequency Slots Distribution

Frequency slot	Discrete uniform	Discrete high	Discrete low
1	0.2	0.1	0.3
4	0.2	0.15	0.25
10	0.2	0.2	0.2
40	0.2	0.25	0.15
100	0.2	0.3	0.1

To evaluate our algorithms, we consider a scenario where the traffic demand includes both unicast unprotected and unicast protected requests; the ratio of unicast protected to unicast unprotected requests varies from 0 % to 50 %, in increments of 10 %, with different traffic demand generation patterns. Note that in the first data point in the graphs, all the requests are unicast unprotected, while in the last data point, half of the requests are unicast unprotected, and half are unicast protected. Table III presents the number of unicast unprotected and unicast protected requests in the scenario.

TABLE III. Number of Requests in the Scenario

Percentage (%)	Number of requests	
	Unicast unprotected	*Unicast protected*
0	182	0
10	164	18
20	146	36
30	128	54
40	110	72
50	91	91

Our proposed algorithms are implemented in C++ using Xcode (version 6.3.1) on a MacBook Pro with OS X El Capitan (version 10.11.4), a 2.2-GHz Intel Core i7 processor, and 16 GB of memory.

C. Performance Analysis and Results

In this subsection, we determine the average percentual improvement in the number of needed subcarriers to evaluate the performances of our proposed algorithms (LWC and AC) when compared with the two existing algorithms proposed in [8] (LFC and WFC). For each data point in our experiment, a large number of random problem instances (up to 8000) were executed, and only the resulting average values are being reported. The averaged results were obtained with 99 % confidence, with a confidence interval smaller than 1 % of the average value.

Figures 4, 5 and 6 show the average number of needed subcarriers versus the percentage of unicast protected requests, for both proposed algorithms and existing algorithms. Table IV presents the performance improvements of our proposed algorithms when compared to LFC and WFC, for different frequency slot distributions.

TABLE IV. AVERAGE PERCENTUAL IMPROVEMENTS

Distribution	LWC		AC	
	LFC	*WFC*	*LFC*	*WFC*
Uniform	8.5 %	6.9 %	8.5 %	6.9 %
Discrete high	9.5 %	7.1 %	9.6 %	7.2 %
Discrete low	6.3 %	6.1 %	6.3 %	6.1 %

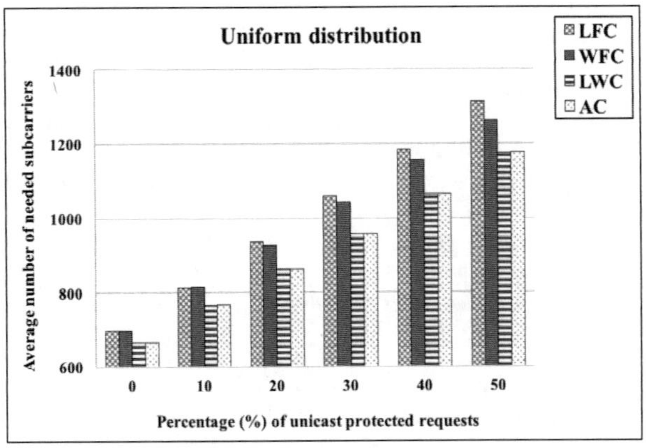

Figure 4. Average number of subcarriers as a function of the percentage of unicast protected requests; uniform frequency slot distribution.

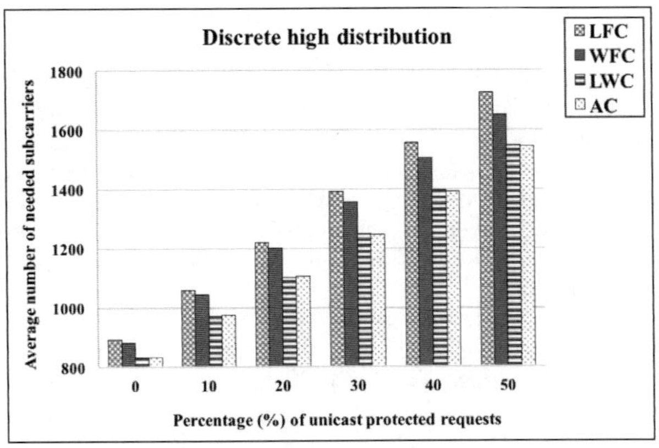

Figure 5. Average number of subcarriers as a function of the percentage of unicast protected requests; discrete high frequency slot distribution.

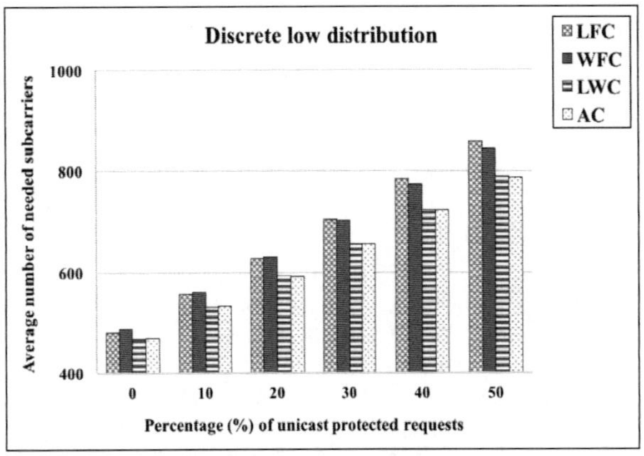

Figure 6. Average number of subcarriers as a function of the percentage of unicast protected requests; discrete low frequency slot distribution.

As shown in the figures, the proposed algorithms performed better than both the LFC and WFC algorithms. In other words, the number of needed subcarriers with our algorithms was less than the number of needed subcarriers with either LFC or WFC. In particular, in the case of a discrete high distribution of the requested frequency slots, LWC and AC improved the results obtained with LFC by 9.5 %, and 9.6 %, respectively; when compared with WFC, improvements of 7.1 % and 7.2 % were respectively obtained. As mentioned previously, considering both dimensions; the amount of spectrum and the number of links; while sorting the requests, affects the number of subcarriers needed to serve the traffic demand. Therefore, our sorting mechanisms outperform the existing mechanisms, and require less number of subcarriers.

V. CONCLUSION

In this paper, we addressed the intractable offline RSA problem in protection-based EONs. We investigated the efficiency of priority allocation algorithms based on the compact scheduling algorithm and the ordering obtained with two different metrics, both of which consider the bandwidth and required number of links of the requests presented to the network, albeit in slightly different ways. Our objective was to minimize the total amount of spectrum needed to serve traffic demand when this demand includes unicast unprotected and unicast protected requests. We evaluated the performance and efficiency of our algorithms across a range of frequency slot distributions. The obtained experimental results have shown that the proposed priority allocation algorithms outperformed other reference algorithms in term of spectrum utilization. The proposed priority allocation algorithms are robust, and can be used in EONs with different setups.

This work can be extended in several interesting directions. For instance, it would be enlightening to investigate the online RSA problem in EONs, in which concerns the reduction of blocking and/or fragmentation obtainable by combining multiple bin packing algorithms (e.g., first fit, best fit, and random fit). Moreover, it would also be very interesting to focus on the problem of how to efficiently handle the multicast protection problem in EONs, by finding the backup tree for a working (multicast) tree with the minimum amount of spectral resources.

REFERENCES

[1] S. Talebi, et al., "Spectrum management techniques for elastic optical networks: a survey," *Opt. Switch. Netw.*, vol. 13, pp. 34-48, July 2014.

[2] M. Jinno, et al., "Spectrum-efficient and scalable elastic optical path network: architecture, benefits, and enabling technologies," *IEEE Commun. Mag.*, vol. 47, no. 11, pp. 66-73, Nov. 2009.

[3] O. Gerstel, M. Jinno, A. Lord, and S. Yoo, "Elastic optical networking: a new dawn for the optical layers?" *IEEE Commun. Mag.*, vol. 50, no. 2, pp. s12-s20, Feb. 2012.

[4] G. Zhang, M. De Leenheer, A. Morea, and B. Mukherjee, "A survey on OFDM-based elastic core optical networking," *IEEE Commun. Surv. Tuts.*, vol. 15, no. 1, pp. 65-87, Feb. 2012.

[5] Y. Wang, X. Cao, and Y. Pan, "A study of the routing and spectrum allocation in spectrum-sliced elastic optical path networks," *Proc. 2011 IEEE INFOCOM*, Shanghai, 2011, pp. 1503-1511.

[6] M. Klinkowski and K. Walkowiak, "Routing and spectrum assignment in spectrum sliced elastic optical path network," *IEEE Commun. Lett.*, vol. 15, no. 8, pp. 884-886, Aug. 2011.

[7] M. Jinno, et al., "Distance-adaptive spectrum resource allocation in spectrum-sliced elastic optical path network," *IEEE Commun. Mag.*, vol. 48, no. 8, pp. 138-145, Aug. 2010.

[8] S. Talebi, E. Bampis, G. Lucarelli, I. Katib, and G. Rouskas, "Spectrum assignment in optical networks: a multiprocessor scheduling perspective," *IEEE/OSA J. Opt. Commun. Netw.*, vol. 6, no. 8, pp. 754-763, Aug. 2014.

[9] M. Klinkowski, "A genetic algorithm for solving RSA problem in elastic optical networks with dedicated path protection," *Adv. Intell. Syst. Comput*, vol. 189, pp. 167-176, 2013.

[10] R. Goscien, K. Walkowiak, and M. Klinkowski, "Tabu search algorithm for routing, modulation, and spectrum allocation in elastic optical network with anycast and unicast traffic," *Comput. Netw.*, vol. 79, pp. 148-165, March 2015.

[11] R.W. Alaskar, I. Ahmad, and A. Alyatama, "Offline routing and spectrum allocation algorithms for elastic optical networks," *Opt. Switch. Netw.*, vol. 21, pp. 76-92, July 2016.

[12] B. Chatterjee, N. Sarma, and E. Oki, "Routing and spectrum allocation in elastic optical networks: a tutorial," *Commun. Surv. Tuts.*, vol. 17, no. 3, pp. 1776-1800, May 2015.

[13] S. Ramamurthy and B. Mukherjee, "Survivable WDM mesh networks, Part I – Protection," *18th Annu. Joint Conf. IEEE Computer and Communications Societies*, New York, 1999, pp. 744-751.

[14] C. Politi, et al., "Dynamic operation of flexi-grid OFDM-based networks," *Optical Fiber Communication Conf. and Expo. and the Nat. Fiber Optic Engineers Conf.*, Los Angeles, CA, 2012, pp. 1-3.

[15] L. Ruan and Y. Zheng, "Dynamic survivable multipath routing and spectrum allocation in OFDM-based flexible optical networks," *J. Opt. Commun. Netw.*, vol. 6, no. 1, pp. 77-85, Jan. 2014.

[16] M. Klinkowski and K. Walkowiak, "Offline RSA algorithms for elastic optical networks with dedicated path protection consideration," *4th Int. Congress on Ultra-Modern Telecommunications and Control Systems and Workshops*, St. Petersburg, 2012, pp. 670-676.

[17] A. Alyatama, "Dynamic spectrum allocation for orthogonal frequency-division multiplexing optical networks with survivability and multicasting," *J. High Speed Netw.*, vol. 22, no. 1, pp. 1-13, Feb. 2016.

[18] A. Tarhan and C. Cavdar, "Shared path protection for distance adaptive elastic optical networks under dynamic traffic," *5th Int. Congr. on Ultra-Modern Telecommunications and Control Systems and Workshops*, Almaty, 2013, pp. 62-67.

[19] M. Klinkowski, "An evolutionary algorithm approach for dedicated path protection problem in elastic optical networks," *Cybern. Syst.*, vol. 44, no. 6-7, pp. 589-605, Aug. 2013.

[20] J. López, Y. Ye, V. López, and F. Jimenez, "Traffic and power-aware protection scheme in elastic optical networks," *XVth Int. Telecommunications Network Strategy and Planning Symposium*, Rome, 2012, pp. 1-6.

[21] K. Walkowiaka, M. Klinkowskib, B. Rabiegaa, and R. Gościeńa, "Routing and spectrum allocation algorithms for elastic optical networks with dedicated path protection," *Opt. Switch. Netw.*, vol. 13, pp. 63-75, July 2014.

[22] M. Liu, M. Tornatore, and B. Tornatore, "Survivable Traffic Grooming in Elastic Optical Networks—Shared Protection," *J. Lightw. Technol.*, vol. 31, no. 6, pp. 903-909, March 2013.

[23] K. Walkowiak and M. Klinkowski, "Shared Backup Path Protection in Elastic Optical Networks: Modeling and Optimization," *9th Int. Conf. Design of Reliable Communication Networks*, Budapest, 2013, pp. 187-194.

[24] C. Yang, N. Hua, and X. Zheng, "Shared Path Protection based on Spectrum Reserved Matrix Model in Bandwidth-Variable Optical Networks," *7th Int. ICST Conf. Communications and Networking in China*, Kun Ming, 2012, pp. 256-261.

[25] G. Shen, G. Guo, and S.K. Bose, "Survivable elastic optical networks: survey and perspective," *Photonic Netw. Commun.*, vol. 31, no. 1, pp. 71-87, Feb. 2016.

[26] M. Fayez, I. Katib, G.N. Rouskas, and H.M. Faheem, "Spectrum assignment in mesh elastic optical networks," *Proc. 24th Int. Conf. Computer Communications and Networks*, Las Vegas, NV, 2011, pp. 1-6.

Design of Composite Routing Metrics in LOADng Routing Protocol for IoT Applications

Deepthi Sasidharan and Lillykutty Jacob

Department of Electronics and Communication Engineering
National Institute of Technology Calicut, India 673 601
Email: deepthi_p140058ec@nitc.ac.in and lilly@nitc.ac.in

Abstract—**Machine to machine communication has gained increasing importance in the context of Internet of Things (IoT). The existing routing protocols for low-power, lossy networks (LLNs) mainly support multipoint to point or point to multipoint communications and have very limited support for point to point communication. The LOADng routing protocol is a source initiated reactive protocol with support for point to point communication. In this paper, a composite routing metric is proposed to improve the packet delivery ratio and the lifetime of a network using LOADng routing protocol. The results obtained through simulation show that using a composite metric can significantly improve the performance of LOADNg routing protocol for low-power, energy constrained networks with sparse traffic.**

Keywords–IoT; LOADng routing protocol; routing metrics, low-power lossy networks.

I. INTRODUCTION

The Internet of Thing (IoT) has gained importance in recent years. The IoT is composed of smartphones, laptops, health-care and home devices, and industry sensors [1]. Machine to machine communication has gained increasing importance in the context of Internet of Things (IoT) [2]. MTC avoids human intervention, and the machines communicate with each other to form an intelligent environment. MTC is an enhancement of the third generation partnership project (3GPP) [3]. Low power devices or sensor nodes constitute the majority of elements in IoT. The sensor nodes are limited in memory, bandwidth and energy requirements and often run on non-rechargeable batteries. These hardware constrained devices form a network known as low power lossy networks (LLNs) and follow IEEE802.15.4 standard [4].

The primary driving force behind the growth of IoT is the effectiveness of Ipv6 over low power lossy personal area networks (6LoWPAN). 6LoWPAN is an adaptation layer between the network layer and the data link layer [5]. The primary function of the 6LoWPAN is to convert IPv6 packets from the network layer into short IEEE802.15.4 frames. To encapsulate IPv6 packets in IEEE802.15.4 frames [4], 6LoWPAN requires performing IPv6 header compression, fragmentation, and defragmentation. The 6LoWPAN adaptation layer also performs routing between the nodes within the network. There exist many protocols for LLNs and consider the network to follow a source - sink architecture. Thus, most of the protocols are designed to support multipoint-to-point (M2P) or point-to-multipoint (P2M) communications. Moreover, they have limited options for point-to-point (P2P) communication.

IoT is more than just connecting a collection of sensor nodes to a common server and making it available from anyplace in the world through the Internet. IoT has enabled machines to communicate with each other without human intervention. So, the demand for one-to-one communication is as much as or even more than that of M2P or P2M. Devices in IoT are mostly low power and hardware constrained. Routing is an important procedure in IoT as the choice of the routing protocol can significantly improve the network performance. The selection of routing protocol is to support the application requirements [6]. Based on the procedure of establishing routes, routing protocols fall into three categories, namely, proactive, reactive and hybrid routing schemes. The proactive routing scheme periodically sends a short probe, such as a HELLO message, to its neighboring node. The node establishes a route to all possible destinations. When there is a data packet ready for transmission to a destination, the node checks its routing table and sends the data packet on the pre-calculated route. The reactive routing scheme, on the other hand, initiates a route discovery only when there is some data packet to be sent across the network over to a destination node and the routing information to the destination is not available at the sending node. The route to the destination is immediately available in proactive routing, but reactive routing needs time to discover a route to the destination. The hybrid routing scheme is a combination of both proactive and reactive routing schemes. The reactive routing scheme is best suited for a network with P2P communication. The Lightweight On-demand Ad hoc Distance-vector Routing Protocol - Next Generation (LOADng) [7] is a routing protocol specifically designed to address P2P communication between energy and hardware constrained nodes.

LOADng is a simplified adaptation of Ad-hoc On-demand Distance Vector (AODV) and is a reactive routing protocol for LLNs. LOADng is a source initiated reactive routing protocol and generates a route discovery when there is some data to be sent to the destination. The route is maintained as long it is in use and nodes discard any idle route from its routing table. Traditionally, LOADng uses hop count as the metric during route discovery. The hop count does not consider the constraints of the nodes in the network leading to the premature death of nodes, reducing the network lifetime.

The impact of different routing metrics on the performance of routing protocols in wireless sensor networks (WSNs) are widely studied in the literature [8]–[11]. Yang et al. [12] discuss the design considerations of routing metrics for multihop wireless networks and Zahariadis et al. [13] discuss the design aspects of primary and composite routing metrics from the LLNs perspective. The Routing Protocol for Low power and Lossy Networks (RPL) is a proactive rank based routing protocol specifically designed for LLNs and is standardized by the Routing Over Low power and Lossy networks (ROLL) working group [14]. RPL calculates the rank of a node using the route metrics. This rank is used to establish the node's position in a destination oriented directed acyclic graph (DODAG). An appropriate choice of RPL routing metrics can significantly improve Quality of Service (QoS) requirements in an LLN [15]–[21]. However, they all consider the LLNs as M2P and P2M networks and have the least support for P2P communication. Routing by Energy and Link quality (REL) is a variant of AODV and uses energy and link quality as the route metrics [22], [23]. The node requires sending periodic HELLO messages to maintain the list of neighbors.

The routing metrics fall into two categories, namely, node based and link based. Node based routing metrics consider the properties of the node such as the remaining energy, number of active connections through the node and transmission queue utilization. Link based routing metrics quantify the link properties between the nodes such as the Received Signal Strength Indicator (RSSI) and the expected transmission count (ETX). Each metric enumerates one or more distinct characteristics needed to enhance the QoS required such as packet delivery ratio, packet loss, latency, reliability, energy consumption and network lifetime. The selection of route metrics depends on the requirement of the application.

In literatures, network lifetime is defined as the time taken in the network for the first node to die or a percentage of nodes to die. Network lifetime can also be defined as the time taken by the network to get partitioned. This definition considers the time period when communication is not possible with one or more nodes in the network. The network can be represented as a fully connected graph where the nodes of the graph are the devices in the network and the connectivity between the devices form the edges of the graph. Efficient utilization of node energy is the prime concern to improve the network lifetime.

A Routing protocol that uses Remaining Energy (RE) metric can find a path with nodes which has maximum remaining energy. However, overusing such paths can quickly deplete the nodes energy. Live routes (LR) metric keeps track of the number of live or active routes through a node. The higher the value of LR, the higher the traffic through the node. Energy consumption rate of a node significantly depends on the energy required for transmitting and receiving data packets. The number of active routes through a node indicates the traffic load which is directly proportional to the energy consumption rate of the node.

LOADng has a provision to incorporate user-defined metrics in its METRIC TLV, and can contain 32-bit dimensionless additive metrics with single precision float value. It is possible to exploit this feature of LOADng to perform route discovery using alternate route metrics. However, there are hardly any works on route metrics design that address the node congestion due to large number of active routes.

In this paper, we propose a composite routing metric for LOADng to improve the lifetime of a network with P2P traffic. The network under consideration has sparse traffic density and the nodes have strict energy constraints. We propose a composite route metrics called LR+RE which combines LR, RE and Hop Count (HC) metrics. The resolution is to deal with the node congestion and the residual energy of the node to improve the network lifetime, improve the reliability of packet transmission and reduce the energy wastage of the nodes. We compare our results with the traditional HC metrics and also with LR and RE as the primary metrics. The rest of the paper is organized as follows. Section II gives a brief overview of the LOADng routing protocol. Section III explains the routing algebra used. Section IV defines and describes the composite routing metrics for LOADng. Section V discusses the numerical results. The conclusion and future works are presented in Section VI.

II. LOADng Routing Protocol

LOADng routing protocol is a simplified version of AODV routing protocol. LOADng has eliminated the HELLO messages of AODV and mandates that only the intended destination replies to the request message. LOADng uses a single message sequence number to uniquely identify its protocol messages. To ensure the freshness of the route, LOADng forces each node to monotonically increase its message sequence number with each protocol message which also ensures a loop-free path [24]. Clausen et al. [7] discuss how each node should process a LOADng protocol message and specifies the condition on which LOADng protocol messages are forwarded.

The route discovery in LOADng starts with the source initiating a Route Request (RREQ) message to a destination when the source has packets to send to the destination and a route entry for the destination is not available in its routing table. The source node will broadcast the RREQ message across the network. The intermediate nodes will process and rebroadcast RREQ messages. The destination node generates Route Reply (RREP) messages which will unicast back to the source node. A Route Reply Acknowledgement (RREP_ACK) message is generated by the intermediate nodes if the route reply acknowledgment required flag in the RREP message is true. This process will establish a bi-directional route between the source and the destination. The Route Error (RERR) message handles the route maintenance and connection failures.

III. Basics of Routing Algebra

In this work, the network is designed with low power wireless nodes. Graph $G(V, E)$ represents the model of the network. Vertices, V, is the set of all low power wireless devices and edges, E, is the set of links that stand for the connectivity between the nodes. An edge is present between two nodes if they are within the transmission range of each other and communication is possible between the two nodes. G is a strongly connected graph. Thus, every node is reachable from every other node through some path in the network.

Routing algebra is formally defined and studied in the literatures [12], [25]–[27], and it is also known as *path weight structure*. The quadruplet $(S, \oplus, \omega, \preceq)$ represents the routing tuple, where, S represents the set of all paths in the network, ω represents the function that maps a path to the weight, and $\oplus$ represents the concatenation operator used for two paths in the network [12]. The fourth element $\preceq$ represents the ordered relation between the paths $p, q \in S$; $\omega(p) \preceq \omega(q)$ means that the path p is lighter than the path q and $\omega(p) \prec \omega(q)$ means p is strictly lighter than q. Here, the lighter route is taken as a better route for routing option.

The optimality, loop-freeness, and consistency are the three essential requirements to ensure a routing protocol is usable. $R(s,d)$ represents the path converged by the routing protocol. A weight structure with route $R(s,d) = p =< s, v_1, v_2, ..., v_{n-1}, v_n, d >$ between the source s and the destination d is consistent if all the intermediate nodes choose the same path to destination d, then, $R(v_i, d) =< v_i, v_{i+1}, v_{i+2}, ..., v_n, d >, \forall v_i \in p$. A path $r =< v_1, v_2, ..., v_{n-1}, v_n >$ is loop-free if $v_i \neq v_j \forall\ i \neq j$. A path structure for a routing protocol, R, is optimal if it finds the lightest path from all the paths between two pair of nodes $(s,d) \in V$. That is, $R(s,d) \preceq p_{s.d}$ where $p_{s,d}$ is any non-empty path between the nodes s and d. This also ensures lightness of the route.

Isotonicity and monotonicity are the two properties of path weight structure. A routing metric must satisfy these two properties to ensure the optimality, loop-freeness, and consistency of the routing protocol. Isotonicity and monotonicity are defined as follows [12]:

> The quadruplet $(S, \oplus, \omega, \preceq)$ is **isotonic** if $\omega(p) \preceq \omega(q)$ implies both $\omega(p \oplus r) \preceq \omega(q \oplus r)$ and $\omega(s \oplus p) \preceq \omega(s \oplus q) \forall\ p, q, r, s \in S$. And, $(S, \oplus, \omega, \preceq)$ is **strictly isotonic** if $\omega(p) \prec \omega(q)$ implies both $\omega(p \oplus r) \prec \omega(q \oplus r)$ and $\omega(s \oplus p) \prec \omega(s \oplus q) \forall\ p, q, r, s \in S$.
>
> The quadruplet $(S, \oplus, \omega, \preceq)$ is **monotonic** if $\omega(p) \preceq \omega(p \oplus q)$ and $\omega(p) \preceq \omega(r \oplus p)$ holds $\forall\ p, q, r \in S$. And, $(S, \oplus, \omega, \preceq)$ is **strictly monotonic** if $\omega(p) \prec \omega(p \oplus q)$ and $\omega(p) \prec \omega(r \oplus p)$ holds $\forall\ p, q, r \in S$.

Isotonicity implies that the order relation will not be affected by prefixing or suffixing a third route. Isotonicity ensures that the path formulated by the routing protocol is optimal and strict optimality ensures the path is consistent. Monotonicity means that the path will not get lighter by prefixing or suffixing another path to it. Monotonicity ensures that the path found using the routing protocol is loop free.

IV. Route Metric for LOADng

In this section, we define the routing metric in two stages. The first stage defines the Remaining Energy (RE) metric and the Live Route (LR) metrics. The second stage is to establish a composite metric called $LR + RE$ and it is designed based on RE, LR, and HC. The RE metric is a ratio of the initial energy and the residual energy of the node.

$$RE = \frac{E_i}{E_{re}} \tag{1}$$

where E_i is taken as the initial energy, and E_{re} is the residual energy of the node. The value of RE increases slowly until residual energy reaches 10% and then increases rapidly after residual energy is less than 10%. This increment in RE will enable the routing protocol to avoid low energy nodes during the route discovery phase.

The LR metric counts the number of active connections through the node and the value of LR can be taken from the nodes routing table.

$$LR = routingTable.GetActiveRouteCount \tag{2}$$

While identifying the existing route from the routing table, any loopback addresses are to be avoided and all interfaces of the node are to be accounted for. Active number of connections per node indicates the traffic congestion through the node. As the value of LR increases for a node, the traffic congestion increases and can lead to dropping of packets. Choosing LR route metric can improve the packet delivery ratio by reducing the packet drop due to traffic congestion at a node.

A composite metric, $LR + RE$ is proposed by combining the RE, LR and HC metrics. Equation 3 gives the $LR + RE$ metrics for the node n.

$$\begin{aligned} \omega(n) &= \alpha RE_n + \beta LR_n + \gamma HC \\ or, \\ \omega(n) &= \alpha\omega_1(n) + \beta\omega_2(n) + \gamma\omega_3(n) \end{aligned} \tag{3}$$

where, RE_n is the ratio of Remaining Energy of the node n, LR_n is the active connections through the node n, HC is the hop count (equal to 1) and provides the minimum hop increment, and α, β, and γ are the tuning factors for RE_n, LR_n, and HC respectively. The route cost is the sum of the hop costs over all nodes along the path.

$$\omega(p) = \sum_{n \in p} \omega(n) \tag{4}$$

Minimum increment (HC) is necessary to ensure a minimum increase in the route cost when a node is added to the path to the destination. The choice of α and β depends on the application. When $\alpha = 0$ and $\beta = 0$, the routing protocol works like the traditional LOADng routing protocol. When $\alpha = 1$ and $\beta = 0$ LOADng works with RE as the routing metric and $\alpha = 0$ and $\beta = 1$ LOADng works with LR as the routing metric. When $\alpha \geq 1$ and $\beta \geq 1$, LOADng routing protocol work with the composite routing metric. $\gamma \geq 1$ is used to ensure there exists a minimum hop cost increment when a new node is added to the existing path and $\omega(n) > 0\ \forall\ n \in V$.

In this work, the concatenation operator $\oplus$ represents an addition of weight calculated by the node to the weight present in the routing packet. Equation 5 defines concatenation operator $\oplus$.

$$\begin{aligned} \omega(p \oplus q) &= \omega(p) + \omega(q) \\ &= \alpha\omega_1(p) + \beta\omega_2(p) + \gamma\omega_3(p) \\ &+ \alpha\omega_1(q) + \beta\omega_2(q) + \gamma\omega_3(q) \end{aligned} \tag{5}$$

Ordered relation $\preceq$ means less than of equal to $(\leq)$ and Equation 6 defines the ordered relation $\preceq$.

$$\omega(p) \preceq \omega(q) \cong \omega(p) \leq \omega(q) \tag{6}$$

The proposed composite routing metric $(LR + RE)$ is additive and should hold the two properties: isotonicity and monotonicity.

Theorem The $LR + RE$ composite routing metric is isotononic.

Proof: Since we add the minimum hop increment $HC = 1$

with $\gamma \geq 1$, $\omega(p) > 0$ and $r \in S$ is a non empty path. Then,

$$\begin{aligned}
\omega(p) \preceq \omega(q) &\Rightarrow \omega(p) + \omega(r) \preceq \omega(q) + \omega(r) \\
&\Rightarrow \alpha\omega_1(p) + \beta\omega_2(p) + \gamma\omega_3(p) \\
&\quad + \alpha\omega_1(r) + \beta\omega_2(r) + \gamma\omega_3(r) \preceq \\
&\quad \alpha\omega_1(q) + \beta\omega_2(q) + \gamma\omega_3(q) \\
&\quad + \alpha\omega_1(r) + \beta\omega_2(r) + \gamma\omega_3(r) \\
&\Rightarrow \omega(p \oplus r) \preceq \omega(q \oplus r) \quad \{from\ Eqn.\ 5\} \\
and, & \\
\omega(p) \preceq \omega(q) &\Rightarrow \omega(r) + \omega(p) \preceq \omega(r) + \omega(q) \\
&\Rightarrow \alpha\omega_1(r) + \beta\omega_2(r) + \gamma\omega_3(r) \\
&\quad + \alpha\omega_1(p) + \beta\omega_2(p) + \gamma\omega_3(p) \preceq \\
&\quad \alpha\omega_1(r) + \beta\omega_2(r) + \gamma\omega_3(r) \\
&\quad + \alpha\omega_1(q) + \beta\omega_2(q) + \gamma\omega_3(q) \\
&\Rightarrow \omega(r \oplus p) \preceq \omega(r \oplus q) \quad \{from\ Eqn.\ 5\}
\end{aligned}$$

$\Rightarrow metric\ is\ Isotonic$

Since $\omega(p) > 0$, the above statements are valid for $\omega(p) \prec \omega(q)$ as well. Hence, $LR + RE$ metric is strictly isotonic.

Theorem The composite routing metrics proposed is monotonic.

Proof: Since we add the minimum hop increment $HC = 1$ with $\gamma \geq 1$, $\omega(p) > 0$ and $r \in S$ is a non empty path. Then,

$$\begin{aligned}
&\omega(p) \preceq \omega(p \oplus r) \\
&\Rightarrow \omega(p) \preceq \alpha\omega_1(p) + \beta\omega_2(p) + \gamma\omega_3(p) \\
&\qquad + \alpha\omega_1(r) + \beta\omega_2(r) + \gamma\omega_3(r) \ \{from\ Eqn.\ 5\} \\
&\Rightarrow \omega(p) \preceq \omega(p) + \omega(r) \\
&since,\ we\ know\ \omega(p) > 0\ and\ \omega(r) > 0, \\
&the\ metric\ is\ right\ monotonic.and, \\
&\omega(p) \preceq \omega(r \oplus p) \\
&\Rightarrow \omega(p) \preceq \alpha\omega_1(r) + \beta\omega_2(r) + \gamma\omega_3(r) \\
&\qquad + \alpha\omega_1(p) + \beta\omega_2(p) + \gamma\omega_3(p) \ \{from\ Eqn.\ 5\} \\
&\Rightarrow \omega(p) \preceq \omega(r) + \omega(p) \\
&since,\ we\ know\ \omega(p) > 0\ and\ \omega(r) > 0, \\
&the\ metric\ is\ left\ monotonic. \\
&\Rightarrow metric\ is\ Monotonic.
\end{aligned}$$

Since $\omega(p) > 0$, the above statements are valid for $\omega(p) \prec \omega(p \oplus r)$ as well and hence, $(LR + RE)$ composite metric is strictly monotonic. Thus, the proposed routing metric satisfies the two properties and it is a suitable candidate for LOADng routing protocol.

LOADng routing protocol is designed to use the $LR + RE$ composite routing metric instead of hop count as its metric. Figure 1 shows the route update rules while processing its route discovery messages.

Algorithm 1 Route Update Rule - LOADng

```
dst := packct_destination;
seqNum := packet_sequence_number;
HC := 1;
RE := node_ResidualEnegry;
LR := node_ActiveRoutes;
nodeCost := α ∗ RE + β ∗ LR + γ ∗ HC;
routeCost := packet_routeCost + nodeCost;
hopCount := packet_hopCount + HC
route := routingT ableEntry(dst); /* Get the routing table entry
                                       for destination*/
if route = N U LL then
    route_seqNum := seqNum;
    route_hopCount := hopCount;
    route_routeCost := routeCost;
    insert(dst, route)
else if route_seqNum < seqNum ||
 (route_seqNum = seqNum && route_routeCost < routeCost) ||
 route_seqNum = seqNum && route_routeCost =routeCost &&
      route_hopCount < hopCount)
then
    route_seqNum := seqNum;
    route_hopCount := hopCount;
    route_routeCost := routeCost;
    update(dst, route)
end if
```

Figure 1. Route Update Rule - LOADng

V. Numerical Results and Discussions

LOADng routing protocol with the proposed metric was implemented and simulated in Network Simulator 3 (NS3). Initially, LOADng protocol was developed using the traditional Hop Count metric and then it was modified to incorporate the composite metric. The results obtained are compared with HC, RE, and LR as the primary metrics for LOADng routing protocol. The packet drop, packet delivery ratio (PDR), the maximum residual energy of any node after the network dies, the energy wastage of the network and the network lifetime are analyzed and compared. The simulation is allowed to run until any of its nodes run out of battery. Network lifetime is taken as the time at which the first node in the network dies off. All values are computed with the assumption that the network is homogeneous, and all nodes start with the same initial energy. The network is uniformly distributed with constant node density. Random traffic is generated between two distinct pairs of nodes where 15% of the nodes are active sources. The paper does not consider mobility and consider all nodes in network static.

Figure 2 shows the percentage of packet dropped versus the total number of nodes in the network. The packet drop over the traditional LOADng with HC route metric is higher compared to the other three options. The LOADng with LR metric performs better than the RE and HC, as the LR metric is capable of identifying the congested nodes in the network and avoid them whenever possible. However, when using $LR + RE$, the packet drop was further reduced. The reduction in the percentage of packet dropped is owing to the ability of

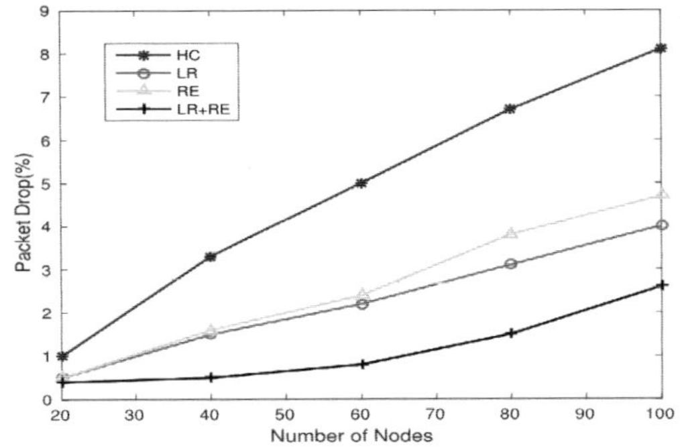

Figure 2. Percentage of Packet Drop

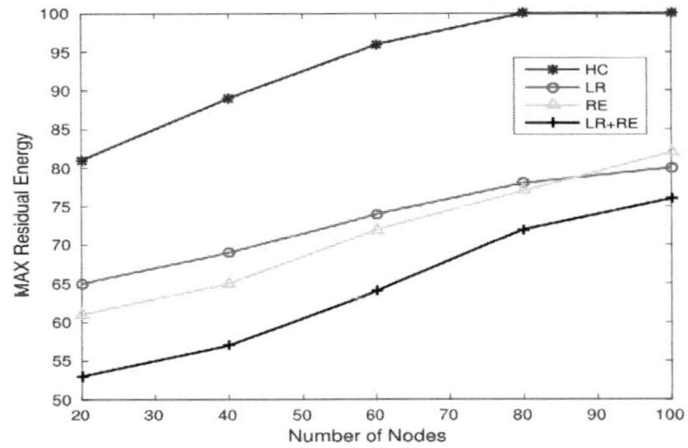

Figure 4. Maximum Residual Energy

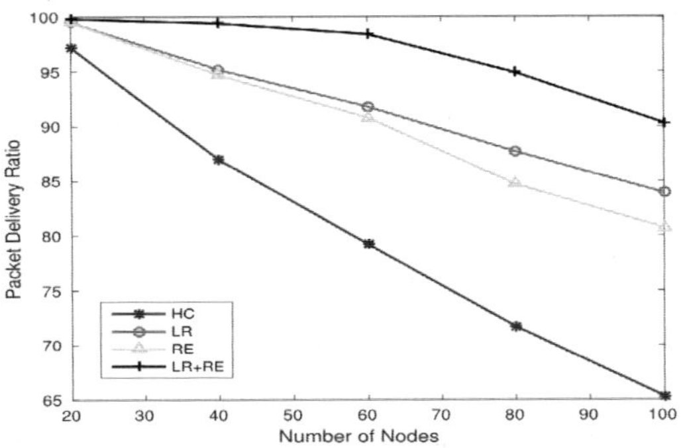

Figure 3. Packet Delivery Ratio

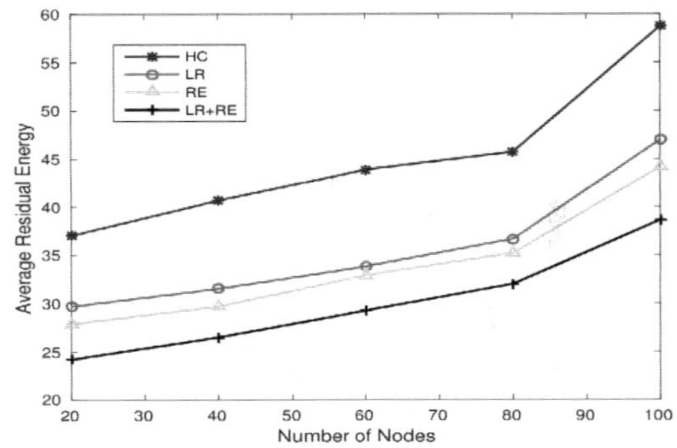

Figure 5. Average Residual Energy

$LR + RE$ to identify the congested node and nodes with low energy and avoid them as much as possible.

The direct consequence of the reduction in percentage packet drop is the improvement in the PDR. Figure 3 shows the PDR versus the number of nodes in the network. PDR decreases when the number of nodes in the network increase and the number of hops required to reach the destination increases. HC has the lowest PDR compared to other three metrics. HC only considers the shortest path towards the destination. PDR is better for the LR metric in comparison to the RE metric. $LR + RE$ outperforms all the other metrics under consideration.

Energy wastage is also a significant concern in a low power network. Energy wastage is the amount of energy remaining in the node after the network reaches its lifetime. Routing protocol should distribute the energy consumption to ensure the minimum energy wastage. Reduced energy wastage also shows the ability of the protocol to distribute the load within the network in a fair manner.

$$E_{max\_residual\_energy} = max(v_i(E_{re}) : \forall v_i \in V) \quad (7)$$

where, $v_i(E_{re})$ is the residual energy of node v_i.

Figure 4 shows the maximum residual energy of some node after the network reaches its lifetime. The corner node in the network remains largely unused in case of the traditional LOADng routing protocol. Thus, the HC metric does not distribute the load in an efficient manner. The RE metric shows a better distribution than LR. However, as the number of nodes in the network grows the routing protocol with LR metric surpasses the performance of RE metric. $LR + RE$ takes the advantage of both LR and RE. The maximum residual energy by any node in the network is lowest for $LR + RE$.

The average residual energy of the network is computed using the Equation 8.

$$E_{net_avg} = \frac{\sum_{i=1}^{N}(v_i(E_{re}))}{N} \quad (8)$$

where N is the total number of nodes in the network.

Simulation results show that the energy distribution of RE metric is better than LR metric. $LR + RE$ has the lowest average network energy. Here, the low values of E_{net_avg} indicate even distribution of the load and reduced energy wastage. This scenario satisfies the primary requirement of LLNs with energy constrained devices. Figure 5 shows the comparison of E_{net_avg} for different metrics.

The network lifetime comparison is given in Figure 6. LOADng with HC metric has the lowest lifetime because it fails to address congestion and energy constraints of the node. Network lifetime of RE metric is better than LR metric as RE metric addresses the energy constraints of the node. The composite metric $LR + RE$ gives the best performance out of all metrics under consideration. $LR + RE$ shows an initial improvement in the network lifetime when the number of nodes in the network is 40. This improvement is attributed to

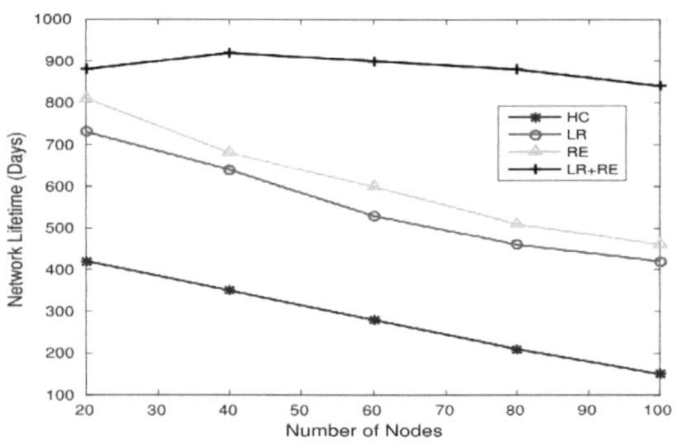

Figure 6. Network Lifetime

higher number of the nodes, and hence more path options available. The network lifetime decreases as the number of nodes increases because the hop distance between the source and destination also has increased. LOADng routing protocol with composite routing metric, $LR+RE$, significantly improves the network lifetime and the PDR compared to the conventional LOADng routing protocol with HC as the routing metrics.

VI. Conclusion and Future Works

In this paper, we consider routing metrics design for LLNs to support machine to machine communication in IoT. The LOADng routing protocol supports point to point communication in a network with sparse traffic. A composite routing metric $LR + RE$ is proposed in this paper which combines the remaining energy and the number of active routes through the node. The packet drop, packet delivery ratio, the maximum energy of any node after the network dies, the energy wastage of the network and the network life are analyzed and compared. The results obtained through simulation show that using composite metric $LR + RE$ with LOADng routing protocol can significantly improve the performance of LLNs with energy constrained devices with sparse traffic. As a future work, we propose to incorporate link quality metrics to improve QoS requirements of the network.

References

[1] L. Atzori, A. Iera, and G. Morabito, "The internet of things: A survey," Computer networks, vol. 54, no. 15, 2010, pp. 2787–2805.

[2] A. Kunz, A. Prasad, K. Samdanis, S. Husain, and J. Song, "Enhanced 3gpp system for machine type communications and internet of things," in 2015 IEEE Conference on Standards for Communications and Networking (CSCN), Oct 2015, pp. 48–53.

[3] T. Taleb and A. Kunz, "Machine type communications in 3gpp networks: potential, challenges, and solutions," IEEE Communications Magazine, vol. 50, no. 3, 2012.

[4] IEEE, "Ieee standard for local and metropolitan area networks–part 15.4: Low-rate wireless personal area networks (lr-wpans) amendment 3: Physical layer (phy) specifications for low-data-rate, wireless, smart metering utility networks," IEEE Std 802.15.4g-2012 (Amendment to IEEE Std 802.15.4-2011), April 2012, pp. 1–252.

[5] N. Kushalnagar, G. Montenegro, and C. Schumacher, "Ipv6 over low-power wireless personal area networks (6lowpans): overview, assumptions, problem statement, and goals," Internet Requests for Comments, RFC 4914, August 2007.

[6] M. Boushaba, A. Hafid, and M. Gendreau, "Source-based routing in wireless mesh networks," IEEE Systems Journal, vol. 10, no. 1, 2016, pp. 262–270.

[7] T. Clausen et al., "The lightweight on-demand ad hoc distance-vector routing protocol-next generation (loadng)," draft-clausen-lln-loadng-15 (work in progress), 2016.

[8] S. D. Odabasi and A. H. Zaim, "A survey on wireless mesh networks, routing metrics and protocols," International journal of electronics, mechanical and mechatronics engineering, vol. 2, no. 1, 2010, pp. 92–104.

[9] N. Javaid, A. Javaid, I. A. Khan, and K. Djouani, "Performance study of etx based wireless routing metrics," in Computer, Control and Communication, 2009. IC4 2009. 2nd International Conference on. IEEE, 2009, pp. 1–7.

[10] M. E. M. Campista et al., "Routing metrics and protocols for wireless mesh networks," IEEE network, vol. 22, no. 1, 2008, pp. 6–12.

[11] M. G. Gouda and M. Schneider, "Maximizable routing metrics," IEEE/ACM Transactions on Networking (TON), vol. 11, no. 4, 2003, pp. 663–675.

[12] Y. Yang and J. Wang, "Design guidelines for routing metrics in multihop wireless networks," in INFOCOM 2008. The 27th conference on computer communications. IEEE. IEEE, 2008.

[13] T. Zahariadis and P. Trakadas, "Design guidelines for routing metrics composition in lln," Internet RFCs- (Expired Internet-Draft), 2012.

[14] T. Winter et al., "Rpl: Ipv6 routing protocol for low-power and lossy networks," Internet Requests for Comments, RFC 6550, March 2012.

[15] W. Xiao, J. Liu, N. Jiang, and H. Shi, "An optimization of the object function for routing protocol of low-power and lossy networks," in Systems and Informatics (ICSAI), 2014 2nd International Conference on. IEEE, 2014, pp. 515–519.

[16] P. Karkazis et al., "Evaluating routing metric composition approaches for qos differentiation in low power and lossy networks," Wireless networks, vol. 19, no. 6, 2013, pp. 1269–1284.

[17] X. Yang, J. Guo, P. Orlik, K. Parsons, and K. Ishibashi, "Stability metric based routing protocol for low-power and lossy networks," in 2014 IEEE International Conference on Communications (ICC). IEEE, 2014, pp. 3688–3693.

[18] T.-H. Lee, X.-S. Xie, and L.-H. Chang, "Rssi-based ipv6 routing metrics for rpl in low-power and lossy networks," in 2014 IEEE International Conference on Systems, Man, and Cybernetics (SMC). IEEE, 2014, pp. 1714–1719.

[19] O. Iova, F. Theoleyre, and T. Noel, "Improving the network lifetime with energy-balancing routing: Application to rpl," in Wireless and Mobile Networking Conference (WMNC), 2014 7th IFIP. IEEE, 2014, pp. 1–8.

[20] P. Karkazis et al., "Design of primary and composite routing metrics for rpl-compliant wireless sensor networks," in Telecommunications and Multimedia (TEMU), 2012 International Conference on. IEEE, 2012, pp. 13–18.

[21] S. Capone, R. Brama, N. Accettura, D. Striccoli, and G. Boggia, "An energy efficient and reliable composite metric for rpl organized networks," in Embedded and Ubiquitous Computing (EUC), 2014 12th IEEE International Conference on. IEEE, 2014, pp. 178–184.

[22] K. Machado et al., "A routing protocol based on energy and link quality for internet of things applications," Sensors, vol. 13, no. 2, 2013, pp. 1942–1964.

[23] J. V. Sobral, J. J. Rodrigues, K. Saleem, J. F. de Paz, and J. M. Corchado, "A composite routing metric for wireless sensor networks in aal-iot," in Wireless and Mobile Networking Conference (WMNC), 2016 9th IFIP. IEEE, 2016, pp. 168–173.

[24] D. Sasidharan and L. Jacob, "Energy and bandwidth efficient multipath-enhanced loadng routing protocol," in 2016 Twenty Second National Conference on Communication (NCC), March 2016, pp. 1–6.

[25] J. L. Sobrinho, "Algebra and algorithms for qos path computation and hop-by-hop routing in the internet," in INFOCOM 2001. Twentieth Annual Joint Conference of the IEEE Computer and Communications Societies. Proceedings. IEEE, vol. 2. IEEE, 2001, pp. 727–735.

[26] Y. Yang, J. Wang, and R. Kravets, "Designing routing metrics for mesh networks," in IEEE Workshop on Wireless Mesh Networks (WiMesh), 2005, pp. 1–9.

[27] J. L. Sobrinho, "An algebraic theory of dynamic network routing," IEEE/ACM Transactions on Networking (TON), vol. 13, no. 5, 2005, pp. 1160–1173.

An Intelligent Agent for Computer Security and Forensic Training

Davi Teles*, André dos Santos† Marcial P Fernandez‡
Universidade Estadual do Ceará
Fortaleza, Ceará, Brazil
Email: *davi@insert.uece.br, †andre@insert.uece.br, ‡marcial.fernandez@uece.br

***Abstract*—The information security and digital forensic training practice is a challenging task because it requires a controlled environment, operating system files and network elements, and is prone to corrupted files. The forensic professional needs to collect and analyze many system logs and historical data to provide a correct identification to unknown attacks. Thus, Shellter, a social network dedicated to teaching and practice of information security and digital forensic training is aimed to help educators, tutors, students and enthusiasts in this area. Shellter offers challenges, educational tracks, materials for studies, information sharing forums and simulations to provide a full arena for hands-on learning. In the simulated environment, one difficulty is motivating users to exploit their knowledge, to learn new things, and to reach the goals presented by the system. This work presents a multi-agent system to provide a realistic training environment, motivating students to learn information security and forensics. The proposed agent was evaluated in the Shellter environment and shows an improvement on creating new tasks to motivate the student.**

Keywords–Information Security and Forensic; Intelligence Agent; Security and Forensic Training; Simulation

I. INTRODUCTION

Human resources training and development in information security and digital forensic requires hands-on training, not just theoretical learning [1]. To practice and perform exercises without broken production systems, a simulated environment is necessary. The training system should be able to create realistic situations, but it should not impact the real world. By attacking your own network or a production network, you may damage the infrastructure. Therefore, it is more appropriate to learn and practice cyber security in an isolated computing environment specially created for this purpose.

Digital Forensics can be defined as the use of scientific methods for the collection, validation, identification, analysis and interpretation of digital evidence for reconstruction events found to be criminal or not, and the identification of unauthorized actions. In the traditional digital forensic training, the instructor needs to present evidence and request the student to identify the attack and discover the authors. This methodology permits discovery of only well-known attacks, deeming it unsuitable for the real world.

Simulation-based games are widely used in training professionals. The simulations start with a well-defined scenario developed during a match. Teams representing different countries begin to attack and react to the situations proposed. Gamification is a motivational technique derived from games. This helps to maintain students interest, thereby increasing their learning. It uses the game dynamic mechanics, as the reward and rank actions taken by a particular participant (computer or not) in a game [2]. It also reinforces the need to use the correct level of difficulty techniques for a specific student knowledge level. Motivating students to learn is an old challenge of educational professionals. Students feel motivated to participate in learning activities if they believe that, with their knowledge, talents, and skills, they can acquire new knowledge, master content, and improve their skills, etc [3].

Learning motivation is always under discussion within the school, pushing students to go further or driving them to go back, even withdrawal in more complex cases. It has a very important role in both, the instructors and the students results. In virtual-learning environments, i.e., non-classroom learning environments, motivating students to study becomes a great challenge because the instructor cannot identify the feelings expressed by the students, for example, their facial expressions or personal conversations [4].

The Shellter system, presented in Section III-C, is a social network for security information training. Shellter offers complete computer systems to solve various challenges in information security, as well as the simulation environment to reproduce raining in actual situations. One of the great challenges to improve the Shellter tool is to create brand new unknown attacks to improve student practice in information security and digital forensic. Another challenge is to motivate students to learn, to test their limits, seek new knowledge and overcome unknown challenges. So, mechanisms to increase learning and motivation in the Shellter system inspired this work.

This paper proposes an intelligent agent system to monitor learning in virtual environments and motivates students using gamification techniques. This system consists of five different agents that work together. This system will analyze student profile, student interests in social networks, success or failure in past challenges and attitudes towards difficulties, to define the techniques applied by the system. Thus, a definition and its requirements of the system will be made, and also, the architecture and interactions between agents. The system validation will be done by the implementation and testing of a prototype of one agent part of the system due to its similarity with the other agents. The choice of the prototype took into account the time available for this work.

This work is organized as follows: in Section II, we present some related work, while the basis of agents and gamification is shown in Section III. In Section IV, we present the proposed agent architecture. Sections V and VI show the prototype, experimental evaluation and the results. Section VIII concludes the paper and presents some intended future work.

II. Related Work

The Tele-Lab project is a hands-on system to practice and train for information security [5]. It offers a virtual environment based on Web accessibility for any place. The system consists of text and video tutorials and practice exercises in a virtual environment in a pool of virtual machines. Students practice the information security exercises by accessing Secure Shell (SSH). For motivation, students are invited to assume the attacker's perspective.

SOFTICE is a proposal which focuses on teaching operating system with hands-on exercises [6]. In particular, its goal is aimed at learning Linux's kernel vulnerabilities focusing on its functions, definitions and implementations. In SOFTICE, students can test their knowledge and implement new Linux's kernel modules in a controlled environment. SOFTICE works by the hypothesis which Linux's kernel code is huge, complex and can make students lose motivation.

Insight is a simulation framework to create and imitate cyber attacks [7]. The attacks are part of scenarios available within the framework. Each scenario has different actors, e.g., network devices, software, network protocols and user. The goal is to simulate attacks from the attacker. With a customized interface, the students can create their own attacks. The attacks are executed inside the Insight framework to guarantee isolation and transparency of the simulated environment. A probabilistic model gives support to decide whether an attack has been successful, based on a combination of virtual machine configurations and attack techniques.

CTF365 is a security training platform for the IT industry with a focus on security professionals, system administrators and Web developers [8]. It provides a real life cyber range where users build their own servers and defend them while attacking other servers [8]. The platform implements Capture The Flag (CTF) concepts and leverages gamification mechanics to improve retention rate and speed up the learning/training curve [8].

III. Background

Given the literature review, in this section, the concepts related to, and influencing the design of the proposed architecture are presented.

A. Inteligent Agent

An Intelligent Agent (IA) is a piece of software that exists in an environment, is not controlled externally, responds (in a timely manner) to changes in its environment, persistently pursues goals, has multiple ways of achieving goals, recovers from failure and interacts with other agents [9].

B. Gamification

Gamification is the capacity to derive in a thoughtful way, the mechanism, fun and addiction of games for other contexts with no relationship with games to motivate people to accomplish results. This brings focus to humans, considering that they don't always feel motivated to accomplish their tasks and a lot of time they need something to become motivated. Gamification is a technique to apply game-design elements and game principles in learning contexts to improve student engagement. It explores the human instinctive natural behaviors to accomplish their goals [3].

C. Shellter

Shellter [10] is a social network dedicated to information security learning. Shellter is idealized, developed and maintained by the Information Security Research Team - Insert, a researching group from Universidade Estadual do Ceará - Brazil. When using Shellter, users can interact in the same way online game users do: building teams or playing solo in challenges so that, in time, they could evolve from novice hackers to pro hackers. In a cloud computing security environment, lab and virtual simulations happen with different types of challenges for distinct types of abilities. With gamification techniques, Shellter builds a space for security information continuing education. Users will test their abilities and can learn new techniques in Shellter's Cyber Warfare environment, providing a real experience in a computer network.

Through virtualization techniques, it will be possible to simulate different scenarios of attacks, defense or attack/defense. The goal is to create an actual hands-on environment for learning. In this simulation environment, users can play alone, against other users or against the intelligent agent system, proposed in this work.

IV. Intelligent Agent for Network Security and Forensic Training

To maintain users' motivation for learning, it is necessary to overcome student limits. Motivating users to seek new acknowledgments and experiences is the goals of Intelligent Agent for Network Security (IANS). The system will monitor users' performance and evolution and will interact with them to encourage continuous study and practice of information security. In addition, it will push them to overcome limits and knowledge. In particular, IANS will classify users according to their knowledge level and their experience with information security. With this classification, it will be possible the choose the most appropriate IA for users profiles.

These two types of IAs discourage the user because it makes the game more difficult rather than easier. The aim is to help users evolve gradually and, in time, they can face more difficult challenges and scenarios. After choosing the correct IAs to play, a second phase begins, namely, the evolution of IAs in the game time. The IAs need to follow users evaluation, because users will be constantly challenged to extend their knowledge. In this second phase, the IAs will use artificial intelligence techniques to learn, in real time, and can accomplish two main goals: (1) evolve according to the user, and (2) evolve according to the environment.

To accomplish these goals, in this work we use the following methodology: (1) Define the IANS architecture, specifying each one of its components and interactions in the system; and, (2) Define, implement, test and validate one of the IAs of IANS. We select the Environment Change Agent (ECA), due to its similar architecture to the others IAs.

A. Proposed Architecture

Figure 1 shows the IANS's architecture of the model based reflex agent that synthesizes the ideas of Russell & Norvig's, related to a reactive agent program [11], as well as the abstract architecture point of view proposed by Wooldridge in [12].

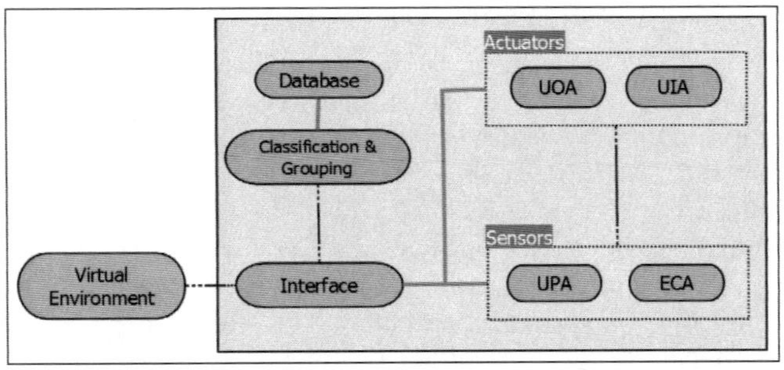

Fig. 1. Intelligent Agent for Network Security Architecture

1) Classification and Grouping - C&G: C&G engine is responsible for classifying users according to their knowledge and experience levels. This classification will be used to choose the appropriate IAs to play and interact with. Before accessing the simulated environment, the users will be asked to allow C&G analyze their social networks data set. With this, we will be able to capture users' interests, experiences and knowledge Some social networks considered are:

- **Facebook:** Users' activities (sharing posts, liked pages, community debates, etc.) will be analyzed to get interests about information security;
- **Github:** Punctuate the users for creation and participation in open source projects;
- **Stackoverflow:** It offers a space to ask about computer science and it sources relevance of issues and answers.
- **Tocoder:** Offers different type of programming challenges;
- **Shellter:** Shellter's profile offers a data set about learning and performance in Shelters environment and challenges, showing the users' strongest and weakest abilitys in information security.

2) User Progress Agent (UPA): In the group of sensor IAs, UPA monitors users' activities. The UPA's actions aim to identify affection and emotional experience that influence the learning process [4]. This IA will be used to compute affective techniques. Lester et. al [4] show some techniques to model emotions to measure the level of engagement and motivation. To capture these emotions, we will use the following plugins:

- **Keyboard plugin**: Will capture all user keyboard entries. These entries represent the user interaction frequency with the environment, access to challenges, number of answers, response time, etc. Keyloggers will be used to capture this information;
- **Video plugin**: It captures facial expressions, gestures, posture and any other body expressions made by the user. Then, it will be possible to identify the user's feelings and emotions [4].
- **Audio plugin**: This plugin will monitor users' sounds during the simulation: sounds emitted and heard. Music favors reasoning, evokes feelings and can change moods, reaching the cognitive and affective dimensions of the human being.
- **Content plugin**: It will be responsible for analyzing what the user is accessing during the simulation: web pages, open study material, etc. The goal is to identify whether users are focusing on solving challenges in a simulated environment.

3) Environment Change Agent (ECA): The ECA is responsible for monitoring and identifying changes in the computer environment for users and IAs which interact with users. ECA will be implemented in this work. Changes in computer environment are necessary to accomplish the most unique information security techniques that need to change files, open/close ports, change configurations, etc. ECA will connect these changes with information security techniques.

To identify these techniques, ECA will use a classification taxonomy, defined in Section V-A1, and a technique catalog of known information security techniques, defined in Section V-A2. To monitor and capture data in computers' environments, ECA will use keyloggers, for users' inputs, and plugins, for use and modifications in computer elements: virtual machines, services, applications, directories, files, virtual networks, switches, routers, firewalls, configurations, etc. It will also consider the access to resources like open and read files.

4) User Opponent Agent (UOA): Starting actuators IAs, UOA will play through attacks and defense actions based on information collected and processed for sensors IAs. This information allows UOA to formulate strategies to play against users and teams:

- What techniques are used to attack/defend in terms of user's knowledge?
- What techniques are used to attack/defend in terms of user's evolution?
- What techniques are used to attack/defend in terms of the modifications in computer environment?

Executing its actions, UOA will use plugins to act in virtual environment and verify the consequences of these actions on the environment. UOA will be analogous to a user, in the sense that it can execute any actions the user can in environment. For example, it can execute shell commands, create and execute scripts, click on icons, etc.

5) User Interaction Agent (UIA): The UIA is also an actuator IA which interacts with users based on the collected information by sensor IAs. However, its purpose is different from UOA. The UIA's goal is for interacting with users to motivate and encourage them to expand their knowledge. It acts like a user's tutor, following their activities to pursue their tasks' accomplishment, always keeping them motivated, even with difficult to complete tasks.

B. Agents Interaction

The use of IAs to improve users' motivation by monitoring simulated environment is a good approach because it can detect changes in environment, acting proactively to execute tasks to reduce negative effects. To achieve this, the IAs have the function to perceive their environment and interact with users and computer environment to maintain the users' motivation. Figure 2 shows the relationship among IAs, users and computational environment. The information exchange among sensors IAs, actuators IAs and monitored environment is a constant activity to achieve the goals of IANS. Figure 3 shows the interaction among IANS's IAs.

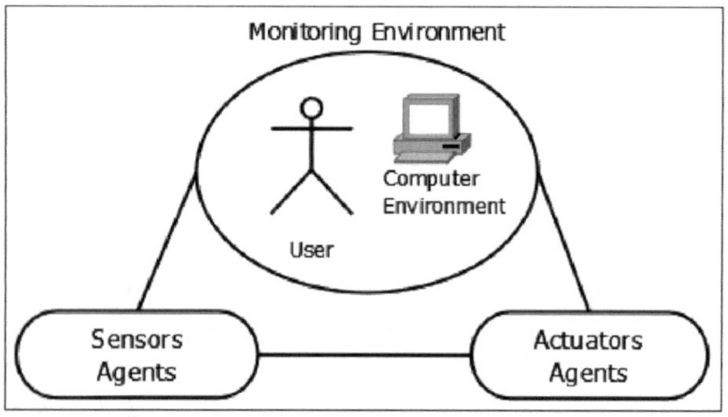

Fig. 2. Relationship among agents vs computer environment vs user

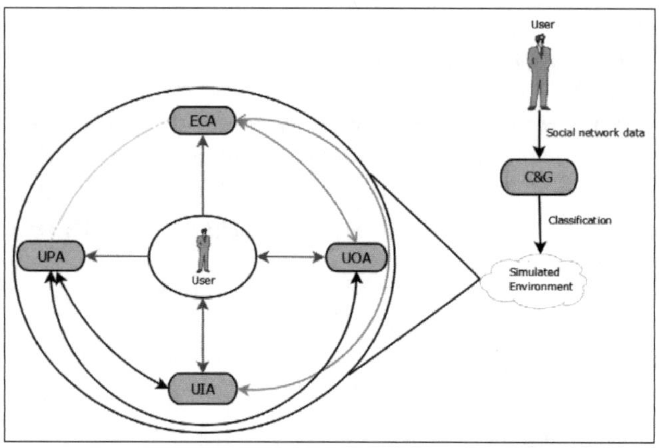

Fig. 3. Interaction among IANS's IAs

Before users gain access to the virtual environment, they need to provide their social network data set to the Classification and Grouping (C&A) engine in order to rank users. The C&A classifies the user and informs IANS's IAs to permit them to gain access to the virtual environment. In the environment, the users will face the most unique security information challenges while IA's sensors monitor their activities. The UPA monitors user's emotion and facial expression to measure motivation and engagement. Meanwhile, ECA monitors the environment modifications made by users to allow IAs to identify appropriate information security techniques. After collecting, processing and analyzing the information, the IAs sensor gives a command to IAs actuators. The UOA plays against the user, applying information security techniques based on data set taken from IAs sensors. At the same time, the UIA uses these data sets to seek the best way to motivate users and apply it, providing study materials, teaching techniques, etc.

V. PROTOTYPE EVALUATION

In order to evaluate the proposed IA, it was developed as a prototype of Environment Change Agent (ECA). The ECA is the most important agent in the architecture. This choice is based on the agent importance for the system and for its influence on other agents. Moreover, ECA's architecture is similar to the others three agents's architecture. C&G use ECA's data to classify users, because the ECA classifies user's abilities and experiences, according to information security techniques applied in virtual environment. The UOA uses this data to analyze, plan and execute attack and defense techniques. The UIA tutoring users with ECA and UOA's data. Finally, UPA is indirectly influenced by ECA, because it depends on user classification and challenge levels, suggested in virtual in environment.

A. Environment Change Agent (ECA) Implementation

To implement ECA, first, it will be necessary to define an information security technique taxonomy and cataloging. Thereafter, we will define the ECA's agent program, the logic formalization, the test and the validations.

1) Security Technique Taxonomy: The proposed taxonomy is shown in Figure 4. Initially, the technique is classified in ***attack*** or ***defense***. Then, the technique is classified according to the information security area: ***Networking***, ***Operating System - OS***, ***Programming*** and ***Database- DB***. Finally, the technique is classified according the difficult level: ***easy***, ***medium*** and ***hard***.

2) Security Technique Cataloging: For cataloging techniques, it is necessary to set an unique identifier for each one. This identifier is formed by a combination of classification criteria and a counter. The first technique, cataloged ***Attack - Network - Hard***, will have the identifier ***ANH1***. Moreover, each identifier will be associated with two information security databases: *CVE* and *Exploit-DB*. The Common Vulnerabilities and Exposures (CVE) is a public dictionary about information security vulnerabilities and exposures, since 2000. Exploit-DB is an exploit repository, i.e., a piece of code which tries to compromise a computer system, created and maintained by Offensive Security [13].

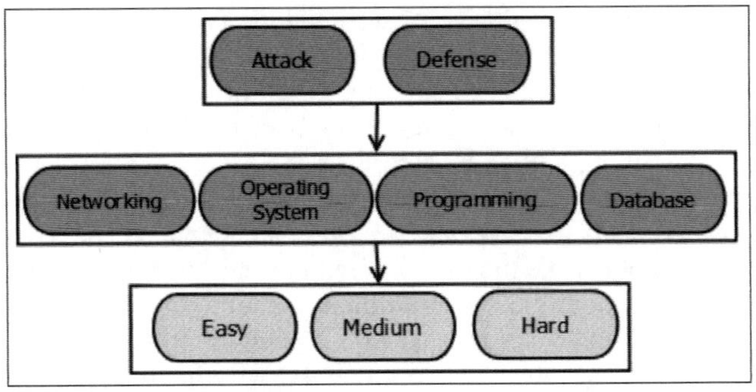

Fig. 4. Taxonomy of information security techniques

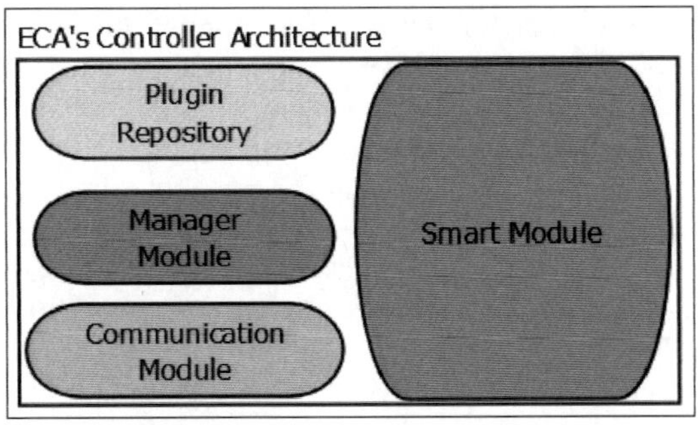

Fig. 5. Intelligent Agent for Network Security Architecture

3) Agent Implementation: The ECA has centralized software architecture for the best plugin's management, in order to provide scalability and resiliency. Another goal is to optimize the number of resources in virtual machines. In the ECA's architecture, it is possible to identify two modules: (1) the controller; and, (2) the plugin. The Controller will implement the ECA's rationality. It will receive the data from plugins, and the decision will be made based on its goals and it will be applied to an actuation (classification). Moreover, it will manage and distribute plugins to the computer environment according to demand. The control of plugins will happen through a table that will be handled with an IP address, operating system and version of computer environment and depending on if the plugins are active in this environment or not. For each unknown environment, a new line will be added to this table and, if an environment is deleted, the line will be marked as deactivated.

The controller, shown in Figure 5, has three modules responsible for agent operation:

- **Plugin Repository**: It is a repository for different types of plugins for distinct types of computer environments. Each environment, depending on platform, architecture and operating system version will have the appropriate plugin for it. Each plugin can be used for one or more environments;
- **Manager Module**: It has the responsibility of managing all plugins in all environments. It controls the entry, exclusion, activation, deactivation and sensor configuration. This module will have information about classification of information security techniques.
- **Communication Module**: It controls the communication between plugins and controller. Receive collected data, send new sensors, send commands and monitor the activity of them;
- **Smart Module**: It is responsible for interpreting and processing data sent from plugins and making a decision about it. The agent modeling will be in this module.

The controller sends a suitable plugin for the target environment to monitor the used information security techniques from the users on it. For this, initially, the Manager Module adds an entry in the control table containing IP address, operating system and OS version from the environment and chooses the appropriate plugin from Plugin Repository. The chosen plugin is sent into the computer environment by Communication Module through File Transfer Protocol (FTP) or Secure Copy Protocol (SCP) and starts the environment monitoring. The plugin has a local database with a set of information security techniques that will be monitored. This database is managed by the Manager Plugin.

The plugin sends the collected data to the Communication Module with their perceptions through REST requests. The received perceptions are passed to the Smart Module where they will be analyzed by ECA's formalization program (Section V-C). If the user received a positive classification for a technique, the plugin do not need to continuous monitoring if the this technique will be applied again. So, after the user is classified based on the information security techniques applied in the environment, the Manager Module checks what techniques were identified. It sends a command to plugin, through the Communication Module, to plugin stop monitoring the identified techniques. This action aims to minimize resources used in the computer environment.

B. Security Treads

The ECA's program will capture the user's commands in simulated environment and will identify and classify information security techniques based on its catalog. The technique shown is based on an Exploit-DB and CVE vulnerability.

1) Security Technique - SSH Root Access: This vulnerability is the capacity to access Linux environment as a root user, based on Debian, through SSH protocol. It is considered a vulnerability because with SSH root access allowed, an attacker can focus on a broken root password with social engineering or brute force techniques. Since root is a default super user in Linux distributions, it is highly recommended to disable remote access to avoid this type of attack. So, an attacker already has the information about a valid user with super powers in the system.

To classify it, ECAs will monitor, through its plugins, two types of user movements:

- **Attack**: ECA will verify if the user applies the following command: ***ssh root@TARGET_IP*** or ***ssh root@TARGET_IP « $password_dictionary***;

- **Defense**: in archive ***/etc/ssh/sshd_config***, ECA will check if parameter ***PermitRootLogin*** is set for ***YES*** or ***NO***. Parameter set to YES allows SSH root access and set to NO disables SSH root access.

This technique will be classified and cataloged as ***Attack, OS, Easy - AOE1*** or ***Defense, OS, Easy - DOE1***, depending on the context.

C. Agent Formalization

Figure 6 shows ECA's formalization algorithm.

```
Algorithm 1: ECA Formalization Algorithm
Data: Perception list - Data collected by plugins
      Expected states list - Expected perception for user
      classification
Begin;
for Perception list do
    for Expected states list do
        if Perception Code X == Expected Perception Code X then
            if Perception != Expected State then
                classified user like FALSE for analyzed
                 technique;
            else
                classified user like TRUE for analyzed technique;
            end
        end
    end
end
return User technique classification list;
End;
```

Fig. 6. ECA Formalization Algorithm

ECA receives the following inputs: (1) Perception list, a list of user's applied techniques received from plugins; and, (2) Expected state list, a list with expected state for user classification. The algorithm returns the user classification technique list, i.e, the user's classification related to the evaluated technique.

D. Prototype Validation

In this section, we will present the tests performed to validate the ECA's program. In other words, we will test the capability of the ECA to classify information security techniques cataloged in its database. For this, we will use the technique defined in Sub-subsection V-B1. ECA's validation tests done using this formalization. Therefore, we created lists to simulate the perceptions of ECA. The chosen perceptions were related to the technique defined in V-B.

In the tests, we tried to create a dataset of different combinations of inputs for the ECA because it would act in a different information security training environment and will find various circumstances, like configurations and users.

Our test scenario was based on *Linux Mint 17.3 64 Bits Debian* and for codification we chose *Python 3.4* and *Prolog*

VI. Results

Table I shows the IA evaluation results considering the expected classification and perception obtained by IA. The first column shows the simulated perceptions; the second column shows expected state for classification, and the third column indicates the results from agent's action. The table structure was made to compare the perception that was used for input of ECA prototype with the expected result of the classification, as this is a simulation, and the result of the ECA's program for classifying the input perception.

The results of the tests show that ECA classified all perceptions correctly, as shown in the *Result* column. In the input list perception, the first information is considered a technique identification. In this identification, the agent's program can find what is the correct state to be compared to the expected state list. Next, the data considers what is in brackets, *[ ]*. These refer to plugins perceptions in environment (simulated in this case).

To detect if the classification needs the combination of one or more parameters and commands, ECA's program searches for *&&* and || separators. They refer to logical operators considered by ECA. The operator *&&* indicates the logical ***AND*** combination, and so, the classification needs combination of one ***AND*** more parameters. The operator || indicates logical ***OR*** combination, and the classification needs one parameter ***OR*** more parameters.

Therefore, different input combinations were tested. For example, AOE1 was tested with distinct methods. Initially, we tested the simple brute force with a single password, then, we executed a more complex brute force test using a combination of multiple password dictionaries.

VII. Forensic Training

For computer forensics, it is important to understand about different areas. In addition to computer science, a forensic examiner needs to know about the local law, best practices, crime scene rules, police procedures, court rules, question from lawyers, etc. The responsibility of a computer forensic examiner goes beyond the limits of computer science.

Therefore, a student can be surprised and unmotivated by all these rules, because he/she is expecting to study and learn forensic computer techniques by learning about the file system, files structures, cryptography, algorithms, operating system, etc.

IANS can be used in all phases of a computer forensic training: preparation of the environment, data collecting, data duplication, data processing, data analysis, data carving, technical explanation, reporting, etc. The system can help students to stay motivated to learn all phases and procedures of a forensic investigation, face new challenges and learn new skills. Furthermore, it can be applied in many other areas, not only in information security knowledge, but also to meet the requirements to form a computer forensic examiner. In addition, ECA will work to identify and classify cataloged forensic techniques applied in a simulated environment.

For example, an advanced student of computer forensics will solve a simulated real-life scenario, where he must follow a specific procedure that will not contaminate evidence , understand the legal aspects and will not let lawyers contest his/her's report. So, IANS will monitor all his/her's performance, looking to monitor, classify, motivate and tutor him/her

TABLE I. INTELLIGENT AGENT EVALUATION RESULTS.

Perception	*Expected Classification*	*Result*
AOE1 - [ssh root@192.168.3.78 && ssh root@192.168.3.78 « $password_dictionary]	AOE1 - TRUE	AOE1 - TRUE
AOE1 - [ssh root@192.168.3.78 « $password_dictionary]	AOE1 - TRUE	AOE1 - TRUE
AOE1 - [ssh root@192.168.3.78]	AOE1 - TRUE	AOE1 - TRUE
AOE1 - [ ]	AOE1 - FALSE	AOE1 - FALSE
DOE1 - [PermitRootLogin YES]	DOE1 - FALSE	DOE1 - FALSE
DOE1 - [PermitRootLogin NO]	DOE1 - TRUE	DOE1 - TRUE
AOE1 - [ssh root@192.168.3.78 && ssh root@192.168.3.78 « $password_dictionary]	AOE1 - TRUE	AOE1 - TRUE
AOE1 - [ssh root@192.168.3.78 « $password_dictionary]	AOE1 - TRUE	AOE1 - TRUE
AOE1 - [ssh root@192.168.3.78]	AOE1 - TRUE	AOE1 - TRUE
AOE1 - [ssh admin@192.168.3.78 && ssh admin@192.168.3.78 « $password_dictionary]	AOE1 - FALSE	AOE1 - FALSE
AOE1 - [ssh admin@192.168.3.78 « $password_dictionary]	AOE1 - FALSE	AOE1 - FALSE
AOE1 - [ssh admin@192.168.3.78]	AOE1 - FALSE	AOE1 - FALSE
AOE1 - [ ]	AOE1 - FALSE	AOE1 - FALSE
DOE1 - [PermitRootLogin YES]	DOE1 - FALSE	DOE1 - FALSE
DOE1 - [PermitRootLogin NO]	DOE1 - TRUE	DOE1 - TRUE
DOE1 - [ ]	DOE1 - FALSE	DOE1 - FALSE

to apply his/her repertoire of forensic techniques and learn new ones, and he/she will do the same for the legal and procedure requirements defined in the scenario.

VIII. Conclusion and Future Work

This work presents a smart logical agent system in the Shellter security training system which was implemented in the synthesis of the architecture proposed in [12] and [11], that works in a rational way. The intelligent agent system monitors the students progress in the virtual environment to motivate them by using gamification techniques. The system analyzes the student profile in social networks searching for student interests, success or failure in past challenges to choose the techniques to be applied, emotional expressions, exceptional information security techniques and intervene in a student's activity to tutor him at the right moment.

A prototype agent was developed in order to show the system's functionality. This prototype was chosen based on the similarity of architecture of the agents that compose the system and its level of importance in the system. The Prolog implementation for the first predicate logic model-based reflex agent was evaluated in the test scenario by condition-action rules. The agent was subjected to a battery of tests, validating its operation using a simulated user case. So, it is possible to use the results from this work in a real-life scenario. The agent notation abstraction was implemented to facilitate the adoption of other security threats in the production system.

In the future, we will develop other agents not evaluated in this work, namely: (1) the UOA, (2) the UIA and (3) the UPA. Furthermore, there is room for considerable improvement in system performance.

Acknowledgments

The authors wish to thank the CAPES (Coordenação de Aperfeiçoamento de Pessoal de Nível Superior) and CNPq (Conselho Nacional de Desenvolvimento Científico e Tecnológico) for supporting this research work through the "Projeto FORTE - Forense digital tempestiva e eficiente - Processo 23038.007604/2014-69" project and Produtividade em Desenvolvimento Tecnológico e Extensão Inovadora - DT – Processo 305905/2016-3 funded by CNPq/Brazil.

References

[1] A. Nagarajan, J. Allbeck, A. Sood, and T. Janssen, "Exploring game design for cybersecurity training," in *Cyber Technology in Automation, Control, and Intelligent Systems (CYBER), 2012 IEEE International Conference on*, May 2012, pp. 256–262.

[2] B. Könings, F. Groh, N. Asaj, M. Poguntke, F. Schaub, B. Wiedersheim, and M. Weber, "Gamification: State of the art definition and utilization," in *Proceedings of the 4th Seminar on Research Trends in Media Informatics*, 2012, pp. 39–46.

[3] C. I. Muntean, "Raising engagement in e-learning through gamification," University of Cluj-Napoca, 1 Mihail Kogalniceanu Street, 400084 Cluj-Napoca, România, 2011, pp. 323–329.

[4] J. C. Lester, E. Y. Ha, S. Y. Lee, B. W. Mott, J. P. Rowe, and J. L. Sabourin, "Serious games get smart: Intelligent game-based learning environments," *AI Magazine*, vol. 34, no. 4, pp. 31–45, 2013.

[5] C. Willems and C. Meinel, "Practical network security teaching in an online virtual laboratory," in *Proceedings of the 2011 International Conference on Security & Management*, 2011.

[6] A. Gaspar, S. Langevin, J. Stanaback, and C. Godwin, "SOFTICE: facilitating both adoption of linux undergraduate operating systems laboratories and students' immersion in kernel code," *Systemics, Cybernetics And Informatics*, vol. 5, no. 3, pp. 30–35, 2007.

[7] A. Futoransky, F. Miranda, J. Orlicki, and C. Sarraute, "Simulating cyber-attacks for fun and profit," in *Proceedings of the 2Nd International Conference on Simulation Tools and Techniques*, ser. Simutools '09. ICST, Brussels, Belgium, Belgium: ICST (Institute for Computer Sciences, Social-Informatics and Telecommunications Engineering), 2009, pp. 4:1–4:9, available in: <http://dx.doi.org/10.4108/ICST.SIMUTOOLS2009.5773>. [retrieved: december, 2016].

[8] M. Corici, "Ctf 365," 2017, available in: <https://ctf365.com/>. [retrieved: february, 2017].

[9] L. Padgham and M. Winikoff, *Developing Intelligent Agent Systems*. Wiley, 2005.

[10] S. Rangel and F. Hachem, "SHELLTER: um ambiente de aprendizado em segurança da informação com abordagem prática," 2015.

[11] S. J. Russell and P. Norvig, *Artificial Intelligence: A Modern Approach*. Prentice Hall, 2010.

[12] M. Wooldridge, *An Introduction to MultiAgent Systems*. Wiley, 2002.

[13] O. Security, "Exploit database," 2015, available in: <https://www.offensive-security.com/>. [retrieved: december, 2016].

Distributed Cross Layer Cooperative MAC Protocol for Multihop Wireless Networks

Shamna Hamsa Rahim, Lillykutty Jacob

National Institute of Technology
Calicut, Kozhikode - 673601
Email: shamnahr@gmail.com, lilly@nitc.ac.in

Abstract—**Extending the battery lifetime of energy constrained devices is a key issue in designing wireless adhoc networks. The existing works focus on using cooperative communications for improving network performance in terms of throughput, delay, spectral efficiency, etc. In this paper, we propose a distributed cross layer cooperative Medium Access Control (MAC) protocol for a multihop network environment that can improve the network lifetime and energy efficiency while not degrading the network throughput and end to end delay. The results show that the proposed protocol can improve the performance of the network in terms of network lifetime, throughput, end-to-end delay, and energy efficiency.**

***Keywords*–Wireless Ad hoc Networks; Cooperative Communication; Cross Layer; Energy Efficiency; Network Lifetime.**

I. INTRODUCTION

Wireless communications have developed tremendously over the past few decades due to the large demand for mobile and wireless access. Compared to wired communications, the signals transmitted over the wireless channels may suffer from severe attenuation. The overall reliability of wireless communication can be significantly improved by transmitting multiple copies of the same signal over multiple independent fading channels. Multiple-Input-Multiple-Output (MIMO) systems achieve spatial diversity by deploying multiple antennas at the transmitter side and receiver side [1]. However, due to size, cost, and hardware limitations, mobile devices may not be able to support multiple antennas.

Recently, cooperative communication is widely used as a transmission strategy for wireless networks. It is a cost effective alternative to the MIMO systems. Here, wireless nodes work together to form a virtual antenna array to achieve diversity gains. It takes advantage of the broadcast nature of the wireless channel to allow communicating nodes to help each other [2]–[4]. Most cooperative transmission schemes involve two phases of transmission - a coordination phase and a cooperation phase. In the coordination phase, the nodes exchange their own source data and control messages with each other. In the cooperation phase, the nodes cooperatively forward their messages to the destination. Cooperative communication improves the network capacity, data transfer delay and Bit Error Rate (BER) performance, reduce battery consumption, and extend the coverage area [5].

When cooperative communication is employed at the physical layer, the receiving node can use physical layer combining to achieve diversity gain and this helps cooperative communication to achieve a higher signal-to-noise ratio (SNR) than the traditional Single-Input-Single-Output (SISO) systems. This SNR advantage can be used to reduce the power of transmitting nodes, which in turn, will increase the lifetime of the network. By using the concept of cooperative communications at the MAC layer, the transmitter (Tx) of a communication link can send the packet to the relay nodes instead of sending it to the receiver (Rx) of that link. Such a communication link is called a cooperative link. Usually, the nodes in between the Tx and Rx are selected as relay nodes. The transmit power or energy required to transmit a packet via cooperative link is comparatively lower than that of transmitting it via direct link. This will effectively improve the network lifetime. So, cooperative MAC can improve the lifetime of energy constrained devices and increase the network lifetime [6], [7].

A proper design of MAC protocols is necessary to exploit the advantages of cooperative diversity in a multiple user cooperative network. The cooperative MAC protocols developed in the past few years show how the MAC layer protocols can be modified to incorporate cooperation in the physical layer and the advantages of cooperative communication from a MAC layer perspective [6]–[12]. Depending on the channel condition, these protocols can apply two hop data transmissions in the MAC layer to achieve higher transmission rates. Most of these protocols aim to improve the overall system throughput and reduce the packet delay. Performance of the protocols in terms of energy efficiency or overall lifetime of the network are not discussed in these works.

The existing works on cooperative communications at physical layer focus on improving spectral efficiency, coverage area, BER, interference reduction, etc. The works on cooperative MAC protocols developed during the past years focus on improving network performance in terms of throughput, delay, and packet delivery ratio. Finally, the works on cooperative routing protocols use the relay nodes to find the energy or power efficient route. In most of the existing cooperative MAC protocols, the resources of the relay nodes (residual energy, queue size, etc.) are not considered while selecting the relay. For each destination, the best relay that can improve the network performance is used for transmitting all the packets generated by the source. This leads to over utilization of resources of some specific relay nodes, while the resources of the other relays are under utilized. In this paper, we propose a distributed cross layer cooperative MAC protocol that can efficiently utilize the resources of the nodes and improve the energy efficiency and network lifetime while maintaining a reasonable throughput and end to end delay.

The rest of the paper is organized as follows. A brief description of the related works is given in Section II. Description about the distributed cooperative MAC is given in Section III. A simple expression for the saturation throughput of the proposed protocol is derived in Section IV. Simulation results are discussed in Section V. Conclusion and future work are presented in Section VI.

II. Related Work

In [7], the authors propose a cross layer distributed energy adaptive location based cooperative MAC protocol with the objective to improve the network performance in terms network lifetime and energy efficiency. In this protocol, the relay selection process is distributed and the best relay is selected based on location information and residual energy. An optimal cross layer power allocation scheme is designed that maintains a constant data rate to meet the desired outage probability requirement. The multi rate capability of 802.11 is not considered in this paper. The throughput of the proposed protocol is even lower than that of legacy 802.11 Distibuted Coordination Function (DCF).

In [13], the authors present a framework for extending the lifetime of energy constrained devices by exploiting cooperative diversity. The cooperation strategy used is based on decode-and-forward (DF) relaying protocol. They formulate an optimization problem with the goal of maximizing network lifetime under a BER constraint, and the solution gives which node to be selected as the relay and how much power to be allocated. The impact of cooperative communications in the higher layers of the protocol stack is not considered in this paper.

In [14], the authors propose an energy efficient cooperative MAC protocol to reduce energy consumption and increase network lifetime by power control. Also, they use a distributed utility based optimal helper selection procedure based on the residual energy and transmission power. They also propose a space and time combination backoff scheme to adjust the power level and contention window in the event of transmission failures. The data and control packets are transmitted using a single data rate. Request-To-Send (RTS) and Clear-To-Send (CTS) messages are transmitted at the highest power level and DATA and Acknowledgement (ACK) are transmitted at the minimum power level.

A low power receiver initiated cooperative MAC for wireless sensor networks is proposed in [15]. The authors compare the energy consumption between SISO, multi hop SISO, and cooperative relay systems for ideal and real MAC protocols to show the impact of MAC layer on the total energy consumption. The performance of the protocol in terms of network lifetime is not considered in this work.

Routing protocols which are based on cooperative communications are known as cooperative routing protocols. In [16], the authors propose cooperative routing protocols that can improve the network lifetime by selecting the energy efficient route. The problem of finding the minimum energy route is formulated as two seperate optimization problems. The first problem is to find the optimal transmission of information between two sets of nodes and the second problem is to decide the neighboring nodes to be selected to route traffic to the destination with minimum overall energy consumption.

A route that requires the minimum transmitted power while maintaining a certain end-to-end throughput is proposed in [17]. The proposed routing protocol makes full use of the cooperation communications to construct the minimum power route. The authors derive a cooperation based link cost formula, which represents the minimum transmitted power that is required to maintain the required end-to-end throughput.

TABLE I. RATE VS RANGE [for IEEE 802.11b]

Data Rate (Mbps)	11	5.5	2	1
Maximum Range (Meter)	60	120	180	250

In most of the existing cooperative MAC protocols, the resources of the relay nodes (residual energy, queue size, etc.) are not considered while selecting the relay. For each destination, the best relay that can improve the network performance is used for transmitting all the packets generated by the source. The protocols that take into account the resources of the relay for the relay selection process explicitly use power control while maintaining a constant data rate. While these protocols improve the network lifetime, the throughput and delay performance degrade to a large extent.

In this paper, we present the design and analysis of a cooperative MAC protocol named DCMAC, which considers the residual energy and the data rate (physical layer parameters)and queue size (total number of packets to be transmitted), of the nodes for the relay selection process. The results show that the protocol improves the performance of the network in terms of energy efficiency, throughput, end-to-end delay, and network lifetime.

III. Distributed Cooperative MAC (DCMAC) Protocol

A. System Model

We consider an IEEE 802.11b/g based mobile ad hoc network where the node transcievers have multi-rate capability. The relationship between the transmission link distance and data rate is shown in Table I for the case of 802.11b transcievers. Two ray ground propagation model is assumed in getting this link length - data rate mapping. The wireless medium is shared among multiple contending mobile nodes. Depending on the distance between the Tx and Rx, a packet could be transmitted at different transmission rates. We assume no power adaptation, so each node transmits its packets using a constant transmission power. The wireless channel between the sender and the receiver is assumed to be almost symmetric. By applying the concept of cooperative communication at the MAC layer, slow one hop transmissions are replaced by fast two hop transmissions if suitable relays are available. Here, cooperative communication is employed only when the direct transmission rate is less than or equal to 2 Mbps and there exist relay nodes such that $\frac{1}{C_{TH}} + \frac{1}{C_{HR}} < \frac{1}{C_{TR}}$, where C_{TH}, C_{HR}, and C_{TR} denote the data rate from source to helper, helper to destination, and source to destination, respectively. In the case of a multi-hop network, Ad hoc On-Demand Distance Vector (AODV) [18] is used as the routing protocol. When a route is established, DCMAC protocol initiates cooperative transmission in a hop-by-hop manner by selecting the relay nodes.

B. DCMAC Protocol Description

DCMAC is based on the IEEE 802.11 DCF. We define one more control frame named Relay Ready To Cooperate (RRTC) to support MAC relaying in addition to the conventional control frames RTS, CTS, and ACK. RRTC is sent by the best relay node to indicate its willingness to act as a relay. The best relay (helper) is the node that can support the highest data rate

Frame Control	Duration	Source Address	Destination Address	Distance

Figure 1. RTS Frame Format

between the Tx and Rx; and is one among the nodes which are within a routing pipe around the direct link between Tx and Rx, with residual energy above a given threshold, and with queue size below a given threshold. All the control frames are transmitted at the basic rate, i.e., 1 Mbps for 802.11b network and 6 Mbps for 802.11g network. The time duration for the transmission of RTS, RRTC, CTS, ACK, and DATA are denoted by T_{RTS}, T_{RRTC}, T_{CTS},T_{ACK}, and T_{DATA}, respectively.

1) Operations at the Sender:

a) When a sender has a packet to transmit, it first checks whether a cooperative link is beneficial or not. In the case of an IEEE 802.11b network, the cooperative link is beneficial if the data rate of the direct link is less than or equal to 2 Mbps. For an 802.11g network, a cooperative link is employed when the direct link data rate is less than or equal to 18 Mbps. *Distance* is a new field introduced in the RTS frame to support cooperative relaying. The format of RTS frame is given in Figure 1. If cooperative link is found beneficial, the node will copy the direct link length (distance in meters) to the destination in the distance field of the RTS message. Otherwise, this field is set to -1. The duration field denotes the time required to transmit the data frame which includes time for CTS, SIFS intervals, and ACK. Even if the sender decides to use cooperative communication, it does not know whether any helper exists to forward its packets. So the duration field in the RTS message is same for direct transmission and cooperative transmission. The duration field is given by

$$Duration = T_{SIFS} + T_{CTS} + \frac{8L}{C_{TR}} + T_{ACK} \tag{1}$$

where L denotes the payload length in bytes.

b) It then senses the channel to check if it is idle. If the channel is idle for DIFS, the node selects a random backoff timer between 0 and minimum contention window (CWmin). When the backoff counter reaches zero, the node sends an RTS to reserve the channel.

c) If the sender does not receive a CTS within $T_{RTS} + T_{SIFS} + T_{CTS} + 2\delta$, it will retransmit the RTS. Here δ denotes the propagation delay. Otherwise, the sender will wait for another $T_{maxbackoff} + T_{SIFS} + T_{RRTC} + \delta$, where $T_{maxbackoff}$ is the maximum backoff time for the relay nodes. If no RRTC is received within this time, it indicates that no relays are available to forward the data. The node will transmit the packet over the direct link and the ACK timeout is set as

$$\frac{8L}{C_{TR}} + 2\delta + T_{SIFS} + T_{ACK}. \tag{2}$$

d) If both CTS and RRTC are received, the sender will forward the data to the relay. The format of the MAC protocol data unit (MPDU) is shown in Figure 2. The sender stores the address of the relay in the destination field and the receiver address is stored in Address 3 field. In this case, the ACK timeout is set as

$$\frac{8L}{C_{TH}} + \frac{8L}{C_{HR}} + 3\delta + 2T_{SIFS} + T_{ACK} \tag{3}$$

The duration field denotes the time required to transmit the data including ACK and SIFS intervals. In the case of cooperative transmission, the value of the duration field in MPDU is given by

$$Duration = 2T_{SIFS} + \frac{8L}{C_{HR}} + T_{ACK} \tag{4}$$

In the case of direct transmission, the value of duration field in MPDU is

$$Duration = T_{SIFS} + T_{ACK} \tag{5}$$

e) If no ACK is received within the ACK timeout duration, the sender resumes the backoff procedure and contends for the channel again. When no ACK is received for cooperative transmission, the sender retransmits the packet directly to the receiver.

Frame Control	Duration	Source Address	Destination Address	Address 3	Sequence Control	Address 4

Figure 2. MAC PDU Header Format

2) Operations at the Relay Nodes:

a) When an RTS message is received with the distance field set to -1, which is an indication that it is decided to use the direct link, the intermediate nodes will set their network allocation vector (NAV) to the duration specified in the duration field of the message.

b) If the distance field contains a non-negative value, the intermediate nodes check whether they can act as a relay. If they cannot act as a relay, they will set their NAVs. Otherwise, the relay nodes will wait for $T_{CTS} + T_{SIFS} + \delta$ duration. If no CTS message is received within this duration, the node will go back to idle state.

c) When the CTS message is received, all the potential relays contend to act as the best relay using the relay selection procedure described in Subsection III-C. The node whose cooperative backoff procedure expires first sends the RRTC message and when this message is heard by other potential relays, they abort the backoff procedure and will set their NAV duration and defer until the channel is idle. The format of RRTC message is given in Figure 3. The duration field denotes the time to transmit the data packet from transmitter to relay and from relay to destination. It also includes the time to send ACK and SIFS intervals. The duration field in the RRTC message is given by

$$Duration = 3T_{SIFS} + \frac{8L}{C_{TH}} + \frac{8L}{C_{HR}} + T_{ACK} \tag{6}$$

d) The best relay will wait for a duration equal to $T_{RRTC} + T_{SIFS} + \frac{8L}{C_{TH}} + 2\delta$ and if no data packet is received within this duration, it will go back to idle state. Otherwise, it will forward the packet to the

Frame Control	Duration	Source Address	Destination Address	Sequence Control

Figure 3. RRTC Frame Format

Frame Control	Duration	Source Address	Destination Address	Sequence Control

Figure 4. CTS Frame Format

destination. Before forwarding the packet, the value of the duration field in MPDU is changed to

$$Duration = T_{SIFS} + T_{ACK} \quad (7)$$

e) The relay waits for a duration of $T_{SIFS} + \frac{8L}{C_{HR}} + T_{ACK} + 2\delta$ to receive an ACK from the receiver. If no ACK is received within this duration, it will go back to idle state.

3) Operations at the Receiver:

a) When the Rx receives an RTS message it will send a CTS back to the source. The format of CTS message is shown in Figure 4. If the distance field is set to -1, the duration field of CTS is set to

$$Duration = 2T_{SIFS} + \frac{8L}{C_{TR}} + T_{ACK} \quad (8)$$

$$Duration = 3T_{SIFS} + T_{maxbackoff} + \frac{8L}{C_{TR}} + T_{ACK} \quad (9)$$

The destination will wait for $2T_{SIFS} + T_{CTS} + T_{maxbackoff} + \frac{8L}{C_{TR}} + 2\delta$ duration to receive either a data packet or an RRTC message. If no data packet or RRTC is recieved within the timeout interval, it will go back to idle state.

b) When a data packet is received, the Rx sends an ACK back to the Tx. If the packet is forwarded by a relay, a copy of the ACK is sent to the relay too.

C. Relay Selection Procedure

The existing cooperative MAC protocols mainly aim at improving network throughput or reducing the end-to-end delay by using cooperative communication. If the channel conditions remain the same, the same relay is selected by the source node every time it has a packet to be transmitted. The same relay may also be used by other source-destination pairs. In addition to this, the relay may also have some packets to be transmitted. These relay nodes run out of battery very quickly and may lead to network disconnection. At the same time, there may be other nodes in the network that are capable to act as relays. The energy consumption can be minimized if a portion of the traffic is relayed through each of the eligible relays. We propose a relay selection procedure to select the best relay based on its residual energy, queue size, and the data rate that it can support over the cooperative link.

When an RTS message is received with the distance field set to a non-negative value, all the neighboring nodes other than the destination check whether they are eligible to act as relays. A node is eligible only if its residual energy is more than 25% of the initial battery level and the following condition is satisfied:

$$\frac{1}{C_{TH}} + \frac{1}{C_{HR}} < \frac{1}{C_{TR}}.$$

All the nodes that satisfy the above condition will start a backoff timer to contend for the optimal relay. The backoff utility function is defined as

$$Backoff = Min\left(\left(\frac{\frac{1}{C_{TH}} + \frac{1}{C_{HR}}}{\frac{1}{C_{TR}}}\right)^{\alpha}\left(1 - \frac{E_r}{E_i}\right)^{\beta}\left(\frac{q_c}{q_{buf}}\right)^{\gamma}, \tau\right) \quad (10)$$

where E_r and E_i denote, respectively, the residual energy and initial energy at the relay node. The terms q_c and q_{buf} denote the number of packets in the queue and the buffer size, respectively. The value τ is used so as to limit the backoff time within an acceptable range. We fix the value of τ in such a way that the backoff time does not exceeds the time to transmit any of the control messages. The variables $\alpha, \beta, and \gamma$ are the weight factors associated with data rate, energy, and queueing parameters. For the results reported in the next section, we give equal weight to all the three parameters.

IV. DCMAC ANALYSIS

In this section, we derive a simple expression for the saturation throughput of DCMAC. A simplified form of the system model presented in III-A is considered for analysis. We consider a single hop network in which all the source-destination pairs are separated by a distance between 120 to 180m. We assume that there exist two helpers between every source-destination pair that can support data rates of (11,5.5) and (5.5,5.5) between the source to helper, and helper to destination, respectively. Only 25% of the total nodes generate traffic and the remaining nodes act as destination and relays. The performance analysis of the IEEE 802.11 DCF presented in [19] and the analysis of CoopMAC [6] are used for analysing the performance of the proposed protocol.

Let Ts denote the transmission time for one packet and L denotes the size of the packet in bytes. For DCMAC protocol, Ts is defined as

$$T_s = (P_{11,5.5} + P_{5.5,5.5})T_{DCMACOH} + \frac{8LP_{11,5.5}}{R_{11}} + \frac{8LP_{11,5.5}}{R_{5.5}} + \frac{16LP_{5.5,5.5}}{R_{5.5}} \quad (11)$$

where $T_{DCMACOH}$ denotes the DCMAC overhead, $P_{11,5.5}$ and $P_{5.5,5.5}$ denote the probability to transmit the packets through the relays that support data rates of (11,5.5) and (5.5,5.5) between the source to helper, and helper to destination, respectively. These probabilities are obtained through numerical approximation.

$$T_{DCMACOH} = 2T_{PLCP} + 5T_{SIFS} + T_{RRTC} + T_{DIFS} + T_{RTS} + T_{CTS} + T_{ACK} + T_{maxbackoff} \quad (12)$$

In the case of EECO MAC protocol [14], Ts is defined as

$$T_s = T_{EECOOH} + \frac{16L}{R_2} \quad (13)$$

where T_{EECOOH} denotes the EECO MAC overhead and it is defined as

$$T_{EECOOH} = 2T_{PLCP} + 5T_{SIFS} + T_{HTS} + T_{DIFS} + T_{RTS} + T_{CTS} + T_{ACK} + T_{eecomaxbackoff} \quad (14)$$

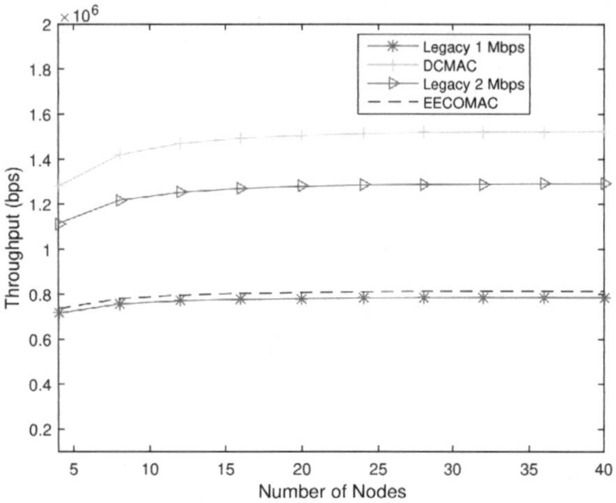

Figure 5. Throughput vs Number of Nodes

R_{11}, $R_{5.5}$, and R_2 represent 11 Mbps, 5.5 Mbps, and 2 Mbps, respectively. From [19], the saturation throughput is defined as,

$$S = \frac{P_s P_{tr} L}{(1 - P_{tr})\sigma + P_s P_{tr} T_s + P_{tr}(1 - P_s)T_c} \tag{15}$$

where P_s is the probability for successful transmission, P_{tr} is the probability that at least one station transmits in a given slot, σ is the slot time, and T_c is the collision time. P_s and P_{tr} are obtained through the Discrete Time Markov Chain (DTMC) analysis of Bianchi [19]; and $T_c = T_{RTS} + T_{DIFS} + \delta$.

Figure 5 compares the saturation throughput performance of the proposed protocol with the legacy DCF that transmits packets at 1 Mbps and 2 Mbps, and EECO-MAC [14]. The throughput of the proposed protocol is higher than that of legacy DCF and EECO-MAC. In the proposed protocol, the packets are forwarded using the relays that support (11,5.5) and (5.5,5.5) data rates in both directions. But in the case of EECO-MAC, the packets are forwarded through the relays at a rate of 2 Mbps.

V. . Simulation Results

The proposed DCMAC protocol described in the previous section is implemented in the NS2 network simulator [?]. A network topology of 600 x $600m^2$ is considered. Nodes are uniformly and independently distributed at random locations. Two ray ground reflected model is considered for wireless channel and IEEE 802.11b parameters are used for the experiments. The data rates for different transmission ranges as per IEEE 802.11b are shown in Table I. The simulation parameters are listed in Table II. EECO-MAC [14] protocol was developed to improve the network lifetime. So, the performance of the proposed protocol is compared with that of EECO-MAC. We also compare the performance of the proposed DCMAC with the legacy 802.11 DCF that transmits packets at a rate of 1 Mbps. 10% of the total nodes are considered as source nodes generating CBR traffic and their destinations are selected randomly.

Figure 6 shows the relationship between the number of nodes and the overall throughput at a fixed payload size (512 bytes). For EECO-MAC and DCMAC protocols, as the number of nodes increases, the availability of helpers for forwarding data packets increases and hence these protocols have better throughput compared to 802.11 DCF. This increase in throughput is due to the increase in availability of helper nodes which results in faster two hop transmission instead of single one hop transmission. The proposed DCMAC protocol has significantly higher throughput than the EECO-MAC. This is because EECO-MAC transmits data at a fixed rate of 2 Mbps.

TABLE II. SIMULATION PARAMETERS

MAC Header	272 bits
PHY Header	192 bits
RTS	352 bits
CTS	304 bits
RRTC	304 bits
ACK	304 bits
Data Rate for MAC Header	1 Mbps
Slot Time	20 μs
SIFS	10 μs
DIFS	50 μs
CWMin	31 Slots
CWMax	1023 Slots
Retry Limit	6

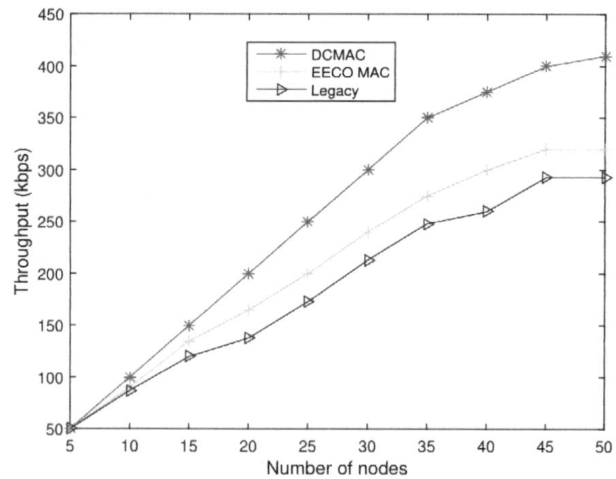

Figure 6. Throughput vs Number of Nodes

Figure 7 shows the relationship between the number of nodes and delay.The delay performance is also better in the case of DCMAC protocol. This is because in EECO MAC, the transmission time is doubled when cooperative communication is employed. In addition to this, the sender node has to wait for a certain amount of time to receive the HTS message. In the case of DCMAC, the source node has to wait for a certain amount of time to get the RRTC message. If cooperative transmission is used, the data is transmitted at higher rates.

The network lifetime and the average energy consumption for different network sizes are shown in Figures 8 and 9, respectively. In EECO MAC, the transmit power is lowered when cooperative communication is used. This leads to a decrease in the total energy consumption and increases the network lifetime. In DCMAC, the relay nodes are selected based on the residual energy level; and as the residual energy of a relay node decreases, other nodes are selected as relays and this leads to an increase in the overall network lifetime. But, in DCMAC, all messages are transmitted with fixed transmit

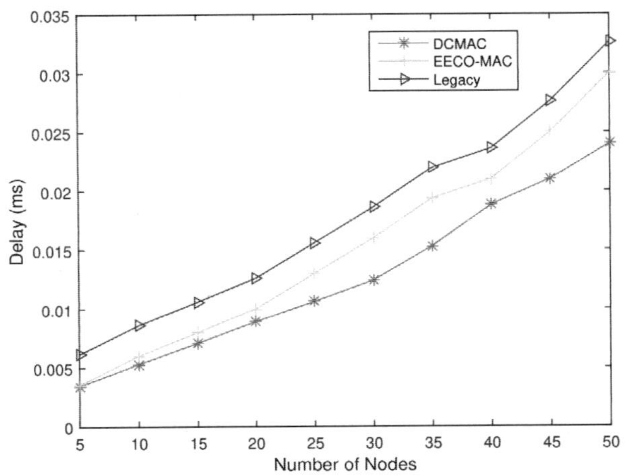

Figure 7. Delay vs Number of Nodes

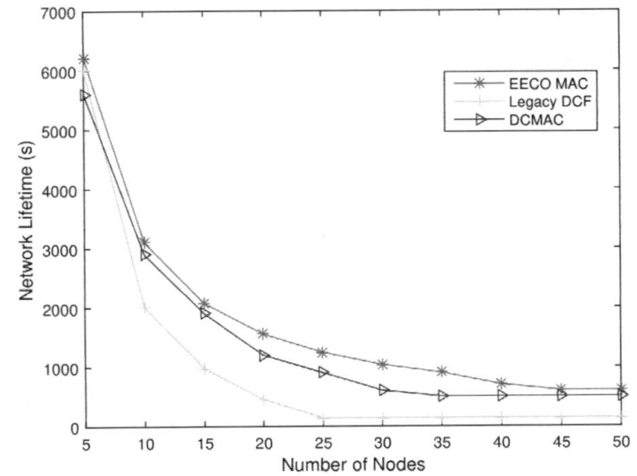

Figure 8. Network Lifetime vs Number of Nodes

power and therefore the energy efficiency and network lifetime is slightly reduced when compared to EECO MAC.

VI. Conclusion

In this paper, we have proposed a distributed cross layer MAC protocol for multihop networks by employing cooperative communication. The relay selection process is distributed and the optimal relay is selected by considering the residual energy, queue size, and location of the potential relays. The simulation results show that the network lifetime and energy efficiency can be improved in multihop networks by using cooperative communication in the MAC layer. The results also show that the proposed protocol can improve the network lifetime and energy efficiency without degrading the network throughput and delay performance.

References

[1] A. Goldsmith, S. A. Jafar, N. Jindal, and S. Vishwanath, "Capacity limits of MIMO channels", *IEEE Journal on Selected Areas in Communications*, 21(5), pp. 684-702, 2003.

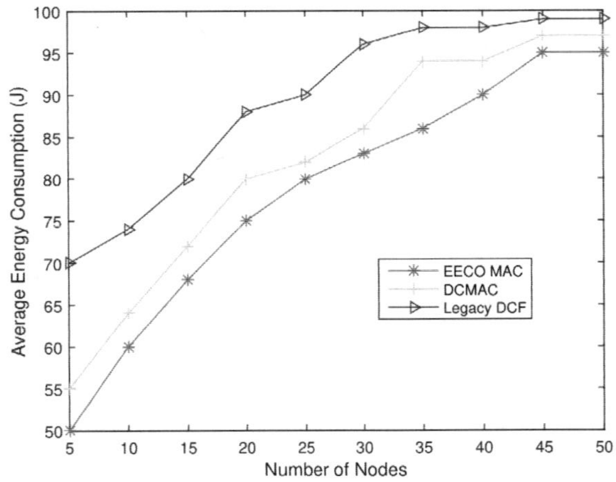

Figure 9. Average Energy Consumption vs Number of Nodes

[2] J. N. Laneman, D. N. C. Tse, and G. W. Wornel, "Cooperative diversity in wireless networks: Efficient protocols and outage behavior", *IEEE Transactions on Information Theory*, 50(12), pp. 3062-3080, 2004.

[3] A. Sendonaris, E. Erkip, and B. Aazhang, "User cooperation diversity-Part I: System description", *IEEE Transactions on Communications*, 51(11), pp. 1927-1938, 2003.

[4] A. Sendonaris, E. Erkip, and B. Aazhang, "User cooperation diversity-Part II: Implementation aspects and performance analysis", *IEEE Transactions on Communications*, 51(11), pp. 1939-1948, 2003.

[5] A. Nosratinia, T. E Hunter, and A. Hedayat, "Cooperative communication in wireless networks", *IEEE Communications Magazine*, 42(10), pp. 74 - 80, 2004.

[6] P. Liu, Z. Tao, S. Narayanan, T. Korakis, and S. Panwar, "CoopMAC: A Cooperative MAC for wireless LANs", *IEEE journal on selected areas in Communications*, 25(2), pp.340-354,2007.

[7] X. Wang and J. Li, "Improving the Network Lifetime of MANETs through Cooperative MAC Protocol Design", *IEEE Transactions on Parallel and Distributed Systems*, 26(4), pp. 1010-1020, 2015.

[8] H. Zhu and G. Cao, rDCF, "A relay enabled medium access control protocol for wireless ad hoc networks", *IEEE Transactions on Mobile Computing*, 5(9), pp 1201-1214, 2006.

[9] J. Zhang, Q. Zhang, and W. Jia, VC-MAC, "A Cooperative MAC protocol in vehicular networks", *IEEE Transactions on Vehicular Technology*, 58(3), pp. 1561-1571, 2009.

[10] H. Shan, W. Zhuang, and Z. Wang, "Distributed Cooperative MAC for Multihop Wireless Networks", *IEEE Communications Magazine*, 47(2), pp. 126-133, 2009.

[11] H. R. Shamna, N. L. Appari, and L. Jacob, "Cooperative MAC protocol: Performance modeling and analysis", *IEEE Recent Advances in Intelligent Computational Systems (RAICS)* , pp. 233-238, 2013.

[12] H. R. Shamna and L. Jacob, "Efficient Cooperative MAC and Routing in Wireless Networks", *Transactions on Networks and Communications*, 3(5), pp. 79-95, 2015.

[13] T. Himsoon, W. P. Siriwongpairat, Z. Han and K. J. R. Liu, "Lifetime maximization via cooperative nodes and relay deployment in wireless networks", *IEEE Journal on Selected Areas in Communications*, 25(2), pp. 306-317, 2007.

[14] X. Zhang, A. Anpalagan, L. Guo, and A. S. Khwaja, "Energy-Efficient Cooperative MAC Protocol Based on Power Control in MANETs", *IEEE 29th International Conference on Advanced Information Networking and Applications*, pp. 48-53, 2015.

[15] L. Q. V. Tran, O. Berder, and O. Sentieys, "RIC-MAC: A MAC protocol for low-power cooperative wireless sensor networks", *IEEE Wireless Communications and Networking Conference (WCNC) Istanbul*, pp. 1944-1949, 2014.

[16] A. E. Khandani, J. Abounadi, E. Modiano, and L. Zheng, "Cooperative

Routing in Static Wireless Networks" *IEEE Transactions on Communications*, 55(11), pp. 2185-2192, 2007.

[17] A. S. Ibrahim, Z. Han, and K. J. R. Liu, "Distributed energy-efficient cooperative routing in wireless networks", *IEEE Transactions on Wireless Communications*, 7(10), pp. 3930-3941, 2008.

[18] C. PERKINS, Ad hoc on demand distance vector (AODV) routing, *Internet-Draft, draft-ietf-manet-aodv-04.txt*, October 1999.

[19] G. Bianchi, "Performance Analysis of the IEEE 802.11 Distributed Cooordination Function", *IEEE Journal on Selected Areas in Communication*, vol. 18, No.3, pp. 535-547, Mar 2000

[20] http://www.isi.edu/nsnam/ns/

Mode Selection, Power Adaptation and Channel Assignment in Device-to-Device Communication

Neeta Ann Ninan

Dept. of Electronics and Communication
National Institute of Technology Calicut, India
Email: neeta.ann93@gmail.com

Lillykutty Jacob

Dept. of Electronics and Communication
National Institute of Technology Calicut, India
Email: lilly@nitc.ac.in

Abstract- **Device-to-Device (D2D) communication is a technique that allows two devices to communicate with each other in the licensed band without the requirement of a base station. The major advantage of D2D communication is that it allows reuse of spectrum resources and thereby improves spectral efficiency. However, it has to deal with interference mitigation and resource allocation. This paper focuses on mode selection, power adaptation and channel assignment for bandwidth efficient and energy efficient D2D communication. In the scheme used here, distributed mode selection is formulated as an evolutionary game and channel allocation uses a graph theoretical approach such that interference is minimum, while power control is performed using channel inversion. The simulations show that the D2D communication improves capacity, reduces power consumption and performs effective bandwidth allocation.**

Keywords-mode selection; evolutionary game; graph theoretical approach; channel inversion.

I. Introduction

Until recent years, cellular communication was having a fixed infrastructure. However, surveys show that 5 billion devices are connected to the cellular network at present [1], global data traffic has increased to 74 % Compound Annual Growth Rate (CAGR) in 2015 and current infrastructure is unable to handle the huge traffic. As a solution to this problem, different methods were suggested [2] like: Device to device (D2D) communication, densification of Base Station (BS), cognitive radio etc. D2D communication is one among the most popular techniques that are used nowadays. In the conventional cellular communication system, even when mobile users are communicating in close proximity, they are required to follow the fixed infrastructure. This proves to be quite complex, in addition to wastage of resources. D2D communication is quite effective in such situations. A properly designed D2D network can have the following advantages [2] [3]: increase in spectral efficiency, reduced latency, increase in throughput, low power consumption, resource conservation, improved capacity etc.

The potential D2D user equipments can operate in one of the following three communication modes [4]:

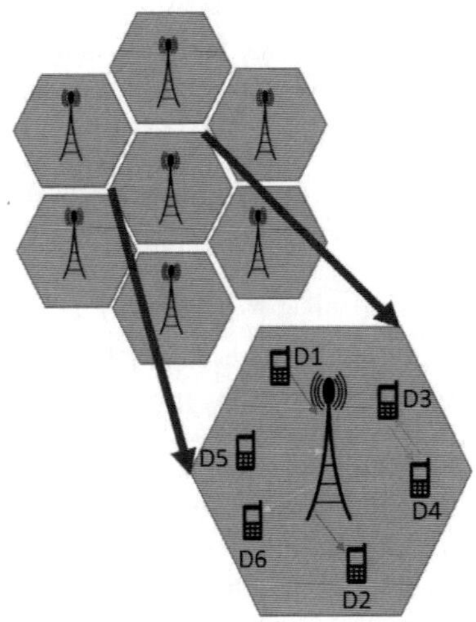

Fig. 1. System Model of D2D Communication

1) Reuse mode: In the reuse mode, the D2D users do not need a BS, instead they communicate directly. They share the resources of the cellular users or the D2D users in cellular mode who have exclusive channels allocated to them.
2) Cellular mode: In cellular mode, the D2D users use the BS to transmit just like the cellular users. Sometimes, even when the transmitter and receiver are in close proximity, a reuse or dedicated mode can not be used due to deep fades. In such cases, those D2D users use the cellular mode.
3) Dedicated mode: The D2D users in dedicated mode can communicate with or without BS but they cannot reuse the spectrum resources. So, they also require dedicated orthogonal frequency bands. This mode is preferred when the signal quality is required to be very high with no interference.

Figure 1 shows the system model where (D1, D2) transmitter-receiver pair are in cellular mode, (D3, D4) are in reuse mode and (D5, D6) are in dedicated mode.

In this paper, we propose a scheme for D2D communication

which includes mode selection, power adaptation and channel assignment. Initially, the users are distinguished into cellular or potential D2D users based on the threshold distance. The potential D2D users will have to choose a suitable mode among the three modes, and for distributed mode selection an evolutionary game model is developed. The utility function used for the game by each user is a function of the rates of all users which are computed based on their respective modes. The transmit power used for rate calculation is a controlled power computed by suitable power control schemes. At the convergence of the evolutionary game, based on the number of users in each mode, the channel allocation is done by the BS.

The rest of this paper is organized as follows. In Section II, we provide a brief literature review on closely related existing works. In Section III, we describe the system model, problem addressed and techniques adopted for mode selection, power adaptation and channel assignment. In Section IV, we describe the simulation setup and results, thus giving a performance evaluation. Section V gives conclusion and future prospects of this work.

II. RELATED WORK

Many works in the literature have addressed one or more of the issues of mode selection, power control and channel allocation in D2D communication. In [5] the authors discuss a joint mode selection and power allocation scheme for D2D communication. They employ an exhaustive search based mode selection, and consider the number of device pairs to be known and the utility used in this case is power efficiency, which is the ratio of capacity to total power. The problem defined is to identify the mode that maximizes the utility. However, the drawback of this model is that the D2D users are assumed to be in reuse modes only and the other possible modes are not considered.

The authors of [6] focus on channel allocation to D2D users while in reuse mode. They consider a centralised algorithm, i.e., the BS makes the decisions. The utility used for channel allocation is the achievable transmission rate of the cellular users. Ultimately, to efficiently allot the resources with minimum interference, we need to maximize the utility. For this, graph theoretical algorithms like maximum and minimum weighted bipartite matching are used and the channels are mapped to the cellular and D2D users in the cell. However, the limitation here is that they consider D2D users only in reuse mode. The cellular and dedicated mode possibilities are not considered. Moreover, there is no power control happening.

Zhu and Hossain [4] discuss an evolutionary dynamic game model for mode selection. The mode selection is first randomly done and then allowed to dynamically adapt according to the performance (average rate) and cost (spectrum access fee). In the real scenario, there is always limited rationality and the evolutionary game model gives the best solution under such situations. The payoff of each user is computed based on his strategy and that decides whether to change or not change his strategy. The steps are repeated until an evolutionary stable state is reached. Wang et al. speak of a stackelberg game in [7]. However, the limitation in these works is lack of power control and channel assignment.

In [8], an evolutionary approach for resource allocation is followed where utilities are formulated in terms of average rate, interference and cost of unit bandwidth and power consumption for each mode. However, multiple D2D users cannot be allotted to the same channel. In [9], joint mode selection, scheduling and power control are together formulated as an optimization problem. The optimization is done using a mixed integer linear programming formulation, which also does not consider all three modes of D2D communication.

This work, however, considers all three possible modes of D2D communication. A multicell scenario is considered for the analysis. But, unlike [4], we do a power adaptation which is lacking in most of the existing works. A channel assignment is also done in addition to the the mode selection using Evolutionary Game Theory (EGT). Along with guarantee on convergence through EGT, the different performance parameters like rate, transmission power, system power efficiency and system spectral efficiency are studied in this work to clearly emphasize the merits of the proposed scheme.

III. PROPOSED WORK

A. System Model and Problem Statement

We consider uplink communication in a multicell scenario with focus on a single cell having a single BS at its centre. There are 'N'number of transmitting users whose positions within the cell are characterized by a Poisson Point Process (PPP) [4]. This PPP model is represented by: $\phi = \{(X_i, y_i)\}$ where X_i gives the spatial location of ith transmitting user and y_i gives the location of receiver of ith transmitting user X_i. The Euclidean distance between the transmitter and the receiver is calculated as D_i=$\|Xi - yi\|$. Based on the distance between transmitter and receiver, the cellular and D2D users can be distinguished. If the Euclidean distance between the transmitting user and its receiver is greater than a threshold distance, then he becomes a cellular user; otherwise, he becomes a potential D2D user. The potential D2D users have to choose one of the three possible modes, namely, cellular mode, reuse mode and dedicated mode. Here a distributed mode selection is done. The populations in cellular, reuse and dedicated modes at any instant are denoted by x_c, x_r and x_d, respectively; and the population state by $\mathbf{x} = (x_c, x_r, x_d)$. The density of users in each mode can be given as in [4]. We consider a general path loss model along with Rayleigh fading. So, the fading channel power gain is exponentially distributed.

In an attempt to enhance the spectral and energy efficiency, we develop a game model for mode selection in D2D communication using evolutionary game theory and also perform a power adaptation using a suitable scheme. This information of population state on convergence of the game is used to model the channel allocation using graph theoretic models. Finally, the performance of this model in doing mode selection, power allocation and channel allocation need to be analyzed in terms on transmission power, rate etc. The notations used in the following subsections are summarized in Table 1.

TABLE I
MAJOR SYMBOLS USED IN THE PAPER

Symbol	Definition
X_i	spatial location of ith transmitting user
yi	location of receiver of the ith transmitting user
D_i	Euclidean distance between transmitter and receiver of ith user
I_c^l	interference experienced by a cellular user on channel 'l '
P_r	transmit power of potential D2D user in reuse mode
$g_{0,i}$	fading gain from interferer 'i 'to target receiver
η	path loss exponent
P_c	transmit power of cellular mode user
ϕ_r^l	set of potential D2D users in reuse mode who cause interference to cellular user on channel 'l '
$\hat{\phi}_c^l$	set of potential out of cell interferers who cause interference to cellular user on channel 'l '
R_c	random variable that denotes the distance between target receiver and its transmitter
h_c	fading gain between target receiver and its transmitter
W	noise power
μ	parameter of exponential fading channel power gain
υ	threshold SINR
λ_r^l	density of users in reuse mode on channel 'l '
λ_b	density of BSs in the multicell scenario
B	amount of bandwidth for each subchannel
F_c	amount of spectrum for cellular users
$E(N_c(A))$	mean number of users in cellular mode
I_r^l	interference experienced by a reuse mode user on channel 'l '
D	random variable that denotes the distance between D2D transmitter and receiver
ξ	learning rate
k	number of channels reused
p	medium access probability
F_d	amount of spectrum for dedicated users
$E(N_d(A))$	mean number of users in dedicated mode
x	population state
$\tau_i(x)$	data rate of user using strategy 'i '
c_i	access fee for strategy 'i '

B. Rate analysis for different D2D communication modes

Initially, the D2D users have all been randomly assigned a mode and corresponding to their mode, the rate of each D2D user needs to be computed. It is to be noted that the D2D users in cellular mode suffer from interference due to D2D users in reuse mode who are using the same channel and also due to out of cell cellular interferers who are using the same channel. Likewise, the D2D users in reuse mode suffer interference from cellular users whose channel is being reused and also from other reuse mode users who reuse the same channel. However, the dedicated mode users suffer no interference. The rate analysis for different communication modes is done to compute the average rate achieved by users, following the approach in [4].

In cellular mode, the net interference of a user on channel *'l'* due to reuse mode users and out of cell interferers is given by (1).

$$I_c^l = \sum_{X_i \epsilon \phi_r^l} P_r g_{0,i} \|X_i\|^{-\eta} + \sum_{X_i \epsilon \hat{\phi}_c^l} P_c g_{0,i} \|X_i\|^{-\eta} \quad (1)$$

It is to be noted that the target receiver is the BS, whose location is assumed to be at the origin. Signal-to-interference-plus-noise ratio (SINR) can be computed as:

$$SINR_c^l = \frac{P_c h_c r_c^{-\eta}}{W + I_c^l} \quad (2)$$

The expected value of Shannons rate with respect to the different random variables involved is given by:

$$\bar{\tau}_c = E_{R_c, h_c, g_{0,i}, \phi_r^l, \hat{\phi}_c^l} \left[log \left(1 + SINR_c^l\right)\right] \quad (3)$$

Therefore, the average spectrum efficiency can be computed using (4):

$$\bar{\tau}_c = \int_0^\infty \frac{p_c\left(\lambda_r^l, \upsilon\right) d\upsilon}{1+\upsilon} \quad (4)$$

where $p_c\left(\lambda_r^l, \upsilon\right)$ can be derived as:

$$p_c\left(\lambda_r^l, \upsilon\right) = \int_0^\infty exp\left(\frac{-W\mu\upsilon r_c^\eta}{P_c}\right) exp\left(-\lambda_r^l r_c^2 \left(\frac{\upsilon P_r}{P_c}\right)^{\frac{2}{\eta}} K(\eta)\right) exp\left(-2\pi\lambda_B \int_R^\infty \left(1 - \frac{\mu}{\mu + sP_c t^{-\eta}}\right) tdt\right) f_{R_c}(r_c) dr_c \quad (5)$$

where,

$$K(\eta) = \frac{2\pi^2}{\eta sin(\frac{2\pi}{\eta})} \quad (6)$$

$$s = \frac{\mu\upsilon r_c^\eta}{P_c} \quad (7)$$

$$f_{R_c}(r_c) = \frac{2r_c}{R^2}, if : x\epsilon[0, R] \quad (8)$$

Equation (8) gives the Probability Density Function (pdf) of the distance from any user to the BS located at the centre, for the PPP model of the user distribution. The expected amount of spectrum resource allocated to cellular users is given by:

$$B_c = \frac{F_c B}{E(N_c(A))} \quad (9)$$

Therefore, the average rate for a user in cellular mode is given by:

$$\tau_c = B_c \bar{\tau}_c \quad (10)$$

Similarly, in reuse mode, the net interference of a user on channel *'l'* from cellular users whose channel is being reused and other reuse users who also reuse the same channel is computed. Accordingly, the interference at the receiver is given by :

$$I_r^l = \sum_{X_i \epsilon \phi_c^l} P_c g_{0,i} \|X_i\|^{-\eta} + \sum_{X_i \epsilon \phi_r^l \setminus \{0\}} P_r g_{0,i} \|X_i\|^{-\eta} \quad (11)$$

The average spectrum efficiency is then found as:

$$\bar{\tau}_r = \int_0^\infty \frac{p_r\left(\lambda_r^l, \upsilon\right) d\upsilon}{1+\upsilon} \quad (12)$$

where $p_r\left(\lambda_r^l, \upsilon\right)$ can be derived as:

$$p_r\left(\lambda_r^l, \upsilon\right) = \int_0^\infty exp\left(\frac{-W\mu\upsilon d^\eta}{P_r}\right) exp\left(-\lambda_r^l d^2 \upsilon^{\frac{2}{\eta}} K(\eta)\right) exp\left(-\lambda_B d^2 \left(\frac{\upsilon P_c}{P_r}\right)^{\frac{2}{\eta}} K(\eta)\right) f_D(d) d_d \quad (13)$$

where,

$$f_D(d) = 2\pi\xi d e^{-\xi\pi d^2}, d \geq 0 \quad (14)$$

which is the Rayleigh pdf of the distance between a potential D2D tx-rx pair, for the PPP model of the user distribution.

The expected amount of spectrum resource for users in reuse mode is given by :

$$B_r = kpB \tag{15}$$

where, k is the number of channels reused and p is the medium accesss probability. Hence, the rate is given by :

$$\tau_r = B_r \bar{\tau}_r \tag{16}$$

In dedicated mode, however, there is no interference since the channel is dedicated completely for that D2D user. Hence, SINR is reduced only due to noise and no interference. The average spectrum efficiency is obtained as:

$$\bar{\tau}_d = \int_0^\infty \frac{p_d\left(\lambda_r^l, \upsilon\right) d\upsilon}{1+\upsilon} \tag{17}$$

The expected amount of spectrum resource for users is:

$$B_d = \frac{F_d B}{E(N_d(A))} \tag{18}$$

Therefore, the rate of transmission is:

$$\tau_d = B_d \bar{\tau}_d \tag{19}$$

C. Mode selection using EGT

For mode selection using evolutionary game, we choose a payoff function which depends on the average achievable rate as well as the cost [4]. The payoff (utility) is given as:

$$U(i, x) = \bar{w}(\tau_i(\mathbf{x})) - c_i \tag{20}$$

where c_i is the price of access per user per unit of time. 'i'represents the strategy (mode) chosen by the user which can be c, r or d. '**x**'represents the population state and $\bar{w}(\tau_i(\mathbf{x}))$ is $\alpha\tau_i(\mathbf{x})$ where 'α' is a constant and $\tau_i(\mathbf{x})$ is the rate of user using strategy i. Using Equations (10) or (16) or (19) the payoff for each user is computed based on his chosen mode. After that, each user sends his utility information to the BS through a control channel and the average population payoff is computed by the BS and broadcast to all potential D2D users. If the payoff of the user is less than the average, then the user randomly selects from the modes other than his present mode such that the payoff is greater than the average payoff. These steps are repeated iteratively until the population state reaches an evolutionary stable state. The corresponding strategy is called the evolutionary stable strategy (mode) for each potential D2D user.

D. Power Control

In this work, a channel inversion is used for power control. The channel inversion method helps to compensate for large scale path loss, but not small scale fading. The main advantage of channel inversion is that it reduces the transmit power consumed by good links and gives more transmit power to only poor links. Also, by means of channel inversion, we can determine the transmit power with limited channel state information. Here, we assume that the received power is unity [10].

E. Channel Allocation

We assume that the channel gain of each cellular mode user is known at the BS so that the maximum bipartite matching can be used to allocate channels to all the cellular mode users. Whatever channels are not allocated to the cellular mode users and are free can now be allocated to the dedicated mode users using again maximum bipartite matching. Further, to allocate channels to the D2D users in reuse mode, we make use of the minimum weighted bipartite matching algorithm. The reuse mode users will be allocated channels that are already allocated to the cellular mode users. However, the channels allocated to the dedicated mode users will not be available for reuse [6].

Bipartite matching is a matching between two sets of vertices such that every edge has one end point in one set and the other end point in the other set. A perfect matching has a maximum number of edges matched between the two sets such that there is a minimum number of free nodes in each set. Maximum matching M is one in which the total weight of selected edges $W_M >$ weight of edges of any other matching M'. Minimum matching M is one in which the total weight of selected edges $W_M <$ weight of edges of any other matching M'. For the maximum bipartite matching algorithm used for channel allocation of cellular mode and dedicated mode users, edge weights are channel gains. And for the minimum bipartite matching algorithm used for reuse mode users, edge weights are the interferences.

IV. NUMERICAL RESULTS

The analysis has been done for the D2D network that has incorporated the algorithms described, and the simulation parameters are listed in Table 2 [4] [10].

TABLE II
SIMULATION PARAMETERS

Radius of the cell R	500m
Total number of users N	40
Total number of channels	40
Out of cell interferers	5
Mode selection threshold distance D_{th}	150m
Intensity of BS λ_b	$(\pi 500^2)^{-1} m^{-2}$
Intensities of user equipments λ	100x$(\pi 500^2)^{-1} m^{-2}$
access fee $[c_c, c_r, c_d]$	[.2, 0, .5]
mean of exponential distribution μ	1
D2D distance parameter ξ	10x$(\pi 500^2)^{-1} m^{-2}$
medium access probability p	1
path loss exponent η	3
Bandwidth of each subchannel B	180KHz
Noise power W	-90dBm

The evolution of population state of all users during mode selection is shown in Figure 2. The initial population of D2D users in each mode is assumed to be known. Using Equation (20) the population state evolves with time. In Equation (20) the values of c_i are chosen such that D2D users will have more incentive to move into the reuse or dedicated rather than the cellular mode. This is because the reuse mode can exploit the proximity gain to achieve a higher average rate

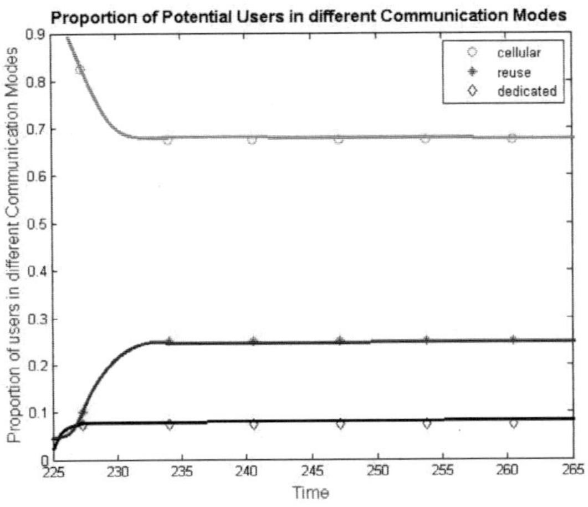

Fig. 2. Proportion of users in each communication mode

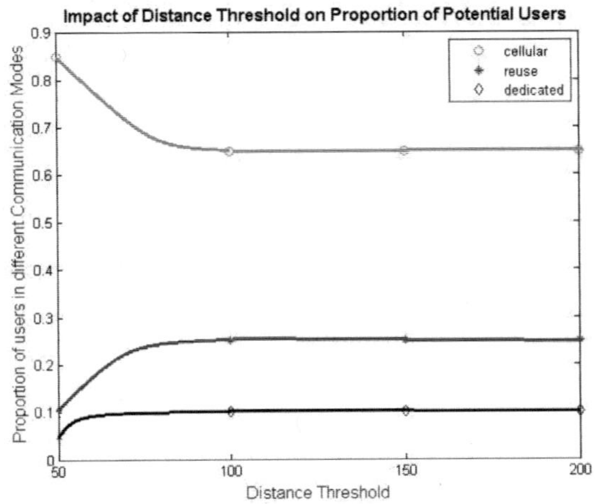

Fig. 3. Impact of distance threshold on proportion of users in different modes

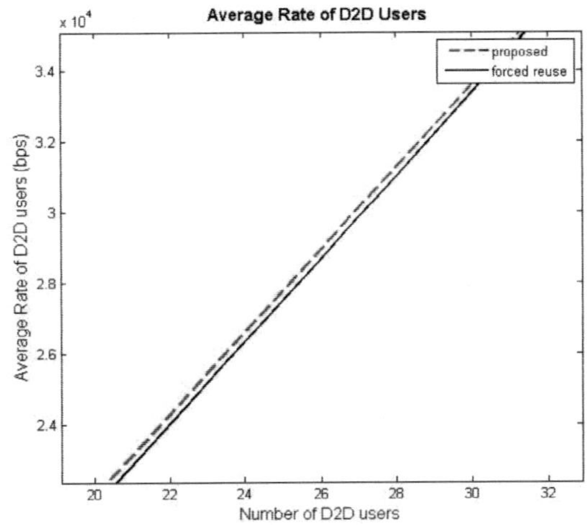

Fig. 4. Average Rate of D2D users

and better spectral efficiency than cellular mode, while using dedicated mode can achieve the best performance. Therefore, the reuse and dedicated modes are the dominant modes in D2D users. Hence, the plots are increasing for reuse and dedicated mode and decreasing for cellular mode. Soon, the population converges to equilibrium at which no user has the incentive to deviate.

The impact of distance threshold on proportion of users in different modes is shown in Figure 3. The threshold distance decides the number of users in cellular and D2D modes. When the threshold distance increases, users who are currently cellular users become D2D users. Since reuse and dedicated modes are dominant, the number of users in these modes increases initially and converges to equilibrium. Similarly, the cellular mode is a dominated strategy and, hence, the population of users in cellular mode decreases.

In Figure 4, we plot the average rate of the D2D users and we see that the average rate in the proposed scheme is much higher than the forced reuse scheme, clearly due to the presence of dedicated mode users in the former. Figure 5 shows that the transmission power decreases when more D2D users arise. This is because transmission power is higher for cellular and dedicated mode than reuse mode according to the power control. In case of forced reuse mode, all D2D users are in reuse and hence the power largely decreases. If we plot the bandwidth utilization, it is clearly a decreasing curve because the bandwidth is consumed only by the cellular and dedicated mode users and as the number of D2D users increase, the population in cellular mode decreases while the population in reuse and dedicated modes increases. However, for a forced reuse mode, bandwidth is consumed only by the cellular users. Likewise, in Figures 6 and 7, we observe increasing plots for system power efficiency (ratio of average data rate to total power) and spectral efficiency (ratio of average data rate to total bandwidth) due to the same reasons. In both the case of spectral efficiency and power efficiency, we see that the proposed scheme gives a better performance.

We consider the total number of users as 40 which includes both cellular (C) and D2D users. They are divided into 28 cellular and 12 D2D users using threshold distance. By mode selection, we can identify the number of D2D users in the respective modes-cellular mode (Cd), dedicated mode (Dd) and reuse mode (Rd). We also consider out of cell interfering cellular users (OE). On reaching the equilibrium of the evolutionary game, all the 28 cellular users are in cellular mode, while the D2D users do not go to cellular mode, instead they prefer reuse and dedicated modes and split into 7 D2D users in reuse mode and 5 D2D users in dedicated mode. The resulting channel allocation is shown in Table 3.

V. CONCLUSION

In this paper, we have investigated some of the problems faced when D2D communication happens in the licensed band; in particular, the mode selection, power adaptation and

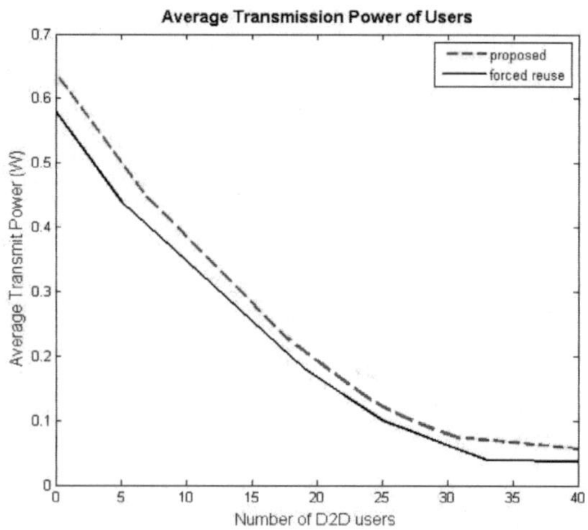

Fig. 5. Average Transmission power of users

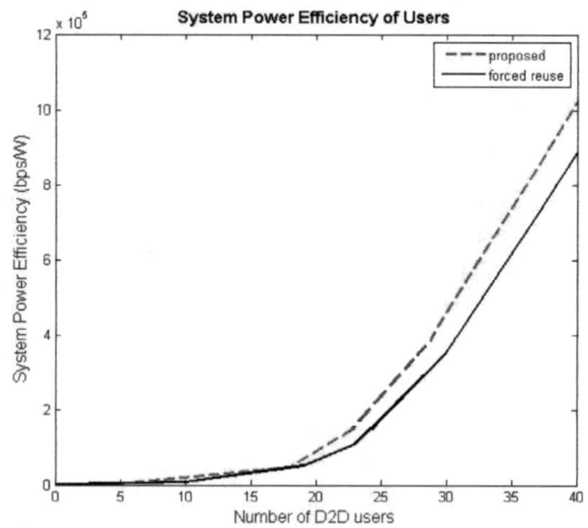

Fig. 6. System Power Efficiency of users

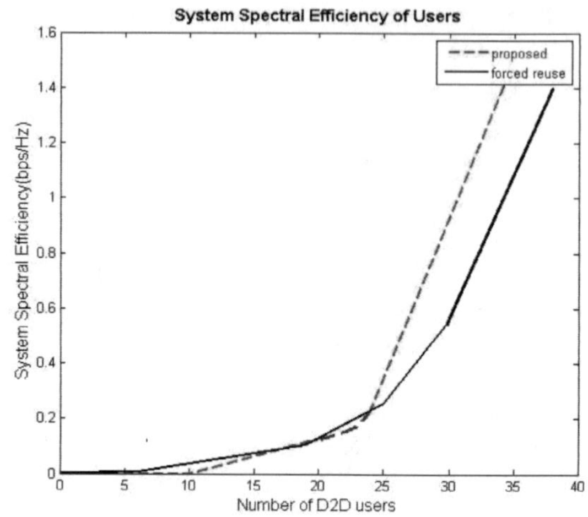

Fig. 7. System Spectral Efficiency of users

TABLE III
CHANNEL ALLOCATION

Channel	User	Channel	User
1	C6	21	C3
2	C5	22	C24
3	C13	23	C26
4	C11	24	C14,Rd6
5	C21,Rd3	25	NOT USED
6	C4,Rd7	26	C9,Rd2
7	C2	27	O4
8	NOT USED	28	C15
9	O3	29	Dd4
10	Dd2	30	C17
11	C23	31	NOT USED
12	C22	32	C8,Rd1
13	C16	33	C10
14	O2	34	C1
15	C25,Rd4	35	C27
16	C19	36	C12
17	C28,Rd5	37	O1,Dd5
18	O5	38	Dd3
19	C18	39	Dd1
20	C20	40	C7

channel assignment. We formulated the mode selection as an evolutionary game under a multicell scenario. The advantage of using evolutionary game model was that it gave room for each user to gradually adapt until it reaches the stable strategy. To save the total transmit power, we have adopted a channel inversion method. Channel allocation was done using a simple graphical approach. Simulation results showed the following. The average rate of D2D is very large for the proposed scheme compared to a forced reuse scheme. Average transmission power is a decreasing function for the scheme and so the system power efficiency is increased for our scheme compared to the pure reuse scheme. However, if we consider the bandwidth usage, the proposed scheme consumes more bandwidth due to the presence of dedicated mode users but is less compared to the high data rate hence achieving better spectral efficiency.

This work can further be improved by introducing the idea of spectrum partitioning so that we can partition the amount of spectrum available to the cellular and dedicated users. Power adaptation can also be done using improved algorithms rather than channel inversion.

REFERENCES

[1] R. Alkurd, R.M. Shubair and I. Abualhaol,"Survey on Device-to-Device Communications: Challenges and Design Issues",in *New Circuits and Systems Conf.(NEWCAS) IEEE 12th International*,October 2014,pp 361-364.

[2] P. Mach, Z. Becvar and T. Vanek,"In-Band Device-to-Device Communication in OFDMA Cellular Networks: A Survey and Challenges",*IEEE Commun. Surveys Tuts*, vol. 17, no. 4, pp 1885-1922,Fourth Quarter 2015.

[3] A. Asadi, Q. Wang and V. Mancuso,"Survey on Device-to-Device Communication in Cellular Networks",*IEEE Commun. Surveys Tuts*, vol. 16, no. 4, pp 1801-1819,Fourth Quarter 2014.

[4] K. Zhu and E. Hossain,"Joint Mode Selection and Spectrum Partitioning for Device-to-Device Communication: A Dynamic Stackelberg Game",*IEEE Trans. On Wireless Commun.*, vol. 14, no. 3, pp 1406-1420,March 2015.

[5] M. Jung, K. Hwang, and S. Choi,"Joint Mode Selection and Power Allocation Scheme for Power-Efficient Device-to-Device (D2D) Communication",in *Proc. Vehicular Technology Conf. (VTC Spring), 2012 IEEE 75th*,July 2012.

[6] S. Maghsudi and S. Stanczak,"Hybrid CentralizedDistributed Resource Allocation for Device-to-Device Communication Underlaying Cellular Networks", *IEEE Trans. on Vehicular Technology*, vol. 65, no. 4, pp 2481-2495,April 2016.

[7] F. Wang, L. Song, Z. Han, Q. Zhao, and X. Wang,"Joint Scheduling and Resource Allocation for Device-to-Device Underlay Communication", in *Proc. Wireless Communications and Networking Conf (WCNC), 2013 IEEE*, pp 134-139,July 2013.

[8] P. Cheng, L. Deng, H. Yu, Y. Xu and H. Wang,"Resource Allocation for Cognitive Networks with D2D communication:An Evolutionary Approach", in *Proc. Wireless Communications and Networking Conf. (WCNC), 2012 IEEE*, pp 2671-2676,June 2012.

[9] M. Belleschi, G. Fodor and A. Abrardo,"Performance Analysis of a Distributed Resource Allocation Scheme for D2D Communication", in *Proc. GLOBECOM Workshops (GC Wkshps), 2011 IEEE*, pp 358-362,March 2012.

[10] X. Lin, J. G.Andrews and A. Ghosh,"Spectrum Sharing for Device -to-Device Communication in Cellular Networks", *IEEE Trans. On Wireless Commun.*, vol. 13, no. 12, pp 6727-6740,December 2014.

A Study on Off-path Caching Scheme by using Successive Interference Cancellation for Information-Centric Network-based Wireless Sensor Network

Shintaro Mori
Department of Electronics Engineering and Computer Science
Fukuoka University
8-19-1, Nanakuma, Jonan-ku, Fukuoka 814-0180, Japan
e-mail: smori@fukuoka-u.ac.jp

***Abstract*— Recently, advanced WSN (Wireless Sensor Network) technologies, such as IoT (Internet of Things) and M2M (Machine to Machine) are widely applicable to various fields. On the other hand, in the network protocols of future wireless networks, it is required to obtain the sensing data from the summarized monitoring values in the large-scale WSN, i.e., it cannot be efficiently built based on the current host-centric scheme. We should redesign based on the content-centric concept. Under these perspectives, we focus on ICN (Information Centric Network)-based WSN. In particular, in this manuscript, we propose a novel off-path caching scheme by using the overhearing sensing data, and we boost the effort of our off-path caching mechanism by using the SIC (Successive Interference Cancellation) technique. In the numerical results, we reveal that the amount of stored sensing data could increase by using exhaustive Monte Carlo computer simulations. As a result, the proposed scheme can be maximally 3.69 times as improved as the comparable system without using any off-path caching method.**

Keywords-Wireless sensor network; Information-centric network; Off-path caching; Successive interference cancellation.

I. INTRODUCTION

A new WSN (Wireless Sensor Network), such as IoT (Internet of Things) and M2M (Machine to Machine), plays a primary role in providing global access by using billions of various devices. In the WSN, the network protocol, as well as the current Internet infrastructures, are founded upon the host-centric architecture. In the view of evolving traditional network frameworks, the ICN (Information Centric Network) architecture is promoting a new communication model [1]. The ICN architecture is fundamentally different from the traditional IP address-based and host-centric network, i.e., a major concept of ICN is the ability to name data independently from a current location (at which the required sensing data are provided). The ICN-based schemes have been investigated not only in the wired networks, but also in the wireless and mobile networks (including IoT, M2M and WSN) [2][3].

In this manuscript, we focus on a novel caching scheme for the important consideration of ICN-based WSN proposal. Regarding the caching mechanism, there are two common principles, such as the on-path and the off-path caching methods [4]. In the on-path caching, the network exploits information caught along the routing path taken by a name resolution request; while in the off-path caching, the network exploits information caught outside those paths. Regarding the related works for the caching schemes, the traditional ICN frameworks, such as DONA (Data-Oriented Network Architecture) [5] and NDN (Named Data Networking) [6] have natively supported the on-path caching method. The authors in [7] have proposed four on-line intra-domain cache management algorithms and [8] have realized an improvement by using the content-space partitioning and the hash-routing techniques.

In particular, we focus on the off-path caching mechanism. Most researchers have introduced an exclusive mechanism, which popular contents are actively and positively replicated. On the other hand, we effectively utilize the specific wireless feature, such as overhearing phenomena, i.e., when the sensor node transmits the sensing data via the wireless link, its neighbor sensor nodes could receive its sensing data due to the free-space radio propagation regardless of necessary or unnecessary. In other words, the proposed scheme can realize the effective off-path caching mechanism without using alternative exclusive data packets and another wireless communication module. Note that, although the signal processing for receiving and decoding transactions need additional energy consumptions, their electrical power is sufficiently smaller than the radio transmission power. Therefore, the cost of extra power consumption could be ignored, unlike the wired network system.

Moreover, regarding the signal processing of overhearing transactions, we utilize the SIC (Successive Interference Cancellation) technique [9] in order to boost the off-path caching capability. Under the SIC-based system, the receiver side tries to decode the strongest signal in the parallel signals from several transmitter sides. If the strongest signal can be successfully decoded, the decoded signal is encoded again and is subtracted from the received signal. Thus, the decoding performance of remaining signal can be improved by removing the strongest interference. The SIC technique has been extensively studied as the physical layer technology; whereas, its performance and behavior in the ICN-based wireless sensor network remain unknown, i.e., our study can demonstrate significant preliminary evaluations.

The rest of this paper is organized as follows. Section II describes the proposed scheme. Section III provides the computer simulation results. Finally, the acknowledgment and conclusions close the article.

II. PROPOSED SCHEME

As shown in Figure 1, the sensor nodes are distributed in the observation area, and every sensor node measures the environmental monitoring values as the sensing data. In the ICN-based system, there is no difference between the original and replicate information when other sensor node requests the same sensing data. Therefore, similar to the traditional ICN studies, the proposed scheme establishes the data transmission link between the subscriber and publisher nodes (that is the routing path). We define the sensor node who transfers and forwards the sensing data along the routing path as the relay node. According to the ICN principles, the relay nodes store the forwarding data into their cache memory as the on-path caching transaction in order to effectively respond to the sensing data in case of a duplicated scenario.

On the other hand, regarding the SIC method, let $P_{i,j}$ denote the signal strength at the j-th sensor node (that is receiver node) based on the overhearing processing from the i-th sensor node (that is a relay node) and let $\mathcal{M}_j$ denote the set of concurrent transmitting sensor nodes that can be heard by the j-th sensor node. If the signal from the i-th sensor node to the j-th sensor node can be decoded correctly, $P_{i,j}$ is satisfied with

$$\mathcal{H}: \frac{P_{i,j}}{\sum_{k \in \mathcal{M}_j}^{k \neq i} P_{k,j} + \sigma^2} \geq \beta \tag{1}$$

where β is the power level of required received signal threshold and σ^2 is the power of ambient noise, respectively. In short, (1) indicates that the j-th sensor node can store the replicated data of the i-th sensor node, if the SINR (Signal to Interfealance plus Noise Ratio) is sufficiently large.

As shown in Figure 2, let y denote the j-th sensor node's received signal strength, which is expressed as

$$y = \sum_{m=1}^{M_j} P_{m,j} \tag{2}$$

where M_j is the amount of $\mathcal{M}_j$'s elements. In the proposed scheme, the decoder works to recover the strongest signal among the input signals (such as the received signal in the first transaction). Therefore, the j-th sensor node tries to decode the signals based on (1), the received signal can be decoded correctly if and only if

$$\begin{aligned}
&\text{Step1:} && \frac{\hat{y}_1}{y} = \frac{P_{1,j}}{\sum_{m=1}^{M_j-1} P_{m,j} + \sigma^2} \geq \beta \\
&\text{Step2:} && \frac{\hat{y}_2}{y - y_1} = \frac{P_{2,j}}{\sum_{m=1}^{M_j-2} P_{m,j} + \sigma^2} \geq \beta \\
&\vdots && \vdots \\
&\text{Step } K: && \frac{\hat{y}_K}{y - \sum_{k=1}^{K-1} y_k} = \frac{P_{K,j}}{\sum_{m=1}^{M_j-K} P_{m,j} + \sigma^2} \geq \beta
\end{aligned} \tag{3}$$

where K denotes the number of successful decoded signals, $\hat{y}_k$ and y_k denote the correct decoded signal and the reconstructed transmission signal based on the decoded signal, respectively. In (2) and (3), we assume that both y_k and $P_{m,j}$ are non-decreasing order as $y_1 \geq y_2 \geq \cdots \geq y_K$ and $P_{1,j} \geq P_{2,j} \geq \cdots \geq P_{K,j}$, respectively.

If we realize the SIC mechanism as shown in Figure 2, we should formulate the detailed protocol design. However, its consideration is out of scope because of analyzing the principal evaluation in this paper. In particular, the considered scheme (with the above terms) should adaptively switch based on the sensor node status, such as not only transmission and receiving modes but also the overhearing mode, which is our future works.

III. NUMERICAL RESULT

Regarding the radio propagation model, we ignore the multi-path fading and shadowing to avoid system complexity. Therefore, the received signal strength can be calculated based on

$$P_{\mathrm{RX}} = P_{\mathrm{TX}} - L_{\mathrm{TX}} + G_{\mathrm{TX}} - L_{\mathrm{P}} + G_{\mathrm{RX}} - L_{\mathrm{RX}} \ \ (\mathrm{dB}) \tag{4}$$

where P_{TX} and P_{RX} are the electrical radio powers, L_{TX} and L_{RX} are the circuit power losses, and G_{TX} and G_{RX} are the antenna gains at the transmitter and receiver terminals, respectively. We determine the above parameters (without P_{RX} and L_{P}) based on the familiar XBee RF module [10]. As shown in Table I, we illustrate the simulation parameters (including above constant values). Note that, the circuit losses at transmitter and receiver sides are not taken into account to avoid system complexity, which occurs in case of the impedance mismatching and power losses at physical circuits as the thermal noise.

In (4), L_{P} is the radio-wave attenuation, which we can calculate L_{P} based on the ratio propagation model [11] with

$$L_{\mathrm{P}} = A + 10\gamma \log_{10}(d/d_0) \tag{5}$$

and

$$A = 20 \log_{10}(4\pi d_0/\lambda) \tag{6}$$

and

$$\gamma = a - bh_0 + c/h_0 \tag{7}$$

where d is the distance between sensor nodes, λ is the radio wavelength, h_0 is the antenna height, and d_0, a, b and c are the constant values depending on the surround environments (see Table I) that are given by [11].

In the computer simulation, the sensor nodes are randomly scattered and the pair of publisher and subscriber nodes is randomly selected. The routing path between the publisher and subscriber nodes is decided based on the minimum physical distance. For eliminating the calculation costs, we utilize the Dijkstra's algorithm [12] (whose algorithm can obtain the optimal path to minimizing the weight links). Regarding the SIC method, we calculate the signal strength based on the distance among sensor nodes, and we assume that the SIC mechanism are ideally conducted and worked.

Figure 3 shows the number of sensor nodes, N, versus the ratio between the sensor nodes that can correctly store the overhearing data and the overall sensor nodes, ρ. As a result, ρ is improved depending on increasing of N, because of increasing the sensor nodes that can store with the overhearing transactions due to increasing a densely deployment. In the case when $170 \leq N$ region, ρ maintains a constant value because of reaching the upper limitation. In comparison with the comparable scheme (without using the off-path caching method), our scheme can improve by 251%, 284%, 341% and 369% at N = 50, 100, 150 and 200, respectively.

IV. CONCLUSION

In this paper, we proposed a novel caching mechanism with the overhearing phenomena and SIC techniques for ICN-WSN. Computer simulation demonstrated that the proposed scheme could have a maximum of 3.69 times improvement over the comparable scheme. In future works, we should consider the detailed protocol design, and demonstrate and discuss under a realistic environment.

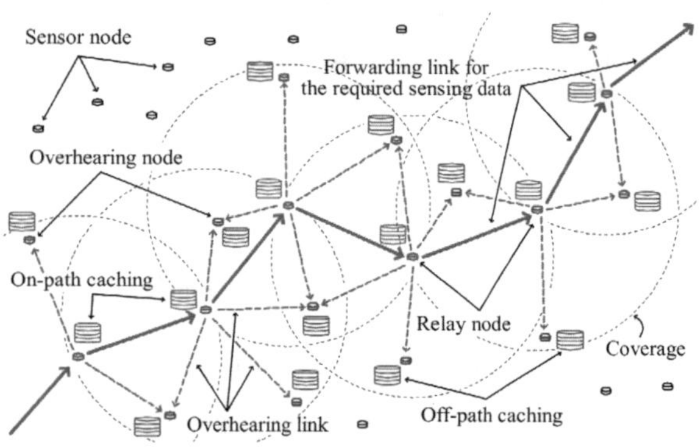

Figure 1. Overview of the proposed scheme.

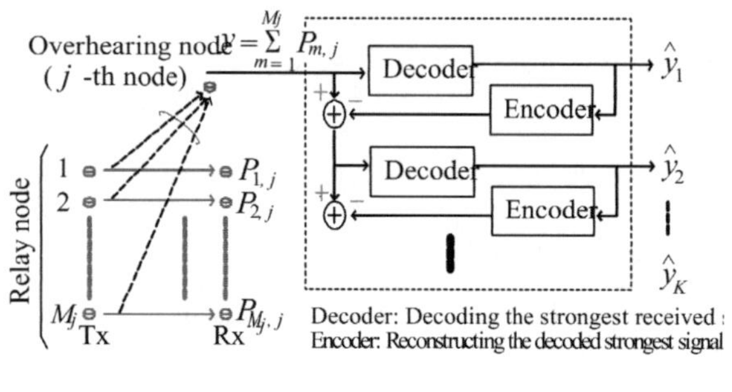

Figure 2. Procedure of SIC process for the proposed caching scheme.

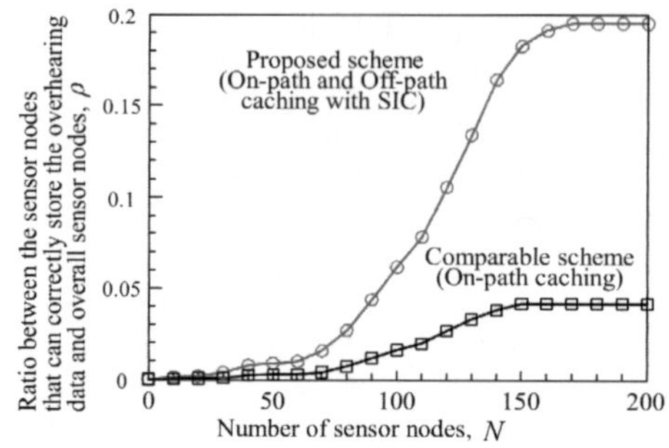

Figure 3. Number of sensor nodes versus the sensor nodes that can correctly store the overhearing data over the number of all sensor nodes.

TABLE I. SIMULATION PARAMETERS

Terms	Values
Transmission power	P_{TX} = 0 dBm (1mW)
Circuit power loss	L_{TX} = 0dB, L_{RX} = 0 dB
Antenna gain	G_{TX} = 0 dBi, G_{RX} = 0 dBi
Parameters in [11]	d_0 = 100, a = 3,6, b = 0.005, c = 20
Antenna height	h_0 = 0.5 m
Radio frequency	2.4 GHz (λ = 0.125 m)
Observation area	1,000 m × 1,000 m
Amount of Pub./Sub. node pair	10

ACKNOWLEDGMENT

A part of this work is supported by the TAF (Telecommunications Advancement Foundation).

REFERENCES

[1] B. Ahlgren, C. Dannewitz, C. Imbrenda, D. Kutscher and B. Ohlman, "A survey of information-centric networking," IEEE Commun. Mag., vol. 50, no. 7, pp. 26–36, July 2012.

[2] C. Liang, F. R. Yu and X. Zhang, "Information-centric network function virtualization over 5G mobile wireless networks," IEEE Network, vol. 29, no. 3, pp. 68–74, May–June 2015.

[3] M. Amadeo, C. Campolo, J. Quevedo, D. Corujo, A. Molinaro, A.Iera, R. L. Aguiar and A. V. Vasilakos, "Information-centric networking for the Internet of Things: Challenges and opportunities," IEEE Network, vol. 30, no. 2, pp. 92–100, Mar.–Apr. 2016.

[4] M. Zhang, H. Luo and H.Zhang, "A survey of caching mechanisms in information-centric networking," IEEE Commun. Surveys and Tutorials, vol. 17, no. 3, pp. 1473–1499, Third-quarter 2015.

[5] T. Koponen, M. Chawla, B. Chun, A. Ermolinskiy, K. H. Kim, S. Shenker and I. Stoica, "A data-oriented (and beyond) network architecture," Proc. ACM Annual Conf. Special Interest Group on Data Commun. (SIGCOM) 2007, Aug. 2007, pp. 181–192, doi:10.1145/1282427.1282402.

[6] http://www.named-data.net/ [retrieved: Mar., 2017]

[7] V. Sourlas, L. Gkatzikis, P. Flegkas and L. Tassiulas, "Distributed cache management in information-centric networks," IEEE Trans. Network and Service Management, vol. 10, no. 3, pp. 286–299, Sept. 2013.

[8] S. Wang, J. B. J. Wu and A. V. Vasilakos, "CPHR: In-network caching for information-centric networking with partitioning and hash-routing," IEEE/ACM Trans. Networking, vol. 24, no. 5, pp. 2742–2755, Oct. 2016.

[9] S. Sen, N. Santhapuri, R. R. Choudhury and S. Nelakuditi, "Successive interference cancellation: A back-of-the-envelope perspective," Proc. ACM Annual Conf. Special Interest Group on Data Commun. (SIGCOM) 2010 WS Hot Topics in Networks, Oct. 2010, doi:10.1145/1868447.1868464.

[10] http://www.digi.com/ [retrieved: Mar., 2017]

[11] V. Erceg, L. J. Greenstein, S. Y. Tjandra, S. R. Parkoff, A. Gupta, B. Kulic and A. A. Julius, "An empirically based path loss model for wireless channels in suburban environments," IEEE J. Sel. Areas in Commun., vol. 17, no. 7, pp. 1205–1211, July 1999.

[12] E. W. Dijkstra, "A note on two problems in connexion with graphs," J. Numerische Mathematik, vol. 1, no.1, pp. 269–271, Dec. 1959.

Adaptive Data Transmission Control for Reliable and Efficient Spatio-Temporal Data Retention by Vehicles

Hiroki Teshiba*, Daiki Nobayashi†, Kazuya Tsukamoto† and Takeshi Ikenaga†
* Graduate School of Computer Science and System Engineering, Kyushu Institute of Technology
† Network Design Research Center, Kyushu Institute of Technology
680-4 Kawazu, Iizuka-shi, Fukuoka, 820-8502, Japan
Email: *teshiba@infonet.cse.kyutech.ac.jp, †{nova, tsukamoto, ike}@ndrc.kyutech.ac.jp

***Abstract*—Vehicles, which have penetrated deeply into society and have become essential to our daily lives, have two major characteristics that are comparable with conventional communication devices (such as cellular phones). First, since each modern vehicle is now equipped with large computational power and vast data storage capacity, they can easily collect, process, and individually store vast amounts of data. Second, they have remarkably high mobility, and can thus transport and spread stored data to everywhere very effectively. Therefore, in this study, we focus on vehicular ad-hoc networks (VANETs) constructed solely with vehicles, and without any support from outside infrastructure. On one hand, although users can usually receive various application services through the Internet, some specific services, such as those handling traffic and local weather information, are strongly dependent on geographical location and time (and so this information is referred to as spatio-temporal data in this paper), which is not readily available via the Internet. Therefore, as a means to providing spatio-temporal data reliably and effectively by exploiting VANET, we propose an adaptive transmission control method in which each vehicle controls data transmission probability by considering the data retention density of neighboring vehicles. Through simulations, we found that our proposed method is effective for retaining spatio-temporal data.**

***Keywords*–VANET, Data retention, Adaptive data transmission control**

I. Introduction

With the progress and widespread dissemination of machine-to-machine (M2M) and Internet of Things (IoT) technologies, the number and types of devices equipped with various wireless modules have expanded rapidly. In current Internet paradigms, most data are first gathered into remote servers connected to networks, after which they are provided to applications as required. However, according to an Organisation for Economic Co-operation and Development (OECD) report [1], the number of M2M devices will grow to fifty billion by 2020, and enormous amounts of small data will flow to the Internet. In order to store and process these data effectively, the acquisition of large-capacity storage modules and high-performance central processing units (CPUs) is essential.

From the viewpoint of data contents, some specific applications such as weather and traffic information are strongly dependent on location and time. Therefore, the utilization of data collected from the IoT devices, which are referred to as *spatio-temporal data* in this paper, can be expected to improve the quality and accuracy of such information. Since the "locally produced and consumed" paradigm of spatio-temporal data use is effective for location-dependent applications, a novel network architecture that can achieve data retention within a specific area is crucial.

In this paper, we focus on vehicular ad-hoc networks (VANETs) as an important network infrastructure that can achieve the required level of spatio-temporal data retention. Modern vehicles have two remarkable features. First, data can be collected by and analyzed within individual vehicles because they are now equipped with significant amounts of storage space, battery power, and high-level computational resources. Second, since there are enormous numbers of highly mobile vehicles operating all over the world, they can provide a foundation from which data can be collected and/or distributed efficiently.

Furthermore, the potential for spatio-temporal information communication between vehicles in a VANET allows us to advocate a new promising network infrastructure. In our study, we utilize vehicles with spatio-temporal data as *regional information hubs*, or *InfoHubs*, in order to disseminate spatio-temporal data within some pre-defined area. The spatio-temporal data are finally received by users (not vehicles). Spatio-temporal data management by *InfoHub* vehicles brings us the following advantages:

- Users can obtain the spatio-temporal information quickly.
- Thanks to distributed data management, an acceptable level of fault tolerance can be achieved.
- Internet server loads can be reduced.

If spatio-temporal data are managed in a distributed manner, users can obtain the data from neighboring vehicles, thereby achieving real-time data acquisition. Moreover, if data are replicated among multiple vehicles in advance, spatio-temporal data retention can be maintained even when some vehicles break down. Finally, data management by InfoHub vehicles has the potential to decrease power consumption by Internet-based (cloud) servers.

However, since all vehicles in a VANET generally utilize the same communication channel, frame (data) collisions are inevitable and a certain level of interference is inherent. In networks with large numbers of vehicles (dense traffic environments), each vehicle could suffer multiple and frequent frame collisions, leading to a decline in communication quality. On the other hand, in networks with small numbers of vehicles (sparse traffic environments), each vehicle must accelerate data transmission activity due to the lack of data transmission timing. With these points in mind, it is clear that the use of adaptive data transmission control in response to vehicle density could provide an indispensable component for distributed data management by exploiting the capabilities of InfoHub vehicles.

Accordingly, in this paper, we propose an adaptive data transmission control method in which vehicles adaptively change data transmission probabilities in response to the density of neighboring vehicles in order to maintain spatio-temporal data retention within a pre-defined area, and thus allow area users to efficiently obtain local spatio-temporal data. In our proposed method, each vehicle estimates not only the number of neighboring vehicles based on the number of beacons but also the number of received data based on the number of data received thus far. Then, based on the estimated values, each vehicle dynamically changes data transmission probability in a way that facilitates overall spatio-temporal data retention within the specified area. Through simulation-based evaluations, we clarified that our proposed method can always achieve an acceptable level of data retention within the target area, irrespective of vehicle density changes.

The rest of this paper is organized as follows. In Section II, we review related works. In Section III, we describe our spatio-temporal data retention system. Section IV shows the detailed mechanisms of our proposed method. Section V provides the simulation model and simulation results. Finally, Section VI is our conclusion.

II. Related Work

Fan Li et al. discussed various VANET-related problems such as data dissemination and data sharing caused by the high mobility of vehicles [2] and proposed the *Geocast Routing-based protocol*, which is basically a location-based multicast routing, in order to deliver data from a source vehicle to all other vehicles within the target area. Maihofer et al. [3] proposed an *abiding geocast* in which data are delivered to all vehicles within the target area and then maintained within them during the lifetime of the network. They provided three solutions for retaining the geocast data within the target area: (1) *server approach*, (2) *election approach*, and (3) *neighbor approach*. We will provide an overview of these approaches in the following paragraph.

In the server approach, a pre-defined fixed server within the target area is used to store and periodically transmit data to other vehicles within the target area based on a geocast routing protocol. Since the server sends data and exchanges location information among all vehicles within the target area, it is susceptible to overloading. Should that occur, the server would not be able to effectively communicate with vehicles if many failures appear, thereby degrading its dissemination performance. In the election approach, only the elected vehicles maintain the data and periodically send the data to other vehicles within the target area. In both of these two approaches, broadcasting from a restricted number of vehicles can result in spatio-temporal data retention performance degradation.

Finally, the neighbor approach, which consists of only the vehicles without a dedicated server or elected vehicle, has been actively studied recently due to its high feasibility, and a number of systems such as that of [4], Floating Content [5], Locus [6], and our previous work [7], have been proposed. In the method of [4], a vehicle exchanges navigation information with neighboring vehicles, identifies other vehicles that are moving towards the target area, and then delivers the data to them. In the Floating Content and Locus systems, each vehicle has a list of data and exchanges its list with the lists of other vehicles that it encounters. If any vehicle has data that are not stored in a neighboring vehicle, the neighboring vehicle can acquire the data from the vehicle that has the data. In this situation, the vehicle that has the data decides what data to send based on the transmission probability. The transmission probability changes dynamically depending on the distance from where the data were generated. More specifically, the transmission probability decreases as the vehicle moves away from the center of the target area, thereby indicating that some outlying recipients will be unlikely to receive the data. In contrast, if there are numerous vehicles near the center of the target area, data collisions tend to occur frequently in VANETs because each vehicle attempts to send high transmission probability data at the same time.

Meanwhile, unlike Floating Content and Locus, our previous work [7] aims to deliver data to all vehicles within a target area at set pre-determined intervals, employing a geolocation-based broadcasting method. In this method, the transmission probability for periodical data dissemination is determined based on the "location information of all neighboring vehicles". Thus, this method needs a complicated calculation by vehicles.

In our research, like [7], we focus on a VANET-based system that disseminates and maintains spatio-temporal data within a target area by adaptively controlling data transmission probability in response to the vehicle density, which is estimated from the number of received data transmissions only. In our proposed method, the decision process of transmission probability is simplified because only the message information are employed without the location information of all vehicles like [7]. More specifically, although existing study [7] requires accurate location information of all vehicles in order to calculate the distance between vehicles, it is quite difficult in terms of computational overhead in a practical environment. Therefore, our proposed method only requires the number of broadcast messages to decide the transmission probability. That is, no complex information (e.g., location information) is required. We refer to our VANET-based system as a *spatio-temporal data retention system.*

III. Spatio-Temporal Data Retention System

In this section, we describe the assumptions behind our spatio-temporal retention system (III-A), the objective of our system design (III-B), and its requirements (III-C).

A. Assumptions

Spatio-temporal data are assumed to have originated at a specific location and have a target area within a predetermined radius. Information related to the data's origination location and target area are hereafter referred to as the "retention requirement" and are included in the spatio-temporal data by the user generating the data.

Since each vehicle can obtain location information by using its GPS receiver and has a unique ID, it can estimate the number of neighboring vehicles based on the received beacon messages broadcast by the InfoHub vehicles. Note that these InfoHub vehicles are equipped with an on-board wireless interface employing IEEE 802.11p specification. Moreover, each vehicle performs an operation that determines whether it is within the target area.

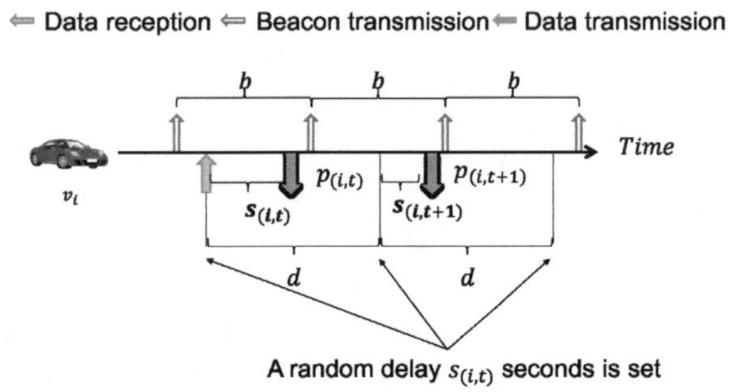

Figure 1. Data transmission procedure.

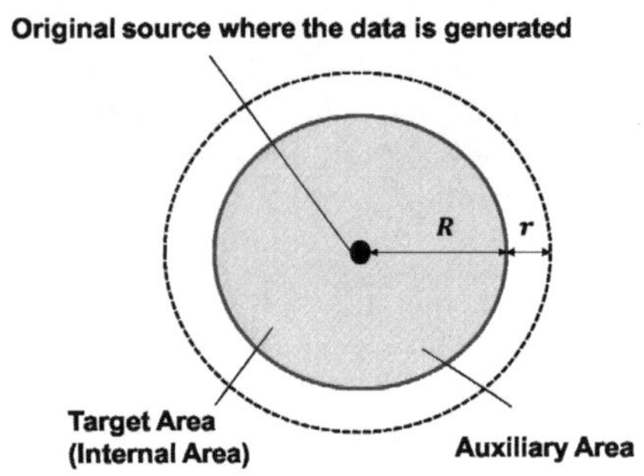

Figure 2. Target area and Auxiliary area.

B. System Objective

The objective of this system is to facilitate data retention, especially for spatio-temporal data such as those on weather and traffic, within a target area. To achieve this, we focus on VANET constructed from vehicles with InfoHub characteristics. By using this system, a user who enters an area can obtain the spatio-temporal data on that area very quickly. Furthermore, since multiple vehicles have the same data, fault tolerance can be achieved. Finally, since the spatio-temporal data are stored only on VANET, there is no burden imposed on Internet (cloud) servers. In the next section, we will discuss the system requirements to achieve our objective.

C. System Requirements

In this paper, we define *coverage rate* as the performance index that indicates how fast users can receive the spatio-temporal data. To facilitate rapid data delivery to users, the entire target area should be covered within the transmission range of InfoHub vehicles. That is, users should be able to obtain the spatio-temporal data from a neighboring vehicle via one-hop broadcast communication. Note that we assume that the transmission range is less than the target area radius, and we calculate the coverage rate at the predetermined interval. The coverage rate formula is shown below:

$$Coverage\ Rate = \frac{S_{DT}}{S_{TA}}$$

where S_{TA} denotes the size of target area, and S_{DT} denotes the size of total area where the user can obtain the data transmitted

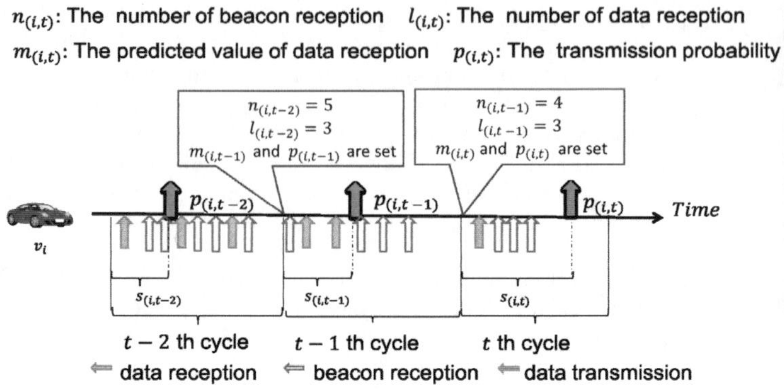

Figure 3. Outline of transmission probability decision.

from either of InfoHub vehicles within the transmission interval. A high coverage rate means that users can automatically receive the spatio-temporal data from anywhere within the target area. Moreover, the slope of the change in the coverage rate indicates the dissemination speed of spatio-temporal data. Therefore, the coverage rate can reveal the responsiveness of the proposed system. Since the proposed system requires rapid acquisition of spatio-temporal data from anywhere within the target area, each vehicle within the area needs to transmit the data as frequently as possible. However, high vehicle density results in frequent data transmissions, which inevitably cause data collisions that can adversely impact the coverage rate. On the other hand, if the vehicle density within the area is low, all vehicles should transmit data as often as possible in order to boost the coverage rate.

In this way, the appropriate transmission probability will change in response to the density of neighboring vehicles. In Section IV, we describe our proposed adaptive transmission control method for achieving the spatio-temporal data retention using InfoHub vehicles.

IV. Node Density-Aware Transmission Control

In this section, we describe our proposed transmission control method, which is based on the number of neighboring vehicles (neighboring vehicle density), and which aims at effective retention of the spatio-temporal data within a target area. Note that, hereafter, InfoHub vehicles are defined as nodes. This method aims to disseminate spatio-temporal data by utilizing the appropriate number of nodes in the target area. Consequently, our spatio-temporal data retention system can maintain a high coverage rate while reducing the total number of data transmissions to the minimum necessary.

A. Data Transmission Timing

In our method, after a node receives data from another node, it needs to re-transmit the received data, as necessary, to ensure spatio-temporal data retention within the target area. However, in order to minimize transmission collisions, the transmission timing of each node is different. This minimizes radio channel collisions among the nodes.

Figure 1 shows the data transmission procedure. In our proposed system, each node periodically transmits the beacon message, but data are only transmitted when necessary. The beacon broadcast interval is fixed at b seconds. On the other hand, the data are transmitted based on the following procedure. When a node v_i receives data from another node, it first checks the transmission intervals of d seconds included in the data. Then, that node randomly determines the next transmission time $s_{(i,t)}$ seconds. Note that the actual transmission time is determined at the start time of the t-th cycle. Here, a cycle lasts d seconds. The random determination within d seconds allows the node to avoid data transmission collisions. This interval d differs between applications, and we assume that the user originating the spatio-temporal data also decides this interval.

B. Adaptive Transmission Control Method

If all nodes are capable of transmitting data at different timing intervals, data collisions can be completely avoided. However, when the number of neighboring nodes within the transmission coverage area is larger than the number of transmission slots, collisions inevitably occur. Accordingly, we designed a new transmission control method in which the transmission probability is dynamically changed based on the neighboring node density, thereby providing a high coverage rate with the minimum number of data transmissions. In our method, nodes around the target area are classified into three types based on distance from the center of the target area (data origin point), as shown in Figure 2. The specific conditions are described below:

$$\begin{cases} 0 \le x \le R: & internal\ area \\ R < x \le R+r: & auxiliary\ area \\ otherwise: & independence \end{cases}$$

where x denotes the distance between the node and the center of target area. This distance is calculated from both GPS information and the data origin point, which is included in the data. R shows the radius of the target area, which is referred to as the *internal area*. r is the range of the *auxiliary area*, which is very close to the internal area. The values of R and r are also contained in the data. In Sections IV-B1 and IV-B2, we show how the transmission probability is determined in each area.

1) Internal Area Nodes: The nodes in the internal area autonomously adjust the transmission probability based on the density of neighboring nodes in order to provide a high coverage rate. Figure 3 shows an outline of the transmission probability decision process. The transmission probability $p_{(i,t)}$, which indicates the transmission probability during the t-th cycle, is always set at the start time of the t-th cycle. Note that i represents a unique node ID and t represents a number of cycle.

In the first step, when a node initially receives the data from other nodes, the transmission probability during the first cycle, i.e., $p_{(i,1)}$, is set to 1. That is, the node makes sure to transmit the data because the other nodes cannot provide the data within the receiving node's transmission coverage. This allows us to improve the coverage rate quickly. In the subsequent cycle (t $\geq$2), $p_{(i,t)}$ is determined based on the number of neighboring nodes $n_{(i,t-1)}$. Here, when the number of neighboring nodes is more than four, the node's own transmission range has the potential to be completely covered by that of all neighboring nodes. For example, when the neighboring four nodes are located to its north, south, west, and south (ideal arrangement), the node's potential transmission cover area is already completely enclosed by that of other nodes. Threfore, the decision method of data transmission probability $p_{(i,t)}$ is classified into the following two cases based on the number of neighboring nodes $n_{(i,t-1)}$.

- **case 1** $n_{(i,t-1)} \leq 3$:

$p_{(i,t)}$ is set to 1. Since the node's own transmission coverage cannot be completely covered by that of the neighboring nodes, it has to transmit, i.e., $p_{(i,t)}$ is set to 1.

- **case 2** $n_{(i,t-1)} \geq 4$:

$p_{(i,t)}$ is determined based on the number of neighboring nodes and the number of received data. However, since such high node density inherently poses transmission collision risks, only the minimum number of nodes required to maintain the high coverage rate should transmit the data. Conversely, in situations where the location of neighboring nodes is radically asymmetrical and has the potential to become imbalanced, the transmission coverage may not be complete, even if there are a large number of neighboring nodes. This can prevent a node from being able to cover its own transmission range.

To solve these abovementioned problems, we define $m_{(i,t)}$ as the estimated value of the number of received data during t-th cycle and adjust the transmission probability based on the $m_{(i,t)}$. The predicted value $m_{(i,t)}$ is given as equation (1), where $m_{(i,t-1)}$ is the predicted value of the previous cycle, $l_{(i,t-1)}$ is the number of received data in the previous cycle (actual value), and α is the moving average coefficient.

$$m_{(i,t)} = \alpha * l_{(i,t-1)} + (1-\alpha) * m_{(i,t-1)} \tag{1}$$

The node adjusts its transmission probability so that the number of data transmissions in the t-th cycle becomes the given target value β. If $m_{(i,t)}$ is less than β, the node can predict that the number of data transmissions is likely to be insufficient to cover the area. Therefore, it must increase its transmission probability. On the other hand, if $m_{(i,t)}$ is more than β, the node needs to decrease its transmission probability because excessive data transmissions will occur in the next cycle. At the start of the t-th cycle, each node estimates $m_{(i,t)}$ and then adjusts its transmission probability. Equation (2) describes how the transmission probability is adjusted.

$$p_{(i,t)} = \begin{cases} p_{(i,t-1)} + \frac{\beta - l_{(i,t-1)}}{n_{(i,t-1)}+1} & (0 < m_{(i,t)} < \beta) \\ p_{(i,t-1)} & (m_{(i,t)} = \beta) \\ p_{(i,t-1)} - \frac{l_{(i,t-1)} - \beta}{n_{(i,t-1)}+1} & (m_{(i,t)} > \beta) \end{cases} \tag{2}$$

In this case, the initial value of transmission probability at the first cycle is set to $\frac{\beta}{n_{(i,t-1)}+1}$. This means the average transmission probability of all nodes (including itself and the number of neighboring nodes $n_{(i,t-1)}$) is set to control the number of data transmissions as β. If $m_{(i,t)}$ is less than β, all $n_{(i,t-1)}+1$ nodes increase their individual data transmission probabilities by $\frac{\beta - l_{(i,t-1)}}{n_{(i,t-1)}+1}$ because their estimates will show that the number of transmitted data does not reach β. On the other hand, if $m_{(i,t)}$ is more than β, the individual nodes

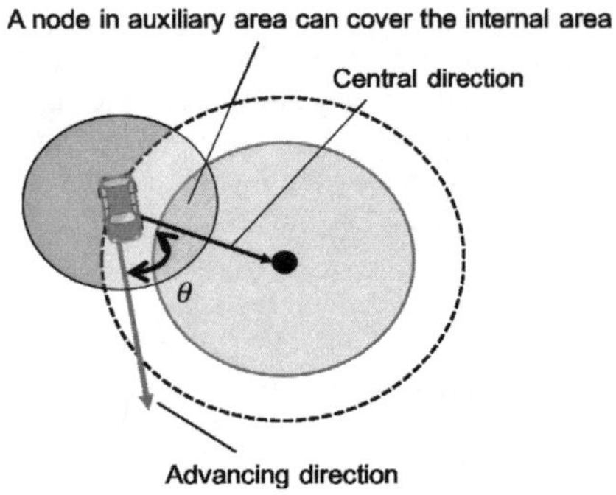

Figure 4. Node behavior in auxiliary area.

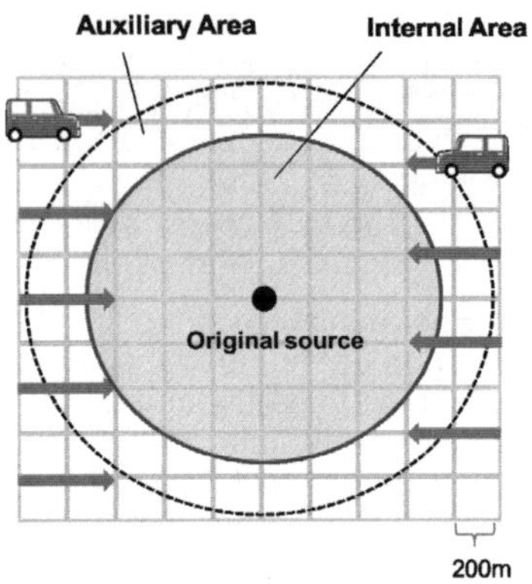

Figure 5. Simulation model.

decrease the transmission probability by $\frac{l_{(i,t-1)}-\beta}{n_{(i,t-1)}+1}$ because they can predict that excessive transmissions will occur. If $m_{(i,t)}$ is equal to β, $p_{(i,t)}$ is set to $p_{(i,t-1)}$ because the current data transmission probability is appropriate. Note that if the value of $\frac{\beta-l_{(i,t-1)}}{n_{(i,t-1)}+1}$ or $\frac{l_{(i,t-1)}-\beta}{n_{(i,t-1)}+1}$ is less than zero, $p_{(i,t)}$ is set to $p_{(i,t-1)}$, and the transmission probability range is varied from $\frac{\beta}{n_{(i,t-1)}+1}$ to 1.

2) Auxiliary Area Nodes: In our proposed method, auxiliary area nodes are also employed to maintain the high coverage rate. To maximize the effect of this extension, just the following two types of nodes are required. The first are nodes that remain in the auxiliary area. The second are nodes approaching the target area (i.e., the angles between the direction of advance and the central direction that are less than θ_{th}, which is the given threshold value, as shown in Figure 4). Since data transmission from these nodes in the auxiliary area can cover the area near the boundary of internal area, these nodes always set $p_{(i,t)}$ to 1. That is, these nodes must transmit the data in order to achieve the high coverage rate.

Finally, the nodes out of the auxiliary area delete the data in order to avoid leaking the spatio-temporal data outside the target area.

V. Performance Evaluation

In this section, we report on a simulation-based performance evaluation of our proposed method. We begin by describing the simulation environment in Subsection V-A. Subsections V-B and V-C present simulation results when the node density and the value of β are changed, respectively. Finally, Subsection V-D shows how the change in node location impacts both the actual number of data transmissions and β. In order to show the effectiveness of our proposed method, we utilized the comparison method called the *naive method*, in which the transmission probability ($p_{(i,t)}$) of all nodes in the simulation area always set to 1.

TABLE I. SIMULATION PARAMETERS.

Internal area	750 m	Auxiliary area	250 m
Transmission range	300 m	α	0.5
Beacon interval	1 s	Transmission interval	5 s

A. Simulation Model

We evaluated our proposed method on the *Veins* [8] simulation platform. The Veins platform implements both the IEEE 802.11p specification for wireless communications and the VANET mobility model, simultaneously. As a result, Veins can combine the network simulator *OMNeT++* [9] and the road traffic simulator *SUMO* [10].

Table I shows our simulation parameters. Here, we assume a grid-shaped road network. The radius of the target area R (distance from the data origination point) is 750 m and the range of the auxiliary area r is set to 250 m, as shown in Figure 5. The velocity of each node on the roads is set to 40 km/h. These nodes run alternately from east to west and from west to east. The communication range of each node is just 300 m. The transmission and the beacon intervals are set to 5 seconds and 1 seconds, respectively.

The moving average coefficient α is 0.5. We evaluated our proposed method from the viewpoint of coverage rate and total data transmission reduction over 100 seconds.

B. Node Density Impact

In this subsection, we set $\beta = 4$ because the minimum number of nodes necessary to provide total transmission coverage over the target area is four. In other words, with four nodes available, users can receive data anywhere within the target area. In this environment, we evaluated the performance of our proposed method in cases where the node density changes. The distance between nodes varies from 100 to 300 m. As a result, the average number of nodes within the transmission range of some node (i.e., 300 m) is also varied from approximately 5.5 to 16.4. Therefore, in this subsection, we investigated how node density impacts the coverage rate and the total number of data transmissions.

Figure 6 (a) shows the average steady state coverage rate. This steady state denotes a period of 75 to 95 seconds because data retention has already been completed. Since the cycle period is five seconds long, the coverage rate is the average value measured over four cycles (i.e., 20 seconds). From this result, it can be seen that a coverage rate of 99 % or more can be maintained regardless of node density changes.

Figure 6 (b) shows the reduction rate in the total number of data transmissions compared with that of the naive method.

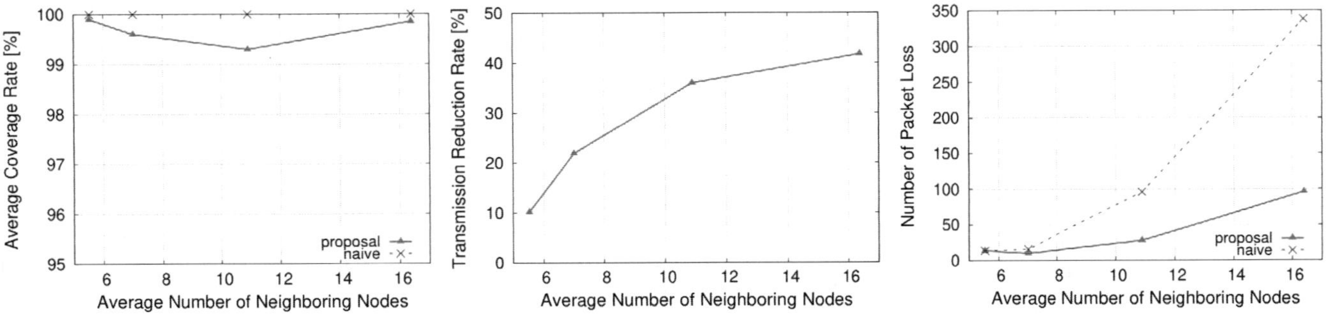

(a) Average coverage rate.

(b) Transmission reduction rate.

(c) Total number of packets lost.

Figure 6. Performance with varying node density.

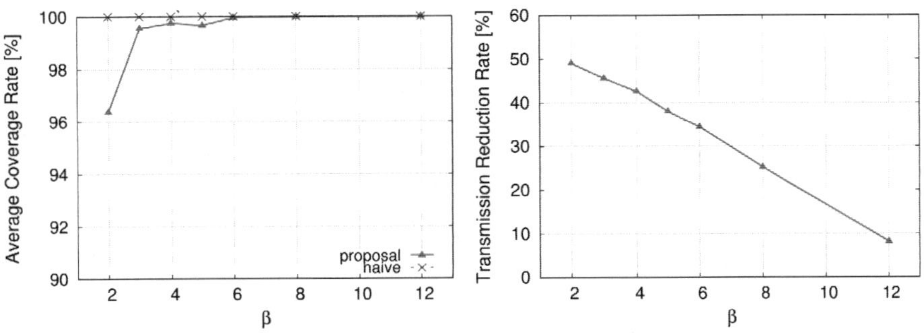

(a) Average coverage rate.

(b) Transmission reduction rate.

Figure 7. Performance achieved by varying the value of β.

Although the reduction rate is limited to 10 % at the low node density, it can be seen that our proposed method can reduce the total number of data transmissions by 42 % at times of high node density (such as in the case of 16.4 neighboring nodes). This result shows that our proposed method can limit redundant data transmissions effectively as the node density increases. We can also confirm that high transmission probability is set with low node density, whereas low transmission probability is set with high node density.

Furthermore, Figure 6 (c) shows the total number of packets lost when the naive and the proposed method are employed. In particular, it can be seen that, compared with the naive method, our proposal method efficiently reduces the number of total packets lost when the node density is high. From these results, we could confirm that our proposed method can adaptively control the data transmission probability in response to the node density changes while maintaining a coverage rate of approximately 100 %.

C. Impact of the Value of β

In this subsection, the number of neighboring nodes is fixed at approximate 16.4 and the value of β is varied from 2 to 12. Figure 7 (a) shows the steady state coverage rate with changes in the value of β. This result shows that our proposed method achieves a coverage rate of nearly 100 % except for the case in which β is two. A low β value creates frequent opportunities for data transmission probability decreases, thereby aggressively limiting transmissions. Therefore, the coverage rate cannot reach 100 % if the value of β is low. Figure 7 (b) shows the reduction in the total data transmission rate when the value of β is varied. This result shows that the rate linearly decreases as the value of β increases, and that our proposed method can reduce transmissions by up to 49 % while maintaining a coverage rate of 100 %.

Since the proposed method dynamically changes the data transmission probability in response to location, it is necessary to investigate the change in the transmission probability that occurs with the location consideration discussed in Section V-D.

D. Discussion: Location-aware Analysis

In this subsection, we investigate the number of data transmissions that result when the location within the internal area is changed. To achieve this, we separate the internal area into two different sub-areas. (1) *Edge Area*: nodes in this area can receive data transmitted from nodes in the auxiliary area; (2) *Center Area*: nodes in this area do not receive data transmitted from the auxiliary area. The radius of the Center Area is 450 m. The Edge Area is defined as the area within a radius of 750 m but outside the Center Area. We evaluate how the difference of location impacts the number of data transmissions.

Figure 8 (a) shows the average number of data transmissions in Center/Edge Areas. From this result, it can be seen that

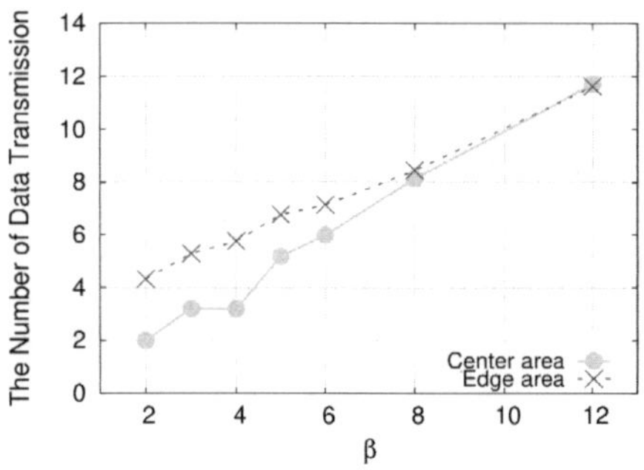

(a) Under proposed method Area.

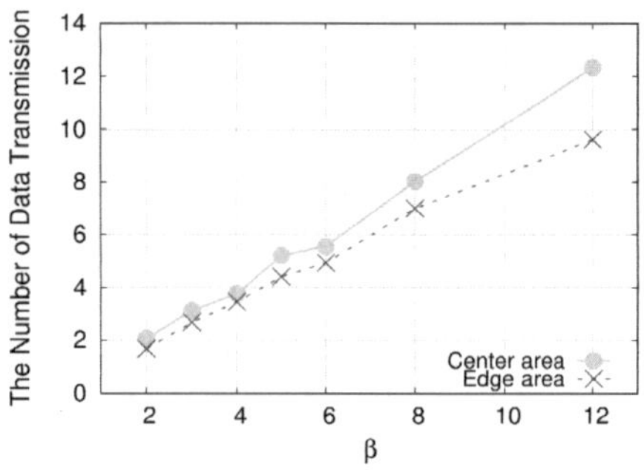

(b) Without data transmissions from auxiliary area.

Figure 8. Average number of data transmissions for nodes in the Center Area and nodes in the Edge Area.

in the Center Area, the number of data transmissions can be controlled to nearly β. However, when the value of β is low, the number of data transmissions in the Edge Area is clearly larger than β. This is because nodes in the Edge Area can receive data from those in the auxiliary area, thereby experiencing many data receptions. Because multiple nodes in the auxiliary area always try to transmit the data, redundant data transmissions occur.

Therefore, to show the contribution of data transmission from nodes in the auxiliary area, we set the probability of those nodes $p_{(i,t)}$ to 0. Figure 8 (b) shows the average number of data transmissions while excluding data transmissions from nodes in the auxiliary area. From this result, we can see that nodes in the Center Area adjust the number of data transmissions to the nearly β. On the other hand, the number of transmitted data from nodes in the Edge Area is insufficient to achieve β, especially in case of high β. This is because the density of nodes in the Edge Area is insufficient and data transmissions from nodes in the auxiliary area are not supported.

From these results, it is clear that the precise control of data transmission from nodes in the auxiliary area is very important for adjusting the number of transmitted data to β. This, in turn, indicates that our proposed method still has an issue that needs to be resolved. Therefore, we will extend our proposed method to permit data transmission probability adjustments for nodes in the auxiliary area, thereby effectively limiting the total number of transmitted data.

VI. Conclusion

In this study, our objective was to achieve spatio-temporal data retention within a target area, which would allow users to automatically receive spatio-temporal data from anywhere within the target area. To achieve this, we proposed a new spatio-temporal data retention system that utilizes a VANET constructed from *InfoHub* vehicles. We also proposed an adaptive decision making method for data transmission probability that is based on the density of neighboring vehicles. In our proposed method, each vehicle first estimates the number of neighboring vehicles based on the received beacon messages. Then, the probability is adaptively set with consideration of both the number of neighboring vehicles and the number of transmitted data during the previous time slot. Furthermore, the decision method used differs depending on the vehicle's location (internal or auxiliary area).

Through simulations, we clarified that our proposed method can roughly control data transmissions in response to vehicle density changes. However, we also confirmed that our proposed method still has a problem in which vehicles in the auxiliary area cannot determine an appropriate transmission probability. Thus, in our future work, we will extend the method and then evaluate the improved method under actual traffic environment conditions (such as by using actual traffic data in a real city). Furthermore, although only one type of data is treated in this paper, various types of data would coexist in real environments. Therefore, we will also extend the proposed method in order to treat various types of data simultaneously.

References

[1] OECD, "M2M Communications: Connecting Billions of Devices," *OECD Digital Economy Papers*, No. 192, 2012.

[2] F. Li, and Y. Wang, "Routing in vehicular ad hoc networks: A survey," *IEEE Vehicular Technology Magazine*, Vol. 2, Issue 2, pp. 12-22, 2007.

[3] C. Maihöfer, T. Leinumüller, and E. Schoch, "Abiding Geocast: Time-stable Geocast for Ad Hoc Networks," In *Proc. ACM VANET*, pp. 20-29, 2005.

[4] I. Leontiadis, P. Costa, and C. Mascolo, "Persistent content-based information dissemination in hybrid vehicular networks," In *Proc. IEEE PerCom*, pp. 1-10, 2009.

[5] J. Ott, E. Hyyti, P. Lassila, T. Vaegs, and J. Kangasharju, "Floating Content: Information Sharing in Urban Areas," In *Proc. IEEE PerCom*, pp. 136-146, 2011.

[6] N. Thompson, R. Crepaldi and R. Kravets, "Locus: A Location-based Data Overlay for Disruption-tolerant Networks," In *Proc. ACM CHANTS*, pp. 47-54, 2010.

[7] T. Higuchi *et al.*, "Regional InfoHubs by vehicles: balancing spatio-temporal coverage and network load," In *Proc. IoV-VoI'16*, pp. 25-30, 2016.

[8] "Veins," [Online]. Available from: http://veins.car2x.org/2017.3.11.

[9] "OMNeT++," [Online]. Available from: https://omnetpp.org/2017.3.11.

[10] "SUMO," [Online]. Available from: http://www.dlr.de/ts/en/desktopdefault.aspx/tabid-9883/16931_read-41000/2017.3.11.

Privacy Token: A Mechanism for User's Privacy Specification in Identity Management Systems for the Cloud

María Elena Villarreal*, Sergio Roberto Villarreal†, Carla Merkle Westphall‡, Jorge Werner§

Network and Management Laboratory
Post-Graduate Program in Computer Science
Federal University of Santa Catarina
Florianopolis, SC, Brazil
Email: maria.villarreal@posgrad.ufsc.br*, sergio@lrg.ufsc.br†,
carla.merkle.westphall@ufsc.br‡, jorge@lrg.ufsc.br§

***Abstract*— With the increasing amount of personal data stored and processed in the cloud, economic and social incentives to collect and aggregate such data have emerged. Therefore, secondary use of data, including sharing with third parties, has become a common practice among service providers and may lead to privacy breaches and cause damage to users since it involves using information in a non-consensual and possibly unwanted manner. Despite numerous works regarding privacy in cloud environments, users are still unable to control how their personal information can be used, by whom and for which purposes. This paper presents a mechanism for identity management systems that instructs users about the possible uses of their personal data by service providers, allows them to set their privacy preferences and sends these preferences to the service provider along with their identification data in a standardized, machine-readable structure, called privacy token. This approach is based on a three-dimensional classification of the possible secondary uses of data, four predefined privacy profiles and a customizable one, and a secure token for transmitting the privacy preferences. The correct operation of the mechanism was verified through a prototype, which was developed in Java in order to be incorporated, in future work, to an implementation of the OpenId Connect protocol. The main contribution of this paper is the privacy token, which inverts the current scenario where users are forced to accept the policies defined by service providers by allowing the former to express their privacy preferences and requesting the latter to align their actions or ask for specific permissions.**

Keywords–Privacy; Cloud Computing; Identity Management.

I. INTRODUCTION

Cloud Computing offers infrastructure, development platform and applications as a service, on demand and charged according to usage. On the one hand, this paradigm gives users greater flexibility, performance and scalability without the need to maintain and manage their own IT infrastructure. On the other hand, it aggravates the problem of application and verification of security and causes users to lose, at least partially, control over their data and applications [1].

With the increasing amount of personal data stored and processed in the cloud, including users' Personally Identifiable Information (PII), economic and social incentives to collect and aggregate such data have emerged. Consequently, secondary use of data, including sharing with third parties, has become a common practice among Service Providers (SPs) [2]. However, since users only interact directly with SPs, which do not provide clear policies to warn them about how their PII can be used, they are usually unaware of secondary use of data and the existence of third parties.

According to the privacy taxonomy defined in [3], secondary use consists in the use of data for purposes other than those for which they were initially collected without the consent of the subject, e.g., the use of personal data collected on social networks for offering personalized advertising. This practice, thus, may violate the privacy of the user and cause damage since it involves using information in a non-consensual and possibly unwanted manner [3]. Nonetheless, whether certain action violates the privacy of a user depends on the perception of such user and his or her willingness to share given types of data. This, therefore, raises the need of collecting and respecting the privacy preferences of users.

An important aspect of the implementation of privacy in the cloud is Identity Management (IdM), which allows Identity Providers (IdPs) to centralize user's identification data and send it to SPs in order to enable the processes of authentication and access control [4]. IdM systems, such as OpenId Connect [5], allow the creation of federations, i.e., trust relationships that make possible for users authenticated in one IdP to access services provided by various SPs belonging to different administrative domains. An example is when users authenticate in different services with their Facebook accounts. In this case, Facebook acts as an IdP.

Even though there are several approaches that are intended to allow users to define their privacy preferences and organizations to express their practices, they are poorly adopted by both users and companies because they do not offer practical methods. In addition, most of them do not consider the decentralized nature of federated cloud environments. Consequently, IdM systems do not offer effective mechanisms to collect user's privacy preferences and to send them to the SP and, therefore, users are still unable to control how their PII can be used, by whom and for what purposes [1].

Werner and Westphall [6] proposed a privacy-aware identity management model for the cloud in which IdPs and SPs interact in dynamic federated environments to manage identities and ensure user's privacy. The model, while allowing users to choose and encrypt the data that can be sent to the SP, does not define a mechanism for determining users' privacy preferences and allowing them to control the use and sharing of their PII.

In order to complement the aforementioned model, this paper presents a mechanism for identity management systems that instructs users about the possible uses of their personal data by service providers and allows them to set their privacy preferences. These preferences are converted into a standardized, machine-readable structure, called privacy token, which is then sent to the SP along with other authentication data.

The remainder of this paper is organized as follows. Section II describes basic concepts relevant to the understanding of the proposal and Section III presents the main related work. In Section IV, the proposed mechanism for user's privacy preferences in IdM systems is introduced and a prototype implementation of the mechanism is described. Finally, conclusion and future work are presented in Section V.

II. Basic Concepts

This section presents the definitions of concepts considered important to the understanding of the proposal of this paper.

A. *Identity Management (IdM)*

IdM is implemented through IdM systems such as OpenId Connect [5], and is responsible for establishing the identity of a user or system (authentication), for managing access to services by that user (access control), and for maintaining user identity profiles [7].

Typical identity management systems involve three parts: users, identity providers, and service providers [7]. The user visits an SP, which, in turn, relies on the IdP to provide authentic information about the user. These systems enable the concept of federated identity, which is the focus of this work and allows users authenticated in various IdPs to access services offered by SPs located in different administrative domains due to a previously established trust relationship [8].

Some important IdM concepts are described next, as defined in [4][9][10]:

1) Personally Identifiable Information (PII): information that can be used to identify the person to whom it relates or can be directly or indirectly linked to that person. Thus, depending on the scope, information such as date of birth, GPS location, IP address and personal interests inferred by the tracking of the use of web sites may be considered as PII.

2) PII Principal: natural person to whom the PII relates.

3) Identity Provider (IdP): party that provides identities to subjects and is, usually, responsible for the process of authentication.

4) Service Provider (SP): party that provides services or access to user's resources and, for that, requires the submission of valid credentials.

B. *Privacy*

In this work, which focuses on IdM systems and federated cloud environments, privacy is considered to be the right of a user to decide if his or her PII can be used, by whom and for what purpose [3][10][11].

1) Privacy policy: set of statements that express the practices of the organizations regarding user data collection, use, and sharing.

2) Privacy preferences: preferences and permissions of a user for the secondary use of his or her PII, i.e., they determine by whom and for what purpose a PII can be used.

There are several approaches that are intended to express policies and privacy preferences, and the ones considered most significant for this work are described in the next section, along with other relevant privacy-concerned studies.

III. Related Work

Platform for Privacy Preferences (P3P) [12] is a protocol designed to inform users about the practices of collecting and using data from websites. A P3P policy consists of a set of eXtensible Markup Language (XML) statements applied to specific resources such as pages, images, or cookies. When a website that has its policies defined in P3P wants to collect user's data, the preferences of that user are compared to the corresponding policy. If this is acceptable, the transaction continues automatically; if not, the user is notified and can opt-in (accept) or opt-out (reject). This work provides a basis for collecting user preferences, but it requires every user and SP to define their policies in this language and does not meet the needs of federated cloud environments.

Enterprise Privacy Authorization Language (EPAL) [13] is a formal language designed to address the industry's need to express organizations' internal privacy policies. An EPAL policy defines a list of hierarchies of data categories, user categories and purposes, as well as sets of actions, obligations, and conditions. These elements are used to formulate privacy authorization rules that allow or reject actions. Nevertheless, as it is specific for internal corporate policies, it does not consider user's preferences and is not suitable for privacy in federated identity environments.

Purpose-to-Use (P2U) [2] was proposed to provide means to define policies regarding the secondary use of the data. It is inspired by P3P, but allows the specification of privacy policies that define the purpose of use, type, retention period, and price of shared data. This language, although it enables user-editable and negotiable policies, is complex for users as it assumes that they have privacy policies and are able to define them in P2U. It also requires the SPs to have their policies defined in the same language.

Basso et al. [14] define a UML profile to assist in the development of applications and services that need to be consistent with the statements of their privacy policies. The authors identify privacy elements, such as policies and statements, through which organizations can define their policies for collecting, using, retaining, and releasing data; and organize their relationships into a conceptual model. This model is then mapped to a UML profile defined by stereotypes, attributes, and constraints that allow modeling statements of actual privacy policies. Although this profile helps application developers, it does not offer practical means for users to set their privacy preferences and transmit them to SPs.

Chanchary and Chiasson [15] performed an online survey to understand how users perceive online tracking for behavioral advertising. They demonstrated that users have clear preferences for which classes of information they would like to disclose online and that some would be more prone to share data if they were given prior control of tracking protection tools. The authors also identified three groups of

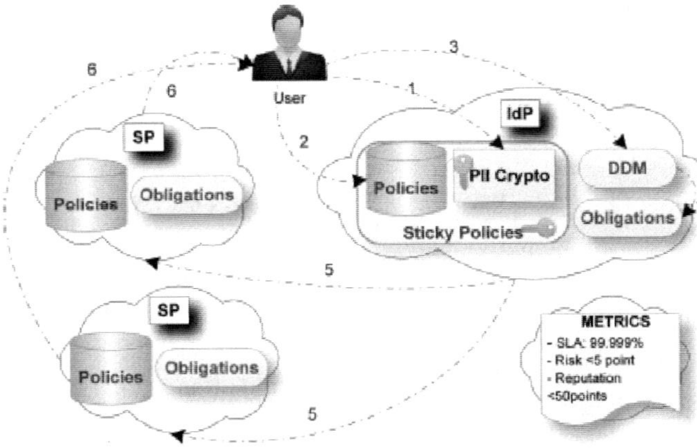

Figure 1. Interaction model between user, IdP and SP proposed in [6].

users according to how their privacy attitudes influenced their sharing willingness. These groups are used as a basis for the privacy profiles of our mechanism and are presented next:

1) Privacy Fundamentalists (30.4%): consider privacy as a very important aspect and they feel very strongly about it.

2) Privacy Pragmatists (45.9%): consider privacy as a very important aspect but also like the benefits of abdicating some privacy when they believe their information will not be misused.

3) Privacy Unconcerned (23.6%): do not consider privacy an important aspect or do not worry about how people and organizations use their information.

Werner and Westphall [6] present an IdM model with privacy for the cloud in which IdPs and SPs interact in dynamic and federated environments to manage the identities and ensure the privacy of users. They propose predefined, customizable privacy settings that help users to declare their desired level of privacy by allowing them to choose the access model, which can be anonymous, pseudonymous, or with partial attributes, and warning them about the reputation of the SP.

The interaction model defined in [6] and shown in Figure 1 proposes the registration in the IdP of the user's attributes and credentials, which may be encrypted (step 1), as well as the privacy policies to regulate the use and dissemination of their PII (step 2). Both the data and the policies are encapsulated in a package called sticky policies, which is sent to the SP along with a data dissemination model and obligations that must be fulfilled by the SP. The idea of the sticky policies is that PII are always disseminated with the policies governing their use and dissemination so that the user's privacy preferences are met by any SP. If the policies of the SP and the sticky policies are compliant, a positive reputation assess is generated for the SP; otherwise, a low reputation score is returned. The authors, however, do not define a mechanism for collecting these preferences, converting them into a machine-executable structure and sending them to the SP.

IV. Proposal for a Privacy Preferences Specification Mechanism

The proposal of this paper consists in a mechanism to incorporate to the OpenId Connect protocol a privacy token, which allows users to have a profile with their privacy preferences that is always sent to the SP along with their data. These profiles are based in a three-dimensional representation of the possible uses of PII.

The proposed mechanism allows users to choose a predefined privacy profile or to create a personalized one by choosing to opt-in or opt-out of each privacy preference. This profile is then transformed into a secure JSON Web Token (JWT), similar to the ID and access tokens already used by the OpenId Connect protocol.

A. Classification of Possible Uses of PII

Due to the large amount of possible actions and methods for collecting and sharing data, it is unfeasible to thoroughly list them. Therefore, this paper proposes a generic model that, on the one hand, is useful for users to set their privacy preferences and, on the other hand, works as a reference for SPs to assess whether the business rules of their data collection applications meet these preferences.

For this purpose, possible uses of the PII were classified in a three-dimensional structure. The dimensions, along with their respective abbreviations, are described next:

1) Data type: category of the PII to which the preference refers. The attributes of this dimension are: *Personal Information (PI)*, which encompasses any kind of information that represents the PII principal, such as name, national identifiers, parents' names, home address, photo and credit card number; *Personal Characteristics and Preferences (PCP)*, which are considered to be the physical attributes of the PII principal and personal options like weight, religious or philosophical beliefs, and sexual orientation; *Location (LO)*, which refers to any information about where the user is or has been and his or her trajectories with any precision degree and obtained by any means, such as GPS, Wi-fi networks or telecommunications systems; *Activities and Habits (AH)*, which are any activities performed by the user and habits inferred from tracking, such as web sites visited, purchases, and behavioral profile; and *Relationships (RS)*, people with whom the PII principal is in a specific moment or interacts through means like social networks, emails, and instant messengers.

2) Purpose: purpose for which the PII can be used. The values of this dimension are: *Service Improvement (SI)*, *Scientific (SC)*, and *Commercial (CO)*.

3) Beneficiary: party that benefits with the use of the PII. The attributes are: *PII Principal (PP)*, *Service Provider (SP)* and *Third Party (TP)*.

The dimensions above define a structure in which each position represents a rule that expresses a user's privacy preference that must be respected by the SP. This way, each of these rules comprises three parts: the type of data the rule refers to, for what purpose it can be used, and for the benefit of whom it can be used. For example, a user can define that his or her location data can be used for the purpose of improving services for the benefit of the PII principal and, in another rule, define that the same type of information for the same purpose cannot be used for the benefit of a third party.

By using this classification, the privacy preferences can be collected in a detailed manner or through four predefined profiles, which are described in the next section.

B. User's Privacy Profiles

Four privacy profiles were defined based on the work in [15], presented in Section III, which classified users into three groups according to their privacy concerns. For offering more privacy options and as it had the highest percentage of users, the Privacy Pragmatist group was divided into two different profiles. Therefore, the proposed profiles are:

1) Privacy Fundamentalist: This profile is aimed at users who have very high concerns with their privacy and do not wish to share any kind of information. Some functionalities or services, however, may not work properly or at all when this profile is chosen.

2) Privacy Aware: This profile represents users who are concerned about their privacy but still want to enable services even though some functionalities are compromised.

3) Privacy Pragmatist: This profile is aimed at users who still want some privacy but also want to enable most of the services and functionalities.

4) Privacy Unconcerned: This profile is for users who are not concerned about their privacy or how their PII are used, hence any data can be disclosed for any purpose and in the benefit of anyone. All services and functionalities should work properly with this profile.

Beside simplifying the process of setting the privacy preferences, these profiles are clarifying for the users as they inform about levels of risks to privacy and the possible uses of their PII and, as a result, assist them in making a conscious decision. In addition, users have the possibility to customize their privacy preferences using any of the profiles above as a basis.

C. Privacy token

Once the profile is chosen or customized, the privacy preferences, along with additional information, are converted by the IdP into a JSON (JavaScript Object Notation) object, which is then used as the payload for creating a signed JWT, called privacy token. This token is encoded into a base 64 URL-safe string for easy transmission to the SP, without compromising performance. After receiving the token, the SP must validate it in order to verify its integrity.

The structure of the privacy token, illustrated in Figure 2, comprises three sections. The first one is the header, which declares that the data structure is a JWT and defines the security algorithm chosen and implemented by the IdP (in this example, SHA-256); the second section consists of the claims set, which is explained next; and the last section contains the signature of the token.

The claims set includes two parts. The first one defines the following claims inherited from the ID token: *sub*, which is the subject identifier, i.e., a sequence of characters that uniquely identifies the PII principal; *iss*, which identifies the authority issuing the token, i.e., the IdP; *aud*, which represents the intended audience, i.e., the SP; and *iat*, which declares the time at which the token was issued.

The second part of the claims set define the privacy preferences of the user. Each claim corresponds to a position of the structure presented in Section IV-A, i.e., a privacy preference, and has a boolean value. The structure of a claim is as follows: the first abbreviation represents the type of data, the second abbreviation refers to the purpose, and the last one represents the beneficiary. For example, if the value of the attribute *LO_CO_SP* is true, it means that location data can be used for commercial purpose in the benefit of the SP.

```
{
  "typ": "JWT",
  "alg": "HS256"
}
{
  "sub"          : "alice",
  "iss"          : "https://openid.c2id.com",
  "aud"          : "client-12345",
  "iat"          : 1488405983,

  "PI_SI_PP"     : true,
  "PI_SI_SP"     : false,
  "PI_SI_TP"     : true,
  "PI_SC_PP"     : true,
  "PI_SC_SP"     : true,
  "PI_SC_TP"     : false,
      ...
}
{
  D7SDQBpVCSRSqVUMP9PAungM0gh7JKjKgXYhUlKMr3Y
}
```

Figure 2. Structure of the privacy token.

The privacy token must always be passed along with the ID token, for instance, when the ID token has expired and a new one is requested to the IdP, when passing identity to third parties or when exchanging the ID token for an access token.This is necessary to ensure that users' PII are always accompanied by the corresponding privacy preferences. This way, with the addition of the privacy token, the OpenId Connect modified flow presented in [6] would be extended, as shown in Figure 3, to encompass the following steps:

1) The user requests access to a resource in the SP;
2) The security manager at the SP asks for the user to authenticate in the IdP where she or he is registered;
3) The IdP asks for the user's credentials;
4) The user provides his or her credentials;
5) The IdP validates user's credentials and returns the ID token and the privacy token to the user, who passes it to the SP;
6) The SP sends the ID and the privacy tokens to the IdP for the proof of validation;
7) The IdP verifies the tokens and confirms their validity to the SP;
8) The SP verifies whether the preferences can be met. If not, the SP asks the user for permission;
9) If the user authorizes, the IdP generates a new privacy token according to the user's response;
10) The IdP sends the new privacy token to the SP;
11) The SP requests additional attributes to the IdP;
12) The IdP shows the data dissemination scopes supported by the SP for the user to choose;
13) The user chooses one of the scopes, and informs the IdP about the selected scope;
14) The IdP provides the data to the SP according to the selected scope;
15) The SP allows the user to access the desired resource.

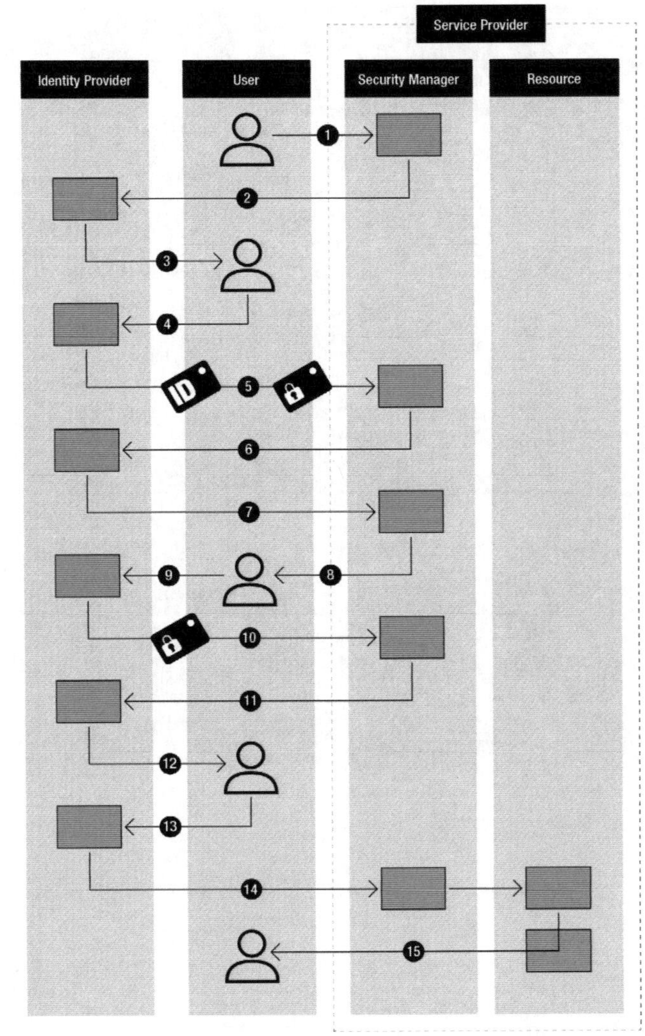

Figure 3. Extension of the IdM flow proposed in [6] with the addition of the privacy token.

The privacy profile that is used for generating the privacy token sent to the SP in Step 5 is chosen or customized by the user during the process of registration in the IdP. In order to offer more flexibility, users can change their choice at any moment requesting it to the IdP.

D. Prototype

In order to verify the correct operation of the proposed mechanism and serve as the base for a future extension of an implementation of the OpenId Connect protocol, a prototype was developed. It is a Web application implemented in Java that performs the processes of collecting the user's privacy preferences through four predefined profiles or a customized one and generating a privacy token from them, as described in Sections IV-B and IV-C, respectively.

The prototype comprises classes representing the IdP, the SP, the user, the user's privacy preferences, and the privacy token. The *User* object is defined by personal data collected through a registration form and the *PrivacyPreferences* attributes are set with the values corresponding to the selected or customized privacy profile, which along with the *IdP* and the *SP* objects form the *PrivacyToken* object. The actual token is then created from this object with Nimbus JOSE+JWT [16], a Java library for the creation and verification of JWTs, and signed with Hash-based Message Authentication Code (HMAC) using SHA-256 algorithm. After generating the token, it is possible to see the output string that should be passed to the SP and to validate it, by verifying the signature.

Figure 4 presents the screen where the user can select a privacy profile. Aiming at usability, each profile is represented by a number, a name, a brief yet expressive description, and an icon. Also, colors are used to help differentiate the profiles and represent the levels of risks to privacy in each of them, being red for the profile with the highest risks and green for the one with the lowest risks. A *See details* button shows the complete profile, i.e., all the privacy preferences of the corresponding profile for more information about the possible uses of the user's PII.

The custom profile option comprises five sections, one for each data type and presents to the user options to opt-in or opt-out of each preference regarding the purpose and the beneficiary of the use of the PII belonging to the given data type. In this option, the user can choose one of the four profiles as the base for personalization.

V. Conclusion and Future Work

In this paper, a practical mechanism that allows users to control how their PII can be used in a federated cloud environment was presented. The mechanism instructs them about the possible uses of PII by SPs, allows them to choose between four predefined privacy profiles or customize one, and sends their privacy preferences to the SP along with their authentication data in a standardized, machine-readable format.

To the best of the authors knowledge, existing work focuses either on low-level approaches, such as privacy policy languages, which can be executed by machines; or on conceptual, high-level specifications, such as UML profiles, which provide a better understanding about privacy requirements in the development of systems and applications. However, these approaches do not offer practical means for users to set their preferences and send them to the SP, and/or require the latter to express all their policies in a specific way.

The main contribution of this work is the privacy token, a secure JWT that inverts the current scenario where users are forced to accept the policies defined by SPs by allowing them to express their privacy preferences. These preferences are stuck together to their data and are used by the SP to align its actions or request specific permissions.

The mechanism does not require SPs to use any specific standards to express and implement their privacy policies. It is only expected for SPs to adapt their data collection systems to interpret and fulfill the preferences expressed in the privacy token, which they can already read and understand once it has the same format as the other tokens used by OpenId Connect.

With the development of this work, it is expected that the model will be implemented in IdM systems and used in federated cloud environments to enable user privacy allowing them to control their PII. Thus, it is also expected to increase

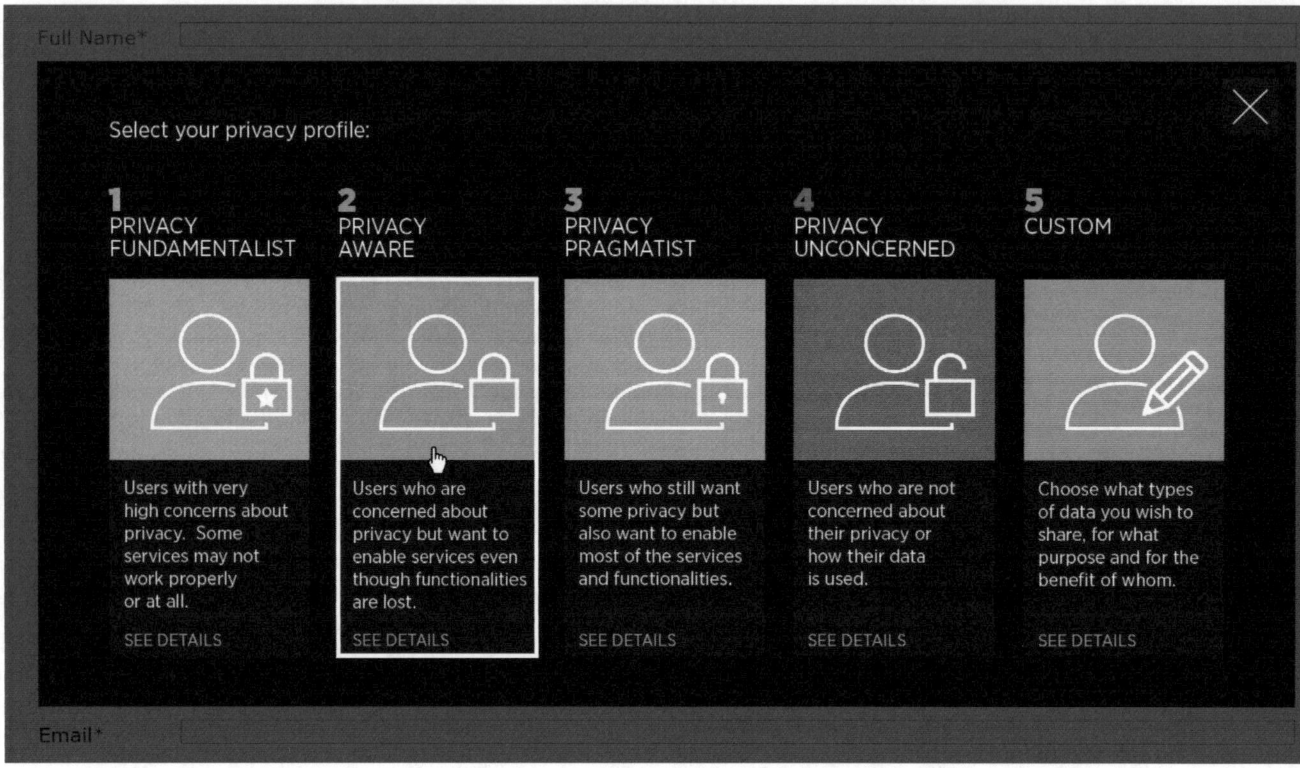

Figure 4. Prototype screen with the four predefined privacy profiles and the customizable one.

their trust in cloud SPs and, consequently, promote greater adoption of the paradigm.

As future work, we intend to verify and improve the classification of possible uses of PII based on privacy standards and case studies. We also intend to extend an implementation of the OpenId Connect to support the presented mechanism. Furthermore, it is proposed to assess the consequences for services, SPs and users of applying this mechanism in real federated cloud scenarios.

REFERENCES

[1] J. Zhao, R. Binns, M. Van Kleek, and N. Shadbolt, "Privacy Languages: Are We There Yet to Enable User Controls?" in Proceedings of the 25th International Conference Companion on World Wide Web, Montreal, Quebec, Canada. International World Wide Web Conferences Steering Committee, Apr. 2016, pp. 799–806, ISBN: 978-1-4503-4144-8.

[2] J. Iyilade and J. Vassileva, "P2U: A Privacy Policy Specification Language for Secondary Data Sharing and Usage," in Proceedings of the 2014 IEEE Security and Privacy Workshops, San Jose, CA, USA. IEEE Computer Society, May 2014, pp. 18–22, ISBN: 978-1-4799-5103-1.

[3] D. J. Solove, "A Taxonomy of Privacy," University of Pennsylvania Law Review, vol. 154, 2006, pp. 477–564.

[4] M. Benantar, Access Control Systems: Security, Identity Management and Trust Models. Springer, New York, 2006, ISBN: 978-0-387-27716-5.

[5] "OpenId Connect," 2015, URL: http://www.openid.net/connect/ [accessed: 2017-03-13].

[6] J. Werner and C. M. Westphall, "A Model for Identity Management with Privacy in the Cloud," in Proceedings of the 2016 IEEE Symposium on Computers and Communication (ISCC), Messina, Italy. IEEE, Jun. 2016, pp. 463–468, ISBN: 978-1-5090-0679-3.

[7] G. Alpár, J. Hoepman, and J. Siljee, "The Identity Crisis. Security, Privacy and Usability Issues in Identity Management," Computing Research Repository, vol. abs/1101.0427, 2011.

[8] D. Temoshok and C. Abruzzi, "Draft NISTIR 8149: Developing Trust Frameworks to Support Identity Federations," 2016, NIST, Gaithersburg, MD, United States.

[9] E. Bertino and K. Takahashi, Identity Management: Concepts, Technologies, and Systems. Artech House, Norwood, 2011, ISBN: 978-1-60807-039-89.

[10] "ISO/IEC 29100. International Standard - Information Technology - Security Techniques - Privacy Framework," 2011, URL: http://www.iso.org/iso/iso_catalogue/catalogue_tc/catalogue_detail.htm?csnumber=45123 [accessed: 2017-03-13].

[11] "OASIS Privacy Management Reference Model and Methodology (PMRM) Version 1.0," 2016, URL: http://http://docs.oasis-open.org/pmrm/PMRM/v1.0/PMRM-v1.0.html [accessed: 2017-03-13].

[12] "The Platform for Privacy Preferences 1.1 (P3P1.1) Specification," 2006, URL: https://www.w3.org/TR/P3P11/ [accessed: 2017-03-13].

[13] "Enterprise Privacy Authorization Language (EPAL 1.2)," 2003, URL: https://www.w3.org/Submission/2003/SUBM-EPAL-20031110/ [accessed: 2017-03-13].

[14] T. Basso, L. Montecchi, R. Moraes, M. Jino, and A. Bondavalli, "Towards a UML Profile for Privacy-Aware Applications," in Proceedings of 2015 IEEE International Conference on Computer and Information Technology; Ubiquitous Computing and Communications; Dependable, Autonomic and Secure Computing; Pervasive Intelligence and Computing (CIT/IUCC/DASC/PICOM), Liverpool, United Kingdom. IEEE, Oct. 2015, pp. 371–378, ISBN: 978-1-509001-552.

[15] F. Chanchary and S. Chiasson, "User Perceptions of Sharing, Advertising, and Tracking," in 11th Symposium On Usable Privacy and Security (SOUPS), Ottawa. USENIX Association, Jul. 2015, pp. 53–67, ISBN: 978-1-931971-249.

[16] "Nimbus JOSE + JWT," 2017, URL: http://www.connect2id.com/products/nimbus-jose-jwt/ [accessed: 2017-03-13].

Entity Title Architecture Pilot: Scaling Out the Deployment of a Clean Slate SDN Based Network at a Telecom Operator

Luiz Cláudio Theodoro, Pedro Henrique A. D. de Melo
Federal University of Uberlândia
Uberlândia, MG, Brazil
Email: {luiz.theodoro, pedro.damaso}@ufu.br

Rogério de Freitas Ribeiro, Flavio de Oliveira Silva, Pedro Frosi Rosa
Federal University of Uberlândia
Uberlândia, MG, Brazil
Email: {rogeriofr, flavio, pfrosi}@ufu.br

Alex Vaz Mendes, João Henrique de Souza Pereira
Innovation, Research and Development
Algar Telecom
Uberlândia, MG, Brazil
Email: {alexvaz, joaohs}@algartelecom.com.br

***Abstract*—The clean-slate approach to new network architectures, named Future Internet Architectures, is a response from the research community to the challenges that the Internet architecture faces today, such as mobility. One major issue in this area is the use of large scale production networks to deploy and test new network architectures. This work extends a previous one and deploys the clean-slate Entity Title Architecture (ETArch) on a production network of a telecom operator. By using Virtual Tunnel (VTun) as an overlay, it was possible to scale out the deployment and connect several customers in different cities. ETArch Pilot shows the feasibility to move forward toward future Internet deployment in order to bring new services and applications to customers.**

Keywords–SDN; ETArch; Network Architecture; VTun; Deployment.

I. Introduction

As the Internet has become fundamental to a huge volume of worldwide activities, there is a need to refine the architecture proposed since the beginning of its operation. Throughout decades of intense use, the protocols which have always supported this huge global network became inadequate regarding new challenges.

The growing demand surrounding multimedia traffic has surprised the most optimistic predictions. Dealing with this volume of media has not been an easy task. Criticism involving information security, a major concern of today's society, has also been widely questioned in relation to the current Internet architecture. Mobility, which is a central requirement for users, is constrained by the current Internet technologies.

Trying to reach solutions, researchers around the world have been proposing new architecture models, new protocols by using a clean-slate approach or the evolution the current ones considering the same network architecture [1]–[5].

To evaluate new proposals, validation in an environment close to the one in the real world is crucial to verify performance, restrictions and benefits when compared to the current network architecture. However, this evaluation is really complicated to be conducted on real production networks considering security aspects and also possible out of service situations.

This work extends a previous one [6] and its goal is to scale out the deployment of a Software-Defined Networking (SDN) based clean-slate network architecture, named Entity Title Architecture (ETArch), in a real network managed by a telecom operator, namely Algar Telecom.

To support a growing number of users and bypass the different access technologies, a tunneling approach, named Virtual Tunnels (VTun), was used. By using VTun, it was possible to connect several Algar Telecom customers located in different cities. Thus, it was possible to deploy a clean-slate network architecture over an operational production network.

This work is organized as follows: Section II presents related work. Section III presents some ETArch basic concepts. Section IV describes the scale out of ETArch deployment at the current network of a telecom operator. Section V describes the experiments conducted and presents the results of the work, and finally, Section VI presents some concluding remarks and forthcoming works.

II. Related Work

Several researches involving SDN and Networking Function Virtualization (NFV) are currently going on in the world and they effectively intend to show the implementation viability in specific scenarios. SDN is applicable in both academic and commercial areas and is effectively viewed as one of the most promising proposals for the networks of the future. NFV, in turn, has gained increasing acceptance as more and more works are being published.

One of the lines of research that challenge researchers is the actual use of these proposals in the world of telecommunications. Specifically, the problem of scalability has directed some work and reflects the effort to make the results extrapolate the boundaries of research labs.

Works such as [7] worried about the ever-increasing adoption of Wi-Fi networks, NFV-fostered middle-boxes, and the avalanche of Internet of Things (IoT)-based devices. For this, it proposes an SDN framework which allows abstracting the Media Access Control (MAC) layer and also the orchestration of WiFi networks. In addition, they present a new architecture named OpenSDWN, exploring the benefits of SDN and NFV for home and enterprise WiFi networks. It presents the design and implementation of a novel WiFi-SDN approach that exploits locality in SDN control plane operations for scalability reasons.

Another important contribution is given by [8] with the R-SDN. It points out that few IT organizations have applied

SDN to their networks. One of the challenges that hinder SDN development lies in the scalability of the control plane. It further states that programmatic interface from a centralized control plane of SDN can meet requirements such as flexibility and manageability, but scalability is questionable. It then proposes a new way of designing the SDN control plan, named R-SDN whose core idea is recursion. This idea originates from network virtualization. At the beginning, it virtualizes the global network as a single logical circle. After that, several local logical circles are derived from the global circle. Finally, it derives the localized circles, layer by layer, until it sees physical switches. This top-down abstraction view can enhance scalability of SDN network.

Many examples of SDN technologies are being applied to commercial cloud services supplied for commercial carrier networks. The use of computing resources on network is becoming active in the Internet and private networks. Openflow is drawing attention as a method to control network virtualization for the cloud computing services and other carrier services. [9] took advantage of the NTT Communications (NTT.com) which aggressively promotes OpenFlow/SDN technology Research and Development. As one of the board members of ONF, NTT watches the trend of NFV closely, as well. This work shows some issues, for instance, limitation of Virtual Lan (VLAN) IDs, intermediate switches MAC address table explosion, large network overhead, inefficient network usage and others. These problems are categorized mainly into scalability, hardware flow table limitation, network stability and operability. SDN is expected to resolve these problems by integrating each independent service network into one physical network, for example within a datacenter, and by reducing cost and delivery lead-time by configuring each virtualized network for each service. With the intention to deploy OpenFlow to commercial networks, this work points out that it is important to consider not only replacing existing network and equipment, but, also, to consider the impact to services and operation. It is necessary to promote investigation of OpenFlow/SDN from these perspectives. The problem with scalability is evaluated together with other issues.

One example is the work published by IBM [10] where challenges related to cross-cloud live migration could not yet be reached. Thus, with the intention of getting an efficient solution, Virtual Wire is proposed, given that this is a system whose providers into the cloud can offer connect and disconnect services which are by far easier to be managed, when compared to virtual network forwarding.

In this context, cloud providers must manage the associated control which specifies how the packets are routed inside a virtual network. For example, providers can implement a distributed virtual switch or logical control embedded in a network controller defined by the software. For this purpose, the Virtual Wire system matches each Virtual Network Interface Card (vNIC) with a point-to-point network tunnel. VNICs belong to Virtual Machines (VMs) that either are implemented in servers or network forwarding components at the level of users like routers and switches. Network users can build complex virtual networks connecting pairs of vNICs together.

By using a tunneling approach, Layer 2 endpoints are made available through Layer 3 network tunnels. In this way, a vNIC is sent through a layer 2 frame, by including an associated endpoint which encapsulates the entire packet (MAC header and VLAN tags in an User Datagram Protocol (UDP) packet). The Internet Protocol (IP) address and socket port number correspond to the physical network address of the endpoint manager. After receiving a package, the endpoint manager parses the headers, examines the ID connector, and then sends the packages to the endpoint destination.

Topics such as Tunneling, SDN and Virtual Switches usually appear in a considerable amount of research developed around the world. Bingham Liu [11] proposes the usage of a virtual switch (Open vSwitch) with the help of General Packet Radio Service (GPRS) Tunneling Protocol (GTP) to explore the SDN evolution in the design of the core of a mobile network by using cloud based computing. This approach has a common idea with our work, the deployment of a clean-slate network architecture in a real operator environment.

Another work [12] focuses precisely on the possible improvements for the SDN applications concerning the infrastructure of mobile networks, by showing current LTE structure, discusses how to simplify the network control and new services offering. In this case, the controller takes functions such as monitoring, Quality of Service (QoS), access control policies, virtual operators, and others, that is, the goal is that it takes the functions of some mobile network elements and the infrastructure's vision. Switches with the capacity to become control local agents are also part of the architecture, since the controller cannot be available to fast answers for local events. Furthermore, they have functions such as daily checking of the traffic counters and change of the queue priorities according to some limit.

This work, besides implementing some concepts of the SDN in a physical network, uses an actual telecom network, accessed by thousands of customers, and shows the flexibility and the simplicity of the ETArch architecture in this real environment, if compared to the regular network infrastructure.

III. ENTITY TITLE ARCHITECTURE (ETARCH)

The architecture of the Internet is not able to meet the requirements of current applications such as mobility, security, QoS. There are several research initiatives toward future Internet architecture [13]. One initiative is the Entity Title Architecture (ETArch), that was initially proposed by our research group. This section presents an overview of ETArch main concepts.

ETArch has a natural match with SDN, since both share the concept that the control plane is separated from the data plane. The ETArch prototype is being created in an incremental way and, currently, researchers from several universities are working with ETArch in order to add an extension to the architecture in order to satisfy several requirements from current applications, such as mobility [14], multicast [15], QoS [16] and routing [17].

An entity is everything which has the capacity to communicate and, this way, the entities can be hosts, smartphones, Network Elements (NE), users, applications, sensors and so on.

Another central concept is the Title, which is a unique identifier independent from the network topology [18]. ETArch uses the title to identify the entities. One Title can also be seen as a credential that can be used to relate the security features [19].

At ETArch, the communication happens by using the Workspace. The Workspace is a logical bus which enables the communication among the entities. Entities attach to a workspace in order to participate in a communication domain.

In ETArch, the Domain Title System (DTS) [20] represents the control plane of the network. Before starting the communication, an entity must register itself at the DTS. The DTS keeps the information about the entities, their titles and Workspaces. The DTS is a distributed system composed by Domain Title System Agents (DTSAs). Each DTSA is capable to control the NEs and is aware of the NE graph. The DTSA is responsible to the communication with other DTSAs. The DTSAs uses Openflow to control the NEs.

IV. ETArch Pilot Scale Out

This work proposes the scale out of the deployment of ETArch by using a real telecom network and their customers, which are geographically distributed in the operator's network. To accomplish this, it was necessary to establish a Layer 2 connection between customers and to have an fully OpenFlow capable infrastructure. Since this last condition was not satisfied in the operator infrastructure, then a tunneling technique was used.

By using the tunnels it was possible to connect geographically distributed clients over the operator's infrastructure. At each physical location, a software based OpenFlow switch was used. Each one of these switches was controlled by the DTSA then creating the conditions to deploy ETArch. Figure 2 shows, in a general way, the protocol tunneling technique that allowed the communication.

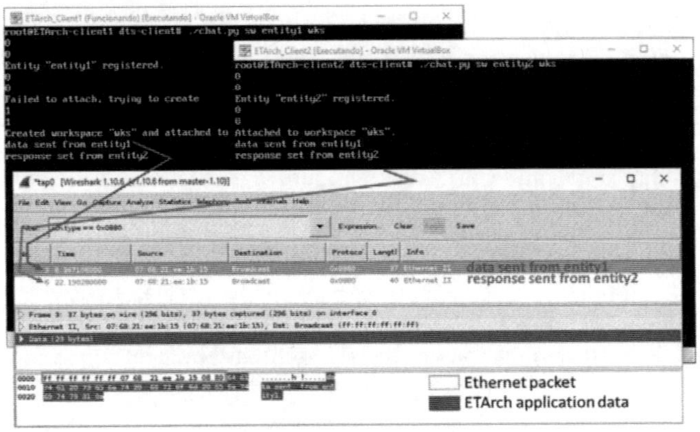

Figure 1. Wireshark capture of ETArch primitives between application instances.

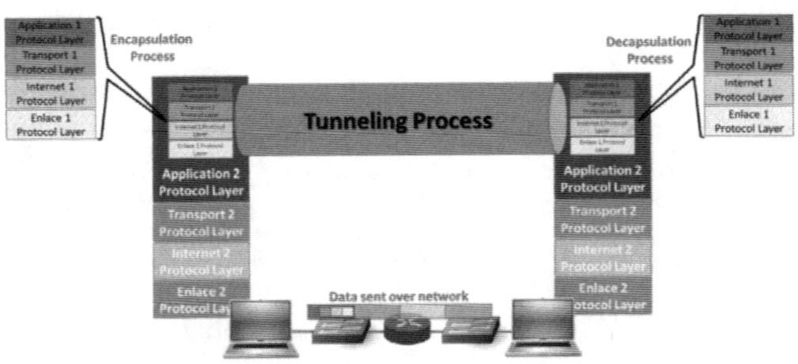

Figure 2. Two hosts communicating with each other using the tunneling technique.

The tunneling concept is commonly used in the computer networking area. Some examples are: Internet Control Message Protocol (ICMP) Tunneling [21], Secure Shell (SSH) Tunneling [22], Generic Routing Encapsulation (GRE) Tunneling [23] and Internet Protocol Security (IPsec) Tunneling [24].

To achieve our objectives, the tunneling technique was based in the VTun software [25]. The Virtual Tunnels (VTun) work in a client/server mode, and are capable to accomplish a point to point connection between the involved hosts. VTun offers a series of functions, like data compression/cryptography, connections access control, besides the bandwidth control. The supported tunneling encapsulation modes by the VTun are: IP Tunnel, Ethernet Tunnel, Serial Tunnel and Pipe Tunnel. This work used the Ethernet Tunnel.

For the traffic to be tunneled by the VTun, one host needs to act as a server, opening a socket in the system and listening to the port 5000. When a client connects to this service, one virtual interface is created in the operating system. This virtual interface is the *access bridge* to the created tunnel.

Any packet sent to that interface will be encapsulated by the Transmission Control Protocol (TCP)/IP protocol stack, and then, will travel through the tunnel to the host connected on the other side of the tunnel, where the decapsulation process will occur, extracting the original packet, which was encapsulated before it enters the tunnel. Figure 3 shows the process of Ethernet tunneling traffic from the ETArch architecture between two hosts connected to the Internet.

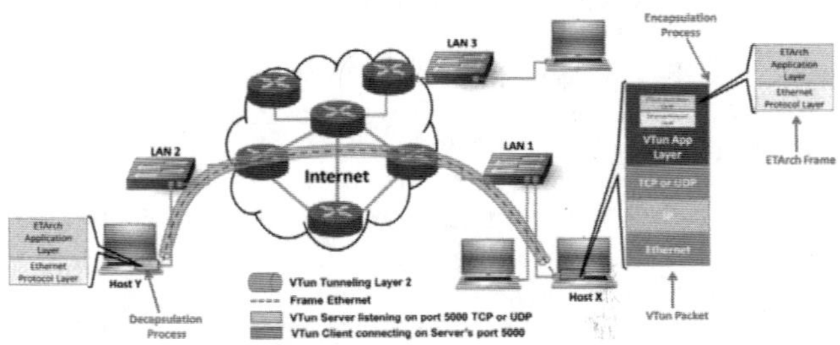

Figure 3. Remote hosts exchanging Ethernet traffic through the Internet.

Compared to our previous work [6], the relevant improvement occurred in the simplification of the tunneling process that occurred due to the use of VTun instead of GRE. That evolution brought to us a major simplicity since the VTun offers less complexity to accomplish the scale out of ETArch deployment. When using GRE, it is necessary to configure the client's modem in *bridge mode*.

By using VTun to produce the tunnel, it was possible to do a smooth deployment and use of ETArch based applications. With this approach, there was no need to change the customer's modem operation mode and in this case the only requirement to use ETArch based applications was to be a customer of the telecom operator. It happens because when the VTun is started, one virtual interface is created in the operating system, which is then responsible to carry the traffic through that interface and also for the created tunnel.

V. ETArch Pilot Experimental Evaluation

To conduct the tests, VTun was used to create the virtual tunnels between the hosts, allowing ETArch based applications to send data to all the hosts connected to the same workspace. Below, it is presented the description of the environment used to perform the initial evaluation, and then, the scale out the ETARch deployment:

- The network operated by Algar Telecom was used to provide the connectivity between several users which are in fact, their customers;
- Ubuntu 14.04 operating system was used in all the computers used in the deployment, in the machine responsible hosting the DTSA, the VTun Server and in the customer's machines to execute the ETArch based application;
- The machines that acted as a VTun client, established a virtual tunnel to the VTun server, which in turn was listening to the port TCP 5000.
- At the VTun server host, Destination Network Address Translation (DNAT) was configured in the modem, redirecting all the traffic destined to the routable IP and port 5000 to the internal IP and keeping the same destination port number.
- For the machine that acted as the DTSA, DNAT was configured in the modem, redirecting the traffic destined to the routable IP and port 6633 to the internal IP while keeping the same destination port number.

Several tests were made and we classified them in two scenarios: Scenario One and Scenario Two. In Scenario one, two hosts have established one tunnel to communicate to each other, one acting as a VTun client and the other as a VTun server. In this scenario, each host also has the role to act as an OpenFlow switch. Each switch was controlled and programmed by the DTSA. The DTSA was responsible to create and modify the flows in order to provide the communication by using the Workspace. This workspace was used to support the chat application used during the test.

Figure 4 shows the detailed topology used in the tests defined in the Scenario One, describing the participating peers and their communications. After the analysis of the results from the tests conducted in the Scenario One, it was noticed that with more than two clients, the approach of establishing a tunnel between each one of the clients in the ETArch architecture would become painful in terms of configuration and troubleshooting. One of the major issues would be the necessity of the Network Address Translation (NAT) configuration in the customer's modems that run the VTun in server mode, which would restrict the participation of clients connected in mobile networks, like 3G and 4G. This restriction would occur because the clients that need to run the VTun in server mode would need additional applications on their cellular phones to create the NAT configurations.

To overcame these issues, Scenario Two was created. In this scenario, the topology was changed to create a concentration tunnel host. The function of this machine was to host the VTun in server mode and to receive all the client's connections from the ETArch architecture. In this scenario, only the VTun concentrator machine was acting like an OpenFlow switch. This made the configuration and troubleshooting process easier since there is only one OpenFlow switch in the topology. On the other side, in Scenario One, it would be necessary to have n OpenFlow switches, one for each connected client. The topology for the tests conducted under Scenario Two is described in detail by in Figure 5.

In order to verify the overhead based on packet capture in the test environment, it was possible to identify that the VTUN encapsulation process caused an overhead of about

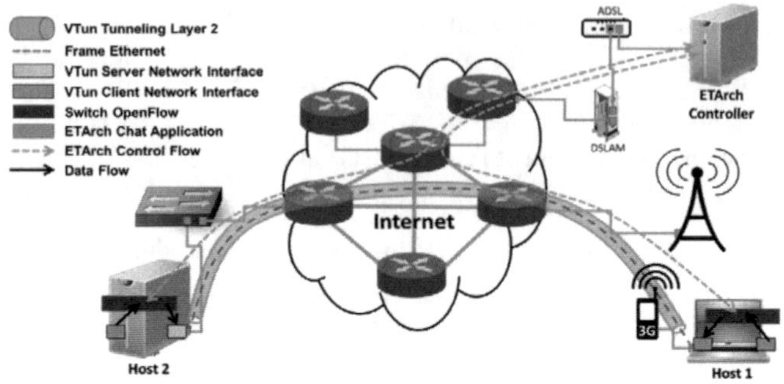

Figure 4. Scenario One - Tunnel between two hosts.

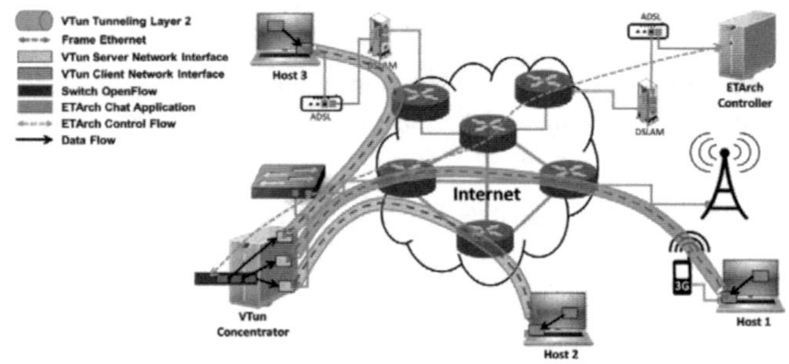

Figure 5. Scenario Two - Tunnel between multiple hosts.

50.4%, equivalent to 56 bytes in each packet generated by the chat application. This overhead of 56 bytes is the result of the subtraction of 111 bytes (Vtun packet) from 55 bytes (chat application packet that contains the text "message of the chat application ETArch"). Figure 6 shows the overhead of the VTun tunneling versus the packet size. The overhead is in a range between 82.35% to 3.73% considering a 1500 Bytes packet.

Figure 7 represents a capture of the VTUN packet, highlighting the VTUN encapsulation data and the packet data of the chat applications in the ETArch environment.

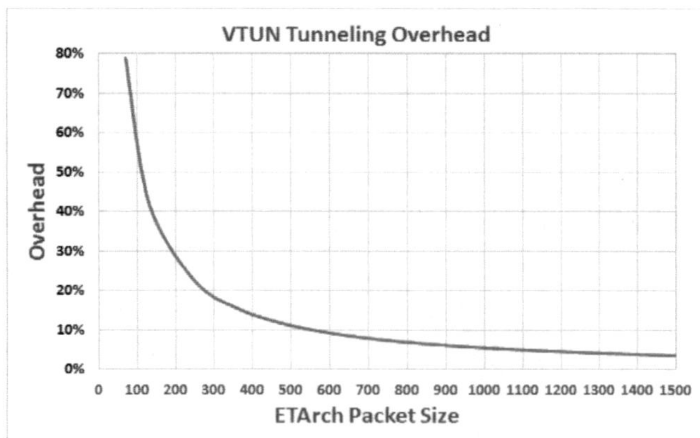

Figure 6. VTun Tunneling Overhead versus Packet Size

Figure 8 shows the result of the package obtained after the decapsulation process is carried out by the VTUN process.

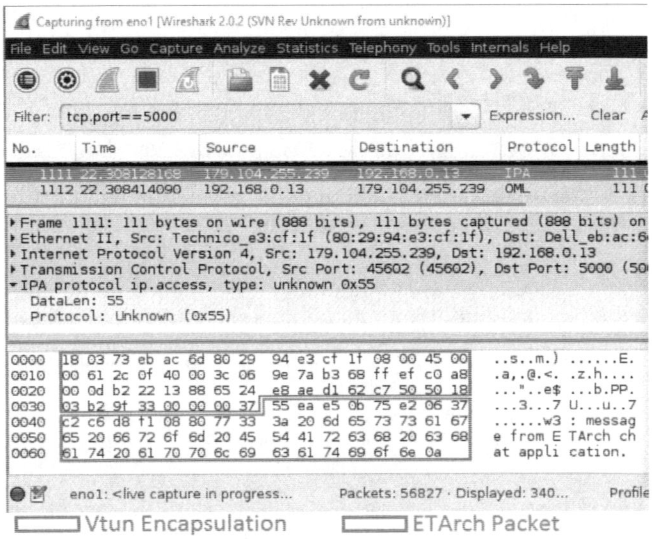

Figure 7. VTUN packet received at the server's network interface before the ETArch packet unpacking process.

After removing the 3 layers of the TCP/IP architecture (media access control, network, and transport) the VTUN process delivers on the virtual interface (tap0) of the server, only the chat application package, as it had been generated in the source.

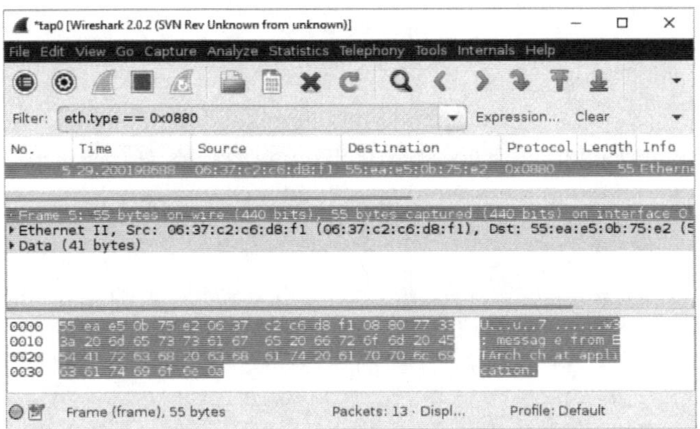

Figure 8. VTUN packet received at the server's network interface before the ETArch packet unpacking process.

Due to the second scenario being developed, it is possible to extend the number of entities in an unlimited geographical area. For this reason, we made a test with more than 40 users connected, distributed in a radius of 600 kilometers from the city of Uberlândia, according to Figure 9 which shows the localization of the machines performed by the chat clients. Most of the users are located in the city of Uberlândia as can be seen partially in Figure 10.

VI. Concluding Remarks and Future Work

This work scaled out the deployment of a clean-slate SDN based network architecture, named ETArch, in the real infrastructure of a network operator, named ALGAR Telecom, with little intervention in the customer environment.

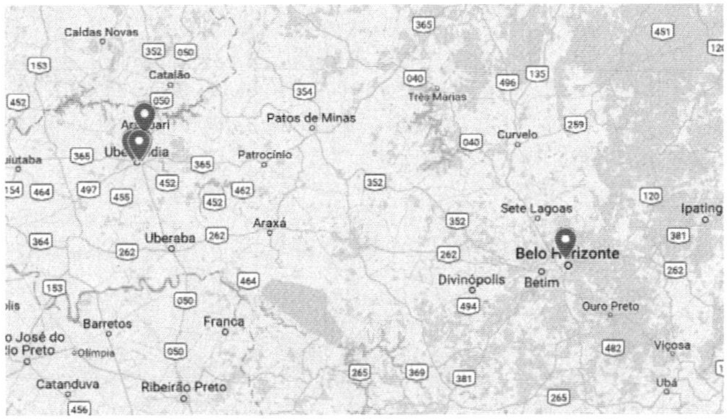

Figure 9. Geographical distribution - second scenario with maximum distance of 600 km

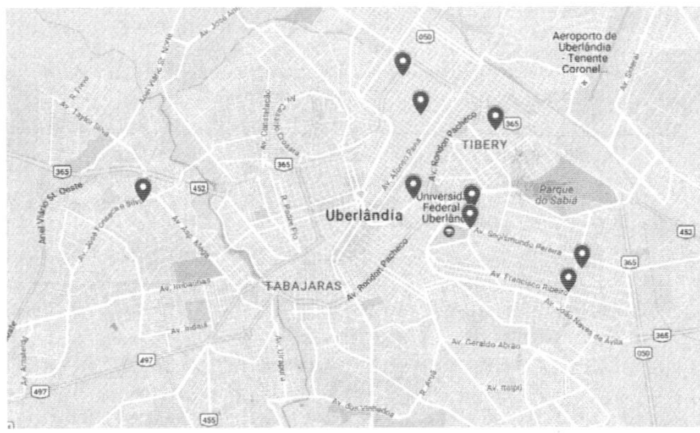

Figure 10. Geographical distribution - second scenario only in Uberlândia

By using VTun to support the tunneling process and to tackle the interconnection issues with the infrastructure, it was possible to use an ETArch based application by several customers located in different cities inside the operator coverage area. The chat application uses natives ETArch's capabilities to support multicast and mobility.

The use of VTun, when compared to the previous approach based on GRE, allowed an easier configuration on each host machine where the application was installed and the use of a VTun server inside the operator infrastructure enabled the scale out of the number of customers that could benefit from the new capabilities provided by ETArch.

The experimental evaluation demonstrated that the overhead imposed by the VTun is in a range between 82.35% to 3.73% of the packet size, by considering a chat application. Applications with greater packet sizes will present less overhead.

As future work, we plan to deploy over the operator network other ETArch based applications, such as a video streaming application which would provide video multicast in a seamless way.

The work demonstrates the feasibility to deploy new network architectures in parallel with current ones and go towards future Internet deployment.

ACKNOWLEDGMENTS

This work has been partially funded by the Brazilian agencies: CAPES, CNPq and FAPEMIG and also by PROPP/UFU. We also would like to thank ALGAR Telecom for the support and partnership on this work.

REFERENCES

[1] F. Bronzino, K. Nagaraja, I. Seskar, and D. Raychaudhuri, "Network service abstractions for a mobility-centric future internet architecture," in *Proceedings of the eighth ACM international workshop on Mobility in the evolving internet architecture*. ACM, 2013, pp. 5–10.

[2] H. Dongsu et al., "Xia: Efficient support for evolvable internetworking." in *NSDI*, vol. 12, 2012, pp. 23–23.

[3] V. Jacobson et al., "Networking named content," in *Proceedings of the 5th international conference on Emerging networking experiments and technologies*. ACM, 2009, pp. 1–12.

[4] T. Anderson et al., "A brief overview of the nebula future internet architecture," *ACM SIGCOMM Computer Communication Review*, vol. 44, no. 3, pp. 81–86, 2014.

[5] Y. Wang, I. Matta, F. Esposito, and J. Day, "Introducing protorina: a prototype for programming recursive-networking policies," *ACM SIGCOMM Computer Communication Review*, vol. 44, no. 3, pp. 129–131, 2014.

[6] L. Claudio et al., "Entity Title Architecture Pilot: Deploying a Clean Slate SDN Based Network at a Telecom Operator," pp. 144–149, Jun. 2015, [retrieved: Mar, 2017]. [Online]. Available: http://www.thinkmind.org/index.php?view=article&articleid=aict_2015_7_40_10152

[7] J. Schulz-Zander, C. Mayer, B. Ciobotaru, S. Schmid, and A. Feldmann, "Opensdwn: Programmatic control over home and enterprise wifi," in *Proceedings of the 1st ACM SIGCOMM Symposium on Software Defined Networking Research*. ACM, 2015, p. 16.

[8] W. Dai, G. Shou, Y. Hu, Z. Guo, and J. Liu, "Extending sdn network with recursive architecture," in *Wireless Personal Multimedia Communications (WPMC), 2014 International Symposium on*. IEEE, 2014, pp. 491–496.

[9] S. Yoichi, I. Fukuda, and T. Fujita, "Deployment of openflow/sdn technologies to carrier services," *IEICE transactions on communications*, vol. 96, no. 12, pp. 2946–2952, 2013.

[10] D. Williams, H. Jamjoom, Z. Jiang, and H. Weatherspoon, "Virtualwires for live migrating virtual networks across clouds," Technical Report RC25378, IBM, Tech. Rep., 2013.

[11] B. Liu, "Software defined networking and tunneling for mobile networks," Master's thesis, kTH Royal Institute of Technology, 7 2013.

[12] L. E. Li, Z. M. Mao, and J. Rexford, "Toward Software-Defined Cellular Networks," in *2012 European Workshop on Software Defined Networking*, Oct. 2012, pp. 7–12.

[13] J. Pan, S. Paul, and R. Jain, "A survey of the research on future internet architectures," *IEEE Communications Magazine*, vol. 49, no. 7, pp. 26–36, Jul. 2011.

[14] C. Guimaraes et al., "IEEE 802.21-enabled Entity Title Architecture for handover optimization," in *2014 IEEE Wireless Communications and Networking Conference (WCNC)*, Apr. 2014, pp. 2671–2676.

[15] M. Amaral Gonçalves et al., "Multicast traffic aggregation through entity title model," pp. 175–180, Jul. 2014, [retrieved: Mar, 2017]. [Online]. Available: https://www.thinkmind.org/index.php?view=article&articleid=aict_2014_7_40_10177

[16] J. Castillo et al., "Additions to the ETArch control plane to support multimedia QoS-guaranteed content transport over OpenFlow-enabled SDN future internet systems," in *Globecom Workshops (GC Wkshps), 2014*, Dec. 2014, pp. 172–177.

[17] N. Vieira de Souza Neto et al., "Control Plane Routing Protocol for the Entity Title Architecture," pp. 185–190, Apr. 2015, [retrieved: Mar, 2017]. [Online]. Available: https://www.thinkmind.org/index.php?view=article&articleid=icn_2015_7_40_30210

[18] J. de Souza Pereira, F. de Oliveira Silva, E. Filho, S. Kofuji, and P. Rosa, "Title model ontology for future internet networks," in *The Future Internet*, ser. Lecture Notes in Computer Science. Springer Berlin Heidelberg, 2011, vol. 6656, pp. 103–114.

[19] ITU, *Security architecture for Open Systems Interconnection for CCITT applications*, International Telecommunications Union, Mar. 1991.

[20] F. Oliveira Silva et al., "On the analysis of multicast traffic over the entity title architecture," in *2012 18th IEEE International Conference on Networks (ICON)*, Dec 2012, pp. 30–35.

[21] J. Postel, "Internet control message protocol," RFC 792 (Standard), Internet Engineering Task Force, September 1981, [retrieved: Mar, 2017]. [Online]. Available: http://www.ietf.org/rfc/rfc792.txt

[22] T. Ylonen and C. Lonvick, "The secure shell (ssh) protocol architecture," RFC 4251 (Proposed Standard), Internet Engineering Task Force, January 2006, [retrieved: Mar, 2017]. [Online]. Available: http://www.ietf.org/rfc/rfc4251.txt

[23] S. Hanks, T. Li, D. Farinacci, and P. Traina, "Generic routing encapsulation (gre)," RFC 1701 (Informational), Internet Engineering Task Force, October 1994, [retrieved: Mar, 2017]. [Online]. Available: http://www.ietf.org/rfc/rfc1701.txt

[24] S. Blake et al., "An Architecture for Differentiated Service," RFC 2475 (Informational), Internet Engineering Task Force, December 1998, [retrieved: Mar, 2017]. [Online]. Available: http://www.ietf.org/rfc/rfc2475.txt

[25] VTUN, "VTun - Virtual Tunnels over TCP/IP networks," Sep. 2016, [retrieved: Mar, 2017]. [Online]. Available: http://vtun.sourceforge.net/

Network Clustering and Cluster Control in Energy Harvesting Wireless Video Sensor Networks

Hwan-hee Lee, Keon-woo Park, Doo-sik Kang and Myeong-jin Lee

Dept. of Electronics and Information Engineering
Korea Aerospace University
Goyang-si, Gyeonggi-do, Rep. of KOREA
Email: hwanhee4777@gmail.com, ko92go@gmail.com, jskg72@nate.com, artistic@kau.ac.kr

***Abstract*—A novel network clustering and cluster control algorithm is proposed for energy harvesting wireless video sensor networks. For inter-cluster energy balance, video sensor nodes are clustered based on their distance from a base station. For intra-cluster energy balance, a cluster head selects a cluster member with the largest residual battery level as the next cluster head. For minimum energy consumption of a cluster, control parameters for all cluster members in each cluster are decided by joint distortion-energy control model of video sensor nodes. From simulation results, the proposed algorithm is shown to keep both inter-cluster and intra-cluster energy balance, and to enable perpetual operation of energy-harvesting wireless video sensor networks.**

Keywords–wireless video sensor network; energy harvesting; energy balance; joint distortion-energy control model.

I. INTRODUCTION

Wireless video sensor networks (WVSNs) for public security and remote monitoring should monitor and record video without interruption [1]. Because they are expected to be installed in a wireless communication environment without stable power supply, energy harvesting is required for perpetual operation. Also, video sensor nodes should control video quality considering their residual energy while keeping network-wide energy balance to prolong the network lifetime.

There have been studies on energy-efficient clustering of wireless sensor networks to improve the lifetime of sensor networks [2][3]. Clusters were organized based on the energy consumption model of data transmission by sensor nodes and a cluster head (CH) was selected based on the selection history and random model [2]. A reactive sensor network routing protocol, TEEN, was proposed to reduce the number of transmission more appropriately in event-driven applications [3]. There have been efforts to extend the lifetime of video sensor networks based on an energy model of a video sensor node [4][5]. Gurses et al. established the energy model of a video codec and radio frequency (RF) transceivers with the energy control parameters of the bit-rate and compression mode of a video codec [4]. Jang et al. also established the energy models of a video codec and RF transceivers with the energy control parameters of routing paths, bit-rate, and aspect ratio of video codecs [5]. However, these studies did not consider the energy consumption of an image sensor which occupies a large portion of the total energy consumption of a video sensor node. Also, energy harvesting function and the corresponding energy consideration in video sensor nodes were not considered to extend the lifetime of WVSNs.

In this paper, a network clustering and cluster control method is proposed for perpetual operation of energy harvesting WVSNs. Sensor nodes are clustered based on their distances to the base station (BS) for inter-cluster energy balance. A video sensor node with the largest residual battery level is selected as the next CH for intra-cluster energy balance. For minimum energy consumption of a cluster, control parameters for all the video sensor nodes in the cluster are calculated by a CH based on joint distortion-energy (JDE) control method of video sensor nodes [6].

The rest of the paper is structured as follows. In Section II, we propose the energy balanced clustering method and WVSN control protocol for the inter-/intra-cluster energy balance. In Section III, we present simulator results verifying the inter-/intra-cluster energy balance. Finally, we conclude the paper in Section IV

II. ENERGY-EFFICIENT NETWORK CLUSTERING AND CLUSTER CONTROL

A. Energy Harvesting Wireless Video Sensor Networks

Energy harvesting WVSNs consist of several clusters where each video sensor node is equipped with energy harvesting and video sensing and encoding functions. Each cluster consists of one CH and several cluster members (CMs). CH aggregates the video data received from CMs and transmits it to the BS. The energy consumption model of a transceiver in [2] is used for our energy modeling and is shown in Table I where $k, d, \epsilon_{elec}, \epsilon_{amp}$ represent the amount of information generated by the cluster, the transmission distance, the energy consumptions by the transceiver and the amplifier, respectively.

TABLE I. ENERGY CONSUMPTION MODEL OF TRANSCEIVER MODULE. [2]

module	energy consumption model
transmitter	$e_{tx}(k,d) = ke_{elec} + kd^2\epsilon_{amp}$
receiver	$e_{rx}(k) = ke_{elec}$

B. Energy Balanced Clustering

For intra-cluster energy balance, the BS estimates the total energy consumption of each cluster by considering its average distance to the cluster and the cluster size.

For the cluster size n, the energy consumption by the cluster head for n rounds is defined as follows:

$$e^{ch}(n, \bar{d}_{bs}) = k(2e_{elec} + \bar{d}_{bs}{}^2\epsilon_{amp}) + e_{proc}, \quad (1)$$

where $\bar{d}_{bs}$ and e_{proc} represent the average distance between the nodes in the cluster and the BS and the energy consumption required for video sensing and encoding in a CH or a CM, respectively.

The energy consumption by a cluster member is defined as follows:

$$e^{cm}(n, \bar{d}_{ch}) = (n-1)\Big\{\frac{k}{n}(e_{elec} + \bar{d}_{ch}^{\,2}\epsilon_{amp}) + e_{proc}\Big\}, \quad (2)$$

where $\bar{d}_{ch}$ represents the average distance between the CH and the CMs in the cluster.

Then, the total energy consumption by a cluster is defined as follows:

$$\begin{aligned} e^{tot}(n, \bar{d}_{bs}) &= k(2e_{elec} + \bar{d}_{bs}^{\,2}\epsilon_{amp}) + ne_{proc} \quad (3) \\ &+ \frac{k(n-1)}{n}\{e_{elec} + (\omega_1 n + \omega_2)^2\epsilon_{amp}\}, \end{aligned}$$

where ω_1 and ω_2 represent the model coefficients. These coefficients model the property of $\bar{d}_{ch}$ growing linearly as the cluster size n.

In conventional studies for sensor networks, the processing energy of a scalar sensor node is negligible compared to the transceiver energy. However, in wireless video sensor nodes, because the bandwidth of sampled data is quite larger than conventional scalar sensors, the processing energy should also be considered for clustering or cluster control. The processing energy in a video sensor node depends greatly on the rate control method of a video codec, and there may exist lots of possible combinations of video sensor node control parameters. Therefore, the processing energy is not considered for clustering, but considered only for cluster control.

In an initialization step, all nodes transmit their ID values, locations, and remaining battery levels to the base station. The number of clusters constructed for the $100 \times 100m^2$ area is chosen to be 5% of the total number of video sensor nodes as in the LEACH [2]. Each cluster is constructed based on the distance between the reference point and the BS with its cluster size proportional to $\bar{d}_{bs}^{\,2}$. The BS selects the size of each cluster to minimize the total energy consumption of the WVSN based on the total energy consumption of (3). The CH is selected right after the clustering. The clustering results are broadcast to all the nodes. An example of clustering is shown in Figure 1.

Figure 2 shows total cluster energy consumption by cluster size n and $\bar{d}_{bs}$ over n rounds. The time duration, n rounds, is same with the cluster size and is the average time for each node to act once CH when cluster size is n. If $\bar{d}_{bs}$ increases, $e^{tot}(n, \bar{d}_{bs})$ increases as the cluster size n decreases. For smaller cluster size n, because nodes in the cluster are more frequently selected as the CH, $e^{ch}(n, \bar{d}_{bs})$ increases while both $\bar{d}_{ch}$ and $e^{cm}(n, \bar{d}_{ch})$ decrease. However, because the effect by $\bar{d}_{bs}$ is more dominant than that of the cluster size n, the overall cluster energy consumption increases.

C. Video Sensor Network Control Protocol

After clustering by the BS, the CM with the highest remaining battery level in each cluster are selected as the CH of each cluster, and the BS broadcasts the clustering result and the CHs to all the nodes in the WVSN. Based on the received information, the CH selects the distortion-energy control parameters of the cluster for each predetermined time interval T. The control parameters are selected by the JDE control method [6] for the CM with the lowest remaining battery level.

Then, each round of the cluster starts with the selected control parameters and the CH performs time scheduling for time division multiple access (TDMA)-based data transmission and broadcasts the results to CMs. This allows each CM to turn off its transmitter if it is not in its assigned time interval, which results in efficient energy dissipation. The CMs transmit the sensed compressed video data, the identifier, and the remaining battery level after each round to the CH at the allocated time interval. The CH finally transmits the video data received from CMs to the BS. The CH selects the next CH, calculates the distortion-energy control parameters based on the remaining battery levels of CMs, and sends the results to all CMs in the cluster.

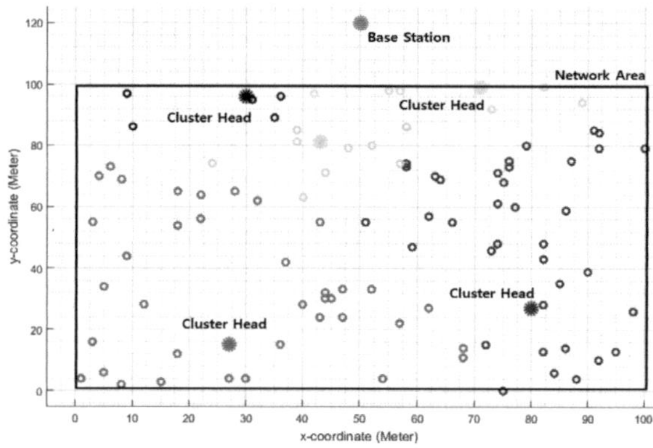

Figure 1. Energy balanced clustering results.

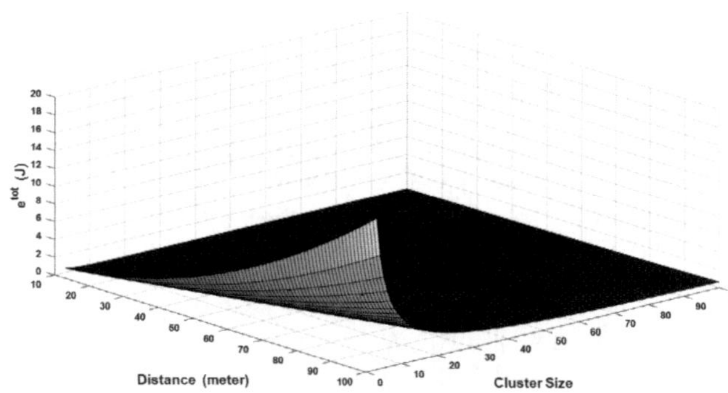

Figure 2. Total energy consumption e^{tot} during n rounds

III. Experimental Results

A simulator is designed to evaluate the sustainability of WVSNs and the inter-/intra-cluster energy balance. Ranges of control parmeters for the JDE control of CMs, such as the operating frequency f of a video sensor node, the quantization parameter q_p and the frame rate r_M of a video codec, are summarized in Table II. Figure 1 shows the clustering results of video sensor nodes randomly distributed in $100 \times 100m^2$ area.

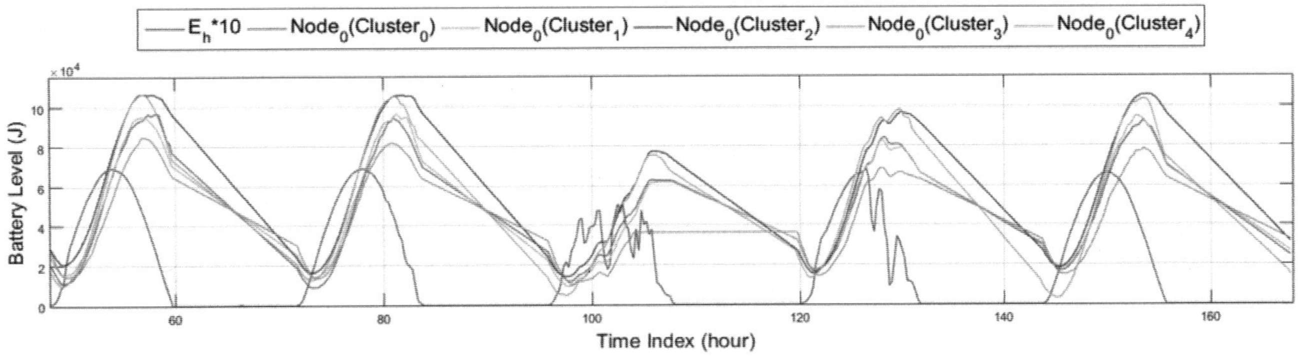

(a) equal sized clustering

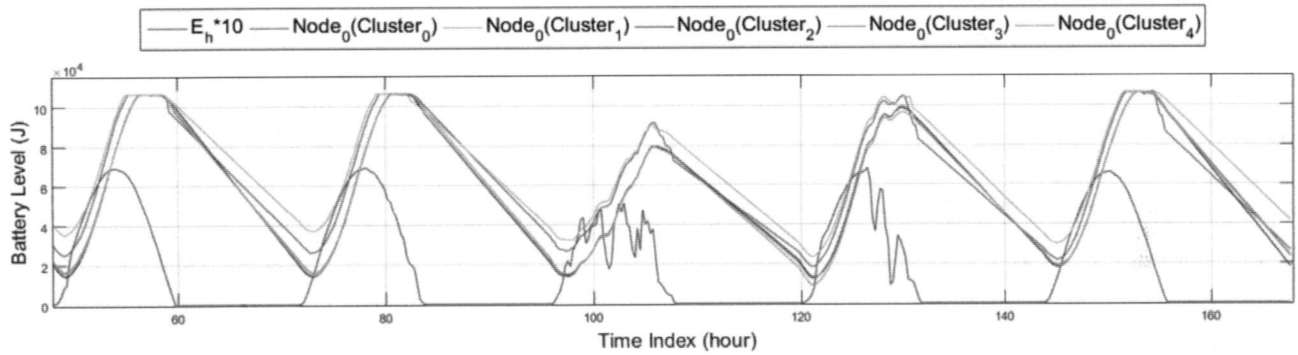

(b) energy balanced clustering

Figure 3. Battery level of CM 0 of each cluster, E_h: harvesting energy.

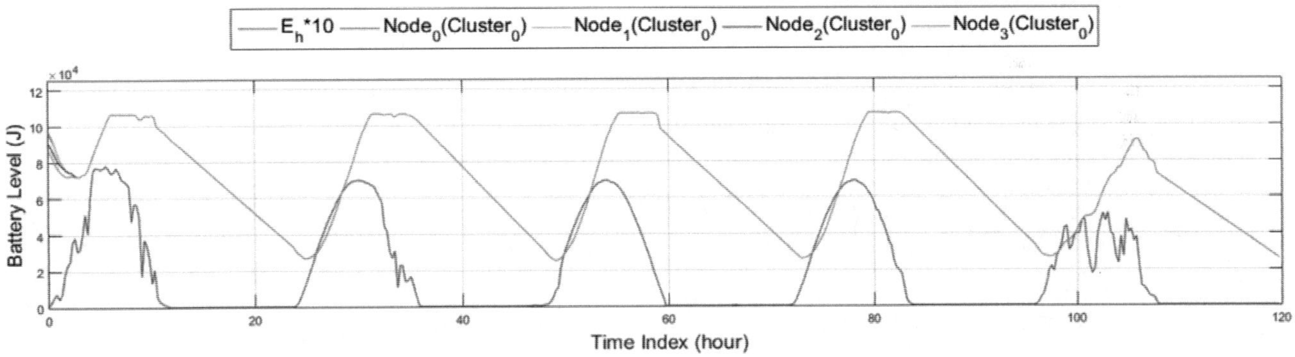

Figure 4. Evaluation of intra-cluster energy balance.

TABLE II. EXPERIMENTAL ENVIRONMENTS.

distortion-energy	$f(MHz)$	q_p	$r_M(fps)$
control parameters	200-1,400	30-45	1-30
time unit for encoding control	900 sec		
energy harvesting	battery capacity	solar panel size	
parameters	106,560J	600 cm^2	
video sequence	hall monitor	CIF (352 x 288)	

Figure 3(a) and Figure 3(b) show the battery levels of CM 0 of each cluster after equal sized clustering and the proposed energy balanced clustering methods, respectively. Although inter-cluster energy imbalance exists in equal sized clustering and operation halt of node 0 in cluster 3 due to the failure of the JDE control, operation halt and energy imbalance is decreased in proposed energy balanced clustering. Figure 4 shows the battery level for cluster members in cluster 0. Although there is difference in the battery levels between CMs in the initial phase, the difference decreases as the proposed cluster control goes on. This is because the proposed cluster head selection selects the next CH considering the remaining battery levels of CMs. The resulting inter-/intra-cluster energy balance enables

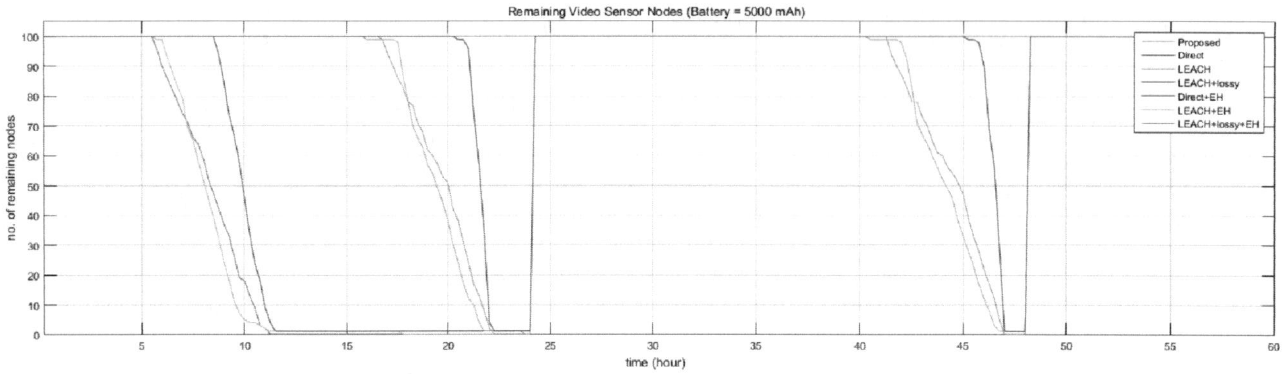

Figure 5. The number of operating CMs.

the perpetual operation of the cluster and the WVSNs.

Figure 5 shows the number of operating CMs for the proposed and the conventional clustering methods. *Direct* and *LEACH* represent the direct transmission without clustering and the clustering method by Heinzelman [2]. Suffixes *lossy* and *EH* represent additive functions, data compression and energy harvesting, respectively. Without EH, CMs die faster due to battery underflow and will not survive because they only use the initially charged energy. With EH, because the conventional clustering method does not consider the amount of harvested energy and the remaining battery level, CMs die during nighttime. However, since the proposed method controls the CMs with the JDE method which predicts the amount of harvesting energy and controls the energy consumption periodically, the CMs can operate perpetually day and night.

IV. CONCLUSIONS

A network clustering and cluster control algorithm is proposed for inter-/intra-cluster energy balance in energy harvesting WVSNs. Based on a ten-day simulation, the proposed distance based clustering, energy level based CH selection, and the cluster control by JDE control of video sensor nodes are shown to enable perpetual operation of energy harvesting WVSNs. The optimum number of clusters and the dynamic clustering should be investigated further for general energy harvesting WVSN applications.

ACKNOWLEDGMENT

This work was supported in part by the National Research Foundation of Korea (NRF) grant funded by the Korea government (MSIP) (NRF-2014R1A2A2A01006294).

REFERENCES

[1] S. Y. Chien and et al, "Power consumption analysis for distributed video sensors in machine-to-machine networks," IEEE Journal on Emerging and Selected Topics in Circuits and Systems, vol. 3, no. 1, March 2013, pp. 55–64.

[2] W. R. Heinzelman, A. Chandrakasan, and H. Balakrishnan, "Energy-efficient communication protocol for wireless microsensor networks," in Proceedings of the 33rd Annual Hawaii International Conference on System Sciences, Jan 2000, pp. 1–10.

[3] A. Manjeshwar and D. P. Agrawal, "Teen: a routing protocol for enhanced efficiency in wireless sensor networks," in Proceedings 15th International Parallel and Distributed Processing Symposium. IPDPS 2001, April 2001, pp. 2009–2015.

[4] E. Gurses, Y. Lin, and R. Boutaba, "Distributed quality-lifetime maximization in wireless video sensor networks," in 2009 IEEE International Conference on Communications, June 2009, pp. 1–6.

[5] J. Jang, G. Kim, and C. M. Kyung, "Lifetime elongation of event-driven wireless video sensor networks," in 2013 IEEE International Symposium on Circuits and Systems (ISCAS2013), May 2013, pp. 437–440.

[6] H. H. Lee, C. H. Lee, and M. J. Lee, "Joint distortion-energy control for energy harvesting video sensor nodes," in Proceedings of the 31st International Conference on Information Networking, Jan 2017.

Resolving Bufferbloat in TCP Communication over IEEE 802.11n WLAN by Reducing MAC Retransmission Limit at Low Data Rate

Masataka Nomoto, Celimuge Wu, Satoshi Ohzahata, and Toshihiko Kato
University of Electro-Communications
Tokyo, Japan
e-mail: noch@net.is.uec.ac.jp, clmg@is.uec.ac.jp, ohzahata@is.uec.ac.jp, kato@is.uec.ac.jp

***Abstract*— IEEE 802.11n wireless local area networks (LANs) provide the data transmission rate of hundreds of Mbps. At the same time, they support multiple data rates and the dynamic rate switching functionality in order to cope with various radio conditions. However, a low data rate may cause a long delay in transmission control protocol (TCP) communications, which is called a bufferbloat problem. In this paper, we infer that one possible reason for the delay is the powerful retransmission capability supported by 802.11n, and propose a method which weakens this capability intentionally for TCP communications when the data rate is low. This paper evaluates the performance of our proposal, the native 802.11n, and CoDel, which is an active queue management approach coping with the bufferbloat problem. It shows that CoDel and our proposal improve the delay performance and that CoDel sometimes reduces the throughput under a high data rate condition.**

Keywords- Wireless LAN; IEEE 802.11n; TCP; Dynamic Rate Switching; Bufferbloat Problem; Block Acknowledgment.

I. INTRODUCTION

Recently, wireless LANs (WLANs) conforming to the IEEE 802.11n standard [1] are being used widely. This type of WLANs can provide a data rate of hundreds of Mbps. In order to realize high throughput, 802.11n has added new physical and media access control (MAC) technologies to the conventional IEEE 802.11. They include multiple-input and multiple-output (MIMO), the channel bonding, the frame aggregation, and the block acknowledgment (Block ACK).

On the other hand, IEEE 802.11n supports multiple data rates and the dynamic rate switching to use the optimal data rate between a terminal and an access point (AP). When a terminal is located close to an AP and the radio condition is good, the high data rate such as 300 Mbps can be used. But, when a terminal moves to the location far from an AP and the receiving radio signal strength becomes weak, the data rate gets lower, for example down to 6.5 Mbps.

In our previous paper [2], we gave a detailed analysis of the performance of TCP communication during which a terminal changes the distance from an AP. As a result, when the distance between the terminal and the AP is large (e.g., 10 m), the packet losses do not increase, but the round-trip time (RTT) increases largely, up to several seconds. This long delay is considered as a sort of bufferbloat problem, which is discussed widely in the networking community [3]-[5]. In order to solve the bufferbloat problem, the active queue management is considered to be effective and an approach named CoDel is proposed [6]. CoDel uses a packet-sojourn time in a queue as a control parameter, and drops a packet in the situation when packets stay too long in the queue.

Our previous paper [2] suggested a different approach from the active queue management. We inferred that one of the reasons for the large queuing delay is the powerful data retransmission function in 802.11n MAC level, which uses the frame aggregation and the Block ACK. So, we proposed that it would be possible to resolve the bufferbloat problem by intentionally weakening the capability of retransmission realized by Block Ack frames, only when the data rate is low in TCP communications. Specifically, we set the retransmission limit to 2 when the data rate is smaller than 80 Mbps, and use 10, which is the default value, when larger than 80 Mbps. Our previous paper showed that this scheme introduces MAC level frame losses and, as a result, reduces the RTT resulting from the shrunk congestion window size. However, this proposal is premature because it uses only two values for the retransmission limit. As for the performance evaluations, our previous work is also premature because it provides only a limited number of measurements.

In this paper, we propose a revised algorithm for reducing the delay in TCP communication over 802.11n WLAN. It defines intermediate values of the retransmission limit corresponding to the data rates between low and high ones, by use of linear interpolation in the semilog relation of data rate and retransmission limit. This paper also presents the detailed performance evaluation of our proposal. In the evaluation, a terminal is located in several positions with different distances from an AP, and the performance is measured for the proposal, CoDel, the native 802.11n, for TCP Reno and CUBIC TCP [7].

The rest of this paper is organized as follows. Section II explains the problem we focused on in this paper and the possible solutions proposed so far. Section III describes our proposed scheme for resolving bufferbloat problem for 802.11n WLAN, and Section IV gives the performance evaluation. In the end, Section V concludes this paper.

II. BUFFERBLOAT PROBLEM AND RELATED WORK

A. *Bufferbloat problem in 802.11n WLAN*

Table I gives the data rates supported by the terminal and the AP used in the experiment. In these data rates, an 802.11n data sender performs retransmission of corrupted frames. During this procedure, the data sender monitors the ratio of retransmissions and selects the lower data rate if the retransmission ratio becomes too large.

In this paper, we focus on the bufferbloat problem in the upload data transfer from a terminal to an AP. Consider the

TABLE I. AVAILABLE DATA RATE IN 802.11N WLAN.

6.5	13.5	27.0	40.5	54	81
108	162	216	243	270	300

Unit: Mbps

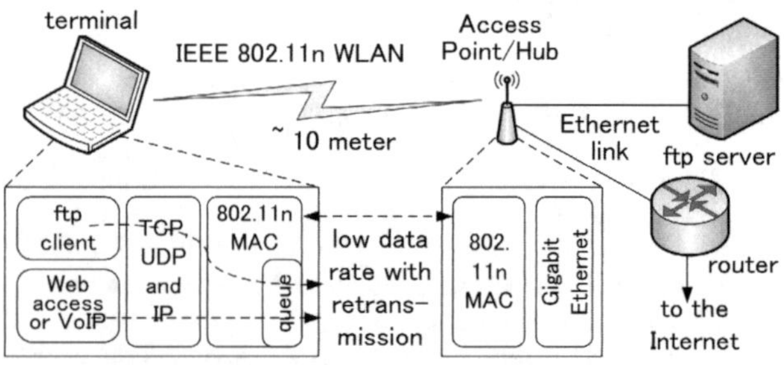

Figure 1. Outline of bufferbloat problem in 802.11n WLAN upload traffic.

situation depicted in Figure 1. A terminal located far from an AP is sending data to the ftp server. The terminal uses a low data rate, such as 6.5 Mbps and 13.5 Mbps. Our previous experiment gave some results that the retransmission at MAC level works well and there are few packet losses at the TCP and IP level [2]. Consequently, the TCP congestion window size grows up, and the data frames corresponding to this size are transmitted contiguously. However, the data rate is low and therefore the data frames are stored in the queue at the MAC level. This brings a large delay in the file transfer. If another application such as web access and voice over IP (VoIP) starts in this situation, the new communication also suffers from the large delay.

B. *Related work*

There are several approaches which can be applied to the problem described above.

The first one is the introduction of IEEE 802.11e [8]. It provides the priorities in the MAC level, i.e., Voice, Video, Best Effort, and Background, by introducing separate queues within a node and separate flows of data frames in a WLAN. In order to introduce separate flows, it discriminates values of arbitration interframe space and contention window boundaries. As for the bufferbloat problem, however, it cannot be always applied. If the second application in Figure 1 is TCP based, such as a web access, the ftp client and the second application are categorized in the same priority in 802.11e. So, the second application will suffer from the delay which the ftp generates.

The second approach is the active queue management. As described above, CoDel uses packet-sojourn time in the queue. Specifically, when any packet stays in the queue longer than a specific duration, called *target* in CoDel, during a predefined interval, called *interval* in CoDel, the last packet in the queue is dropped. As for the value of *target*, 5 msec is used in [6]. For the *interval*, 100 msec is used as the beginning of the procedure and, if a packet is dropped, the value is decreased in inverse proportion to the square root of the number of drops since the dropping state was entered. Some simulation results are shown in [6] over WiFi links whose data rate changes among 100Mbps, 50Mbps and 1Mbps, and tell that the per-packet queue delay in CoDel is smaller than that in random early discard (RED) [9] and Tail Drop.

The third approach is the adoption of TCP based on non-loss based congestion control. As described above, the grown congestion window size is the reason for queued data frames, and no loss situation allows the window size to grow. So, the introduction of non-loss based congestion control, such as TCP Vegas [10], might be effective. With the current values of congestion window size and RTT, TCP Vegas estimates the buffer size in the bottleneck node. A TCP sender increases the congestion window size when the bottleneck buffer size is small and decreases when the buffer size is large.

In contrast with those approaches, our scheme uses the retransmission limit adjustment. There are several studies focusing on this topic [11]-[13]. However, all of them focus on the relationship between the transmission delay and the retransmission limit. On the other hand, our scheme aims at causing a packet loss intentionally by changing the retransmission limit.

III. PROPOSAL

The basic idea of our scheme is that a MAC data sender tunes up the retransmission limit in response to the data rate used for data frame transmission. The lower data rate, the smaller retransmission limit. This adjustment is done only if the sending data frame contains a TCP segment by checking the protocol field in IP header. The followings give the points of our scheme.

A. *Focusing on Block Ack based retransmission*

As for the reception confirmation, IEEE 802.11n adopts an approach called High Throughput (HT)-immediate Block Ack [1]. A sender aggregates multiple data frames into one frame (aggregated MAC protocol data unit: A-MPDU) and sends it out. A receiver checks the correctness of individual received data frames, and returns a Block Ack frame. The Block Ack frame is sent out immediately after the receiver received the A-MPDU, and indicates individual data frames are received successfully or not in the Block Ack Bitmap field.

If the Block Ack Bitmap field indicates loss of some data frames, the sender side retransmits the lost frames (*the Block Ack based retransmission*). On the other hand, in the case when A-MPDU itself is corrupted or the returning Block Ack frame is lost, the A-MPDU is retransmitted again (*the timeout based retransmission*).

In general, the timeout based retransmission is controlled by a WLAN hardware chip and the Block Ack based retransmission is controlled by a WLAN device driver. They are managed independently. In the case of the WLAN device driver we use in this paper, the retransmission limit is 19 for the timeout based, and 10 for the Block Ack based retransmission.

Since our scheme is implemented in a WLAN device driver, we focus on the Block Ack based retransmission. Our scheme decreases the limit for the Block Ack based retransmission when the data rate becomes low.

B. *Determining retransmission limit for individual data rate*

The next point is what value is selected as the retransmission limit for an individual data rate. As described above, the maximum value of the Block Ack based retransmission is 10. On the other hand, our experiment described in [2] showed that 2 is appropriate as the retransmission limit for the data rate 6.5 Mbps and 13.5 Mbps. So, in this proposal, we focus on determining the in-between retransmission limit values.

We have decided to define the Block Ack based retransmission limit in the following way.

- For the data rate equal to and higher than 100 Mbps, the limit is 10.
- For the data rate equal to and lower than 10 Mbps, the limit is 2.
- As a first step, we introduce a linear relationship between the limit and the data rate between 10 Mbps and 100 Mbps over a semilog scale. This is depicted as a dashed line in Figure 2.
- Based on this result, we have selected stepwise values for the retransmission limit as shown by a solid line in the figure.

That is, the Block Ack based retransmission limit is

10 if $rate \geq 100$ Mbps,
8 if 50 Mbps $\leq rate <$ 100 Mbps,
5 if 25 Mbps $\leq rate <$ 50 Mbps, and
2 if $rate <$ 25 Mbps.

It should be noted that this limit value selection is not based on a specific theory. However, the results given in Section IV show that our scheme works well using those limit values.

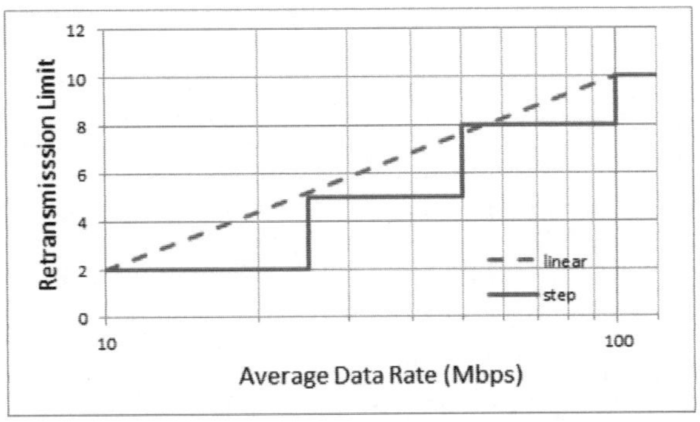

Figure 2. Retramission limit adopted by our scheme.

C. *Using moving average for data rate*

The last point is what data rate is to use for determining the retransmission limit. The data rate for a specific data frame is determined when the device driver handles the corresponding data transfer request. The data rate will be changed according to the physical layer status between the terminal and AP. So, we decided to introduce the exponential moving average with coefficient 0.25. That is, the *rate* described above is calculated at each of data transfer request by the following equation.

$$rate \leftarrow 0.75 \times rate + 0.25 \times actual\ data\ rate$$

The retransmission limit is determined using this rate and is applied when a data frame is retransmitted according to the Block Ack based retransmission.

IV. Performance Evaluation

A. *Experimental settings*

Figure 3 shows the network configuration of our experiment. A terminal and an AP use 5GHz band WLAN conforming to IEEE 802.11n. The AP and a server are connected via Gigabit Ethernet link through a bridge. The bridge is used to add a delay to emulate a communication via the Internet.

The experiment is performed in a two-storied Japanese style house built of wood. The server, the AP and the bridge are located in the 2nd floor. The terminal is located in various locations in the 1st and 2nd floors, and the stairs between them. The distance between the terminal and the AP is about 1.2 meter at the nearest position and about 10 meter at the far most position. At one position, the terminal is fixed and sends data to the server for 60 seconds. The data communication is done by use of iperf [14].

The specification of the terminal is given in Table II. The AP is commercially available and its model number is WZR-HP-AG300H manufactured by Buffalo Inc., Japan. This AP supports multi-rate up to 300 Mbps. In the experiment, we used all of the 12 levels of data rate given in Table I.

In the experiment, the performance of the proposed scheme, CoDel and the native 802.11n are evaluated. The detailed conditions of the experiment are as follows.

- The proposed scheme is implemented in the ath9k device driver [15].
- The CoDel used is that for Linux 3.5. We ported this version of CoDel to Linux 3.2.38. As the performance parameters in CoDel, we used default parameters, e.g., 5 msec as the target and 100 msec as the interval.

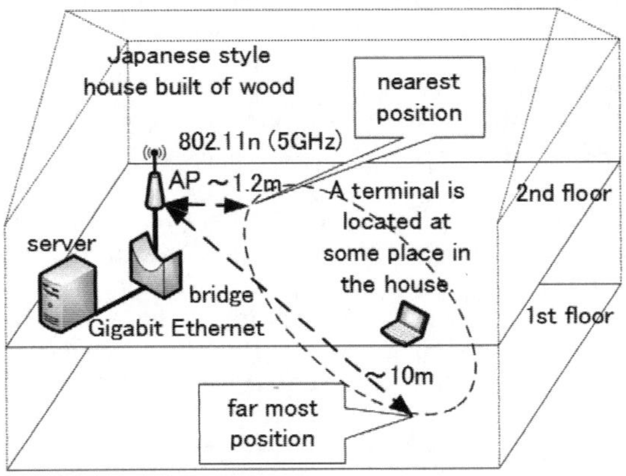

Figure 3. Experiment configuration.

TABLE II. SPECIFICATION OF TERMINAL.

Linux kernel	3.2.38 (self build)
Manufacturer/model	Lenovo ThinkPad X61
WLAN card	NEC Aterm WL300NC
WLAN device driver	ath9k

- As for TCP versions, we adopted TCP Reno, as a conventional scheme, and Cubic TCP, as the default in Linux.
- In the experiment, two cases without and with additional delay are evaluated. The delay is inserted by the bridge. In the case of additional delay, 100 msec round-trip delay (50 msec one way delay) is used. The insertion is done using netem in Linux [16].
- During a 60 sec. TCP communication, the following data are collected;
  - o packet trace at the terminal, by use of tcpdump,
  - o TCP connection information, such as the congestion window size (cwnd) at the terminal, by use of tcpprobe [17], and
  - o WLAN transfer information, such as data rate, from WLAN device driver.

  From these data, the average of data rate, RTT, throughput, and cwnd for an individual TCP communication are calculated.
- As for the parameter which characterizes the position of the terminal, the distance between the terminal and AP is not appropriate. The reason is that the distance is only meaningful in our experimental environment. On the other hand, the data rate used in one position is rather stable. So, we use the average data rate during a TCP communication as the parameter which specifies the location of the terminal. The other measured values are mapped with the average data rate.

B. Comparison among proposal, CoDel and native 802.11n

Figure 4 shows the results when Cubic TCP is used and no additional delay is inserted at the bridge. In this figure, (a), (b) and (c) show the average throughput, the average RTT, and the average cwnd versus the average data rate, respectively. An individual point in the figure shows a result of one evaluation for one 60 sec. TCP communication. From Figure 4 (a), it can be said that our proposal, CoDel, and the native 802.11n give a similar TCP throughput.

But, Figure 4 (b) indicates that the average RTT of the native 802.11n is large, about 1000 msec, when the average data rate is lower than 30 Mbps. The average RTT of CoDel is smaller than that of the native 802.11n for all values of the average data rate. The average RTT for the native 802.11n and CoDel maintains a linear relationship with the average data rate in the log-log scale. On the other hand, our proposal shows different features. In our proposal, the average RTT is similar with that of the native 802.11n while the average data rate is larger than 80 Mbps. For the average data rate smaller than 80 Mbps, however, the average RTT of our proposal becomes smaller than that of the native 802.11n, and even that of CoDel.

Figure 4 (c) shows the reason of those results for RTT. In the native 802.11n, the average cwnd is large, 700 to 900 segments, for all values of the average data rate. This large cwnd causes the queue to build up. In the case of CoDel, the average cwnd is small throughout all the range of the average data rate. This is caused by dropping packets against the built up queue. On the contrary, in our proposal, the average cwnd is similar with that of the native 802.11n while the average data rate is 100 Mbps or larger. When the average data rate becomes smaller than 100 Mbps, the average cwnd also becomes smaller, and in the range of below 40 Mbps, it is smaller than that of CoDel. It can be said that the proposed scheme to decrease the MAC level retransmission limit at the low data rate works well for a TCP communication.

When TCP Reno is used, the results were similar when no additional delay is inserted.

Figure 5 shows the results when Cubic TCP is used and 100 msec additional delay is inserted at the bridge. As for the average RTT, the native 802.11n has a large value and the CoDel is smaller than that of the native 802.11n, while the average data rate is smaller than 100 Mbps. On the other hand,

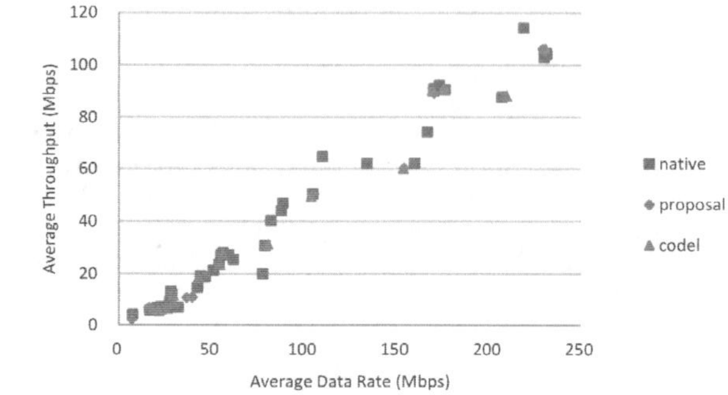

(a) Average throughput versus average data rate

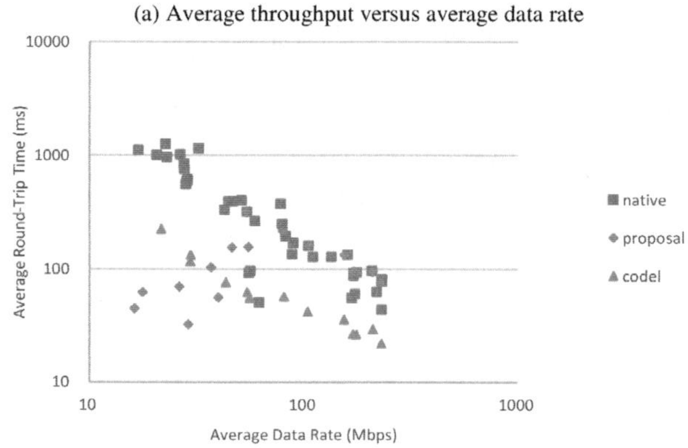

(b) Average RTT versus average data rate

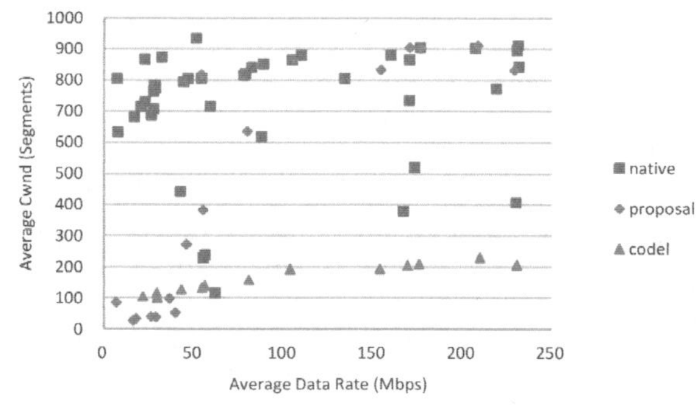

(c) Average congestion window size versus average data rate

Figure 4. Results for Cubic TCP without any additional delay.

our proposal has similar average RTT values with the 802.11n while the average data rate is larger than 80 Mbps. For the average data rate smaller than 80 Mbps, however, the average RTT of our proposal becomes smaller than that of the native 802.11n, and even that of CoDel. This is similar with the case of Figure 4.

Figure 5 (c) gives a different result from Figure 4 (c). The average cwnd of CoDel in the case of additional delay is larger than the case without additional delay. The average cwnd of CoDel is similar with the native 802.11n and our proposal for 100 Mbps and larger average data rate. This brings the similar TCP throughput.

Figure 6 shows the results when TCP Reno is used and when 100 msec additional delay is inserted at the bridge. Figure 6 (b) shows that the average RTT is similar with that in Figure 5 (b). From Figure 6 (a), however, the average throughput of CoDel is lower than the other schemes in the range of the average data rate with larger than 100 Mbps. Figure 6 (c) shows that the average cwnd of CoDel is also smaller than those of our proposal and the native 802.11n for the average data rate larger than 100 Mbps. This is the reason for the low throughput. In order clarify the situation, Figure 7 shows the timeline of throughput and cwnd when the average data rate is 216 Mbps. Figure 7 (a) shows that the throughput of CoDel becomes low at time 15 sec. Figure 7 (b) indicates that, at this timing, a packet loss causes slow start and, after that, cwnd grows up only slowly. This result says that CoDel may drop packets unnecessarily and the TCP version with the moderate congestion increasing may suppress the throughput.

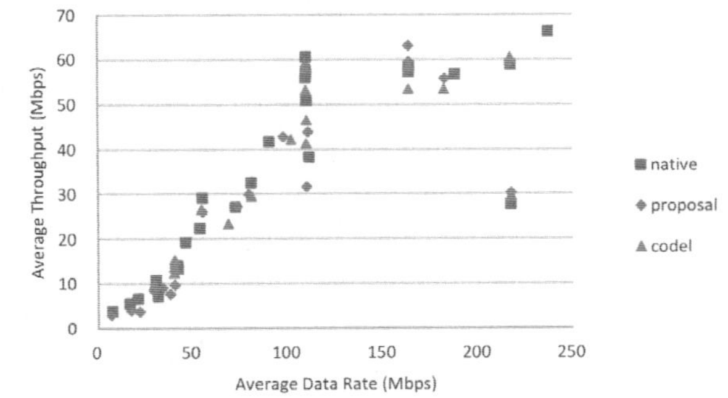

(a) Average throughput versus average data rate

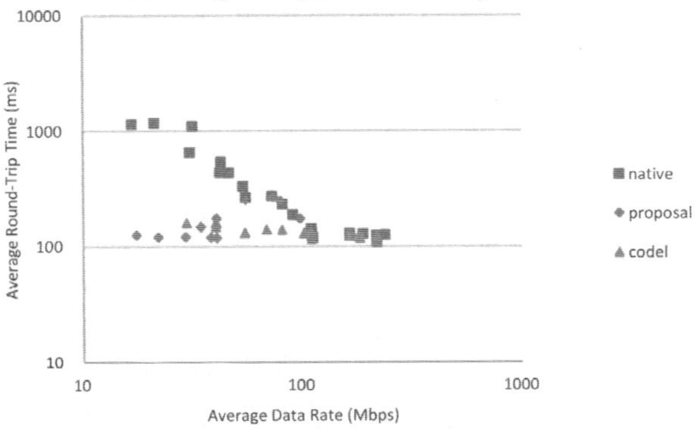

(b) Average RTT versus average data rate

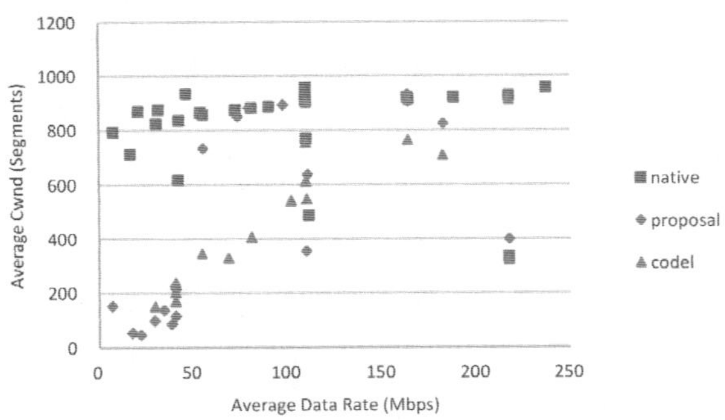

(c) Average congestion window size versus average data rate

Figure 5. Results for Cubic TCP with 100 msec additional delay.

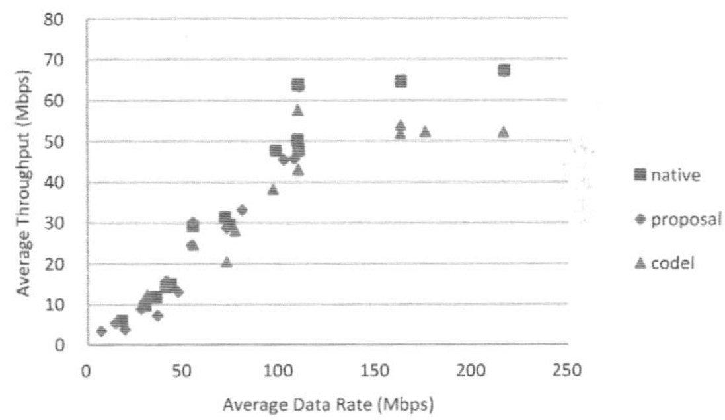

(a) Average throughput versus average data rate

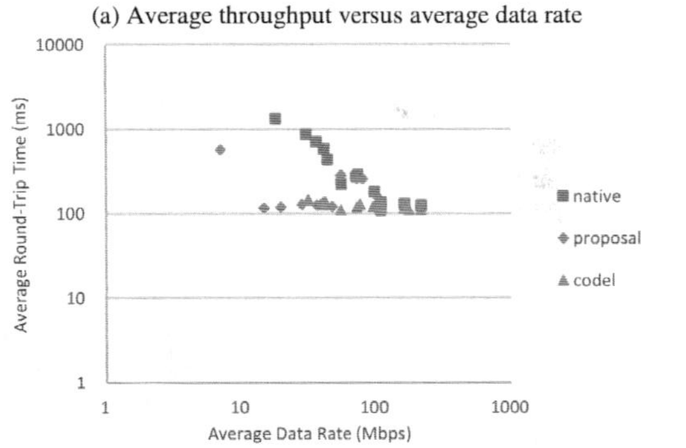

(b) Average RTT versus average data rate

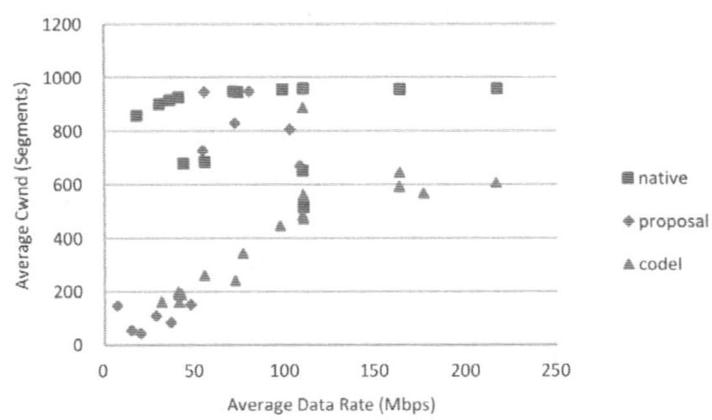

(c) Average congestion window size versus average data rate

Figure 6. Results for TCP Reno with 100 msec additional delay.

V. CONCLUSIONS

This paper proposes a scheme for reducing the delay in TCP communication over 802.11n WLAN. Our scheme decreases the retransmission limit of the Block Ack based retransmission gradually according to the data rates becoming low. This paper also presents the detailed performance evaluation of our proposal, CoDel using the active queue management, and the native 802.11n with Cubic TCP and TCP Reno. The results show that our proposal and CoDel decrease the delay at a low data rate which the native 802.11n suffers from. The results also show that there are some cases where CoDel drops packets unnecessarily and the throughput in CoDel becomes lower at a high data rate. These results show that our proposal, which weakens the MAC level retransmission function can solve the bufferbloat problem specific for 802.11n WLAN.

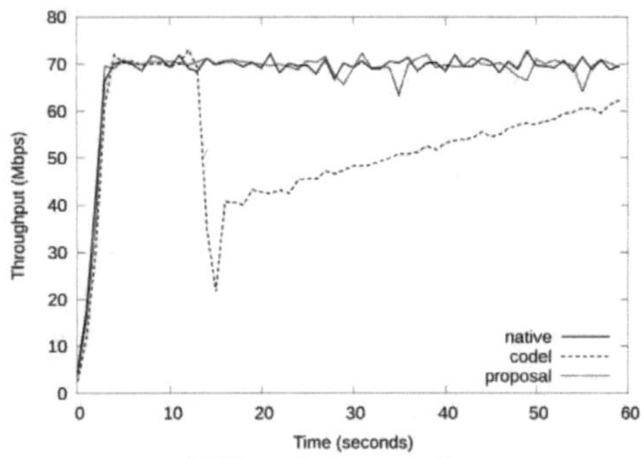

(a) Throughput versus time

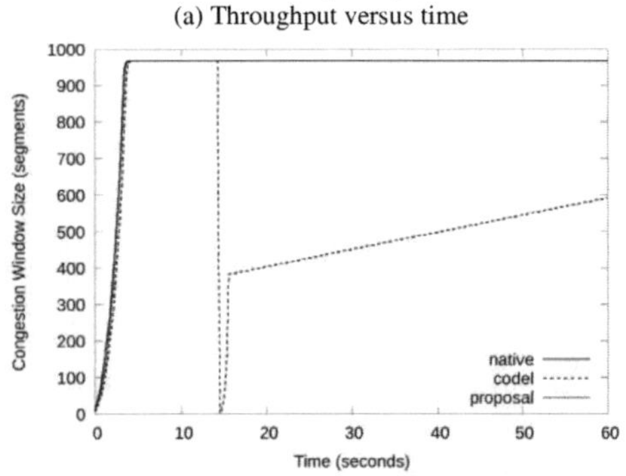

(b) Congestion window size versus time

Figure 7. Results for individual TCP Reno communications with 216 Mbps data rate (100 msec additional delay).

REFERENCES

[1] IEEE Standard for Information technology,"Local and metropolitan area networks Part 11: Wireless LAN Medium Access Control (MAC) and Physical Layer (PHY) Specifications," 2012.

[2] M. Nomoto, T. Kato, C. Wu, and S. Ohzahata, "Resolving Bufferbloat Problem in 802.11n WLAN by Weakening MAC Loss Recovery for TCP Stream," Proc.12th IASTED PDCN, pp. 293-300, Feb. 2014.

[3] J. Gettys and K. Nichols, "Bufferbloat: Dark Buffers in the Internet," ACM Queue, Virtualization, vol. 9, no.11, pp. 1-15, Nov. 2011.

[4] M. Allman, "Comments on Bufferbloat," ACM SIGCOMM Computer Communication Review, vol.43, no.1, pp. 31-37, Jan. 2013.

[5] A. Showail, K., Jamshaid, and B. Shihada, "An Empirical Evaluation of Bufferbloat in IEEE 802.11n Wireless Networks," Proc. IEEE WCNC '14, pp. 3088-3093, Apr. 2014.

[6] K. Nichols and V. Jacobson, "Controlling Queue Delay," ACM Queue, Networks, vol.10, no.5, pp. 1-15, May 2012.

[7] I. Rhee and L. Xu, "CUBIC: a new TCP-friendly high-speed TCP variant," SIGOPS Operating Systems Review, vol.42, no. 5, pp. 64-74, July 2008.

[8] IEEE Standard for Information technology, "Local and metropolitan area networks--Specific requirements--Part 11: Wireless LAN Medium Access Control (MAC) and Physical Layer (PHY) Specifications - Amendment 8: Medium Access Control (MAC) Quality of Service Enhancements," 2005.

[9] S. Floyd and V. Jacobson, "Random Early Detection Gateways for Congestion Avoidance," IEEE/ACM Trans. On Networking, vol.1, no.4, pp. 397-413, Aug. 1993.

[10] L. Brakmo and L. Perterson, "TCP Vegas: End to End Congestion Avoidance on a Global Internet," IEEE J. Selected Areas in Commun., vol. 13, no. 8, pp. 1465-1480, Oct. 1995.

[11] J. Bai, E. P. Eyisi, Y. Xue, and X. D. Koutsoukos, "Dynamic Tuning Retransmission Limit of IEEE 802.11 MAC Protocol for Networked Control Systems," Proc. 2010 IEEE/ACM Int. Conf. on Green Computing and Comunications, pp. 666-672, Dec. 2010.

[12] W. Wen and D. Liu, "An adaptive retry scheme for delay-constrained service transmission in 802.11n system," Proc. IEEE ICCP 2011, pp. 97-101, Oct. 2011.

[13] M. Kim and C. Choi, "Joint Rate and Fragment Size Adaptation in IEEE 802.11n Wireless LANs," Proc. 2011 IEEE CCNC, pp. 942-947, Jan. 2011.

[14] iperf, https://github.com/esnet/iperf, [retrieved: Nov. 2016].

[15] ath9k Linux Wireless, http://wireless.kernel.org/en/users/Drivers/ath9k, [retrieved: Nov. 2016].

[16] S. Hemminger, "Network Emulation with NetEm," Proc. 6th Australia's National Linux Conference (LCA2005), pp. 1-9, Apr. 2005.

[17] Linux foundation: tcpprobe, http://www.linuxfoundation.org/collaborate/workgroups/networking/tcpprobe, [retrieved: Nov. 2016].

Preserving Privacy with Fine-grained Authorization in an Identity Management System

Gerson Luiz Camillo* Carla Merkle Westphall†, Jorge Werner‡, Carlos Becker Westphall§

Post-graduate Program in Computer Science (PPGCC)
Networks and Management Laboratory (LRG-UFSC)
Federal University of Santa Catarina - UFSC
P.O. Box 476, 88040-970, Florianópolis, SC, Brazil
Email: *gerson.camillo@posgrad.ufsc.br †carla.merkle.westphall@ufsc.br
‡j.werner@posgrad.ufsc.br §westphall@lrg.ufsc.br

Abstract—**In policy-based management, service providers want to enforce fine-grained policies for their resources and services. Besides the assurance of digital identity, service providers usually need personal data for evaluation of access control policies. The disclosure of personal data, also known as Personally Identifiable Information (PII), could represent a privacy breach. This paper proposes an architecture that allows an individual to obtain services without the need of releasing all personal attributes. The architecture achieves that outcome evaluating the targeted policy in the domain of the identity provider, that is, policies are sent from service providers to identity providers to be evaluated, without the need of releasing some PIIs to the service provider side. We also present an implementation of a prototype using XACML 3.0 for fine-grained authorization and OpenID Connect for identity management. The prototype was evaluated through an use case representing an hypothetical scenario of a bookstore. The project demonstrated that for certain situations an user can restrict the release of PII data and still gain access to services.**

Keywords–Privacy; Identity Management; OpenID Connect; Fine-grained Authorization; XACML.

I. Introduction

The data that identifies and distinguishes the users have acquired invaluable importance in the digital society, to the extent that any online transaction usually requires some information to be disclosed. These data are known as Personally Identifiable Information (PII) and they are represented by attributes.

The risks to personal information in service providers (SP) are totally related to the amount of collected attributes of individuals [1]. In addition, the personal identification data can be collected by the service providers to identify users and create profiles for business. Many Internet companies grew up selling personally identifiable information and behavioral data. These two situations represent attacks on the privacy of individuals and the risks increase with the amount of personal attributes in the SP.

Thus, privacy aims to minimize the release of personal information and/or prevent that attributes are linked to the user [2][3][4]. Privacy can be achieved by law, techniques, and mechanisms, aiming to empower the individuals in controlling their personal information. This work presents a technique that aims to minimize the disclosure of PII data.

The access control is a central security point and the authorization systems evolved from identity-based to attribute-based. The attribute is an assertion describing a quality, state, appearance, and characteristic of some entity in the context of authorization. There can be attributes of the subject, resource, action, and environment. The Attribute-Based Access Control (ABAC) model [5] is a formalization of the requirements for an attribute-based authorization. The ABAC evaluates rules and policies against the attributes of the entities (subjects, resources, actions, and environment). The model is characterized as policy-based authorization, because the logic of access control is represented by rules that compose policies.

The architecture of ABAC is constituted by functional points, which were already defined in [6]. The Organization for the Advancement of Structured Information Standards (OASIS) specified the *eXtensible Access Control Markup Language* (XACML) [7] as an implementation for the ABAC model and for the authorization framework [6]. The XACML is a policy language for fine-grained authorization which provides a request-response protocol and a reference architecture. The functionality of the model starts with the request that arrives at the Policy Enforcement Point (PEP), which acts protecting the resource. The PEP receives user's request and asks the Policy Decision Point (PDP) for an access control decision. The PDP evaluates the policy that matches the request and returns a decision to PEP for enforcement. Also, there is the Policy Administration Point (PAP), which manages the repository of policies and the Policy Information Point (PIP), which searches for the attributes that are not present in the request.

Service providers (SP) need user's attributes to enforce fine-grained policies and to perform appropriate authorization decisions. One solution for the SP is to use the authentication token to get attributes from an identity management system (IdM). An IdM is the process and technology that enables the creation, management, use, and removal of digital identities. Digital identities are electronic representations of the real identities and can be characterized by a subset of values of attributes [8]. Thus, IdM systems were created in order to maintain PII data in an identity provider (IdP) and to securely transport attributes and identity assertions among different parties.

In this paper, we will present the scenario of a bookstore to explain the problem to be solved. The Web service of the bookstore sells materials online but the company is seeking to include a competitive edge in the field of user privacy. The bookstore has included the possibility to view books online, but some of them with restricted access. Firstly, users have to login in the IdP and then the SP will evaluate XACML policies against user's attributes to generate an access decision. Consequently, the SP needs to obtain the personal data from the user maintained by the IdP. However, this situation creates a privacy risk to the individual because the bookstore could increase the amount of collected personal attributes. This problem led us to propose an architecture to preserve user's privacy.

The proposal of this paper is an approach that maintains the SP needs for fine-grained authorization while protecting user's privacy. To ensure privacy of users, the architecture will evaluate the service policy in the domain of the IdP. Thus, the complete set of personal attributes are not conveyed from the IdP to the SP to evaluate the policies. The trust relationship that enables the SP to rely on assertions from IdP is used by the architecture to obtain an access control decision from the same IdP. The development of our architecture is based on recent protocols and specifications: OAuth 2.0 [9], OpenID Connect (OIDC) [10], and RESTful Web services. In addition, the SP applies fine-grained authorization using XACML architecture and policies.

One of the main contribution of this work is the introduction of an architecture that evaluates attribute-based access control policies in the IdP side, returning to the SP only the result of the evaluation, aiming to prevent the service provider from obtaining private user data. The other contribution is the enforcement of fine-grained access control policies using XACML by the SP while keeping user's privacy regarding PII. The proposal and development of a prototype to test a use case scenario can also be considered a contribution of this work.

The remaining of this paper is arranged as follows: Section II presents the related work; the problem statement is in Section III; in Section IV, the proposed architecture is presented; the Section V describes the implementation of a prototype and the results from the test case; Section VI discusses the findings; and Section VII sums up the text.

II. Related Work

Different works and Privacy Enhancing Technologies (PETs) have the purpose of increasing or establishing privacy in the relationship between users and service providers in IdM environment. This section restricts the descriptions of the works that aim to provide privacy of personal data, as defined in EU Directive 95/46/EC [11]. The directive defines personal data as a piece of information that identifies directly or indirectly a natural person.

The Privacy-preserving Attribute-based Credentials (Privacy-ABC) is an approach to authentication with private credentials in IdM scenarios, which provides user privacy. The Privacy-ABC are technologies which enable users to obtain credentials and derive unlinkable tokens that reveal only a subset of attributes. They are based on cryptographic primitives, and two examples of them are the schemes of Brand [12] and Camenisch-Lysyanskaya [13].

The Privacy-ABC were developed in the European projects PRIME [14] and PRIMELife [15]. IBM Identity Mixer (Idemix) [16][17] and the Microsoft U-Prove [18] are commercial deployments based on Privacy-ABC. Those technologies do not have a widespread use, owing to the fact that the areas of user interface, policy languages, and infrastructure need further research [19][20]. In addition, the Privacy-ABC have difficult understanding and use [21]. The ABC4Trust [22] project was created to overcome some of those technical issues.

The User-Managed Access (UMA) [23] is a profile of OAuth 2.0 and its principal aim is to enable users to manage the policies of their protected resources (personal data, content, and services). The users are central in UMA, however, they may be confronted with complex policies in Web scenarios, that require complicated authorization choices and could negatively affect the user's privacy decisions.

Chadwick and Fatema [24] proposed an architecture that aims to provide authorization services in cloud infrastructure. Privacy is addressed by the use of *sticky* policies that consist of privacy policies that are attached to the data. The premise was that the SPs in the cloud are reliable in such a way that they will honor the privacy policies defined in *sticky* policies.

Architectures for policy decomposition [25] and policy federation [26][27] aimed to provide confidentiality and privacy when enforcing access control policies in distributed environments. The proposed works are supported by the XACML architecture because the entities of XACML are specified to be easily distributed. The entities use SOAP/SAML protocols to convey the request/response messages and the policies, all defined in XACML specification [7]. Despite the privacy achieved in some scenarios, the models do not explicitly include user authentication through identity management.

The Shibboleth 2.0 [28] is a well-known example of implementation of the Security Assertion Markup Language (SAML) protocol [29] for IdM. However, some characteristics of Shibboleth 2.0 limit its use in our architecture: the set of attributes are predefined between the SP and IdP and there is no consent mechanism (this was included natively in IdPv3). Thus, the SAML/Shibboleth 2.0 has a difficult integration with RESTful Web API and mobile applications. The OpenID Connect (OIDC) [10] is a recent specification for IdM and was developed on the top of OAuth 2.0. The main advantages are the use of RESTful Web APIs and the transport of data through Javascript Object Notation (JSON) format. OIDC is a natural choice for identity management in Web 2.0 environments.

Werner and Westphall [30] defined a model for an IdM with privacy in cloud infrastructure. Even though the authors have presented a model that tries to help users to make decisions about their privacy, the architecture still depends on SP to enforce the privacy policy.

Ma and Sartipi [31] proposed an infrastructure that integrates the OIDC to XACML for sharing diagnostic images in cloud deployments. Their solution transfers to the end user the management of policies, which could be administrative burden when users have data in different types of services.

III. Problem Statement

The main problem that this work aims to solve is the amount of PII data released in IdM scenarios. The proposed solution transfers the policy from the SP to the IdP. For this work, the words Service Provider (SP), Relying Party (RP), and Client have the same functional definition.

The externalization and distribution of policy evaluation have been studied before [26][27]. Those references adopted the XACML for the architecture and for the policy language. The XACML and the ABAC were defined for distributed environments [5], but considered in a single domain of security. This work proposes the inclusion of a PDP in an IdP domain to evaluate policies that need end-users attributes. However, the approach is unusual when considering the IdM scenarios. The proposed architecture uses the trust agreement created to support a federated identity management to federalize the authorization concerning PII data.

The architecture proposed can be defined as a PET solution. The taxonomy of PETs [3] defined the aspect of privacy that is targeted by PET, and that can be the *identity*, the *content*, or the *behavior*. The proposal of this paper aims to protect the data that represents the identity of the user stored in an IdP. The architecture does not include mechanisms to protect the content of data that are created, stored, and manipulated during service interaction. The aspect of behavior is related to access pattern and it is obtained by correlating actions with identities. The proposed architecture only can guarantee such aspect if the underlying IdM provides transient pseudonyms identifiers or anonymity.

The following set of trust relationships were assumed for this work: the IdP is trustworthy for management of end user attributes; the RP is untrustworthy, which follows the protocol but wants more information than is really necessary; and, the RP relies on the IdP to provide the identity claims about the end user.

The previous definition leads to the configuration of the architecture in security domains. There is the domain of the SP and the domain of the IdP. The classification is regarding to the protection of the PII data. The IdM technologies adopted the concept of minimization of data releasing only the attributes required for the purpose of the service. The trust relationship between IdP and RP includes agreement on what attributes of IdP are needed to what services of SP during transactions related to identity and authorization management. The trust agreement can be static or dynamic. Static agreements are used by IdMs based on SAML. In that type of IdM, the user has little or no control about the personal data released to the SP.

On the other hand, recent specifications of architectures and protocols for authorization and identity are more dynamic. They define the user as the central entity for controlling data access and the main mechanism is the consent management [11][1]. Examples of systems that include user's consent: OAuth 2.0, OIDC, UMA [32], Shibboleth IdPv3 [33]. This demonstrates that consent is relevant in IdM scenarios and it is why this proposal can be considered for increasing the privacy of personal data.

IV. Proposed Architecture for Privacy Preserving User Attributes

The architecture proposed here includes elements and flows in a network-based IdM. This type of IdM provides the functionality of Web authentication, known as Web Single Sign-on (SSO). The proposed architecture is depicted in Fig. 1. The elements of ABAC model are included in the RP and in the IdP. The ABAC functional points provide the following features: evaluation of fine-grained policies; request/response authorizations; and, distribution of the functional points. Those characteristics enable the creation of a loosely-coupled architecture for authorization and a means to convey the policies to the IdP.

Fig. 1 shows that there are the domain of RP and the domain of IdP. The end user trusts the IdP to be the provider of personal data (attributes). The RP trusts the IdP for end-user authentication. This trust relationship can be statically agreed upon or dynamically created. The dynamic mechanism occurs through some form of discovery and metadata exchange for registration. The elements included in the architecture are: PDP and PAP in RP domain; and, PDP in IdP domain. The PEP in RP must enforce the result of PDP evaluation of policies managed by the PAP. The PAP stores the authorization policies for the RP. This scheme defines an externalized architecture of authorization.

The inclusion of the PDP and PAP points for authorization purposes are common scenarios in ABAC models. However, inclusion of a PDP point in IdP is a novel proposal. This creates another point of policy evaluation in the domain of IdP. In ABAC model, the same policy that is evaluated by the PDP in RP domain can be evaluated in the domain of IdP, because of its distributed architecture. If the service policy requires user attributes, then the policy can be conveyed to the IdP domain for evaluation. This approach eliminates the release of personal data from IdP to RP domain.

The flows highlighted in Fig. 1 will be now described. The steps 1 to 4 are related to the process of authentication (Web SSO). An end user through user agent (Web browser) requests services from RP (step 1). The RP redirects the end user to IdP via Web browser (step 2). The end user is authenticated by IdP (step 3) and the IdP generates a token that is redirected to RP (step 4). The token is an authentication assertion and the token corresponds to the user credentials.

The next phase (step 5) only occurs when end users have decided to release personal attributes to the RP through the consent dialog. The RP uses the token obtained in the phase of authentication to get those user released attributes. Those attributes can be used by the RP to enrich the user experience on the Web and create authorization with fine-grained controls. However, this consent phase can also increase the risks to the privacy of the user because the risk is directly related to the amount of personal data transferred to the RP.

The next steps are concerned with the description of the contribution of this proposal. The RP implements the ABAC model to protect resources using fine-grained policies. The end user's demand is captured by the PEP which generates a XACML request with the available attributes. The PEP sends the XACML request to the PDP for an access decision (step 6). The PDP chooses the applicable policy based on the attributes of different categories: subject, object, action, and environment. If the end user have denied access to the subject attributes, the PDP cannot evaluate the applicable policy to the XACML request and thus the PDP returns the "Indeterminate" response. Besides, the PDP includes the status of missing attributes in response. With that outcome, the PEP could deny the user's request to resources. However, in the proposed architecture, this lack of necessary attributes starts the phase of the evaluation of the RP policy in the IdP domain.

The RP discovers that the IdP can evaluate XACML policies when the IdP announces the PDP endpoints through

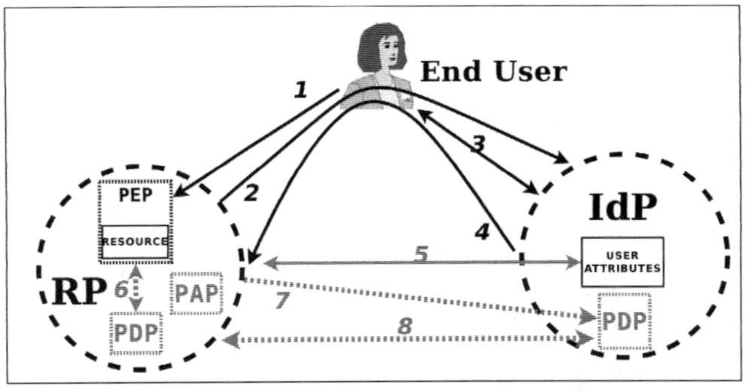

Figure 1. Proposed architecture. Our contribution is highlighted and comprises PDP/PAP points and steps 6, 7 and 8 for conveying policies.

metadata information. The implementation of the XACML standard is not specified because the policy-based XACML language does not rely on the technical engine that will run it. In consequence, the architecture is ready to evaluate the authorization policy in IdP domain.

The response from PDP also contains the identification of the target policy. The PEP uses that information to retrieve the policy from the PAP and then sends it to the endpoint of the PDP in the IdP (step 7). The PEP sends the same XACML request to the PDP at IdP for evaluation (step 8). The PDP starts the evaluation of the policy against the attributes that come from the following sources: XACML request for the resource, action, and environment attributes; and, the subject attributes from the IdP. The subject attributes refer to the attributes about end users at IdP. As the PDP figures out an authorization decision, it is returned to the PEP in the domain of RP for enforcement (step 8).

V. Prototype Results

The prototype consists of an IdM and the elements of the ABAC authorization model. Fig. 2 shows the entities grouped in security domains along with the principal steps. The steps may represent one or more flows of interaction among the entities. The diagram also depicts which flows are related to OIDC, XACML, and those provided by the contribution of this work.

The domain of RP was built with the following elements: PEPClientApp, PDP-rp, and PAP. The PEPClientApp is the application that owns and protects the access to resources or services through the PEP. It intercepts the end-user request and generates a XACML request for the PDP-rp to obtain an access control decision. The PEPClientApp was constructed using base code of a sample application which is included in the MITREid project. It uses the Spring Framework to provide the security elements for protection of the services.

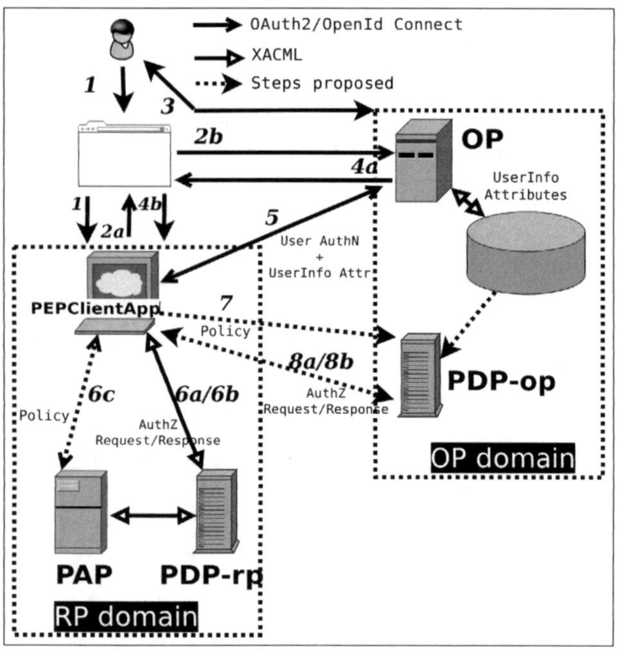

Figure 2. Prototype of the proposed architecture.

The PDP-rp evaluates the XACML request against the policies, which protect the services and resources. The PAP manages the access control policies for the RP.

In the security domain of OP, there were the following elements: OP, PDP-op, and *UserInfo*. The OP is the IdP provider, which will authenticate the end user and will provide claims about the user to the RP. The MITREid Connect [34] was defined for the IdP because it is an implementation of the OIDC standard. The PDP-op is the PDP point of the XACML architecture that evaluates the RP policies that are sent by the PEPClientApp. The *UserInfo* is the repository of end-user attributes, which are stored in a database, that enables both the OP and the PDP-op to retrieve attribute information.

The OpenAZ [35] is a reference implementation of the XACML 3.0 standard and it was chosen because it supports REST interfaces and JSON messages for communication among PDP, PAP, and PEP. This REST support makes it more easy to distribute the XACML points as RESTful Web services. It also enabled the integration of the XACML with the OIDC. The OpenAZ, MITREid Connect, and PEPClientApp are all open-source software based on the Java language, and they performed on the Tomcat Web server.

A. *Test Case*

The scenario used for this test case was based on an online bookstore that sells books and offers some other services. One service allows users to view and read books online from their catalog. However, there are titles that need different types of authorization because they are restricted material.

The bookstore adheres to an IdM and obtains the authentication result from an identity provider (IdP). The authorization system needs the following characteristics: policy-based, fine-grained controls, and dynamic management of access controls. In addition, the outsourced authentication and authorization need to adopt principles of RESTful architecture style. These requirements are complied by XACML 3.0 standard for fine-grained authorization and OpenID Connect for identity management.

The following fine-grained policy was defined to assess the use case and that was identified as P1: users authenticated by an IdP and whose residence is in either of Japan, China, or South Korea can view online books restricted by locality. Besides, the books are only available between December 1st and December 31, 2016. The policy is expressed in the XACML 3.0 language, which is deployed in PAP. It will protect the resources at RP domain besides other policies.

The steps in the test are described below. First, it was assumed that the end user "Jackie" was registered in the OP. And similarly, the RP identified as PEPClientApp was already registered as a client application in the same OP. The steps 1 to 4 are related to the phase of authentication of the end user to the OP. After that, a page of consent was presented to him.

The consent phase is shown in Fig. 3. It sets up the user's decision about his privacy. It is where the user has the power of choice on the release of personal attributes to the RP domain. In our example, the end user "Jackie" authorized the PEPClientApp to access resources on his behalf. However, he does not want to share his personal information with the RP. Thus, "Jackie" just chose to release the *sub* claim to RP, clicking in the option "login using your identity". The claim *sub* identifies the end user at the issuer (OP) and it is included in the assertion that OP sends to the RP.

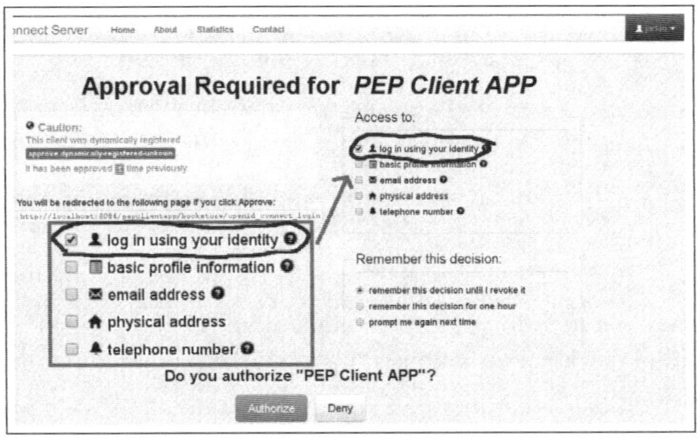

Figure 3. Screen of consent at OP.

The PEPClientApp generated a XACML request with the attributes available at RP. The request contains the attributes from resource, action, environment, and subject. The attributes of the subject contained only the identifier of OP and the identifier of subject ("subject-id"). The PEPClientApp sent the XACML request to the PDP-rp for an access control decision (step 6a). The PDP-rp evaluated the request against the applicable P1 XACML policy to renders an authorization decision. The main rule of P1 policy contains the element *Condition* that has two set of functions. The parameters are the attributes *country* and *current-dateTime*. However, the value of the attribute *country* was missing and was not available for evaluation by the PDP-rp. Thus, the PDP-rp returned the response "Indeterminate" with the status "missing-attribute" (step 6b). That resulted in a new authorization step.

The next phase is where the proposal of preserving privacy is included in the architecture. The XACML response included the identification of the policy and in sequence the PEPClientApp obtained it from PAP (step 6c). Considering that the targeted policy was sent to the cache of PDP-op (step 7), the PEPClientApp performed the same request to the RESTful endpoint of PDP-op (step 8a).

The PDP-op evaluated the request against the policy and arrived in the XACML *Condition*, which contained a function that needed the attribute *country*. Thus, the PDP-op consulted the PIP through Context Handler for the missing attribute. The PIP obtained a value for the attribute *country* making a query using the end user identified by *sub* in the *UserInfo* database. Then, the PDP-op evaluated the rule and arrived a decision. The response containing the decision "Permit" was returned to the PEPClientApp for enforcement (step 8b).

VI. Discussion

The results from the test case (Section V-A) showed that the architecture allowed an end user to access the protected resources without releasing personal attributes to the RP. In the test case, the end user "Jackie" has not released the attribute *country* to the RP. However, the PDP-op arrived at decision "Permit" because it obtained the value of attribute *country* from the OP domain. Summarizing, an architecture was proposed in this paper that transferred the authorization service from RP to the OP and that achieved the outcome of avoiding to release personal information to RP.

The prototype presented low complexity to implement the proposed architecture. Besides, there was no need to change flows and specifications of the OIDC and XACML. In contrast, the works and systems [14]-[20] that use private credentials have to deal with the complexity of the Public Key Infrastructure (PKI) and with questions related to integration, data formats, and user interfaces.

Organizations that collect and store PII data should establish security controls to provide the confidentiality of this information [36][37]. This represents an administrative and operational costs for those companies. However, when an organization can provide service without the need for personal attributes, it can minimize these costs. This is a benefit that can be achieved with the use of the proposed architecture.

The test case also demonstrated the usability of the prototype, because the end users did not need to establish privacy policies to manipulate their personal data. The users only needed to deny the release of attributes to protect their PII data. The outcome is that the SPs can modify their authorization logic without updating them in the agreement with the IdP. The proposals [23][24][30][31], which depend on the user's ability to define policies, may create risks to privacy of PII due to an increase in management complexity.

The aspects of confidentially, integrity, threats and security risks are directly related to the measures adopted when implementing the IdM infrastructure. If the architecture uses the OpenID Connect for IdM, as in the prototype, the security measures are those specified in the [10] and in the [38]. The [38] presents the threat model and security considerations when implementing systems and protocols that use the underlying protocol OAuth 2.0.

There is a potential limitation in the confidentiality concerning service provider policies in our work. There is a need of security mechanisms to protect the policy when it leaves the domain of RP, because it may contain sensitive information about the service provider. This problem can be minimized considering the trust relationship established between the OP and RP.

There is another issue that needs to be considered. The privacy feature of anonymity depends on the IdM system used in the architecture. Pseudonymity and anonymity can be obtained in OIDC by the use of Pairwise Pseudonymous Identifier (PPID) [10] for the value of *sub* claim. PPID is an identifier that identifies the end user to an RP that cannot be correlated with the end-user PPID at another RP. The PPID can be used in OIDC without any problem in the proposed architecture.

There is a performance limitation regarding the authorization actions. As the architecture included steps to evaluate the policy in the domain of OP, the decision time increases. Moreover, there are concerns regarding the runtime of the XACML policies. However, there are works [39][40] that aim to optimize PDP performance. In addition, the mechanism of caching can be used for the PDP and PAP points of the architecture. The question of performance can be considered a valid trade-off between user privacy and the performance penalty to get an authorization decision. The end user can assume the performance impact considering that the request can be denied in the absence of the proposed architecture.

VII. Conclusion and Future Work

The proposed architecture presents a new way of obtaining privacy to users, when dealing with fine-grained resource permissions. The SP policies are carried out and assessed in the domain of the IdP to avoid the release of personal attributes to SP domain. This approach allows users to deny the release of personal data to SP while getting a decision for accessing resources or services. The outcome of the architecture is the minimization of use, collection, and retention of personal data (PII), that attends the principle of collection limitation from OECD privacy guideline. Future work might go towards research on the inclusion of the decomposition of policies to protect the confidentiality of some elements of the policy.

REFERENCES

[1] K. Cameron. The laws of identity. [retrieved: March, 2017]. [Online]. Available: http://myinstantid.com/laws.pdf

[2] S. Gürses, C. Troncoso, and C. Diaz. (2011) Engineering privacy by design. [retrieved: March, 2017]. [Online]. Available: http://www.cosic.esat.kuleuven.be/publications/article-1542.pdf

[3] J. Heurix, P. Zimmermann, T. Neubauer, and S. Fenz, "A taxonomy for privacy enhancing technologies," *Computers & Security*, vol. 53, pp. 1–17, 2015.

[4] C. Landwehr *et al.*, "Privacy and cybersecurity: The next 100 years," *Proceedings of the IEEE*, vol. 100, no. Special Centennial Issue, pp. 1659–1673, May 2012.

[5] V. C. Hu *et al.*, "Guide to Attribute Based Access Control (ABAC) Definition and Considerations," *NIST SP 800-162*, 2014.

[6] J. Vollbrecht *et al.*, "AAA Authorization Framework," RFC 2904, Tech. Rep., August 2000.

[7] E. Rissanen, "eXtensible Access Control Markup Language (XACML) version 3.0 OASIS standard," January 2013.

[8] A. Pfitzmann and M. Hansen, "A terminology for talking about privacy by data minimization: Anonymity, unlinkability, undetectability, unobservability, pseudonymity, and identity management," 2010.

[9] D. Hardt, "The OAuth 2.0 Authorization Framework (RFC 6749)," RFC 6749, Internet Engineering Task Force, Proposed Standard, October 2012, [retrieved: March, 2017]. [Online]. Available: https://tools.ietf.org/html/rfc5849

[10] N. Sakimura, J. Bradley, M. B. Jones, B. d. de Medeiros, and C. Mortimore. (2014) OpenID Connect Core 1.0. [retrieved: March, 2017]. [Online]. Available: http://openid.net/specs/openid-connect-core-1_0.html

[11] EU, *Directive 95/46/EC of the European Parliament and of the Council*, 1995.

[12] S. A. Brands, *Rethinking public key infrastructures and digital certificates: building in privacy.* MIT Press, 2000.

[13] J. Camenisch and A. Lysyanskaya, "An efficient system for non-transferable anonymous credentials with optional anonymity revocation," in *Advances in Cryptology – EUROCRYPT 2001*, ser. Lecture Notes in Computer Science. Springer, 2001, vol. 2045, pp. 93–118.

[14] (2016) PRIME. The PRIME Consortium. [retrieved: December, 2016]. [Online]. Available: https://www.prime-project.eu/

[15] (2016) PrimeLife. PrimeLife Project Consortium. [retrieved: March, 2017]. [Online]. Available: http://primelife.ercim.eu/

[16] J. Camenisch and E. Van Herreweghen, "Design and Implementation of the Idemix Anonymous Credential System," in *Proceedings of the 9th ACM Conference on Computer and Communications Security*, ser. CCS '02. New York, NY, USA: ACM, 2002, pp. 21–30. [Online]. Available: http://doi.acm.org/10.1145/586110.586114

[17] Identity Mixer. IBM Research. [retrieved: March, 2017]. [Online]. Available: http://www.research.ibm.com/labs/zurich/idemix/

[18] U-Prove. Microsoft Research. [retrieved: March, 2017]. [Online]. Available: https://www.microsoft.com/en-us/research/project/u-prove/

[19] C. A. Ardagna *et al.*, "Enabling Privacy-preserving Credential-based Access Control with XACML and SAML," in *10th IEEE International Conference on Computer and Information Technology.* IEEE, 2010, pp. 1090–1095.

[20] P. Bichsel *et al.*, "H2.2 - ABC4Trust Architecture for Developers," *ABC4Trust*, 2013.

[21] J. Camenisch *et al.*, "Concepts and languages for privacy-preserving attribute-based authentication," *Journal of Information Security and Applications*, vol. 19, no. 1, pp. 25–44, 2014.

[22] ABC4Trust - Project description. ABC4Trust EU Project. [retrieved: March, 2017]. [Online]. Available: https://abc4trust.eu/download/ABC4Trust-Project-Description.pdf

[23] T. Hardjono, E. Maler, M. Machulak, and D. Catalano, "User-Managed Access (UMA) Profile of OAuth 2.0," Internet Engineering Task Force, Internet-Draft, January 2016, work in Progress.

[24] D. W. Chadwick and K. Fatema, "A privacy preserving authorisation system for the cloud," *Journal of Computer and System Sciences*, vol. 78, no. 5, pp. 1359–1373, 2012.

[25] D. Lin, P. Rao, E. Bertino, N. Li, and J. Lobo, "Policy decomposition for collaborative access control," in *Proceedings of the 13th ACM symposium on Access control models and technologies.* ACM, 2008, pp. 103–112.

[26] M. Decat, B. Lagaisse, and W. Joosen, "Toward Efficient and Confidentiality-aware Federation of Access Control Policies," in *Proceedings of the 7th Workshop on Middleware for Next Generation Internet Computing*, ser. MW4NG '12. New York, NY, USA: ACM, 2012, pp. 4:1–4:6. [Online]. Available: {http://doi.acm.org/10.1145/2405178.2405182}

[27] ——, "Middleware for efficient and confidentiality-aware federation of access control policies," *Journal of Internet Services and Applications*, vol. 5, no. 1, pp. 1–15, 2014. [Online]. Available: http://dx.doi.org/10.1186/1869-0238-5-1

[28] M. Erdos and S. Cantor, "Shibboleth architecture draft v05," *Internet2/MACE, May*, vol. 2, 2002.

[29] N. Ragouzis *et al.*, "Security Assertion Markup Language (SAML) v2.0 Technical Overview," 2008.

[30] J. Werner and C. Westphall, "A Model for Identity Management with Privacy in the Cloud," in *2016 IEEE Symposium on Computers and Communication (ISCC)*, Messina, Italy, June 2016, pp. 463–468.

[31] W. Ma and K. Sartipi, "Cloud-based Identity and Access Control for Diagnostic Imaging Systems," in *Proceedings of the International Conference on Security and Management (SAM).* Athens: The Steering Committee of The World Congress in Computer Science, Computer Engineering and Applied Computing (WorldComp), 2015, pp. 320–325.

[32] E. Maler, "Extending the Power of Consent with User-Managed Access," in *2015 IEEE Security and Privacy Workshops.* IEEE, May 2015, pp. 175–179.

[33] (2016) Shibboleth IdPv3 Consent Configuration. Shibboleth Consortium. [retrieved: March, 2017]. [Online]. Available: https://wiki.shibboleth.net/confluence/display/IDP30/ConsentConfiguration

[34] (2016) MITREid Connect. MIT Consortium for Kerberos and Internet Trust (MIT-KT). [retrieved: March, 2017]. [Online]. Available: http://kit.mit.edu/projects/mitreid-connect

[35] (2016) OpenAZ. [retrieved: March, 2017]. [Online]. Available: https://github.com/apache/incubator-openaz

[36] OECD, *Guidelines on the Protection of Privacy and Transborder Flows of Personal Data.* Organisation for Economic Co-operation and Development, 1981.

[37] E. McCallister, T. Grance, and K. Scarfone, "Guide to Protecting the Confidentiality of Personally Identifiable Information (PII)," *NIST SP 800-122*, 2010.

[38] T. L. (ed.), M. McGloin, and P. Hunt, "OAuth 2.0 Threat Model and Security Considerations (RFC 6819)," RFC 6819, Internet Engineering Task Force, Informational, January 2013, [retrieved: March, 2017]. [Online]. Available: {https://tools.ietf.org/html/rfc6819}

[39] S. Marouf, M. Shehab, A. Squicciarini, and S. Sundareswaran, "Adaptive reordering and clustering-based framework for efficient XACML policy evaluation," *IEEE Transactions on Services Computing*, vol. 4, no. 4, pp. 300–313, 2011.

[40] A. Mourad and H. Jebbaoui, "Towards efficient evaluation of XACML policies," in *Privacy, Security and Trust (PST), 2014 Twelfth Annual International Conference on.* IEEE, 2014, pp. 164–171.

Throughput Analysis in Cognitive Radio Networks with Imperfect Sensing Using Slotted Aloha and CSMA Protocols

Pedro Ivo de Almeida Guimarães
National Institute of Telecommunications-INATEL
Santa Rita do Sapucaí, Brazil
email: pedroguimaraes11@gmail.com

José Marcos Câmara Brito
National Institute of Telecommunications-INATEL
Santa Rita do Sapucaí, Brazil
email: brito@inatel.br

Abstract— **Cognitive radio is a promising technology for the next generation of wireless networks. Performance analysis of multiple access protocols in cognitive radio networks has been presented in the literature, but only considering the unreal situation of perfect channel sensing. In this paper, we extend an analytical model previously proposed to evaluate the performance of a cognitive radio network using Slotted Aloha and CSMA (Carrier Sense Multiple Access) multiple access protocols. In our new model, we consider imperfect channel sensing, resulting in more realistic performance analysis. After that, we investigate the influence of the parameters related to the performance of the channel sensing process in the performance of the network.**

Keywords— Cognitive Radio; Multiple Access; Imperfect sensing; Throughput; Performance analysis.

I. Introduction

Cognitive Radio (CR) is a new paradigm for the design of wireless communications systems, which aims to enhance the utilization of the Radio Frequency (RF) spectrum [1][2]. The motivation behind CR is the scarcity of radio frequency spectrum due to the increase in traffic in wireless networks. A study made by the Spectrum Policy Task Force (SPTF) of the Federal Communications Commission (FCC) has shown that some frequency bands are heavily used by licensed systems, in some particular locations and periods of time, but there are also many frequency bands that are only partly occupied or largely unoccupied [2]. A way to overcome these limitations is to promote changes in the current licensing model, by allowing secondary users (SUs) to access spectrum opportunities, also called spectrum holes, without causing harmful interference to the licensed users or primary users (PUs).

Cognitive Radio is defined as a radio that can change its transmission parameters based on the environment in which it is operating. The main functions of CR include spectral detection, spectrum management, spectral mobility and spectrum sharing [2]. Its paramount objective is to provide adaptability to wireless transmission systems through Dynamic Spectrum Access (DSA) in order to optimize the performance of the system and improve the use of spectrum.

The components of the cognitive radio network architecture can be classified into two groups: primary network and secondary network. The primary network is the licensed network infrastructure, which is authorized to exploit a certain band of the frequency spectrum. The secondary network is not licensed to operate in the designated band and its stations can access the spectrum in an opportunistic way, exploring the bands unused by PUs.

Medium Access Control (MAC) is a key issue in Cognitive Radio Networks (CRN). In the primary network, the MAC protocols are important in order to organize the access to the channel of different PUs. In the secondary network, the MAC protocols have the responsibility to organize the access of SUs to the idle channels of the primary network and prevent the licensed network from harmful interference [3].

In [3], the performance of CRN is analyzed for several MAC protocols, including the analysis that considers Slotted Aloha in the primary network and Slotted Carrier Sense Multiple Access (CSMA) in the secondary network. In these analyses, the capture effect is taken into account in the primary and secondary networks. However, the analyses presented in [3] do not consider the Packet Error Rate (PER) due to simultaneously transmission of two or more stations. This lack in the performance analysis has been solved by the extension presented in [4]. However, the analyses presented in [3] and [4] do not consider one important aspect, the imperfect sensing in the secondary network, and therefore can lead to unrealistic results. Thus, the main goal of this paper is to extend the analyses presented in [3] and [4], by considering the effect of imperfect sensing in the mathematical formulation.

The remainder of this paper is organized as follows: in Section II, we present the proposal of a new analytical model to compute the performance of the primary and secondary networks considering the effect of imperfect sensing; Section III presents numerical results and a comparison between the results obtained with our model with the results previously presented in [4]; the conclusions are given in Section IV.

II. The Proposed New System Model

In the network architecture considered in this paper, the primary network uses Slotted Aloha as multiple access protocol and the secondary network uses Slotted-CSMA. The primary access point (PAP) and the secondary access point (SAP) provide services for primary and secondary networks, respectively. In the primary network, there are N_p PUs and, among these, I_p stations are attempting to transmit their data packets during a time slot. On the other hand, the secondary network has N_s SUs and during a given time slot there are J_s SUs attempting to transmit their packets [3][4].

A. Structure of Time Slot and Mini-Slot

The channel is time slot based on the primary network and mini-slot based on the secondary network. So, each time slot of Slotted Aloha is subdivided into mini-slots. The duration of each mini-slot is equal to the maximum propagation delay (τ) found in the primary and secondary networks and corresponds to the distance from point *a* to *b* in Figure 1 [3][4].

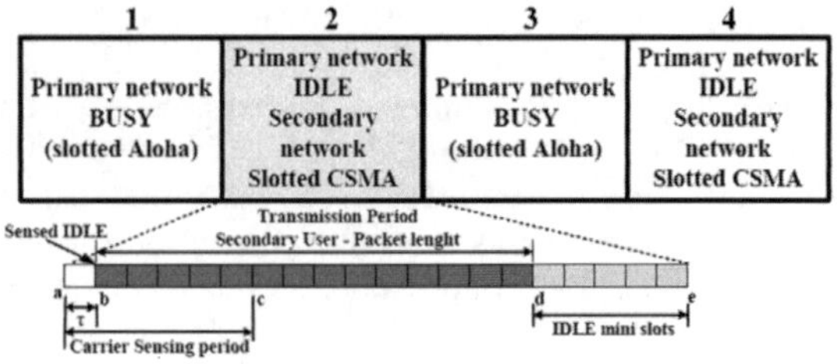

Figure 1. Slots structure of Slotted Aloha for primary users and Slotted CSMA for secondary users.

There are two types of mini-slots: a few intended for carrier sensing, defining the carrier sensing period (S_{mi}), and the most of them intended for packet transmissions, defining the transmission period (T_{mi}) to the SUs, as illustrated in Figure 1 [3][4]. According to Figure 1, the maximum sensing period allowed is from point *a*, i.e., in the beginning of a time slot, to point *c;* the sensing point is set to happen at the beginning of each mini-slot. The distance between point *c* and point *e* is specified as the maximum length of the data packets (T_{mi}) from the secondary network in terms of the number of mini-slots. Therefore, the packet length of the secondary network is shorter than the packet length of the primary network due to the carrier sensing period [3][4].

B. Fading Model for Primary and Secondary Network

In this paper, following [3] and [4], a quasi-static fading model is used, according to the Rayleigh statistical model, wherein the instantaneous power of the received signal have an exponential distribution, as represented by (1):

$$p(\delta) = \frac{1}{\Delta} e^{-\delta/\Delta}. \tag{1}$$

where Δ is the mean power of the received signal and δ is the instantaneous power of the received signal.

C. Channel Sensing

The spectral sensing is one of the most critical parts of the CRN. Before transmit, the secondary network performs channel sensing, which can be modeled as a hypothesis testing problem. We assumed that H_0 denotes the hypothesis that the channel is inactive, and H_1 denotes the hypothesis that the channel is active. Thus, $\hat{H}_0$ denotes the decision that there are not primary users in the channel and $\hat{H}_1$ denotes the decision that there are primary users in the channel. With the result of the decision and the true nature of the activity of the primary network, we can define the probability of a correct decision about the channel when a PU is active, given by (2), and the probability of false alarm when the primary network is inactive, given by (3) [5][6]:

$$P_d = \Pr\left[\hat{H}_1 \middle| H_1\right] \tag{2}$$

$$P_f = \Pr\left[\hat{H}_1 \middle| H_0\right] \tag{3}$$

D. The Interfering Model

In the model used in [4], denominated original model, the sensing process is considered perfect. As a consequence, if the primary network uses a time slot, the SUs do not transmit in that slot. Thus, only other PUs can interfere with the transmission of a given PU. Similarly, the SUs will transmit only in idle slots (slots without transmission of PUs) and, as a consequence, only other SUs can interfere with the transmission of a given SU. In the model proposed in this paper, we consider imperfect sensing, resulting in that SUs and PUs can transmit simultaneously and therefore can interfere with each other.

E. Traffic Model for the Primary and Secondary Network

During a time slot, any PU that is not in a retransmission state can generate a new packet with probability σ_p. Therefore, the probability that a PU does not generate any packet is $(1-\sigma_p)$. If a new packet is generated in the network, it is transmitted immediately in the next time slot. If the packet is not successfully transmitted during a time slot, it is retransmitted with probability σ_p in the following time slots until that packet is successfully transmitted. Users in the retransmission state cannot generate new data packets.

In the secondary network, using Slotted CSMA multiple access protocol, each SU can generate a new packet with probability (σ_{mi}) during a mini-slot. Consequently, the probability of an SU does not generate a new packet is ($1-\sigma_{mi}$). Whether an SU is in the retransmission state, it cannot generate a new packet. In the beginning of a time slot, the SAP senses the channel and decides if it is idle or busy by the PU. If the decision is given as busy, a SU with a packet to transmit does not use the channel, stores the packet in a buffer and try again to transmit the packet in the next time slot. If the SAP decision regarding of the channel is idle, an SU with a packet to transmit has permission to sense the channel in the next detection point inside the carrier detection period. If the decision of the SU is idle, the packet is transmitted immediately. If the decision of the SU is busy, the packet is stored in a buffer and the SU attempts to transmit it again in the next time slot. If an SU generates a packet outside of the carrier detection period, this packet is stored and the transmission is attempted in the next time slot. If an SU transmits a packet and a collision occur, the SU goes to the retransmission state and tries to retransmit the packet in the next time slot.

When the channel state is busy, the SAP and SU have P_{dSAP} and P_{dSU} as the detection probability of the channel state, respectively. However, if the channel state is idle, the

SAP and SU have P_{fSAP} and P_{fSU} as the probability of false alarm, respectively.

F. Probability of Secondary User Transmissions in a Given Time Slot

To compute the performance of primary and secondary networks, we need to calculate the probability mass function (PMF) of the number of SUs attempting to transmit in a given time slot.

The computation of the probability of J_s SUs attempting to transmit in a time slot ($P_{tx}(J_s)$) depends on the state of the channel. If the channel is busy, the transmission will only occur if the SAP miss detects the status of the channel, which occurs with probability $1-P_{dSAP}$, and the SU also miss detect the status of the channel, which occurs with probability $1-P_{dSU}$. If the channel is idle, the SU only transmits if the SAP correctly detects the status of the channel, with occurs with probability $1-P_{fSAP}$, and the SU also correctly detects the status of the channel, with occurs with probability $1-P_{fSU}$. In both hypotheses, channel busy or idle, this probability can be computed by (4), where $P_{SAP} = P_{dSAP}$ if the channel is busy and $P_{SAP} = P_{fSAP}$ if the channel is idle and $P_{SU} = P_{dSU}$ if the channel is busy and $P_{SU} = P_{fSU}$ if the channel is idle.

In (4), S_{mi} denotes the number of mini-slots that compose the carrier detection period, numbered from 0 to S_{mi-1}. The number of stations that will detect the carrier at the beginning of mini-slot i is equal to the number of stations that generated packets during the mini-slot $i-1$. The stations that generated packets in the S_{mi-1} mini-slot will detect the carrier in the beginning of the S_{mi} mini-slot, which already belongs to the transmission period. Still in (4), Bi $(i = 0,1,2 \ldots, S_{mi})$ denotes the maximum number of stations that can generate packets to be transmitted starting from the mini-slot i; X_i $(i = 0,1,2 \ldots, S_{mi})$ denotes the number of stations that effectively generated packets to be transmitted starting from the mini-slot i; j_i $(i = 0,1,2 \ldots, S_{mi})$ denotes the number of stations that missed detected the status of the channel and effectively transmitted starting from the mini-slot i. The other parameters define the limits in the sums and are defined in Table (1).

$$P_{tx}(J_s) = (1-P_{PAS}) \sum_{x_0=0}^{B_0=N_s} \sum_{j_0=C_0}^{D_0} \sum_{x_1=A_1}^{B_1} \sum_{j_1=C_1}^{D_1} \cdots \sum_{x_{s_{mi}-1}=A_{s_{mi}-1}}^{B_{s_{mi}-1}} \sum_{j_{s_{mi}-1}=C_{s_{mi}-1}}^{D_{s_{mi}-1}} \sum_{x_{s_{mi}}=A_{s_{mi}}}^{B_{s_{mi}}}$$
$$\left(\left(\binom{B_0}{x_0}\sigma_{mi}^{x_0}(1-\sigma_{mi})^{B_0-x_0}\right)\left(\binom{x_0}{j_0}(1-P_{SU})^{j_0}(P_{SU})^{x_0-j_0}\right)\right)$$
$$\left(\left(\binom{B_1}{x_1}\sigma_{mi}^{x_1}(1-\sigma_{mi})^{B_1-x_1}\right)\left(\binom{x_1}{j_1}(1-P_{SU})^{j_1}(P_{SU})^{x_1-j_1}\right)\right)\cdots$$
$$\left(\left(\binom{B_{s_{mi}-1}}{x_{s_{mi}-1}}\sigma_{mi}^{x_{s_{mi}-1}}(1-\sigma_{mi})^{B_{s_{mi}-1}-x_{s_{mi}-1}}\right)\left(\binom{x_{s_{mi}-1}}{j_{s_{mi-1}}}(1-P_{SU})^{j_{s_{mi-1}}}(P_{SU})^{x_{s_{mi}-1}-j_{s_{mi-1}}}\right)\right)$$
$$\left(\left(\binom{B_{s_{mi}}}{x_{s_{mi}}}\sigma_{mi}^{x_{s_{mi}}}(1-\sigma_{mi})^{B_{s_{mi}}-x_{s_{mi}}}\right)\left(\binom{x_{s_{mi}}}{j_{s_{mi}}}\left((1-P_{SU})^{j_{s_{mi}}}\right)(P_{SU})^{x_{s_{mi}}-j_{s_{mi}}}\right)\right). \quad (4)$$

TABLE 1. VALUES THAT THE LOWER AND UPPER BOUNDS CAN ASSUME IN EACH MINI-SLOT OF THE CARRIER SENSING PERIOD

Mini-Slots	Lower and Upper Bounds in the Packet generation	Lower and Upper Bounds in the Packet transmission
$N=1$	$A_0=0.$ $B_0=N_s$ $0 \leq x_0 \leq B_0$	*if* $(N_s - x_0) \geq J_s$ $C_0=0$ *else* $C_0 = J_s - (N_s - x_0).$ *if* $x_0 \leq J_s$ $D_0 = x_0$ *else* $D_0 = J_s$ $P_{SU} = P_f$ $C_0 \leq j_0 \leq D_0$
$N=2$	*If* $(Ns - x_0) \geq (Js - j_1)$ $A_1=0$ *Else* $A_1=(Js-j_1)-(Ns-x_0).$ $B_1=(Ns-x_0).$ $A_1 \leq x_1 \leq B_1$	*If* $(Ns - x_0 - x_1) \geq (J_s - J_0)$ $C_1=0$ *Else* $C_1 = (J_s - j_0) - (Ns - x_0 - x_1).$ *If* $x_1 \leq (J_s - j_0)$ $D_1 = x_1$ *Else* $D_1 = (J_s - j_0).$ *If* $j_0 > 0$ $P_{SU} = P_d$ *Else* $P_{SU} = P_f$ $\{C_1 \leq j_1 \leq D_1\}.$
…	…	….
$N=S_{mi}-1$	*if* $(Ns-x_0-x_1-\ldots x_{Smi-2}) \geq (Js-j_1-j_2-\ldots j_{Smi-2})$ $A_{Smi-1}=0$ *Else* $A_{Smi-1}=(Js-j_1-j_2-\ldots j_{Smi-2})-(Ns-x_0-x_1-\ldots x_{Smi-2}).$ $B_{Smi-1}=(Ns-x_0-x_1-\ldots x_{Smi-2}).$ $A_{Smi-1} \leq x_{Smi-1} \leq B_{Smi-1}$	*If* $(N_s - x_0 - x_1 - \ldots x_{Smi-2} + x_{Smi-1}) \geq (Js - j_0 - \ldots j_{Smi-2})$ $C_{Smi-1}=0$ *Else* $C_{Smi-1} = (J_s - j_0 - \ldots j_{Smi-2}) - (N_s - x_0 - x_1 - \ldots x_{Smi-2} + x_{Smi-1}).$ *If* $x_{Smi-1} \leq (J_s - j_0 - \ldots j_{Smi-2})$ $D_{Smi-1} = x_{Smi-1}$ *Else* $D_{Smi-1}=(Js-j_0-\ldots j_n + j_{Smi-2})$ For any of the j $(j_0, j_1, j_2 \ldots j_{Smi-2}) > 0$ $P_{SU}=(P_d)$ *Else* $P_{SU}=(P_f)$ $C_{Smi-1} \leq j_{Smi-1} \leq D_{Smi-1}$
$N= S_{mi}$	$\{A_{Smi}=Js-J_0-J_1-\ldots-j_{Smi-1}\}$ $B_{mi}=(Ns-x_1-x_2-\ldots x_{Smi-1})\}.$ $\{A_{Smi} \leq x_{Smi-1} \leq Bs_{mi}$	$\{C_{Smi}=Js-J_0-J_1-\ldots J_{Smi}\}$ For any of the j $(j_0, j_1, j_2 \ldots j_{Smi-1}) > 0$ $P_{SU}=(P_d)$ *Else* $P_{SU}=(P_f)$ $\{J_{Smi} = J_s - j_0 - j_1 - \ldots j_{Smi-1}\}$

To validate the PMF expressed by (4), we compare the results obtained with the equation with the results obtained using Monte Carlo simulation.

G. Power Level Applied in the Network

Let X_p and X_s be the mean values of instantaneous power of the concerned packet from primary and secondary networks, respectively. Let Y and Z be the mean values of the interfering powers of one packet from the primary and secondary networks, respectively. Following [3], we define $X_p=Y$ and $X_s=Z$. Having in mind that the SUs work with lower levels of transmission powers, in order to minimize interference in the PU's, denoting the relation between the powers in the primary and secondary networks by γ, we have [3]:

$$\gamma = \frac{X_p}{Z} = \frac{Y}{X_s}. \tag{5}$$

H. Analysis of the Capture Effect

According to [7], the signals arriving at the receiver have different power levels due to different transmission powers practiced by the users and also due to the fading in the wireless channel.

If the ratio between the received power of the concerned packet and the sum of the received powers of all interfering packets is greater than a given threshold, called capture ratio (R), then the concerned packet is captured by the access point.

The capture probabilities for the primary and secondary networks have been analyzed in [4] considering perfect sensing. In this paper, we modify the analyses presented in [4] in order to consider the effect of imperfect sensing.

In the primary network, if a given time slot is occupied by a PU, there are two scenarios in terms of interfering power: the SAP correctly detect the channel as occupied and the interfering power comes only from other PUs; the SAP miss detect the channel as idle and the interfering power comes from other PUs and also from SUs that miss detect the channel as idle too. In this latter case, the PMF of the number of SUs attempting to transmit in a given time slot is given by (4) considering that the channel is busy. Considering these scenarios, the capture probability can be computed by (6).

$$\mathrm{P}_{\mathrm{pcap}\rightarrow\mathrm{PAP}}(I_p,J_s) = \left(\frac{x_p}{\sum_{i=1}^{I_p-1} y_i + \sum_{j=1}^{J_s} z_j} > R\right) = \left[\left(\left(\frac{\gamma}{R+\gamma}\right)^{J_s} P_{tx}(J_s)\left(\frac{1}{R+1}\right)^{I_p-1}\right) + \left(\frac{1}{R+1}\right)^{I_p-1} P_{dSAP}\right] \tag{6}$$

In the secondary network, if a given time slot is occupied by a PU, there is a transmission from SUs only if the SAP and some SUs miss detect the channel as idle. In this case, the interfering power comes from PUs and other SUs; the PMF of the number of SUs attempting to transmit in a given time slot is given by (4) considering that the channel is busy. On the other hand, if a given time slot is idle, there are transmissions from SUs only if the SAP correctly detect the channel as idle and the transmissions come from SUs that correctly detect the channel as idle; the PMF of the number of SUs attempting to transmit in a given time slot is given by (4) considering that the channel is idle. Considering these scenarios, the capture probability can be computed by (7).

$$\mathrm{P}_{\mathrm{pcap}\rightarrow\mathrm{PAS}}(I_p,J_s) = \left(\frac{x_s}{\sum_{i=1}^{I_p} y_i + \sum_{j=1}^{J_s-1} z_j} > R\right) = \left(\left[\left(\frac{1}{R\gamma+1}\right)^{I_p} + \left(\frac{1}{R+1}\right)^{J_s-1} P_{tx(J_s)}\right] + \left(\frac{1}{R+1}\right)^{J_s-1} P_{tx(J_s)}\right) \tag{7}$$

I. Packet Error Rate Analysis

In this paper, following [4], the PER is calculated for a fading channel as a function of SIR, through the use of a fairly accurate upper bound presented in [8]. The SIR in the primary and secondary networks depends on the number of PUs and SUs attempting to transmit and are given, respectively, by (8) and (9), which I_p is the number of PUs attempting to transmit and J_s is the number of SUs attempting to transmit, whose PMF is given by (4).

$$\Delta_p = \frac{1}{(I_p - 1) + J_s/\gamma}, \tag{8}$$

$$\Delta_s = \frac{1}{\gamma I_p + J_s - 1}. \tag{9}$$

Let $f(\delta)$ be a function that relates the PER with the instantaneous SIR at the receiver in an Additive White Gaussian Noise Channel (AWGN), and $p(\delta)$ the probability density function of the SIR in the receiver, considering a Rayleigh channel, which has an exponential distribution, as represented in (1).

According to [8], the PER, represented by $P_{ave}(\Delta)$, can be calculated by (10):

$$P_{ave}(\Delta) = \int_0^{\infty} f(\delta) p(\delta) \, d\delta, \tag{10}$$

Considering the modulation techniques, packet lengths and coding schemes, it is difficult to compute (10) for a general case. An approximation is then proposed for the upper bound of the PER, according to the following inequality [8]:

$$P_{ave}(\Delta) \cong 1 - e^{-w_0/\Delta}. \tag{11}$$

The Packet Success Rate (PSR) is then given by:

$$PSR(\Delta) \cong e^{-w_0/\Delta}, \tag{12}$$

where w_0 is a constant value for Rayleigh channel and its value can be computed by [8]:

$$w_0 = \int_0^{\infty} f(\delta)\, d\delta. \tag{13}$$

Not considering channel coding and considering n-bit packets, $f(\delta)$ can then be obtained as follows [8]:

$$f(\delta) = \left\{1 - [1 - b(\delta)]^n\right\}, \tag{14}$$

where $b(\delta)$ is the BER in AWGN channels. Considering a BPSK modulation with coherent detection, $b(\delta)$ can be calculated by [8]:

$$b(\delta) = \frac{1}{2} erfc(\sqrt{\delta}). \tag{15}$$

Applying (15) in (14) and then (14) in (13), we can compute (using Mathcad software) w_0. Considering $n=127$ *bits* per packet, the same value used in [8], we obtain $w_0 = 3.4467$.

J. The Primary Network Throughput for the New model

The primary network throughput (V_{np}) is defined as the mean number of packets transmitted by the PUs and correctly received by the PAP during a time slot and can be computed by:

$$V_{np} \cong \left[\begin{array}{l} \left(\sum_{i=0}^{N_p} \binom{N_p}{i} \sigma_p^i (1-\sigma_p)^{N_p-i} .i\left[\left(\frac{1}{R+1}\right)^{i-1} .e^{-w_0(i-1)}(P_{dSAP})\right]\right) + \\ \left(\sum_{i=0}^{N_p}\sum_{Js=0}^{N_s} \binom{N_p}{i} \sigma_p^i (1-\sigma_p)^{N_p-i}. \right. \\ \left. .i\left[\left(\frac{1}{R+1}\right)^{i-1}\left(\frac{\gamma}{R+\gamma}\right)^{J_s} P_{tx(J_s)}.\, e^{-w_0\left(\left(\frac{J_s}{\gamma}\right)+(i-1)\right)}\right]\right) \end{array}\right] \tag{16}$$

K. The Secondary Network Throughput for the New Model

The definition of the secondary network throughput (V_{ns}) is similar to the definition for the primary network: the mean number of packets transmitted by the SUs and correctly received by the SAP during a time slot. However, to consider the overhead due to the detection period used by the CSMA protocol, it is necessary to consider an additional factor, which is the length of the packet in terms of mini-slots (T_{mi}) divided by the total number of mini-slots used in the transmission process, including both transmission period and carrier sensing period (T_{mi} + S_{mi}). The secondary network throughput can be computed by:

$$V_{ns} \cong \left[\begin{array}{l} \left[\frac{T_{mi}.(1-\sigma_p)^{N_p}}{T_{mi}+S_{mi}} .\sum_{J_s=0}^{N_s} J_s\left[\left(\frac{1}{R+1}\right)^{J_s-1} e^{-w_0(J_s-1)} P_{t(J_s)}\right]\right] + \\ \left[\frac{T_{mi}}{T_{mi}+S_{mi}} .\sum_{i=1}^{N_p}\sum_{J_s=0}^{N_s} \binom{N_p}{i} \sigma_p^i (1-\sigma_p)^{N_p-i}. \right. \\ \left. .J_s\left[\left(\left(\frac{1}{R\gamma+1}\right)^{i}\left(\frac{1}{R+1}\right)^{J_s-1} P_{t(J_s)}.\, e^{-w_0((i\gamma)+(J_s-1))}\right)\right]\right] \end{array}\right] \tag{17}$$

III. NUMERICAL RESULTS

The curves presented in Figures 2, 3, 4 and 5 show the throughput for the primary network and secondary network. They are plotted as a function of the primary traffic load, defined as $G_p = N_p\sigma_p$, considering the original model presented in [4] and the new model proposed here, which take into account the imperfect sensing of the channel. To compare the numerical results between the models, we considered the same parameters used in [4], i.e., $N_p=N_s=10$, $w_0=3.4467$, $\gamma=10$ and R=3 *dB*, $S_{mi}=5$ and $T_{mi}=10$. For the new model, we set additionally the values of P_{dSAP}, P_{dSU}, P_{fSAP} and P_{fSU} as specified in the figures.

In Figures 2 and 3, we plotted the throughput in the primary network varying P_{dSAP} and P_{dSU}, respectively. Analyzing the figures, we can conclude that the performance of primary network tends to decrease as the values of P_{dSAP} or P_{dSU} decreases. The results obtained with the original model are optimistic due to consider a perfect sensing process. Also, we can observe that the effect of imperfect sensing can not be neglected in the performance analysis of the system.

In Figure 4, we plotted the throughput in the secondary network varying P_{fSAP}. The performance of the network tends to decrease according to the value of P_{fSAP} increase. Comparing the models, it is verified that the original model presents an optimistic result in relation to the results obtained with the new model. Again, the effect of the imperfect sensing process can not be neglected in the performance analysis of the system.

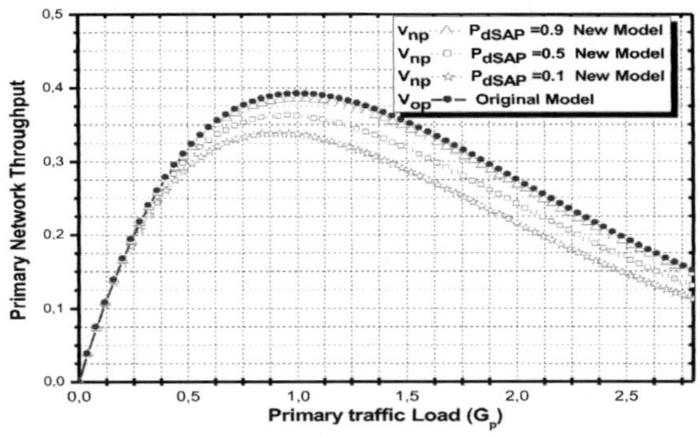

Figure 2. Influence of P_{dSAP} in the primary throughput with $P_{dSU}=0.9$.

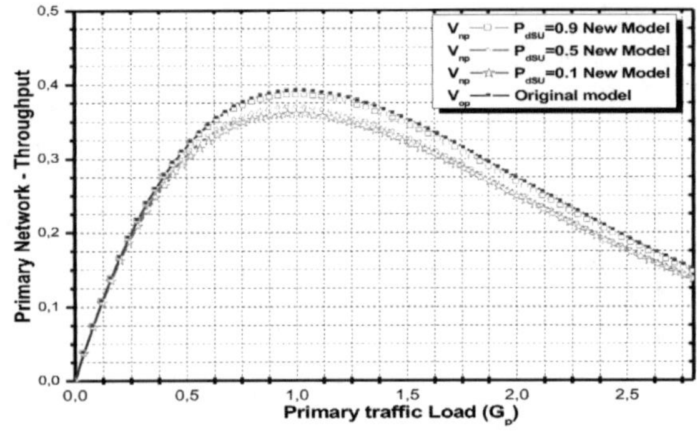

Figure 3. Influence of P_{dSU} in the primary throughput with $P_{dSAP}=0.9$.

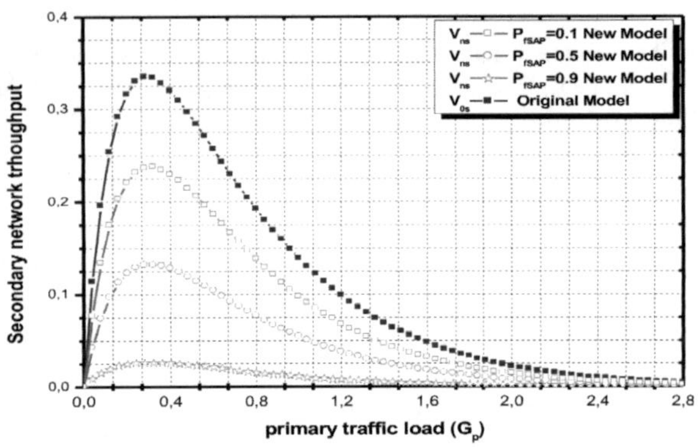

Figure 4. Influence of P_{fSAP} in the secondary network throughput with $P_{dSU}=P_{dSAP}=0.9$ and $P_{fSU}=0.1$.

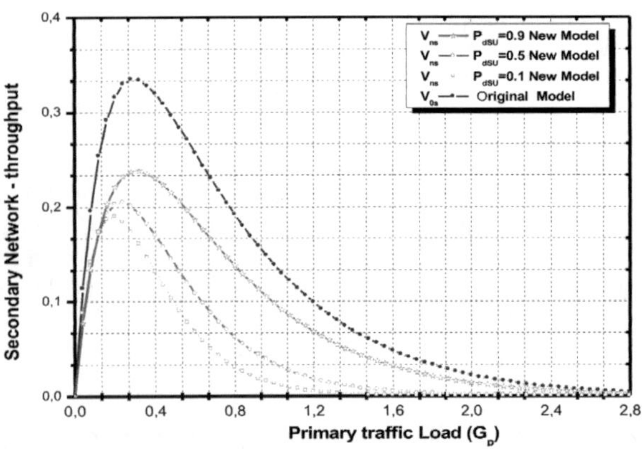

Figure 5. Influence of P_{dSU} in the secondary network throughput with $P_{dSAP}=0.9$ and $P_{fSU}=P_{fSAP}=0.1$.

In Figure 5, we plotted the throughput in the secondary network varying P_{dSU}. Analyzing the figure, we can conclude that the performance of the network tends to decrease as the value of P_{dSU} decreases. Once more, the original model presents an optimistic result in relation to the results obtained with the new model and the effects of the imperfect sensing process can not be neglected in the performance analysis of the network.

IV. CONCLUSIONS

In this paper, we extended the analysis presented in [4], considering the effect of imperfect sensing in the throughput of a cognitive radio network that uses Slotted Aloha and CSMA multiple access protocols in the primary and secondary network, respectively. We conclude that the throughput in the primary and secondary network reduces when we consider the effects of the imperfect sensing and, therefore, the effect of the imperfect sensing in the performance of the networks can not be neglected. Also, we analyze the influence of the parameters P_{dPAS}, P_{dSU} , P_{fPAS} and P_{fSU} in the performance of the system. As a future study, one can investigate the influence of channel coding and cooperative sensing techniques in the performance of the system. Also, one can analyze the performance of the system in terms of delay.

ACKNOWLEDGMENT

This work was partially supported by Finep, with resources from Funttel, Grant No. 01.14.0231.00, under the Radiocommunication Reference Center (*Centro de Referência em Radiocomunicações* - CRR) project of the National Institute of Telecommunications (*Instituto Nacional de Telecomunicações* - Inatel), Brazil.

REFERENCES

[1] F. Akyildiz, W. Lee, M. C. Vuran, and S. Mohanty, "Next Generation/Dynamic Spectrum Access/ Cognitive Radio Wireless Networks: A Survey," Computer Networks, Elsevier, vol. 50, pp. 2127- 2159, May 2006.

[2] E. Hossain, D. Niyato, and Z .Han, "Introduction to Cognitive Radio Dynamic Spectrum Access and Management in Cognitive Radio network", New York: Cambridge University Press, P.39-73. 2009.

[3] Z. Yang, "Investigations of Multiple Access Protocols in Cognitive Radio Networks", Ph.D. dissertation, Dept. of Elect. and Computer Engineering., Stevens Inst. of Technology, Hoboken, NJ. 2010.

[4] A. Faria and J.M.C. Brito, " A New Throughput Analysis in Cognitive Radio Networks Using Slotted CSMA", COCORA The Third International Conference on Advances in Cognitive Radio, 2013, 6 pages.

[5] G. Ozcan, M.C. Gursoy, and S. Gezici, "Error Rate Analysis of Cognitive Radio Transmissions with Imperfect Channel Sensing," IEEE Transactions on Wireless Communication vol. 13, pp.1642-1655 March 2014.

[6] D. S. Chaves, "Analysis of Spectral Sensing Power Detection", dissertation Master's dissertation in Electrical Engineering, Publishing PPGEE.DM-502/2012, Dep. of Engineering. Electrical. Univer. Of Brazilian, pp. 103, 2012.

[7] Y. Onozato, J. Liu, and S. Noguchi, "Stability of a Slotted Aloha system with Capture Effect," IEEE Transactions. on Vehicular Technology, vol. 38, February 1989, pp.31-36.

[8] Y. Xi, A. Burr, J. Wei, and D. Grace, "A General Upper Bound to Evaluate Packet Error Rate over Quasi-Static Fading Channels". IEEE Transactions on Wireless Communication, vol. 10, May 2011, pp. 1373-1377.

Recursive Least-Squares Algorithms for Echo Cancellation An Overview and Open Issues

Camelia Elisei-Iliescu and Constantin Paleologu

University Politehnica of Bucharest
Bucharest, Romania
Email: pale@comm.pub.ro

Abstract—**The recursive least-squares (RLS) algorithm is very popular in many applications of adaptive filtering, especially due to its fast convergence rate. However, the computational complexity of this algorithm represents a major limitation in some applications that involve high length adaptive filters, like echo cancellation. Moreover, the specific features of this application require good tracking capabilities and double-talk robustness for the adaptive algorithm, which further implies an optimization process on its parameters. In case of most RLS-based algorithms, the performance can be controlled in terms of two main parameters, i.e., the forgetting factor and the regularization term. The goal of this paper is to outline the influence of these parameters on the overall performance of the RLS algorithms and to present several solutions to control their behavior, taking into account the specific requirements of echo cancellation application.**

Keywords–Adaptive filters; Echo cancellation; Recursive least-squares (RLS) algorithm.

I. INTRODUCTION

The recursive least-squares (RLS) algorithm [1][2] is one of the most popular adaptive filters. As compared to the normalized least-mean-square (NLMS) algorithm [1][2], the RLS offers a superior convergence rate especially for highly correlated input signals. Of course, there is a price to pay for this advantage, which is an increase in the computational complexity. For this reason, it is not very often involved in echo cancellation [3][4], where high length adaptive filters (e.g., hundreds of coefficients) are required.

The performance of the RLS algorithm is mainly controlled by two important parameters, i.e., the forgetting factor and the regularization term. Similar to the attributes of the step-size from the NLMS-based algorithms, the performance of RLS-type algorithms in terms of convergence rate, tracking, misadjustment, and stability depends on the forgetting factor [1][2]. The classical RLS algorithm uses a constant forgetting factor (between 0 and 1) and needs to compromise between the previous performance criteria. When the forgetting factor is very close to one, the algorithm achieves low misadjustment and good stability, but its tracking capabilities are reduced [5]. A small value of the forgetting factor improves the tracking but increases the misadjustment, and could affect the stability of the algorithm [6]. Motivated by these aspects, a number of variable forgetting factor RLS (VFF-RLS) algorithms have been developed, e.g., [7]–[10] (and references therein).

It should be mentioned that in the context of system identification (like in echo cancellation), where the output of the unknown system is corrupted by another signal (which is usually an additive noise), the goal of the adaptive filter is not to make the error signal goes to zero, because this will introduce noise in the adaptive filter. The objective instead is to recover the "corrupting signal" from the error signal of the adaptive filter after this one converges to the true solution. This was the approach behind the VFF-RLS algorithm proposed in [9], which is analyzed in Section II.

As compared to the forgetting factor, the regularization parameter has been less addressed in the literature. Apparently, it is required in matrix inversion when this matrix is ill conditioned, especially in the initialization stage of the algorithm. However, its role is of great importance in practice, since regularization is a must in all ill-posed problems (like in adaptive filtering), especially in the presence of additive noise [11]–[14]. Consequently, in Section III, we focus on the regularized RLS algorithm [2]. Following the development from [12], a method to select an optimal regularization parameter is presented, so that the algorithm could behave well in all noisy conditions. Since the value of this parameter is related to the echo-to-noise ratio (ENR), a simple and practical way to estimate the ENR in practice is also presented, which leads to a variable-regularized RLS (VR-RLS) algorithm.

The simulation results (presented in Section IV) are performed in the context of echo cancellation and support the theoretical findings. Finally, the conclusions are outlined in Section V, together with some open issues related to future works.

II. VARIABLE FORGETTING FACTOR RLS ALGORITHM

Let us consider a system identification problem (like in echo cancellation), where the desired signal at the discrete-time index n is obtained as

$$\begin{aligned} d(n) &= \mathbf{h}^T\mathbf{x}(n) + v(n) \\ &= y(n) + v(n), \end{aligned} \quad (1)$$

where $\mathbf{h} = [\ h_0 \quad h_1 \quad \cdots \quad h_{L-1}\ ]^T$ is the impulse response (of length L) of the system that we need to identify (i.e., the echo path), superscript ^{T} denotes transpose of a vector or a matrix,

$$\mathbf{x}(n) = [\ x(n) \quad x(n-1) \quad \cdots \quad x(n-L+1)\ ]^T \quad (2)$$

is a vector containing the most recent L samples of the zero-mean input signal $x(n)$ (i.e., the far-end signal), $v(n)$ is a zero-mean additive noise signal [which is independent of $x(n)$], and $y(n)$ represents the output of the unknown system (i.e., the echo signal). In the context of echo cancellation, the output of the echo path could be also corrupted by the near-end speech (besides the background noise), which is usually known as the double-talk scenario [3][4]. The main objective is to estimate or identify $\mathbf{h}$ with an adaptive filter $\widehat{\mathbf{h}}(n) = \left[\ \widehat{h}_0(n)\ \ \widehat{h}_1(n)\ \ \cdots\ \ \widehat{h}_{L-1}(n)\ \right]^T$.

Using the previous notation we may define the a priori error signal as

$$\begin{aligned} e(n) &= d(n) - \mathbf{x}^T(n)\widehat{\mathbf{h}}(n-1) \\ &= \mathbf{x}^T(n)\left[\mathbf{h} - \widehat{\mathbf{h}}(n-1)\right] + v(n). \end{aligned} \tag{3}$$

In this context, the relations that define the classical RLS algorithm are:

$$\mathbf{k}(n) = \frac{\mathbf{P}(n-1)\mathbf{x}(n)}{\lambda + \mathbf{x}^T(n)\mathbf{P}(n-1)\mathbf{x}(n)}, \tag{4}$$

$$\widehat{\mathbf{h}}(n) = \widehat{\mathbf{h}}(n-1) + \mathbf{k}(n)e(n), \tag{5}$$

$$\mathbf{P}(n) = \frac{1}{\lambda}\left[\mathbf{P}(n-1) - \mathbf{k}(n)\mathbf{x}^T(n)\mathbf{P}(n-1)\right], \tag{6}$$

where λ $(0 < \lambda \leq 1)$ is the exponential forgetting factor, $\mathbf{k}(n)$ is the Kalman gain vector, $\mathbf{P}(n)$ is the estimate of the inverse of the input correlation matrix, and $e(n)$ is the a priori error signal defined in (3). The a posteriori error signal can be defined using the adaptive filter coefficients at time n, i.e.,

$$\begin{aligned} \varepsilon(n) &= d(n) - \mathbf{x}^T(n)\widehat{\mathbf{h}}(n) \\ &= \mathbf{x}^T(n)\left[\mathbf{h} - \widehat{\mathbf{h}}(n)\right] + v(n), \end{aligned} \tag{7}$$

Using (3) and (5) in (7), it results in

$$\varepsilon(n) = e(n)\left[1 - \mathbf{x}^T(n)\mathbf{k}(n)\right]. \tag{8}$$

In the framework of system identification, it is desirable to recover the system noise from the error signal [5]. Consequently, we can impose the condition:

$$E\left[\varepsilon^2(n)\right] = \sigma_v^2, \tag{9}$$

where $E[\cdot]$ denotes mathematical expectation and $\sigma_v^2 = E\left[v^2(n)\right]$ is the power of the system noise. Furthermore, using (9) in (8) and taking (4) into account, it finally results in

$$E\left\{\left[1 - \frac{\theta(n)}{\lambda(n) + \theta(n)}\right]^2\right\} = \frac{\sigma_v^2}{\sigma_e^2(n)}, \tag{10}$$

where $\theta(n) = \mathbf{x}^T(n)\mathbf{P}(n-1)\mathbf{x}(n)$. In (10), we assumed that the input and error signals are uncorrelated, which is true when the adaptive filter has started to converge to the true solution. We also assumed that the forgetting factor is deterministic and time dependent. By solving the quadratic equation (10), it results a variable forgetting factor

$$\lambda(n) = \frac{\sigma_\theta(n)\sigma_v}{\sigma_e(n) - \sigma_v}, \tag{11}$$

where $E\left[\theta^2(n)\right] = \sigma_\theta^2(n)$. In practice, the variance of the error signal can be recursively estimated based on

$$\widehat{\sigma}_e^2(n) = \alpha\widehat{\sigma}_e^2(n-1) + (1-\alpha)e^2(n), \tag{12}$$

where $\alpha = 1 - 1/(KL)$, with $K \geq 1$. The variance of $\theta(n)$ is evaluated in a similar manner, i.e.,

$$\widehat{\sigma}_\theta^2(n) = \alpha\widehat{\sigma}_\theta^2(n-1) + (1-\alpha)\theta^2(n). \tag{13}$$

The estimate of the noise power, $\widehat{\sigma}_v^2(n)$ [which should be used in (11) from practical reasons], can be estimated in different ways, e.g., [9][15][16].

Theoretically, $\sigma_e(n) \geq \sigma_v$ in (11). Compared to the NLMS algorithm (where there is the gradient noise, so that $\sigma_e(n) > \sigma_v$), the RLS algorithm with $\lambda(n) \approx 1$ leads to $\sigma_e(n) \approx \sigma_v$. In practice (since power estimates are used), several situations have to be prevented in (11). Apparently, when $\widehat{\sigma}_e(n) \leq \widehat{\sigma}_v$, it could be set $\lambda(n) = \lambda_{\max}$, where $\lambda_{\max}$ is very close or equal to 1. But this could be a limitation, because in the steady-state of the algorithm $\widehat{\sigma}_e(n)$ varies around $\widehat{\sigma}_v$. A more reasonable solution is to impose that $\lambda(n) = \lambda_{\max}$ when

$$\widehat{\sigma}_e(n) \leq \rho\widehat{\sigma}_v, \tag{14}$$

with $1 < \rho \leq 2$. Otherwise, the forgetting factor of the VFF-RLS algorithm [9] is evaluated as

$$\lambda(n) = \min\left[\frac{\widehat{\sigma}_\theta(n)\widehat{\sigma}_v(n)}{\zeta + |\widehat{\sigma}_e(n) - \widehat{\sigma}_v(n)|}, \lambda_{\max}\right], \tag{15}$$

where the small positive constant ζ prevents a division by zero. Before the algorithm converges or when there is an abrupt change of the system, $\widehat{\sigma}_e(n)$ is large as compared to $\widehat{\sigma}_v(n)$; thus, the parameter $\lambda(n)$ from (15) takes low values, providing fast convergence and good tracking. When the algorithm converges to the steady-state solution, $\widehat{\sigma}_e(n) \approx \widehat{\sigma}_v(n)$ [so that condition (14) is fulfilled] and $\lambda(n)$ is equal to $\lambda_{\max}$, providing low misadjustment. It can be noticed that the mechanism that controls the forgetting factor is very simple and not expensive in terms of multiplications and additions.

III. Variable Regularized RLS Algorithm

In this section, a different version of the RLS algorithm is presented, which allow us to outline the importance of the regularization parameter. Let us consider the regularized least-squares criterion:

$$J(n) = \sum_{i=0}^{n}\lambda^{n-i}\left[d(i) - \widehat{\mathbf{h}}^T(n)\mathbf{x}(i)\right]^2 + \delta\left\|\widehat{\mathbf{h}}(n)\right\|_2, \tag{16}$$

where λ is the same exponential forgetting factor, δ is the regularization parameter, and $\|\cdot\|_2$ is the ℓ_2 norm. From (16), the update of the regularized RLS algorithm [2] results in

$$\widehat{\mathbf{h}}(n) = \widehat{\mathbf{h}}(n-1) + \left[\widehat{\mathbf{R}}_{\mathbf{x}}(n) + \delta\mathbf{I}_L\right]^{-1}\mathbf{x}(n)e(n), \tag{17}$$

where

$$\begin{aligned} \widehat{\mathbf{R}}_{\mathbf{x}}(n) &= \sum_{i=0}^{n}\lambda^{n-i}\mathbf{x}(i)\mathbf{x}^T(i) \\ &= \lambda\widehat{\mathbf{R}}_{\mathbf{x}}(n-1) + \mathbf{x}(n)\mathbf{x}^T(n) \end{aligned} \tag{18}$$

is an estimate of the correlation matrix of $\mathbf{x}(n)$ at time n, $\mathbf{I}_L$ is the identity matrix of size $L \times L$, and

$$\begin{aligned} e(n) &= d(n) - \widehat{\mathbf{h}}^T(n-1)\mathbf{x}(n) \\ &= d(n) - \widehat{y}(n) \end{aligned} \tag{19}$$

is the a priori error signal as defined in (3); the signal $\widehat{y}(n)$ represents the output of the adaptive filter, which should be an estimate of the echo signal. We will assume that the matrix $\widehat{\mathbf{R}}_{\mathbf{x}}(n)$ has full rank, although it can be very ill conditioned. As a result, if there is no noise, regularization is not really required; however, the more the noise, the larger should be the value of δ.

Summarizing, the regularized RLS algorithm is defined by the relations (17)–(19). In the following, we present one reasonable way to find the regularization parameter δ. It can be noticed that the update equation of the regularized RLS can be rewritten as [12]

$$\widehat{\mathbf{h}}(n) = \mathbf{Q}(n)\widehat{\mathbf{h}}(n-1) + \widetilde{\mathbf{h}}(n), \tag{20}$$

where

$$\mathbf{Q}(n) = \mathbf{I}_L - \left[\widehat{\mathbf{R}}_{\mathbf{x}}(n) + \delta \mathbf{I}_L\right]^{-1} \mathbf{x}(n)\mathbf{x}^T(n) \tag{21}$$

and

$$\widetilde{\mathbf{h}}(n) = \left[\widehat{\mathbf{R}}_{\mathbf{x}}(n) + \delta \mathbf{I}_L\right]^{-1} \mathbf{x}(n)d(n) \tag{22}$$

is the correctiveness component of the algorithm, which depends on the new observation $d(n)$. In this context, we can notice that $\mathbf{Q}(n)$ does not depend on the noise signal and $\mathbf{Q}(n)\widehat{\mathbf{h}}(n-1)$ in (20) can be seen as a good initialization of the adaptive filter. In fact, (22) is the solution of the noisy linear system of L equations:

$$\left[\widehat{\mathbf{R}}_{\mathbf{x}}(n) + \delta \mathbf{I}_L\right] \widetilde{\mathbf{h}}(n) = \mathbf{x}(n)d(n). \tag{23}$$

Let us define

$$\widetilde{e}(n) = d(n) - \widetilde{\mathbf{h}}^T(n)\mathbf{x}(n), \tag{24}$$

the error signal between the desired signal and the estimated signal obtained from the filter optimized in (22). Consequently, we could find δ in such a way that the expected value of $\widetilde{e}^2(n)$ is equal to the variance of the noise, i.e.,

$$E\left[\widetilde{e}^2(n)\right] = \sigma_v^2. \tag{25}$$

This is reasonable if we want to attenuate the effects of the noise in the estimator $\widetilde{\mathbf{h}}(n)$.

For the sake of simplicity, let us assume that $x(n)$ is stationary and white. Apparently, this assumption is quite restrictive, even if it was widely used in many developments in the context of adaptive filtering [1][2]. However, the resulting VR-RLS algorithm will still use the full matrix $\widehat{\mathbf{R}}_{\mathbf{x}}(n)$ and, consequently, it will inherit the good performance feature of the RLS family in case of correlated inputs. In this case and for n large enough (also considering that the forgetting factor λ is on the order of $1 - 1/L$), we have

$$\begin{aligned}\left[\widehat{\mathbf{R}}_{\mathbf{x}}(n) + \delta \mathbf{I}_L\right] &\approx \left[\frac{\sigma_x^2}{1-\lambda} + \delta\right] \mathbf{I}_L \\ &\approx \left[L\sigma_x^2 + \delta\right] \mathbf{I}_L \end{aligned}\tag{26}$$

and $\mathbf{x}^T(n)\mathbf{x}(n) \approx L\sigma_x^2$, where $\sigma_x^2 = E\left[x^2(n)\right]$ is the variance of the input signal. Next, from (1), we can define the echo-to-noise ratio (ENR) as

$$\text{ENR} = \frac{\sigma_y^2}{\sigma_v^2}, \tag{27}$$

where $\sigma_y^2 = E\left[y^2(n)\right]$ is the variance of $y(n)$. Developing (25) and based on the previous approximations, we obtain the quadratic equation:

$$\delta^2 - 2\frac{L\sigma_x^2}{\text{ENR}}\delta - \frac{\left(L\sigma_x^2\right)^2}{\text{ENR}} = 0, \tag{28}$$

with the obvious solution:

$$\begin{aligned}\delta &= \frac{L\left(1+\sqrt{1+\text{ENR}}\right)}{\text{ENR}}\sigma_x^2 \\ &= \beta\sigma_x^2, \end{aligned}\tag{29}$$

where

$$\beta = \frac{L\left(1+\sqrt{1+\text{ENR}}\right)}{\text{ENR}} \tag{30}$$

is the normalized regularization parameter of the RLS algorithm.

As we can notice from (29), the regularization parameter δ depends on three elements, i.e., the length of the adaptive filter, the variance of the input signal, and the ENR. In most applications, the first two elements (L and σ_x^2) are known, while the ENR can be estimated. Using a proper evaluation of the ENR, the algorithm should own good robustness features against the additive noise.

Let us assume that the adaptive filter has converged to a certain degree, so that we can use the approximation

$$y(n) \approx \widehat{y}(n). \tag{31}$$

Hence,

$$\sigma_y^2 \approx \sigma_{\widehat{y}}^2, \tag{32}$$

where $\sigma_{\widehat{y}}^2 = E\left[\widehat{y}^2(n)\right]$. Since the output of the unknown system and the noise can be considered uncorrelated, (1) can be expressed in terms of power estimates as

$$\sigma_d^2 = \sigma_y^2 + \sigma_v^2, \tag{33}$$

where $\sigma_d^2 = E\left[d^2(n)\right]$. Using (32) in (33), we obtain

$$\sigma_v^2 \approx \sigma_d^2 - \sigma_{\widehat{y}}^2. \tag{34}$$

The power estimates can be evaluated in a recursive manner as

$$\widehat{\sigma}_d^2(n) = \alpha\widehat{\sigma}_d^2(n-1) + (1-\alpha)d^2(n), \tag{35}$$

$$\widehat{\sigma}_{\widehat{y}}^2(n) = \alpha\widehat{\sigma}_{\widehat{y}}^2(n-1) + (1-\alpha)\widehat{y}^2(n), \tag{36}$$

where $\alpha = 1 - 1/(KL)$, with $K \geq 1$ [similar to (12) and (13)]. Therefore, based on (32), (34), and (35), an estimation of the ENR is obtained as

$$\widehat{\text{ENR}}(n) = \frac{\widehat{\sigma}_{\widehat{y}}^2(n)}{\left|\widehat{\sigma}_d^2(n) - \widehat{\sigma}_{\widehat{y}}^2(n)\right|}, \tag{37}$$

so that the variable regularization parameter results in

$$\begin{aligned}\delta(n) &= \frac{L\left[1+\sqrt{1+\widehat{\text{ENR}}(n)}\right]}{\widehat{\text{ENR}}(n)}\sigma_x^2 \\ &= \beta(n)\sigma_x^2, \end{aligned}\tag{38}$$

where

$$\beta(n) = \frac{L\left[1+\sqrt{1+\widehat{\text{ENR}}(n)}\right]}{\widehat{\text{ENR}}(n)} \tag{39}$$

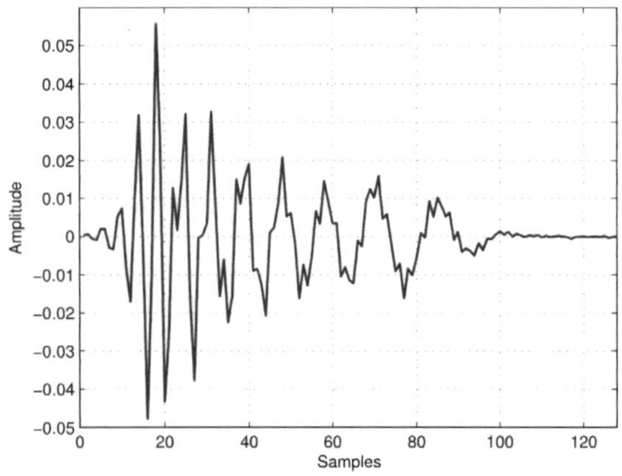

Figure 1. Impulse response used in simulations (the fourth echo path from G168 Recommendation [17]).

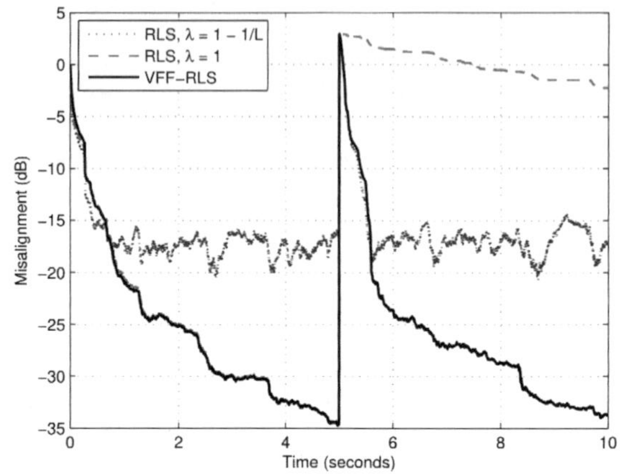

Figure 2. Misalignment of the RLS algorithm (using different constant values of the forgetting factor) and VFF-RLS algorithm in a single-talk scenario, including echo path change.

is the variable normalized regularization parameter. Consequently, based on (38), we obtain a variable-regularized RLS (VR-RLS) algorithm, with the update:

$$\widehat{\mathbf{h}}(n) = \widehat{\mathbf{h}}(n-1) + \left[\widehat{\mathbf{R}}_{\mathbf{x}}(n) + \delta(n)\mathbf{I}_L\right]^{-1} \mathbf{x}(n)e(n), \quad (40)$$

where $\widehat{\mathbf{R}}_{\mathbf{x}}(n)$ is recursively evaluated according to (18) and $\delta(n)$ is computed based on (35)–(38).

Finally, some practical issues should be outlined. The absolute values in (37) prevent any minor deviations (due to the use of power estimates) from the true values, which can make the denominator negative. It is a non-parametric algorithm, since all the parameters in (37) are available. Also, good robustness against the additive noise variations is expected. The main drawback is due to the approximation in (32). This assumption will be biased in the initial convergence phase or when there is a change of the unknown system. Concerning the initial convergence, we can use a constant regularization parameter δ in the first steps of the algorithm (e.g., in the first L iterations).

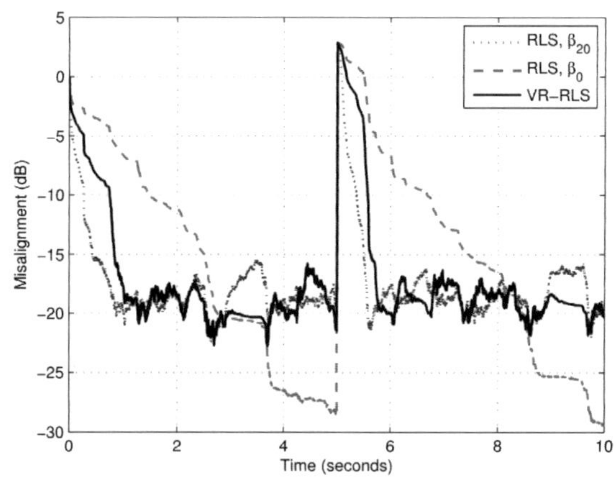

Figure 3. Misalignment of the regularized RLS algorithm (using different constant values of the regularization parameter) and VR-RLS algorithm in a single-talk scenario, including echo path change.

IV. Simulation Results

Let us consider a network echo cancellation scenario, in the framework of G168 Recommendation [17]. The echo path is depicted in Figure 1; it is the fourth impulse response (of length $L = 128$) from the above recommendation. The sampling rate is 8 kHz. All adaptive filters used in the experiments have the same length as the echo path. The far-end signal (i.e., the input signal) is a speech signal. The output of the echo path is corrupted by an independent white Gaussian noise with 20 dB ENR. An echo path change scenario is some experiments (in order to evaluate the tracking capabilities of the algorithms), by shifting the impulse response to the right by 8 samples in the middle of simulation. The performance measure is the normalized misalignment (in dB) evaluated as

$$\text{Mis}(n) = 20\log_{10}\frac{\left\|\mathbf{h}(n) - \widehat{\mathbf{h}}(n)\right\|_2}{\left\|\mathbf{h}(n)\right\|_2}. \quad (41)$$

In the first the experiment, the performance of the VFF-RLS algorithm (presented in Section II) is evaluated, as compared to the classical RLS algorithm defined in (4)–(6), which uses different constant values of the forgetting factor. A single-talk case is considered and the echo path changes in the middle of simulation. It can be noticed in Figure 2 that the VFF-RLS algorithm achieves the same initial misalignment as the RLS with its maximum forgetting factor, but it tracks as fast as the RLS with the smaller forgetting factor. As expected, the classical RLS algorithm using constant forgetting factors has to compromise between these performance criteria, i.e., the larger the value of λ, the better the misalignment level but worse the tracking capability.

Next, the performance of the VR-RLS algorithm (from Section III) is investigated, as compared to the regularized RLS algorithm defined in (17)–(19), using different constant values of the regularization parameter. In real-world applications, the value of ENR is not available. However, based on

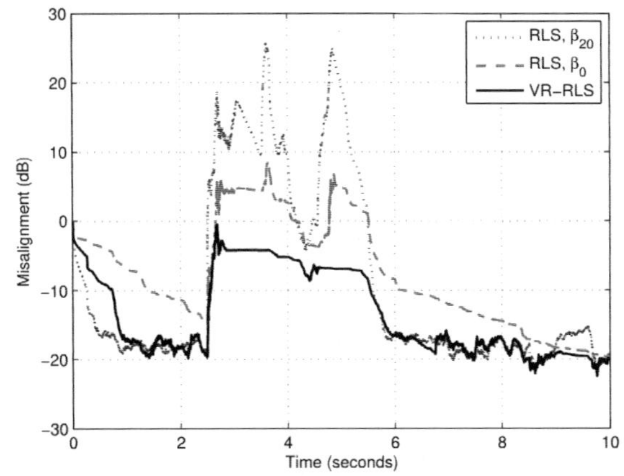

Figure 4. Misalignment of the regularized RLS algorithm (using different constant values of the regularization parameter) and VR-RLS algorithm in a double-talk scenario.

(30), we can determine the values of the optimal normalized regularization parameter of the RLS algorithm for different cases; for example, let us consider two values of the ENR, i.e., 20 dB (the true one) and 0 dB. Using appropriate notation, we obtain $\beta_{20} = 14.14$ and $\beta_0 = 309.01$, respectively. In the next set of experiments, we compare the regularized RLS algorithm using these constant regularization parameters with the VR-RLS algorithm. The constant forgetting factor is set to $\lambda = 1 - 1/(3L)$ for all the algorithms.

In Figure 3, a single-talk scenario is considered and an echo path change is introduced in the middle of the simulation. It can be noticed that the VR-RLS algorithm behaves similarly to the RLS algorithm using the constant parameter β_{20}, which is associated to the value of the true ENR. Also, it can be noticed that a larger value of the normalized regularization parameter (β_0) improves the misalignment but affects the convergence rate and tracking.

In Figure 4, a double-talk scenario [3][4] is considered. The near-end speech appears between time 2.5 and 5 seconds, so that the signal $v(n)$ is now non-stationary, since it contains both noise and speech. It is clear that the VR-RLS algorithm is more robust in this case as compared to the regularized RLS using constant values of β. It should be outlined that we do not use any double-talk detector (DTD) [3][4] with the VR-RLS algorithm, which is the regular approach in a double-talk situation. Therefore, the VR-RLS algorithm owns good robustness features against double-talk, which is an important gain in practice.

V. Conclusions and Perspectives

The RLS algorithms are very appealing due to their fast convergence rate. In this paper, we have focused on the main parameters that control the performance of these algorithms, i.e., the forgetting factor and the regularization term. In order to achieve a better compromise between the performance criteria (i.e., convergence and tracking versus misadjustment and robustness), these parameters could be controlled. In this context, the solutions presented in Sections II and III led to the VFF-RLS and VR-RLS algorithms, respectively.

The experiments were performed in the context of echo cancellation, which is a very challenging system identification problem. According to the simulation results, the VFF-RLS and VR-RLS algorithms perform very well as compared to their classical counterparts (which use constant values of the key parameters). On the other hand, the complexity of the RLS-based algorithms is $O(L^2)$, which represents a problematic issue for high values of L (like in echo cancellation). The alternative is to combine these VFF and VR methods with low-complexity versions of the RLS algorithm, e.g., [18]. Also, another interesting issue to address in future works could be a combination between the VFF and VR approaches, in order to inherent the advantages of both methods.

Acknowledgment

This work was supported by UEFISCDI Romania under Grant PN-II-RU-TE-2014-4-1880.

References

[1] S. Haykin, *Adaptive Filter Theory*. Fourth Edition, Upper Saddle River, NJ: Prentice-Hall, 2002.

[2] A. H. Sayed, *Adaptive Filters*. New York, NY: Wiley, 2008.

[3] J. Benesty, T. Gaensler, D. R. Morgan, M. M. Sondhi, and S. L. Gay, *Advances in Network and Acoustic Echo Cancellation*. Berlin, Germany: Springer-Verlag, 2001.

[4] C. Paleologu, J. Benesty, and S. Ciochină, *Sparse Adaptive Filters for Echo Cancellation*. Morgan & Claypool Publishers, 2010.

[5] S. Ciochină, C. Paleologu, J. Benesty, and A. A. Enescu, "On the influence of the forgetting factor of the RLS adaptive filter in system identification," in *Proc. IEEE ISSCS*, 2009, pp. 205–208.

[6] S. Ciochină, C. Paleologu, and A. A. Enescu, "On the behaviour of RLS adaptive algorithm in fixed-point implementation," in *Proc. IEEE ISSCS*, 2003, pp. 57–60.

[7] S. Song, J. S. Lim, S. J. Baek, and K. M. Sung, "Gauss Newton variable forgetting factor recursive least squares for time varying parameter tracking," *Electronics Lett.*, vol. 36, pp. 988–990, May 2000.

[8] S.-H. Leung and C. F. So, "Gradient-based variable forgetting factor RLS algorithm in time-varying environments," *IEEE Trans. Signal Processing*, vol. 53, pp. 3141–3150, Aug. 2005.

[9] C. Paleologu, J. Benesty, and S. Ciochină, "A robust variable forgetting factor recursive least-squares algorithm for system identification," *IEEE Signal Processing Lett.*, vol. 15, pp. 597–600, 2008.

[10] Y. J. Chu and S. C. Chan, "A new local polynomial modeling-based variable forgetting factor RLS algorithm and its acoustic applications," *IEEE/ACM Trans. Audio, Speech, Language Processing*, vol. 23, pp. 2059–2069, Nov. 2015.

[11] P. C. Hansen, *Rank-Deficient and Discrete Ill-Posed Problems: Numerical Aspects of Linear Inversion*. Philadelphia, PA: SIAM, 1998.

[12] J. Benesty, C. Paleologu, and S. Ciochină, "Regularization of the RLS algorithm," *IEICE Trans. Fundamentals*, vol. E94-A, pp. 1628–1629, Aug. 2011.

[13] Y. V. Zakharov and V. H. Nascimento, "Sparse sliding-window RLS adaptive filter with dynamic regularization," in *Proc. EUSIPCO*, 2016, pp. 145–149.

[14] C. Elisei-Iliescu, C. Stanciu, C. Paleologu, J. Benesty, C. Anghel, and S. Ciochină, "Robust variable regularized RLS algorithms," in *Proc. IEEE HSCMA*, 2017, pp. 171–175.

[15] C. Paleologu, S. Ciochină, and J. Benesty, "Variable step-size NLMS algorithm for under-modeling acoustic echo cancellation," *IEEE Signal Processing Lett.*, vol. 15, pp. 5–8, 2008.

[16] M. A. Iqbal and S. L. Grant, "Novel variable step size NLMS algorithms for echo cancellation," in *Proc. IEEE ICASSP*, 2008, pp. 241–244.

[17] *Digital Network Echo Cancellers*, ITU-T Rec. G.168, 2002.

[18] Y. V. Zakharov, G. P. White, and J. Liu, "Low-complexity RLS algorithms using dichotomous coordinate descent iterations," *IEEE Trans. Signal Processing*, vol. 56, pp. 3150–3161, July 2008.

The Impact of the Acoustic Environment on Recovering Speech Signals Drowned in Loud Music

Robert Alexandru Dobre, Radu-Mihnea Udrea, Cristian Negrescu, Dumitru Stanomir
Telecommunications Department
Politehnica University of Bucharest
Bucharest, Romania
email: rdobre@elcom.pub.ro, mihnea@comm.pub.ro, negrescu@elcom.pub.ro, dumitru.stanomir@elcom.pub.ro

Abstract—**In many trials, multimedia materials, video or audio, brought as evidence could make the difference between "guilty" or "not guilty" verdicts. Most multimedia content is stored in a digital form nowadays, therefore, with so many free editing software at anyone's disposal, it is very easy to be forged. In other situations the critical evidence, even if recorded, it can be heavily masked by other signals and declared inappropriate. This paper is a contribution to the multimedia forensic domain presenting the impact of the acoustic environment on a computer software based on adaptive filtering, which can be used to recover a speech signal drowned in loud music. The results help to decide if placing a microphone in a certain room could be useful or not given the proposed solution for recovering the speech is to be used afterwards.**

Keywords-multimedia forensic; noise reduction; adaptive filtering.

I. INTRODUCTION

There are many ways in which criminals could act in order to turn the tables on their side in a trial. For example, they could do basic editing of audio recordings in order to change the meaning of the message and present the forged material as evidence. This audio signal must be authenticated before taken into account. The direction of multimedia forensics that study these problems is called multimedia authentication. In other situations, the suspects can be tapped. If some people would like to discuss something of great importance and they are afraid that a microphone can be placed in the room where the dialogue is about to take place, the simplest solution that would come into mind to make the conversation private is to turn very loud any nearby audio system. This way the speech signal would be drowned in the loud music and the recording, at a first glance, could be considered useless. There are very high chances that the musical material would be represented by a radio station program or the studio versions of some songs recorded on a CD or any other storage form. With all the advances in musical material identification, the melody can be precisely determined and a studio quality version of it can be acquired. The problem in this stage is as follows: given the speech and loud music mixture recorded using the microphone placed in the tapped room and the studio quality of the song that masks the dialogue in the recording, can these signals be processed in such way that the speech signal can be recovered? This is a typical adaptive noise reduction problem and its configuration is depicted in Figure 1.

In Figure 1 $s_{speech}(t)$ represents the ideal speech signal, or the speech that would be recorded in open space conditions and $n_{music}(t)$ is the masking melody in studio quality. $h(t)$ is a finite impulse response (FIR) filter that models the acoustic environment in which the recording took place and $r(t)$ is the actually recorded signal, the sum of the aforementioned signals affected by the room's acoustics. In the recorded mixture, given the intention of the speakers to hide their conversation, the musical signal dominates. The recorded signal is fed into a music identification software like Shazam or SoundHound and the masking song is identified. Furthermore, the louder the music is turned in the room (with the purpose to achieve better masking), the easier is the job of the identification software, so the speakers may even help the forensic engineer without knowing it. After the successful identification, the studio quality version of the song is acquired. In order to be able to remove the musical signal from the recorded mixture, an estimate for the impulse response of the room [$h_{est}(t)$] is needed. In the mentioned conditions this can be found using an adaptive algorithm [recursive least squares (RLS)[1][2] and variable forgetting factor RLS (VFF-RLS) are used]. In the end, the error signal of the adaptive algorithm denoted $e(t)$ will be a good estimate for $s_{speech}(t)$. More precisely, it will represent the speech signal affected by the room's acoustics, but that is what everyone hears when talking to other persons in a closed acoustic environment every day, so it is clearly intelligible. The problem that arises is how large can be the room [which translates into how long the $h(t)$ impulse response can be] for the proposed solutions

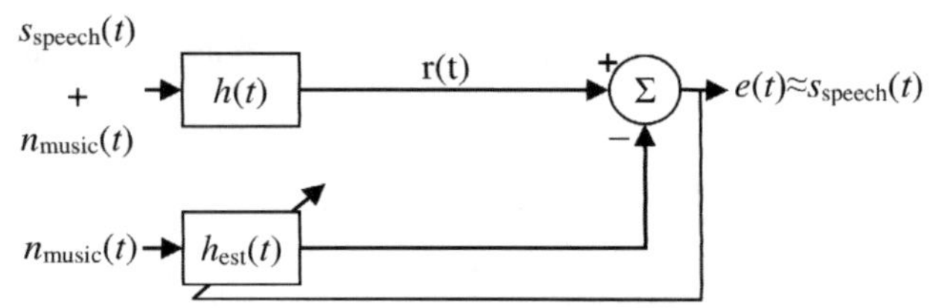

Figure 1. The adaptive noise reduction configuration.

to still work with good performances (the recovered signal is clearly intelligible).

Besides this brief introduction, the paper consists of another four sections: Section II presents the algorithms that were used in the speech recovering software, Section III details the actually speech recovery solution along with some experimental results, in Section IV the impact of the room size on the proposed solution is described and the results of the conducted experiments are presented and Section V concludes the paper.

II. RLS AND VFF-RLS ALGORITHMS

The speech recovery software is mainly built around a system identification problem. The chosen algorithms were RLS and VFF-RLS because of their very fast convergence speed, property which is important in the presented application. The recovered signal would not be intelligible when the adaptive algorithm is not in steady state (the room's impulse response is not accurately determined) so, if the convergence speed would be low, the unusable part could be too large and corrupt the meaning of the message. In the following equations the largely accepted adaptive filtering notations will be used: x – the input signal, d – the desired signal, $\mathbf{w}$ – the adaptive filter's coefficients vector, e – the error signal.

A. The RLS algorithm

The RLS algorithm uses a totally different approach compared to the classical least mean squares (LMS) or the normalized LMS (NLMS) detailed in [1] and [2]. It uses more than just one sample of the error signal to update the adaptive filter's coefficients. Its cost function is described by (1):

$$c_N(\mathbf{w}_N) = \sum_{k=0}^{n} \lambda^{n-k} \left|e_N(k,n)\right|^2 \tag{1}$$

where λ is a constant called forgetting factor, N is the length of the adaptive filter and

$$0 < \lambda \leq 1, \tag{2}$$

$$e_N(k,n) = d(k) - \mathbf{w}_N^{\mathrm{T}}(n)\mathbf{x}_N(k), \tag{3}$$

$$\mathbf{x}_N(k) = [x(k), x(k-1), ..., x(k-N+1)]^{\mathrm{T}} \tag{4}$$

where $(\cdot)^{\mathrm{T}}$ is the transposition operator (only real signals are taken into consideration). The solution to the minimization of the cost function with respect to $\mathbf{w}$ is:

$$\mathbf{R}_N(n)\mathbf{w}_N(n) = \mathbf{D}_N(n), \tag{5}$$

where $\mathbf{R}_N$ is a correlation matrix computed using:

$$\mathbf{R}_N(n) = \sum_{k=0}^{n} \lambda^{n-k} \mathbf{x}(k)\mathbf{x}^{\mathrm{T}}(k) \tag{6}$$

and the cross-correlation vector $\mathbf{D}_N$ can be computed using:

$$\mathbf{D}_N(n) = \sum_{k=0}^{n} \lambda^{n-k} \mathbf{x}(k) d(k) \tag{7}$$

The name of the RLS algorithm comes from its property that the vector $\mathbf{w}$ can be determined recursively. It is clearly more computationally complex that the aforementioned classical adaptive algorithms, but its convergence speed is much greater.

B. The VFF-RLS algorithm

The performance of an adaptive algorithm in estimating an unknown filter is given mainly by two indicators: the misalignment and the convergence speed. The misalignment is defined as the norm of the difference vector between the vector containing the coefficients of the filter to be estimated and the vector containing the estimated coefficients. Using the notations introduced in Figure 1 this translates as:

$$m(n) = \left|h(n) - h_{est}(n)\right|^2 \tag{8}$$

The convergence speed gives an information about the amount of time the adaptive algorithm needs to reach its minimum misalignment.

The choice of the forgetting factor parameter in RLS algorithm is done by making a compromise: a small λ will give very fast convergence speed, but the convergence will not be very strong (the misalignment will have large values) while a larger λ will give better misalignment performances, but will decrease the convergence speed [3]. An algorithm with variable forgetting factor is desirable, which could detect large misalignment and decrease the λ parameter in order to speed up the convergence and progressively increase it as the misalignment decreases.

In [4] and [5] new ways in which λ can be computed are shown:

$$\lambda(n) = \begin{cases} \min\left(\dfrac{\sigma_q(n)\sigma_v(n)}{\xi + \left|\sigma_e(n) - \sigma_v(n)\right|}, \lambda_{max} \right), & \sigma_e(n) \leq \gamma\sigma_v(n) \\ \lambda_{max}, & \sigma_e(n) > \gamma\sigma_v(n) \end{cases}, \tag{9}$$

$$0 < \gamma \leq 1, \tag{10}$$

where ξ is a small positive constant to avoid division by zero, λ_{max} is a preset maximum value for the forgetting factor and

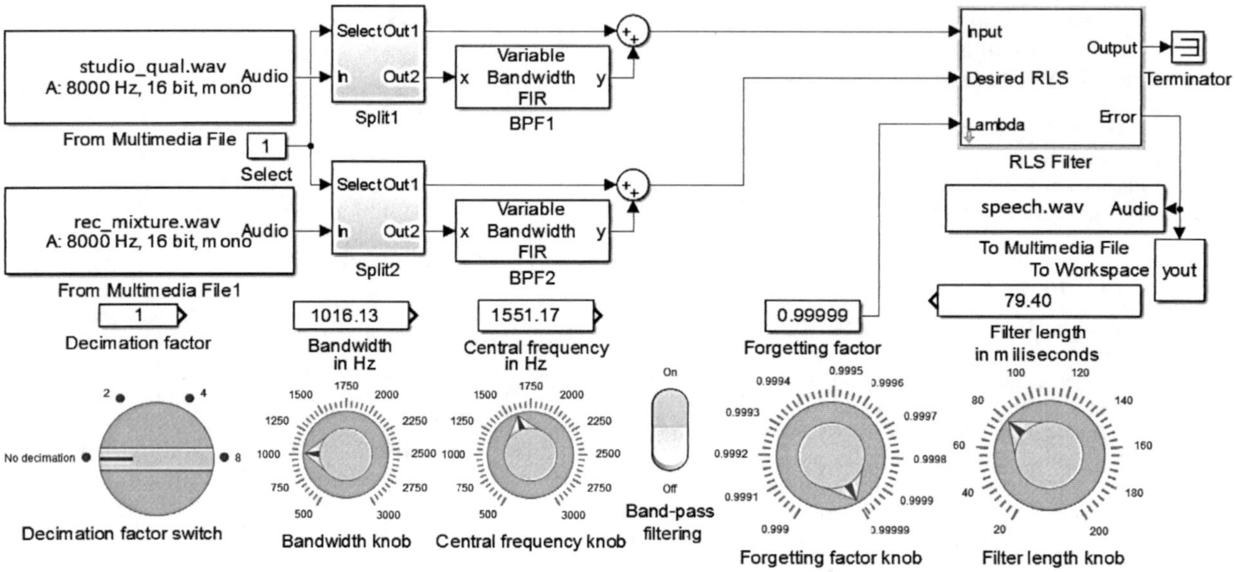

Figure 2. The forensic software for speech recovering based on the RLS algorithm.

$$\sigma_e^2(n) = \left(1 - \frac{1}{\mathrm{K}N}\right)\sigma_e^2(n-1) + \left(\frac{1}{\mathrm{K}N}\right)e^2(n), \quad (11)$$

$$\sigma_q^2(n) = \left(1 - \frac{1}{\mathrm{K}N}\right)\sigma_q^2(n-1) + \left(\frac{1}{\mathrm{K}N}\right)q^2(n), \quad (12)$$

$$\sigma_v^2(n) = \left(1 - \frac{1}{\mathrm{K}_\beta N}\right)\sigma_v^2(n-1) + \left(\frac{1}{\mathrm{K}_\beta N}\right)v^2(n), \quad (13)$$

$$\mathrm{K}_\beta > \mathrm{K} \geq 1, \quad (14)$$

$$q(n) = \mathbf{x}^{\mathrm{T}}(n)\mathbf{R}_N^{-1}(n)\mathbf{x}(n), \quad (15)$$

where K=2 and $\mathrm{K}_\beta=5\cdot\mathrm{K}$ for noise input or K=6 and $\mathrm{K}_\beta=3\cdot\mathrm{K}$ for speech input.

III. DESCRIPTION OF THE FORENSIC SOFTWARE

The forensic software for recovering speech signals drowned in loud music was briefly described in the introduction. The details are presented onwards.

A sample rate equal to 8 kHz is considered sufficient for the acquisition of a speech signal while musical signals are sampled using much higher rates ranging from 44.1 kHz to 192 kHz in very rare cases. Because the speech signal is the sought one, there is no need to assume that the recording sample rate would be larger than 8 kHz. The first step is to equalize the sample rates of the two available signals: the recorded mixture and the identified studio quality musical signal. This is achieved by decimating the latter.

Since there is a high chance that the source of the musical signal is a radio station, it is known that the songs are usually crossfaded, so parts (especially the beginning and the end) of the melody will miss from the recording. Since the available studio quality melody contains also these parts, some preprocessing must be done to the signals before applying the adaptive filtering. Particularly, the musical signals must be aligned. In theory, the adaptive filter can handle this aspect by itself, but it will greatly increase the computational effort and since both RLS and VFF-RLS are not very computationally light, avoiding this additional task from the main processing becomes a necessity. A method for aligning the signals based on the cross-correlation function can be imagined and it was detailed in [6]. Since the adaptive filter can intervene in this aspect, the alignment does not need to be perfect.

The RLS based forensic software that was developed using Simulink is presented in Figure 2. The signals to be processed are loaded in two multimedia files readers named "From Multimedia File" and "From Multimedia File1". For uncommon situations or for speeding the processing especially useful in initial testing a decimation control was provided. The user can select if the signals are decimated before processing or not and the value of the decimation factor.

Two tunable band-pass filters can be switched on or off as needed. The role of these filters is to preselect the spectral band occupied by the speech signals having the effect of reducing the work of the adaptive filter. Their parameters, i.e., the central frequency and the bandwidth, can be set using the corresponding knobs named suggestively "Central frequency knob" and "Bandwidth knob". The on and off switching of the filters is done using the rocker switch named "Band-pass filtering". Finally, the parameters of the adaptive filter (the forgetting factor and the filter length) are set using the "Forgetting factor knob" and the "Filter length knob". The recovered speech signal is saved using a dedicated block named "To Multimedia File".

In order to test the implemented forensic software, it was proceeded as follows: a speech signal was mixed with a musical signal (in the role of the masking noise) in a very harsh signal to noise ratio, –40 dB. Then the mixture was processed using an impulse response that models an acoustic environment illustrated in Figure 3. The variation of the misalignment for the RLS algorithm can be observed in Figure 4, confirming its very fast convergence. The forgetting factor was set at 0.999999 and the length of the adaptive filter matched the length of the impulse response t models the acoustic environment. The recovered signal is a very good estimate for the initial speech signal as it can be seen in Figure 5.

The RLS algorithm gives very good results in this situation as shows the absolute recovery error (the absolute value of the difference between the normalized initial speech signal and

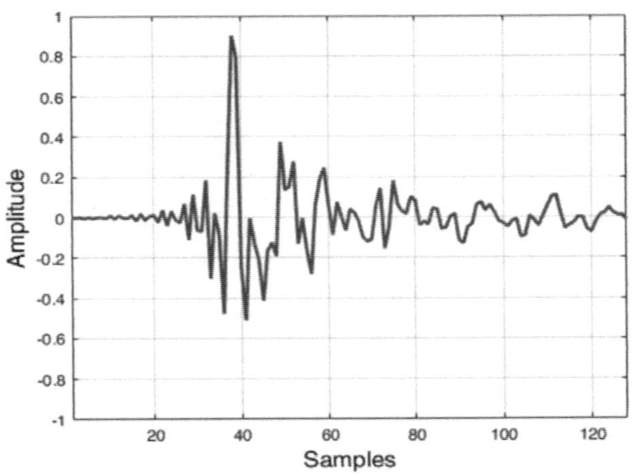

Figure 3. The impulse response used to model the acoustic environment.

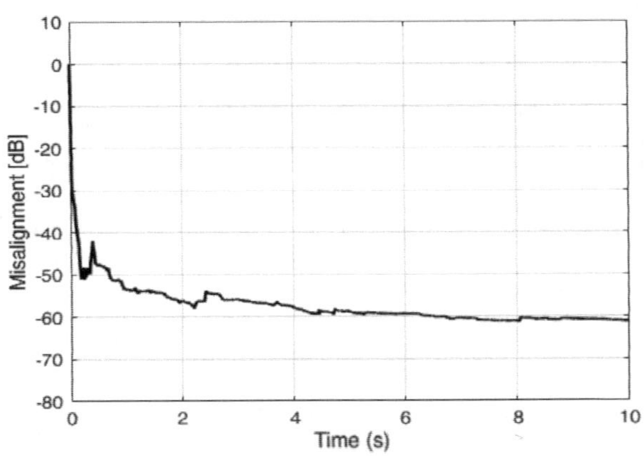

Figure 4. The variation of the misalignment for the RLS algorithm.

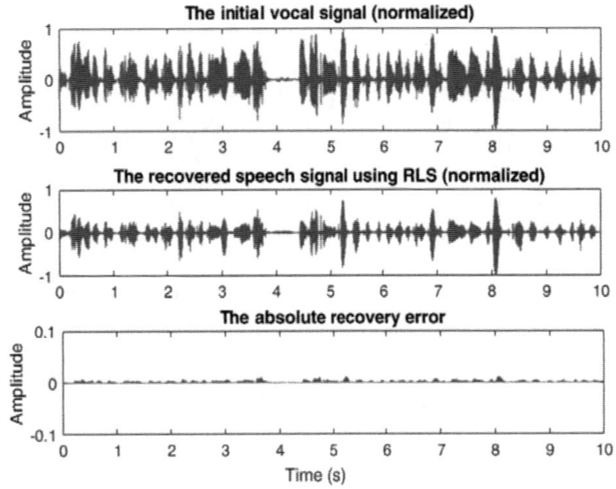

Figure 5. The performances of the RLS algorithm in the given situation.

the normalized recovered speech signal), which is negligible. However, this particular solution can be applied only if the acoustic properties do not change over time, which is not very often in real situations.

The situation in which the acoustic properties change over time was studied. After 5 seconds the impulse response of the room was modified (shifted with 8 samples). The results presented in Figu re 6 show that the RLS algorithm, because of its large and constant forgetting factor, cannot recover from this sudden change (the absolute recovery error is much greater than the reference signal after the moment of the change), while the VFF-RLS algorithm recovers very quickly (in about 10 ms). The reason why the VFF-RLS behaves this way is its ability to modify the forgetting factor. The variation of the VFF-RLS parameters can be observed in Figure 7, and,

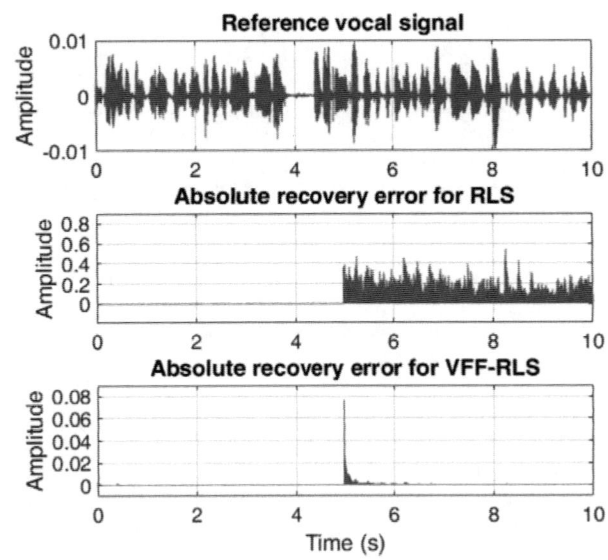

Figure 6. The performances of the RLS and VFF-RLS algorithms in the case in which a change in the acoustic parameters occurs.

in Figure 8, the evolution of the forgetting factor is depicted. It can be observed that λ is equal to the maximum value (0.999999) for most of the time and a very sudden change occurs at the moment when the impulse response is modified. The forgetting factor λ drops to very small values in order to grant the algorithm a fast convergence speed, then its value grows to assure the sought low misalignment. Figure 9 shows the variation of the misalignment for the two algorithms and confirms the conclusions drawn above. Other parameters are K=6 and $K_\beta=3 \cdot K$.

IV. ACOUSTIC ENVIRONMENT IMPACT ON THE PROPOSED SOLUTION

From the previous experiments it resulted that the preferred algorithm to be used for recovering a speech signal drowned in loud music is VFF-RLS. Its disadvantage of being more computationally complex than the RLS (which is already demanding from this point of view compared to the classical algorithms) is compensated by its ability to follow changes in the acoustic parameters. Changes in the acoustic parameters could mean the moving of the speakers through the room, opening doors, people entering or leaving etc.

The length of the chosen impulse response for the tests conducted above was 128 samples, which at a sample rate of 8 kHz would mean 16 ms. A room that can be characterized by such a small impulse response is either very small or it is

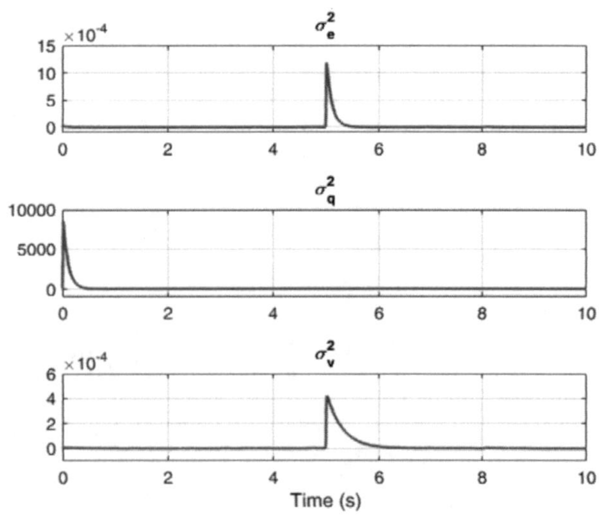

Figure 7. The variation of the VFF-RLS parameters.

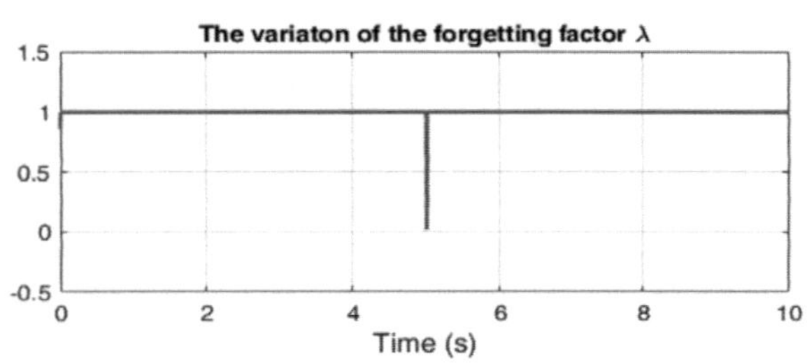

Figure 8. The variation of the forgetting factor.

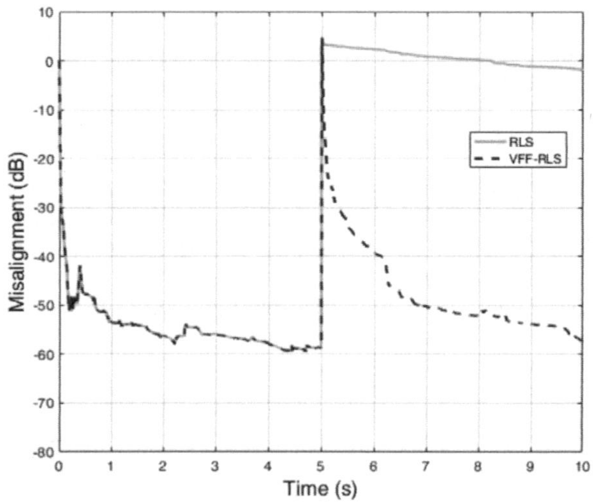

Figure 9. The variation of the misalignment for the two adaptive algorithms.

acoustically treated (typically only studios and professional audio spaces are treated, so it is not a very common situation) or both.

The purpose of this paper is to investigate the maximum length of the impulse response that characterizes a room for which the presented software gives good results. It is clear that the computational complexity will increase with the length of the impulse response.

For this, a longer (i.e., 512 samples) impulse response was considered, depicted in Figure 10. The length of the impulse response used in the experiment was progressively increased starting from 128 samples in order to determine the length at which the performances of the adaptive algorithm are not

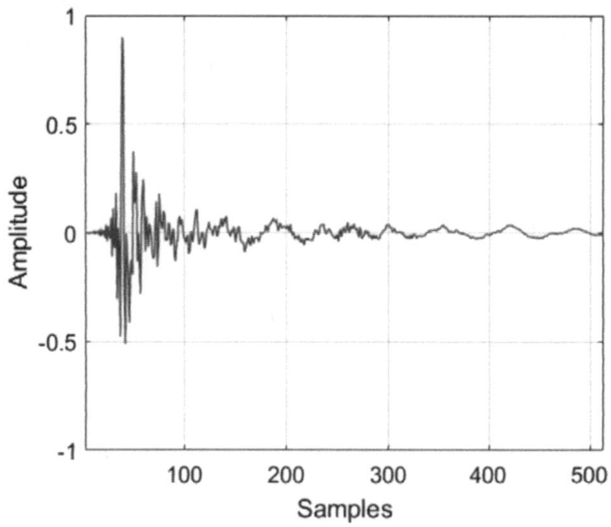

Figure 10. The impulse response used for studying the impact of acoustic parameters on the proposed solution.

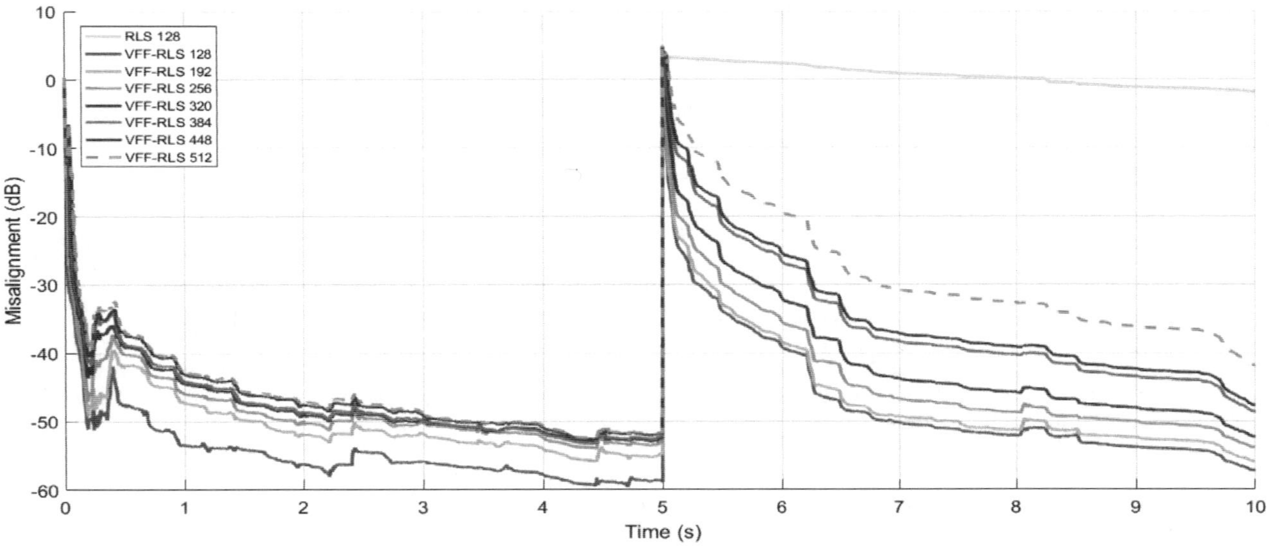

Figure 11. The variation of the misalignment for the two adaptive algorithms with respect to the length of the impulse response.

satisfactory anymore. The impulse response from Figure 10 was truncated from the start to various lengths and the previous experiments were rerun.

In Figure 11, the misalignment of the two adaptive algorithms with respect to the length of the impulse response can be observed. The RLS algorithm works very well until the acoustic parameters are changed, then it loses convergence and, because the forgetting factor is large and fixed, its convergence speed is slow. The VFF-RLS shows promising results for following the impulse response change for low filter lengths, then, for longer filters, its performance slightly degrades, but it is still usable for the whole impulse response of 512 samples.

V. Conclusion and Future Work

In this paper, the problem of recovering a speech signal drowned in loud music was described and its importance in the field of multimedia forensic was highlighted.

It was shown how adaptive filters can be used in order to solve the stated problem. A software developed using Simulink, which uses adaptive algorithms for recovering speech drowned in loud music, was presented and characterized from the performance point of view.

The RLS algorithm gives very good results if the acoustic properties of the room in which the recording takes place does not vary over time. Since this is a rare situation, a change in these parameters was simulated and the performances fell drastically. Another algorithm, VFF-RLS, was tested in these more realistic conditions and its results are promising.

The length of the impulse response is in close relation with the size of the room or the quality of the acoustic treatment that could exist in it, but very few rooms are treated. Tests were conducted in order to determine the longest impulse response for which the VFF-RLS algorithm is still usable.

The maximum length of the impulse response for which the VFF-RLS gives usable results was concluded to be 512 samples. This information along with basic knowledge of acoustics (Sabine's reverberation time formula) can help to decide if placing a microphone in a certain room it's worth it or not.

Future work will include testing the algorithms using other types of impulse response changes than time shifting.

Acknowledgment

This work was supported by UEFISCDI Romania under Grant PN-II-RU-TE-2014-4-1880, and under Grant PN-III-P2-2.1-PED-2016-1465/No. 32PED/2017.

References

[1] S. Haykin, Adaptive Filter Theory. Fourth Edition, Upper Saddle River, NJ:Prentice-Hall, 2002.

[2] A. H. Sayed, Adaptive Filters. New York, NY: Wiley, 2008.

[3] S. Ciochina, C. Paleologu, J. Benesty, and A. A. Enescu, "On the influence of the forgetting factor of the RLS adaptive filter in system identification," in Proc. IEEE ISSCS, 2009, pp. 205–208.

[4] C. Paleologu, J. Benesty, and S. Ciochină, "A robust variable forgetting factor recursive least-squares algorithm for system identification," IEEE Signal Processing Letters, vol. 15, pp. 597–600, 2008.

[5] C. Paleologu, J. Benesty, and S. Ciochină, "A practical variable forgetting factor recursive least-squares algorithm," in Proc. ISETC, 2014, pp. 1–4.

[6] R. A. Dobre, C. Negrescu, and D. Stanomir, "Development and testing of an audio forensic software for enhancing speech signals masked by loud music," Advanced Topics in Optoelectronics, Microelectronics, and Nanotechnologies 2016, pp. 100103A-100103A-7, 2016.

On the FPGA Implementation of the VR-RLS Algorithms

Cristian Anghel, Silviu Ciochina
Telecommunications Department
University Politehnica of Bucharest
Bucharest, Romania
e-mail: {canghel, silviu}@comm.pub.ro

Abstract—**This paper presents the main elements proposed for an efficient implementation on Field Programmable Gate Array (FPGA) of our novel Variable-Regularized Recursive Least Squares (VR-RLS) algorithm. The followed performance axes are the overall processing speed and the amount of used hardware resources. We also focus on this adaptive algorithm performance in the scenario of acoustic echo cancellation (AEC), from the finite precision implementation degradation point of view.**

Keywords- VR-RLS; FPGA; efficient implementation; adaptive algorithms

I. INTRODUCTION

Adaptive algorithms are very popular in many signal processing fields. One of the most known examples is the acoustic signal scenario, especially for the echo cancellation purposes. There are many studies in the literature referring to this topic. Our research team proposed in the last years several modified versions for the classic adaptive algorithms, pointing out the importance of variable step size (VSS) approach for the Least Mean Squares (LMS) family [1]-[4], respectively the variable regularized (VR) for Recursive Least Squares (RLS) ones [5]-[7]. The proposed algorithms were proved to be more robust from performance point of view on echo path change, double talk situations and noisy environments.

But, starting from these promising simulation results, obtained manly using Matlab, a question appeared: are these proposed algorithms stable enough when finite precision format is used in real implementation on digital signal processors (DSPs) or field programmable gate arrays (FPGAs)? We tried to answer to this question analyzing from theoretical point of view the quantization effect in [8][9]. More accurate results were presented in [10]-[13].

Starting from this previous experience, a new algorithm called Variable-Regularized Recursive Least Squares (VR-RLS) was proposed in [14]. The purpose of this paper is to present the main ideas used in order to obtain an efficient FPGA implementation of this algorithm. The efficiency is checked on two axes, one referring to the overall clock frequency and the other to the amount of used resources. The implementation targets a XC5VFX70 chip from Xilinx Virtex5 family [15] found on the evaluation board ML507 [16] from Xilinx. The synthesis results are obtained using Xilinx XST tool from Xilinx ISE 14.7.

The rest of this paper is organized as follows. Section II describes the equations belonging to VR-RLS algorithm. Section III describes the main proposed solutions for the hardware implementation. Section IV addresses the obtained results when synthesizing the very high speed description language (VHDL) source code. Section V highlights the conclusions of this paper.

II. VR-RLS ALGORITHM

Out of the four possible scenarios, one of the most common situations for an adaptive algorithm is the system identification problem. Figure 1 depicts this configuration in an acoustic echo canceller (AEC) context.

Considering the discrete time n, we can introduce the desired signal as:

$$d(n) = \mathbf{h}^T \mathbf{x}(n) + v(n) = y(n) + v(n), \qquad (1)$$

where $\mathbf{h} = [h_0 \;\; h_1 \;\; \ldots \;\; h_{L-1}]^T$ is the impulse response of length L of the unknown system (that is to be identified), and superscript ^{T} denotes transpose of a matrix (or vector). The input vector is formed with the most recent L samples of the zero-mean input signal $x(n)$

$$\mathbf{x}(n) = [x(n) \;\; x(n-1) \;\; \ldots \;\; x(n-L+1)]^T, \qquad (2)$$

and $v(n)$ is a zero-mean additive noise signal, which is independent of $x(n)$.

The goal for the configuration in Figure 1 is to estimate $\mathbf{h}$ with the adaptive filter $\hat{\mathbf{h}}(n) = \left[\hat{h}_0(n) \;\; \hat{h}_1(n) \;\; \ldots \;\; \hat{h}_{L-1}(n)\right]^T$. In order to do this, a solution would be to use the cost function $J(n)$ corresponding to regularized least-squares criterion:

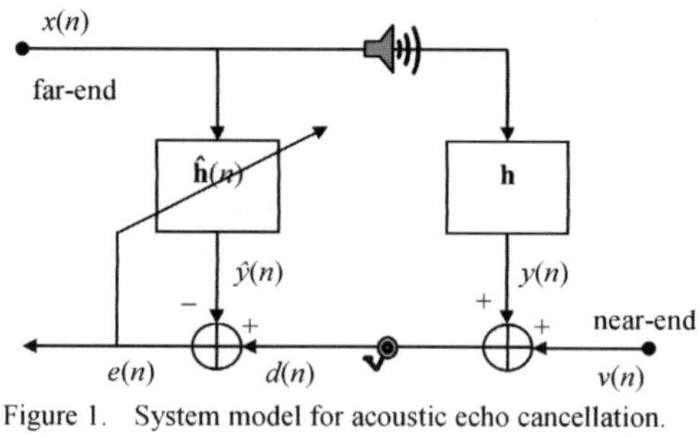

Figure 1. System model for acoustic echo cancellation.

$$J(n) = \sum_{i=0}^{n} \lambda^{n-i} \left[d(i) - \hat{\mathbf{h}}^T(n)\mathbf{x}(i) \right]^2 + \delta \left\| \hat{\mathbf{h}}(n) \right\|_2 \quad (3)$$

where $\lambda(0 < \lambda < 1)$ is the exponential forgetting factor, δ is the regularization parameter, and $\|\cdot\|_2$ is the ℓ_2 norm. Based on (3) it is shown in [14] that the update of the regularized RLS algorithm can be expressed as:

$$\hat{\mathbf{h}}(n) = \hat{\mathbf{h}}(n-1) + \left[\hat{\mathbf{R}}_{\mathbf{x}}(n) + \delta \mathbf{I}_L \right]^{-1} \mathbf{x}(n)e(n), \quad (4)$$

where

$$\hat{\mathbf{R}}_{\mathbf{x}}(n) = \sum_{i=0}^{n} \lambda^{n-i} \mathbf{x}(i)\mathbf{x}^T(i) = \lambda \hat{\mathbf{R}}_{\mathbf{x}}(n-1) + \mathbf{x}(n)\mathbf{x}^T(n) \quad (5)$$

is an estimate of the correlation matrix of $\mathbf{x}(n)$, $\mathbf{I}_L$ is the identity square matrix (of size L), and the a priori error signal is given by:

$$e(n) = d(n) - \hat{y}(n) = d(n) - \hat{\mathbf{h}}^T(n-1)\mathbf{x}(n). \quad (6)$$

Starting from this classic RLS algorithm described above, we introduced in [14] the VR-RLS form, which proposes a mean to find the regularization parameter δ.

If we consider the convergence of the adaptive filter (of course, keeping in mind that a certain misalignment will exist always), this will allow us to introduce the approximation:

$$y(n) \approx \hat{y}(n) \text{ and } \sigma_y^2 \approx \sigma_{\hat{y}}^2, \quad (7)$$

where $\sigma_u^2 = E\left[u^2(n)\right]$ is the variance of $u(n)$ (u being replaced here by d, y, v, $\hat{y}$), with $E[\cdot]$ denoting mathematical expectation. With these notations, and with the assumption that $y(n)$ and $v(n)$ are uncorrelated, we can write from (1) and (7)

$$\begin{aligned} \sigma_d^2 &= \sigma_y^2 + \sigma_v^2, \\ \sigma_v^2 &\approx \sigma_d^2 - \sigma_{\hat{y}}^2 \end{aligned} \quad (8)$$

For the power estimates a sliding window can be used as recursive computational method:

$$\hat{\sigma}_u^2(n) = \gamma \hat{\sigma}_u^2(n-1) + (1-\gamma)\hat{\sigma}_u^2, \quad u \in \{d, \hat{y}\} \quad (9)$$

where $\gamma = 1 - 1/(KL)$, with $K \geq 1$, and the initial values for the two power estimates from (9) are initialized with 0.

From (1) we can define the Signal to Noise Ratio (SNR)

$$\text{SNR} = \frac{\sigma_y^2}{\sigma_v^2}, \quad (10)$$

and from (9) we can rewrite an estimate of it as:

$$\hat{\text{SNR}}(n) = \frac{\hat{\sigma}_{\hat{y}}^2(n)}{\left| \hat{\sigma}_d^2(n) - \hat{\sigma}_{\hat{y}}^2(n) \right|} \quad (11)$$

With this approach, following the demonstration from [14], the variable regularization parameter is obtained as:

$$\delta(n) = \frac{L\left[1 + \sqrt{1 + \hat{\text{SNR}}(n)}\right]}{\hat{\text{SNR}}(n)} \sigma_x^2 = \beta(n)\sigma_x^2, \quad (12)$$

where $\beta(n)$ is the ratio from (12) and it represents the variable normalized regularization parameter. Introducing (12) in (4), we obtain the VR-RLS algorithm, with update:

$$\hat{\mathbf{h}}(n) = \hat{\mathbf{h}}(n-1) + \left[\hat{\mathbf{R}}_{\mathbf{x}}(n) + \delta(n)\mathbf{I}_L \right]^{-1} \mathbf{x}(n)e(n). \quad (13)$$

III. PROPOSED ARCHITECTURE

Let's evaluate now the algorithm described in the previous section from implementation complexity point of view. We consider the fractional 2's complement format, with variables on N bits, the bit N-1 indicating the sign. One can observe that complex operations, such as square root, high-order matrix inversion, fractional divider, and product with vector, are to be executed.

A. *Fractional divider*

There are several classic schemes for computing the fractional division. However, for fractional operations, it is very important to verify that the results are still in the accepted range of [-1, 1). This check has to be done also for division. If the *dividend* is bigger than the *divisor*, a *quotient* outside the range is obtained. For example, 0.8 divided by 0.5 equals 1.6. So we need a pre-divider module in order to make sure that we will have always the dividend less than the divider. If this is not the case, a certain number of shifts to the right will be applied to the dividend, until the condition becomes true. This number of shifts is counted and compensated afterwards, on another part of the algorithm. We consider a maximum possible number of shifts *lim*, obtained from Matlab simulations. This approach provides constant latency for this module.

On the other hand, if the dividend is less than the divisor, we may perform another action to improve the precision of the quotient. More precisely, usually we have the variables on a larger number of bits than needed. The most relevant example is the multiplication result: a number on N_a bits multiplied with a number on N_b bits will produce a result on N_a+N_b-1 bits. Since the multiplication appears periodically (with each new input sample), a truncation is needed after each such operation in order to keep the variables size constant. And since the product of two fractional numbers produces a result even smaller than the two operands, we can conclude that the truncation shall be carefully applied. In this context, considering that the dividend and the divider are obtain from such multiplication operations (for example)

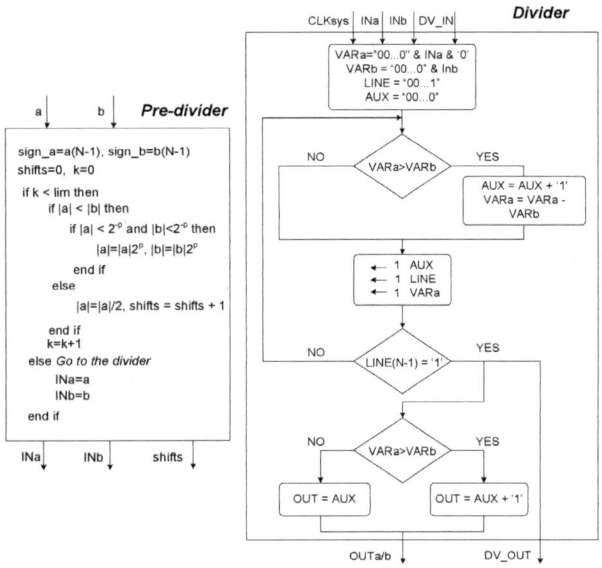

Figure 2. Pre-divider procedure and divider block scheme.

even if the dividend is less than the divider, a truncation applied to both of them before the division may lead to un-accurate results. So, we will check first if not both operands can be shifter a certain number of times to the left, and only after we truncate and then we divide. The complete idea is described in Figure 2, where a classic model of booth divider is also included.

B. *Square root unit*

The square root appears in (12), when computing the variable regularization parameter. In order to execute this operation, the approximation algorithm described in Figure 3 is used.

The algorithm is based on the property of the sequence $c_n = (c_{n-1} + a/c_{n-1})/2$ which converges to $a^{1/2}$. The simulations show that a number *Niter* = 12 iterations produces a very good approximation of the square-root function. When the result is ready before *Niter*, the algorithm ends and the result is buffered in order to produce the same processing delay. We can efficiently use the number *Niter* by choosing a proper value of the threshold 2^{-r} (see Figure 3).

```
function sqrt_a=sqrt(a)
  x=1; k=0;
  y=(x+a/x)/2
  if k<Niter then
    if (|x-y|>2^-r) then
       x=y; y=(x+a/x)/2;
    else
       x=x;
    end
    k=k+1;
  end
  sqrt_a=x
```

Figure 3. Square-root approximation algorithm.

C. *High-order matrix inversion*

The last two most complex operations are in (5), respectively in (13).

In order to better understand (5), we may consider the first cases n=0, 1, 2 and 3 for a simplified scenario with L=3. One will observe that the matrix $\hat{\mathbf{R}}_{\mathbf{x}}(n)$ is symmetric, and moreover always the upper-left sub-matrix (L-1)x(L-1) from matrix $\hat{\mathbf{R}}_{\mathbf{x}}(n-1)$ is identical with the lower-right sub-matrix (L-1)x(L-1) from matrix $\hat{\mathbf{R}}_{\mathbf{x}}(n)$. In other words, it is enough to compute only the first column of the new matrix $\hat{\mathbf{R}}_{\mathbf{x}}(n)$ using the first column of matrix $\hat{\mathbf{R}}_{\mathbf{x}}(n-1)$:

$$\hat{\mathbf{R}}_{\mathbf{x}}^{(1)}(n) = \lambda \hat{\mathbf{R}}_{\mathbf{x}}^{(1)}(n-1) + \mathbf{x}(n)x(n) \quad (14)$$

and then to obtain the complete matrix $\hat{\mathbf{R}}_{\mathbf{x}}(n)$, as shown in Figure 4.

The last and the most complex remaining operation is the high-order matrix inversion. Usually, L may be equal to 1024. This means that we have to compute the inverse of a matrix 1024 x 1024. This operation, besides the amount of required resources for processing, is also very time consuming. This is the reason why others alternative solutions were studied till now. One of the most efficient methods is the dichotomous coordinate descent (DCD) algorithm [17][18]. Our research team also obtained very good results in terms of FPGA implementation efficiency, the most important ones being presented in [8] and [10]. For this reason, we will not enter into details here about this already exposed solution.

IV. OBTAINED RESULTS

The proposed solutions described in the previous section fulfill both the requirements for high system clock frequency, respectively for reduced amount of used hardware resources. In order to show this, we propose an implementation on XC5VFX70 chip from Virtex 5 family. This FPGA has an architecture based on Configurable Logic Blocks (CLBs). Each such CLB contains 2 slices, one slice being formed of four flip-flops and four 6-inputs look-up tables.

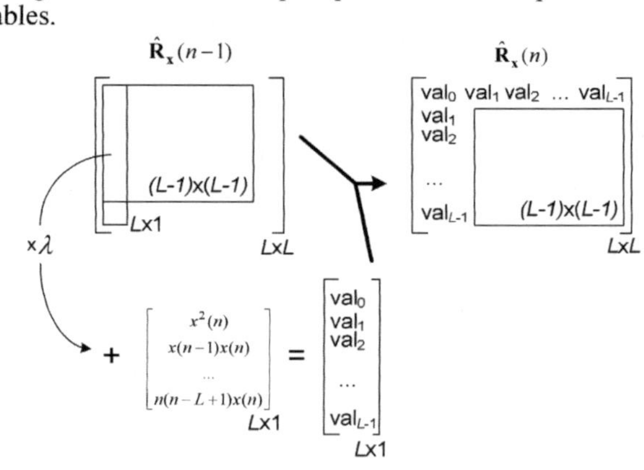

Figure 4. Matrix $\hat{\mathbf{R}}_{\mathbf{x}}(n)$ update.

The proposed AEC implementation, without the DCD part, uses 4620 flip flops (from a total of 44800), 5551 LUTs (from a total of 44800), and 3 block RAMs. The maximum frequency reported after placing and routing the design is 271.3 MHz. The results above were obtained when using a 16 bit representation for the AEC inputs, while all the other variables (including the coefficients) being computed using 31 bits. These variables are used at full width in summing units and only on the first 16 most significant bits on multipliers and dividers. This numerical format was selected based on the misalignment variation. The misalignment is defined as:

$$m(n) = 20\log_{10}\left(\left\|\mathbf{h} - \hat{\mathbf{h}}(n)\right\|_2 / \left\|\mathbf{h}\right\|_2\right) \tag{15}$$

and we accepted a degradation of maximum 2 dB between the 2 curves obtained in infinite precision, respectively in finite precision formats.

V. CONCLUSIONS

We presented in this paper the most important theoretical aspects related to VR-RLS algorithm. Starting from the obtained equations, and considering a fractional 2's complement numerical format, we identified the most complex operations. These were the divider, the square root, the matrix update and the matrix inversion. For each of them, an efficient solution from FPGA implementation point of view was proposed, except the matrix inversion, for which our research team proposed and presented previously an architecture based on the DCD algorithm.

The elements described in this paper can represent a solid ground for the efficient FPGA implementation of any adaptive algorithm.

ACKNOWLEDGMENT

The work has been funded by the Internal Research Grants Program offered by University Politehnica of Bucharest called "Excellency Research Grants UPB-EXCELENTA-2015".

REFERENCES

[1] C. Paleologu, J. Benesty, and S. Ciochina, "A variable step-size affine projection algorithm designed for acoustic echo cancellation," *IEEE Trans. Audio, Speech, Language Processing*, vol. 16, pp. 1466-1478, Nov. 2008.

[2] C. Paleologu, S. Ciochina, and J. Benesty, "Variable step-size NLMS algorithm for under-modeling acoustic echo cancellation," *IEEE Signal Processing Lett.*, vol. 15, pp. 5-8, 2008.

[3] S. Ciochina, C. Paleologu, and J. Benesty, "An optimized NLMS algorithm for system identification," *Signal Processing*, vol. 118, pp. 115-121, Jan. 2016.

[4] C. Paleologu, S. Ciochina, J. Benesty, and S. L. Grant, "An overview on optimized NLMS algorithms for acoustic echo cancellation," *EURASIP Journal Advances Signal Processing*, 2015, 2015:97 (19 pages).

[5] J. Benesty, C. Paleologu, and S. Ciochina, "On regularization in adaptive filtering," *IEEE Trans. Audio, Speech, Language Processing*, vol. 19, pp. 1734-1742, Aug. 2011.

[6] J. Benesty, C. Paleologu, and S. Ciochina, "Regularization of the RLS algorithm," *IEICE Trans. Fundamentals*, vol. E94-A, pp. 1628-1629, Aug. 2011.

[7] C. Paleologu, J. Benesty, and S. Ciochina, "A robust variable forgetting factor recursive least-squares algorithm for system identification," *IEEE Signal Processing Lett.*, vol. 15, pp. 597-600, 2008.

[8] C. Stanciu, C. Paleologu, J. Benesty, and S. Ciochina, "On a robust dual-path DCD-RLS algorithm for stereophonic acoustic echo cancellation," *Trans. Electronics and Communications*, vol. 58, pp. 9-14, Dec. 2013.

[9] C. Paleologu, S. Ciochina, and A. A. Enescu, "A family of recursive least-squares adaptive algorithms suitable for fixed-point implementation," *International Journal Advances in Telecommunications*, vol. 2, no. 2&3, pp. 88-97, 2009.

[10] C. Stanciu, C. Anghel, and L. Stanciu, " Efficient FPGA Implementation of the DCD-RLS Algorithm for Stereo Acoustic Echo Cancellation," *2015 International Symposium on Signals, Circuits and Systems (ISSCS)*, Iasi, 2015, pp. 1-4. doi: 10.1109/ISSCS.2015.7204008

[11] C. Stanciu, C. Anghel, C. Paleologu, J. Benesty, F. Albu, and S. Ciochina, "FPGA implementation of an efficient proportionate affine projection algorithm for echo cancellation," in *Proc. European Signal Processing Conference (EUSIPCO)*, 2011, pp. 1284-1288, Barcelona, Spain.

[12] C. Anghel, C. Paleologu, J. Benesty, and S. Ciochină, "FPGA Implementation of a Variable Step-Size Affine Projection Algorithm for Acoustic Echo Cancellation", in *Proc. European Signal Processing Conference (EUSIPCO)*, 2010, pp 532-536, Aalborg, Denmark

[13] C. Anghel, C. Paleologu, J. Benesty, and S. Ciochină, "FPGA Implementation of an Acoustic Echo Canceller Using a VSS-NLMS Algorithm", in *Proc. IEEE International Symposium on Signals, Circuits and Systems* (ISSCS), 2009, pp. 369-372, Iasi, Romania.

[14] C. Stanciu, C. Iliescu, C. Paleologu, J. Benesty, C. Anghel, "Robust Variable-Regularized RLS Algorithms", in Proc IEEE HSCMA, March 2017, San Francisco, USA, pp. 171-175

[15] "Xilinx Virtex 5 family user guide," www.xilinx.com, retrieved: February, 2017

[16] "Xilinx ML507 evaluation platform user guide," www.xilinx.com retrieved: March, 2017

[17] J. Liu and Y. Zakharov, "Dynamically regularized RLS-DCD algorithm and its FPGA implementation", Asilomar Conference on Signals, Systems and Computers, 2008, pp. 1876-1880

[18] Z. Quan, Y. Zakharov, J. Liu, "DCD-based simplified matrix inversion for MIMO-OFDM", IEEE International Symposium on Circuits and Systems (ISCAS), 2011, pp. 2389-2392

Low Complexity Recursive Least-Squares Algorithm for Adaptive Noise Cancellation

Cristian Stanciu, Lucian Stanciu, Roxana Mihăescu
Politehnica University of Bucharest, Romania
Email:{cristian,lucians}@comm.pub.ro
roxana.2010.mihaescu@gmail.com

***Abstract*—Adaptive Noise Cancellation (ANC) belongs to the interference cancellation class. It employs an adaptive filter to estimate a perturbation signal, which corrupts a primary acoustic source. In most of the corresponding applications, the goal is to imitate an original speech signal. This paper proposes the use of a low complexity recursive least-squares (RLS) adaptive algorithm for the ANC procedure. The combination between the RLS method and the dichotomous coordinate descent (DCD) iterations offers good performance with acceptable arithmetic costs. Simulation results are provided in order to demonstrate the validity of the ANC system based on the RLS-DCD adaptive algorithm.**

Keywords: adaptive noise cancellation; recursive least-squares; dichotomous coordinate descent.

I. Introduction

Modern technology allows the deployment of telecommunication networks in problematic environments, which frequently introduce strong acoustic interference. The high quality communication performed in extremely noisy surroundings, such as airplane cockpits or social gatherings, requires the real-time estimation of corrupted acoustic signals (usually speech sequences).

With the development of adaptive algorithms, the field of Adaptive Noise Cancellation (ANC) has also been the subject of intensive study [1][2]. The workhorse of signal processing systems employing adaptive methods is the Least Mean Squares (LMS) family [1]-[5]. Although the classical LMS adaptive algorithms were improved to a certain degree, their performances are limited when working with highly correlated signals. A new generation of efficiently implementable adaptive systems is required to increase the noise cancellation capabilities.

The standard recursive least-squares (RLS) adaptive methods have attractive convergence properties [1]-[5]. However, the classical solutions for directly solving the corresponding matrix inversion problem have high arithmetic complexities and require large amounts of computational resources. Moreover, the implementations employing the traditional RLS algorithms suffer from occasional numeric instability caused by higher order arithmetical operations, such as divisions. Although the Fast RLS (FRLS) [4] considerably reduces the arithmetic effort, it is not stable when working with nonstationary signals, such as speech.

In [6]-[8], the prohibitive nature of the RLS methods was approached using the combination with the dichotomous coordinate descent (DCD) iterations. The DCD portion of the algorithm replaces the classical matrix inversion problem with an auxiliary system of equations, which is solved using only additions and bit-shifts. The solution is based on the statistical properties of the input signals and reduces the overall arithmetic complexity to a value proportional to L, which is used to denote the adaptive filter's length. The resulting RLS-DCD algorithm is a numerically stable alternative, offering comparable results in terms of adaptation speed and precision, with a considerably reduced computational effort [6]-[10]. By comparison, the classical RLS method has a complexity of $O(L^3)$, which can be reduced using Woodburry's identity to $O(L^2)$ – both methods are considered prohibitive for practical applications [1][4].

The original RLS-DCD solution was rarely tested with colored signals, such as speech sequences [7][8]. It was later successfully applied for stereophonic acoustic echo cancelation (SAEC) setups requiring the estimation of multiple unknown systems [9]. This paper proposes the use of the RLS-DCD method for ANC systems employed in real-time recovery of speech signals. A theoretical model is presented and tested using different types of acoustic interference, with low Signal-to-Noise Ratio (SNR). Although the number of adaptive filter coefficients associated with ANC applications is lower than the case of acoustic echo cancellation (AEC) scenarios, the reduction in terms of computational workload (in comparison to the classical RLS) is valuable for mobile devices (i.e., headphones, mobile phones, etc.). As a consequence, the compromise between arithmetic complexity and performance is analyzed, and a comparison is performed with the classical RLS.

The paper is organized as follows. In Section II, the theoretical model of the ANC setup is defined. Section III describes a low complexity RLS-type adaptive algorithm which is suitable for the ANC procedure. The performances of the proposed adaptive method are demonstrated using simulations in Section IV. The classical RLS adaptive algorithm is employed as a reference. Finally, in Section V, a few conclusions are stated regarding the compromise between arithmetic complexity and the performance of the ANC system using a low complexity RLS method.

II. THEORETICAL MODEL

Figure 1 illustrates the ANC scheme. We denote by $\hat{\mathbf{h}}(n)$ the L x 1 vector comprising the adaptive filter's variable coefficients at time index n, i.e.:

$$\hat{\mathbf{h}}(n) = \left[h_0(n),\ h_1(n),\ \ldots, h_{L-1}(n)\right]^T, \tag{1}$$

where ^{T} is the transpose of a matrix. The desired signal $d(n)$ is the combination between the relevant signal $s(n)$ and the corrupting sequence $q(n)$ (also called the interference signal). The input of the adaptive algorithm $x(n)$ is a reference signal, which is linearly correlated with the interference $q(n)$. The theoretical model of the adaptive algorithm is completed with the L dimensional vector $\tilde{\mathbf{x}}(n)$ formed with the most recent L input samples:

$$\tilde{\mathbf{x}}(n) = \left[x(n),\ x(n-1),\ \ldots, x(n-L+1)\right]^T. \tag{2}$$

In literature, the relation between $x(n)$ and $q(n)$ is usually modelled through a finite impulse response (FIR) filter, which generates $q(n)$ using $x(n)$ as the input. In practical ANC applications, the samples corresponding to $x(n)$ and $d(n)$ are available through microphones [2]. The influence of the physical distance between the two acoustic sensors is represented in Figure 1 through the delay factor D, associated with the length of the mentioned FIR filter.

The purpose of the ANC system is to output an estimate $y(n)$ of $q(n)$ and subtract it from the desired signal. Consequently, the error signal $e(n)$ is an estimate of s(n), i.e. $e(n) \rightarrow s(n)$. The *error* of the adaptive algorithm is used to adjust the coefficients of the adaptive filter in order to minimize the noise interference. In an optimal situation, $e(n)$ is composed of the signal $s(n)$, free of the noise interference $q(n)$.

III. THE RLS-DCD ADAPTIVE METHOD

The core of the ANC system presented in Figure 1 is the adaptive algorithm. The usual methods employed for the update of $\hat{\mathbf{h}}(n)$ are the LMS-type adaptive algorithms, which have reduced performance when working with highly correlated input signals. In the ANC case, the samples of input signal $x(n)$ can be associated with speech, music, engine noise or other (usually highly correlated) acoustic signals. In such circumstances, the RLS-based systems can generate superior performance through their de-correlation properties. Despite the attractive features of the RLS algorithms, the classical versions use direct methods for computing the corresponding matrix inverse and solving the

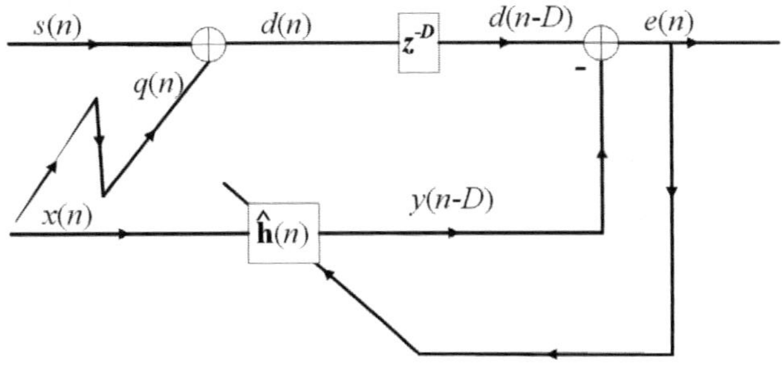

Figure 1. The ANC scheme

associated system of equations. Consequently, prohibitive workloads are imposed on signal processing chips, which usually handle multiple tasks.

The RLS-DCD adaptive algorithm was proposed as a stable alternative for other low-complexity RLS versions (such as the FRLS). Initially, the method was mostly employed for processing weakly correlated signals and later for the identification of long unknown acoustic systems (e.g., the AEC/SAEC scenarios). We propose to use the method for real time retrieval of speech signals in ANC scenarios. Table 1 illustrates the RLS-DCD adaptive algorithm [6]-[9], where we denote by $\lambda\left(0 \ll \lambda < 1\right)$ the forgetting factor associated with the memory of the algorithm [1]. The L x L correlation matrix $\tilde{\mathbf{R}}_{\tilde{x}}(n)$ has the transpose property, i.e. $\tilde{\mathbf{R}}_{\tilde{x}}(n) = \tilde{\mathbf{R}}_{\tilde{x}}^T(n)$. It can be updated by copying the upper-left L-1 x L-1 block of $\tilde{\mathbf{R}}_{\tilde{x}}(n-1)$ to the lower-right L-1 x L-1 submatrix of $\tilde{\mathbf{R}}_{\tilde{x}}(n)$, and by computing only the first corresponding column [7][9]. The main diagonal of $\tilde{\mathbf{R}}_{\tilde{x}}(n)$ is initialized using the identity matrix $\mathbf{I}_L$ and the constant value δ, in order to avoid processing a singular matrix in the initial stages of the adaption course. The statistical properties of the matrix allow a significant reduction of complexity in step 1, to a value proportional to the adaptive filter's length.

The RLS-DCD method exploits the statistical properties of the input signals and solves an auxiliary system of equations using only additions and bit-shifts of the operands, therefore completely eliminating divisions. In steps 3 and 4, the DCD portion of the adaptive algorithm takes into account the results obtained at time index n-1 and generates, using a limited number of updates, the solution vector $\Delta\hat{\mathbf{h}}(n)$ (with values represented in the numerical interval [-H, H] using M_b bits). The updates are conditioned by the comparisons performed between the values comprising the residual vector $\mathbf{r}(n)$ and the values positioned on the main diagonal of $\tilde{\mathbf{R}}_{\tilde{x}}(n)$ [6]-[9]. It was demonstrated in [10] that the vector $\mathbf{r}(n)$ becomes almost null, as the adaptive filter reaches convergence state. Correspondingly, the vector values oscillate in a large dynamic range in the adaptation stages. The arithmetic complexity associated with step 4 is upper

TABLE I. THE RLS-DCD ALGORITHM

Step	Computations
Init	$\hat{\mathbf{h}}(0)=\mathbf{0},\ \mathbf{r}(0)=0,\ \mathbf{R}_{\tilde{\mathbf{x}}}(0)=\delta\mathbf{I}_L$
For n = 1, 2, …	
1	$\hat{\mathbf{R}}_{\tilde{\mathbf{x}}}^{(1)}(n)=\lambda\hat{\mathbf{R}}_{\tilde{\mathbf{x}}}^{(1)}(n-1)+x(n)\mathbf{x}(n)$
2	$e(n)=d(n)-\hat{\mathbf{h}}^T(n-1)\mathbf{x}(n)$
3	$\mathbf{r}(n)=\lambda\mathbf{r}(n-1)+e(n)\mathbf{x}(n)$
4 {**DCD method**}	$\hat{\mathbf{R}}_{\tilde{\mathbf{x}}}(n)\Delta\hat{\mathbf{h}}(n)=\mathbf{r}(n)\Rightarrow\Delta\hat{\mathbf{h}}(n),\ \mathbf{r}(n)$
5	$\hat{\mathbf{h}}(n)=\hat{\mathbf{h}}(n-1)+\Delta\hat{\mathbf{h}}(n)$

limited by $2N_uL$ possible additions, where N_u is the number of *successful iterations* (or solution vector updates) performed by the DCD (usually N_u<10; one iteration uses only additions and bit-shifts) [7][9]. The value of N_u is usually low and represents a sufficient number of *successful* DCD iterations performed for the computation of $\Delta\hat{\mathbf{h}}(n)$ in order to achieve good RLS-DCD performance. The algorithm also updates $\hat{\mathbf{h}}(n-1)$ in step 5, through an addition to $\Delta\hat{\mathbf{h}}(n)$.

The overall complexity of the RLS-DCD can be reduced by choosing the forgetting factor as $\lambda=1-1/(KL)$, where K and the filter length L are powers of 2. Therefore, any multiplication with λ can be replaced by a bit-shift and one subtraction. The total amount of arithmetic operations corresponding to the algorithm described in Table I is represented by $3L$ multiplications and less than $6L$+$2N_uL$ additions for every time index n [8]. We notice that the value of M_b has no direct influence on the number of arithmetic operations (the parameter is relevant only for their complexity).

IV. SIMULATIONS

Simulations results are presented for the context illustrated in Figure 1, using the RLS-DCD and RLS adaptive algorithms. The performance of the ANC system is analyzed using spectrogram plots with 256 points Fourier Transforms for the generated error signals.

The acoustic test signals are sampled with a frequency of 8 kHz, using 16 bits/sample. The goal is to recover interference-free speech sequences available in the $s(n)$ waveforms [11]. The desired signal is generated by filtering the interference $x(n)$ with a Matlab *fir1* 12th order low-pass impulse response and adding the output $q(n)$ to $s(n)$.

The length of the adaptive filter is L=25 and the corresponding forgetting factor is set to $\lambda=1-1/(16L)$. Correspondingly, the L values comprising the RLS-DCD solution vector are represented in the numerical interval [-H, H]=[-1,1] using M_b bits. The parameter M_b directly influences the precision of the adaptive system and is varied in order to establish a compromise between the performance and complexity. Furthermore, $\Delta\hat{\mathbf{h}}(n)$ is updated for a maximum number of N_u=4 times per every time index n.

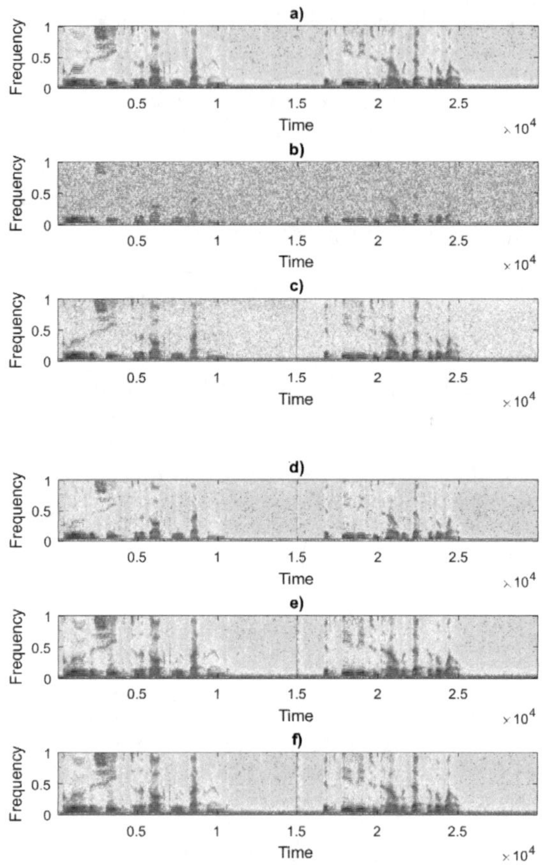

Figure 2. Spectrograms with 256 Fourier Transforms – the interference is Gaussian noise (SNR=0 dB): a) The speech sequence to be recovered; RLS-DCD error signal with b) M_b=3, c) M_b=6, d) M_b=8, e) M_b=16; f) RLS error signal

The first simulation compares the performance of the RLS-DCD and RLS algorithms using Gaussian noise as acoustic interference. The $s(n)$ and $q(n)$ signals have the same power (i.e., the corresponding SNR has the value 0 dB). It can be noticed in Figure 2 that increasing the number of bits used for the representation of the adaptive filter coefficients leads to better estimates of interference samples and a better reduction in noise level. Additionally, the comparison performed with the RLS spectrogram indicates that higher values of the parameter M_b provide similar performance from the RLS-DCD method, with lower arithmetic effort.

For the second simulation (Figure 3), the interference signal $x(n)$ is acoustic engine noise. The same value is used for the SNR (0 dB). In comparison to the previous scenario, it can be noticed that the settings M_b=8 and M_b=16 do not provide the same performance rating anymore. The properties of the second interference type require more

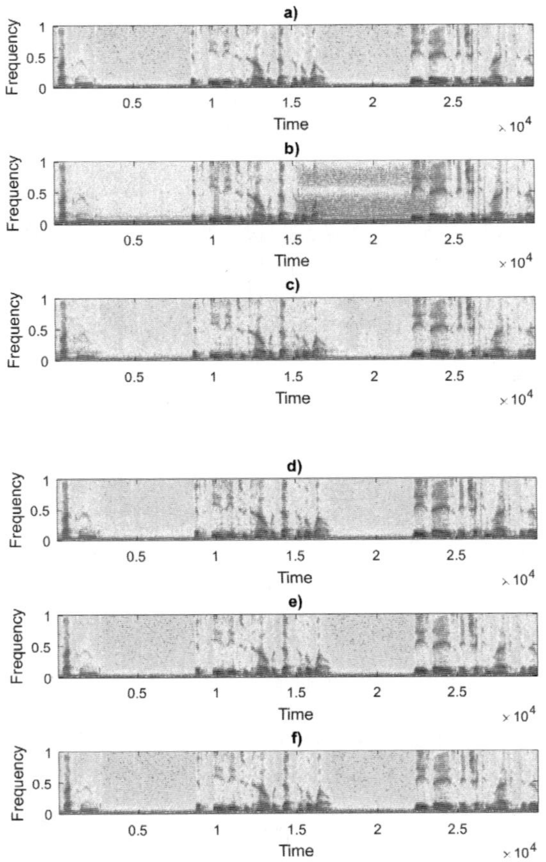

Figure 3. Spectrograms with 256 Fourier Transforms – the interference is engine noise (SNR=0 dB): a) The speech sequence to be recovered; RLS-DCD error signal with b) M_b=3, c) M_b=6, d) M_b=8, e) M_b=16; f) RLS error signal

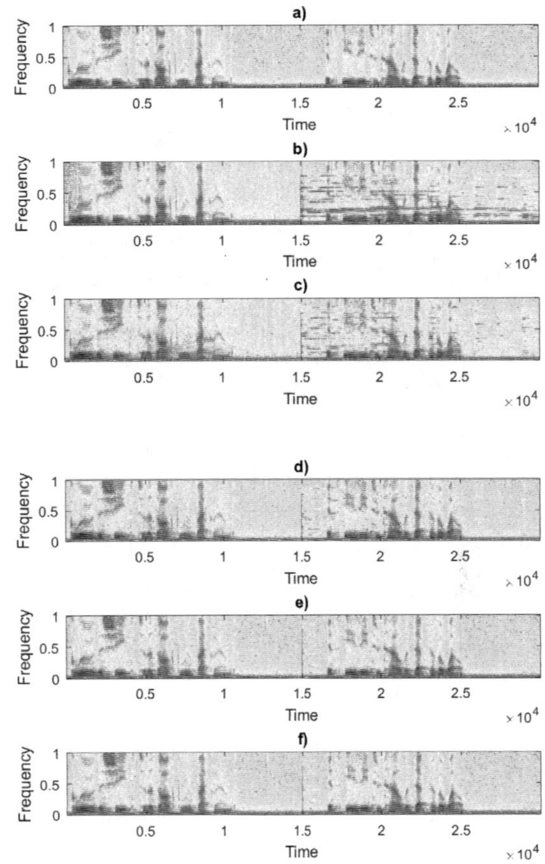

Figure 4. Spectrograms with 256 Fourier Transforms - the interference is engine noise, which changes to music at time index 15000 (SNR=-10 dB): a) The speech sequence to be recovered; RLS-DCD error signal with b) M_b=3, c) M_b=6, d) M_b=8, e) M_b=16; f) RLS error signal

precision in order to generate the similar results between the RLS-DCD and the RLS methods.

The spectrograms corresponding to a third experiment are illustrated in Figure 4. The speech $s(n)$ is corrupted for the first half of the simulation by engine sound, which is afterwards replaced by music. The SNR is set to -10 dB for the entire scenario. The change in interference produces a spike in each error spectrogram and the adaptive algorithms require an adaptation period. It can also be noticed that the music is harder to eliminate from the desired signal (the corresponding interference leaves easier noticeable traces in the error signal). As a consequence, the correlation properties of the interference signals have an important influence on the performance of the adaptive algorithms.

V. CONCLUSIONS

In this paper, the low-complexity RLS-DCD adaptive algorithm was employed for ANC scenarios with low SNR conditions. Simulations were performed in order to analyze the behavior of the proposed system, which indicated that the RLS-DCD has attractive performance, computational efficiency and is suitable for ANC hardware implementations.

ACKNOWLEDGMENT

This work has been funded by University Politehnica of Bucharest through the "Excellence Research Grants" Program, UPB – GEX; Identifier: UPB–EXCELENȚĂ–2016 NOVEL – AUTO, Contract number 100/26.09.2016, code 220. This work was also supported by the UEFISCDI under Grant PN-II-RU-TE-2014-4-1880.

REFERENCES

[1] S. Haykin, *Adaptive Filter Theory*. Fourth Edition, Upper Saddle River, NJ: Prentice-Hall, 2002.

[2] E. Hänsler and G. Schmidt, *Acoustic Echo and Noise Control – A Practical Approach*. John Wiley & Sons, Inc., Hoboken, New Jersey, 2004.

[3] A. H. Sayed, *Adaptive Filters*. New York, NY: Wiley, 2008.

[4] J. Benesty, C. Paleologu, T. Gänsler, and S. Ciochină, *A Perspective on Stereophonic Acoustic Echo Cancellation*, Springer-Verlag, Berlin, Germany, 2011.

[5] B. Farhang-Boroujeny, *Adaptive Filters - Theory and Applications*. Second Edition, John Wiley & Sons, Inc., Hoboken, New Jersey, 2013.

[6] Y. V. Zakharov and T. C. Tozer, "Multiplication-free iterative algorithm for LS problem," *IEE Electronics Lett.*, vol. 40, pp. 567–569, Apr. 2004.

[7] Y. V. Zakharov, G. P. White, and J. Liu, "Low-complexity RLS algo-rithms using dichotomous coordinate descent iterations," *IEEE Trans. Signal Processing*, vol. 56, pp. 3150–3161, July 2008.

[8] J. Liu, Y. V. Zakharov, and B. Weaver, "Architecture and FPGA design of dichotomous coordinate descent algorithms," *IEEE Trans. Circuits and Systems I: Regular Papers*, vol. 56, pp. 2425–2438, Nov. 2009.

[9] C. Stanciu, J. Benesty, C. Paleologu, T. Gänsler, and S. Ciochină, "A widely linear model for stereophonic acoustic echo cancellation," *Signal Processing*, vol. 93, pp. 511–516, Feb. 2013.

[10] C. Stanciu and C. Anghel, "Numerical of the DCD-RLS Algorithm for Stereo Acoustic Echo Cancellation," in *Proc. COMM*, 2014, pp.65–68.

[11] The Open Speech Repository, http://www.voiptrouble shooter. com/open_speech/ [last accessed: 30.03.2017].

Modeling Handover Latency in PMIPv6-based Protocols with Timed Petri Nets

Nivia Cruz Quental
Department of Computer Science, Centro de Informática (CIn)

Universidade Federal de Pernambuco (UFPE)
Recife, Brasil
Email: ncq@cin.ufpe.br

***Abstract*—Performance evaluation of networking protocols is generally related to metrics like latency, signaling overhead, packet loss, throughput, among others. Specifically for latency modeling, most of analytical modeling techniques involve considering the handover latency as a sum of all delays of each signaling message in the handover. However, it may not reflect the reality of various protocols based on *Proxy Mobile Internet Protocol version 6* (PMIPv6), which may consider asynchronous and parallel messages. Petri Nets are state-transition systems capable of expressing parallelism, synchronization, and allowing evaluation of properties of the systems modeled. The Timed Petri Net extension can additionally express time elapsing, which makes it a powerful tool for performance evaluation. This paper proposes to employ Timed Petri Nets to model PMIPv6-based protocols, and, therefore, to bring attention to the main advantages of this formalism for performance evaluation.**

Keywords–PMIPv6; Timed Petri Nets; Mobility; Modeling.

I. INTRODUCTION

The Internet Engineering Task Force (IETF) has proposed the PMIPv6 [1] protocol to address issues related to energy saving and high latency found in Mobile IP (MIP). PMIPv6 considers two entities: the Mobile Access Gateway (MAG), which tracks the current Mobile Node (MN) location; and Local Mobility Anchor (LMA), which plays a similar role as the MIP's Home Agent for its domain. Signaling between MAG and LMA is responsible for the MN binding update. Several PMIPv6 extensions have been proposed to reduce packet loss during handover, as in *Fast Handovers for PMIPv6* (FPMIPv6) [2]. Other proposals handle localized routing as in *Optimized* PMIPv6 (O-PMIPv6) [3]. Multihoming aspects are considered by the *Transient Binding for PMIPv6* (TPMIPv6) protocol [4].

In order to evaluate these protocols, one may use measurements, simulation, or analytical modeling techniques. While measurements and simulation may give fine-grained details about network behavior, the use of analytical modeling may raise protocol design issues in earlier stages of the development in a shorter time than the other techniques.

This paper presents a proposal for modeling network-based mobile protocols at the IP layer using Timed Petri Nets. Petri Nets are a formalism generally employed to analyze the behavior of various types of systems, from product lines to programming languages. Petri Nets are capable of expressing parallelism and synchronization, and to check for possible deadlocks in systems [5]. Timed Petri Nets are an extension to that formalism that allows performance assessment [6]. Applying Timed Petri Nets to these protocols allows protocol designers to anticipate important issues about reliability, robustness and performance in an expressive and simple way.

The remainder of this paper is organized as follows. Section II presents some of the main PMIPv6-based protocols; in Section III, we discuss related work on modeling the handover latency for those protocols; in Section IV, we introduce a proposal for modeling some PMIPv6-based protocols using Timed Petri Nets, followed by the conclusion in Section V.

II. IPV6 MOBILITY MANAGEMENT

In order to accomplish handover between two different networks, in addition to link layer procedures, it is necessary to update routing tables, IP addressing, and handle authentication issues. These mobility management procedures are done by mobility protocols at the network layer. The most well-known mobility protocol is the MIP, which proposes the MN to keep the original IP address while moving beyond its original network, also known as *Home Network*. The *Home Agent* (HA) entity is the coordinator of the network. When the MN visits a foreign network, it receives a *Care-of address* (CoA) in order to be reachable by its HA in the foreign network. MIP has standards for both IPv4 and IPv6. Figure 1 presents the signaling for the MIP handover. After a new attachment, the MN receives the CoA information. Then, the *Binding Update* (BU) and *Binding Acknowledgment* (BA) messages are exchanged. They are responsible for the update of the HA's binding table.

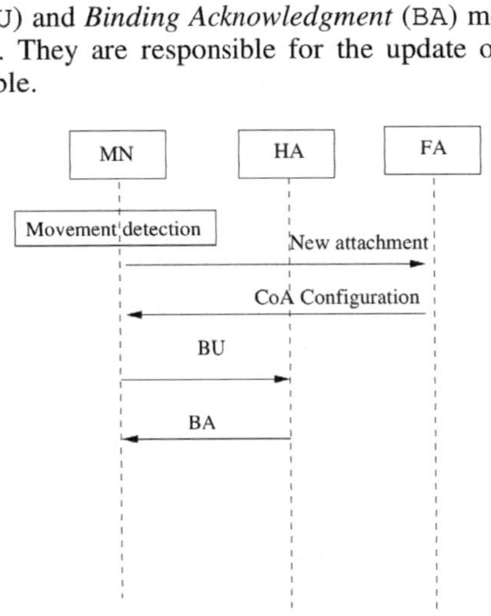

Figure 1. Mobile IP signaling flow.

The *MIPv6 Fast Handovers* (FMIP) [7] is a MIP extension that intends to reduce handover latency through anticipation of the address configuration step during the movement detection phase. The *Hierarchical MIPv6* [8] protocol seeks to reduce latency handling local and global mobility separately. This avoids unnecessary signaling overhead while there is intra-domain mobility with the help of a *Mobility Anchor Point*.

Since MIP requires that the MN has the protocol implementation in its operational system and, therefore, leads to an additional energy consumption, the IETF *Distributed Mobility Management* (DMM) working group proposed the PMIPv6 protocol [1]. PMIPv6 introduces two types of entities: MAG and LMA. A MAG detects movements of MNs and, thus, start binding update signaling. The LMA plays a similar role to the HA from MIP. Thus, PMIPv6 reduces the signaling overhead and the energy consumption on the MN side. Additionally, PMIPv6 does not require modifications in the operating system of the MN, being more adaptable to legacy devices. Figure 2 presents the PMIPv6 message flow for the handover. After the link layer handover, the previous MAG (PMAG) detects the detachment of the MN. Then, the MN asks the new MAG (NMAG) for a new route through the `Rtr Sol` message from the *Internet Control Message Protocol* (ICMP). Then, the NMAG requests the binding update to the LMA through the *Proxy Binding Update* (PBU) message. The LMA then responds with the *Proxy Binding Acknowledgment* (PBA) message. Finally, the NMAG may announce the new route to the MN sending the `Rtr Adv` ICMP message.

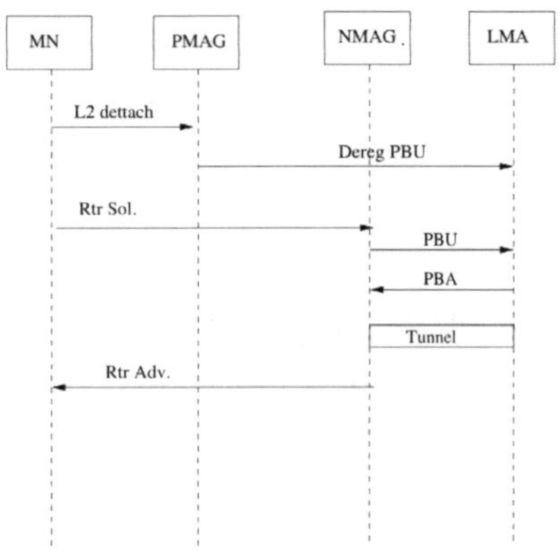

Figure 2. PMIPv6 signaling flow.

The FPMIPv6 protocol [2] adds a buffering scheme and a new tunnel between the PMAG and the NMAG while handover control messages are being exchanged. The main purpose of FPMIPv6 is to reduce packet loss during handover. FPMIPv6 may work in two modes: predictive or reactive. In the predictive mode, shown in Figure 3, PMAG sets up a tunnel with the NMAG through the `HI` (*Handover Indication*) and `HACK` (*Handover Acknowledgment*) messages as the link of the MN is about to be switched. After the node associates with the new network, NMAG exchanges signaling with the LMA, just like in PMIPv6. In the reactive mode, the tunnel setup occurs after the node connects to the link of the new network. In that case, the NMAG starts the signaling with the PMAG in order to configure the tunnel. This can be seen in Figure 4. The rest of the signaling is as in PMIPv6. Although FPMIPv6 may reduce packet loss, the signaling overhead introduced may increase the handover latency.

III. HANDOVER LATENCY MODELING AND RELATED WORK

Analytical modeling is a very powerful technique for performance evaluation of mobile network protocols. This is based on mathematical concepts and helps to predict systems behavior in a variety of scenarios in a short time.

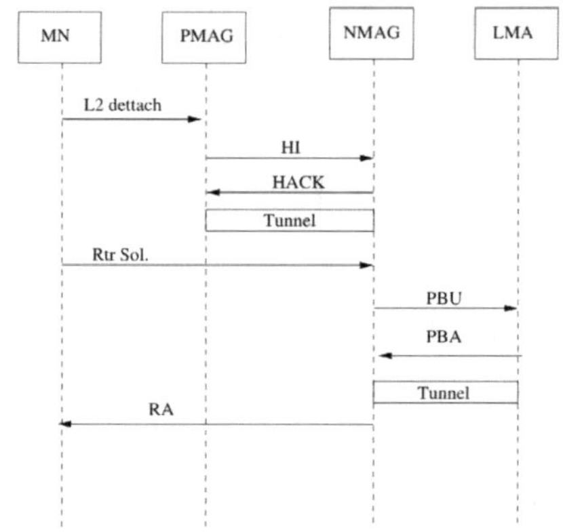

Figure 3. FPMIPv6 signaling flow in the predictive mode.

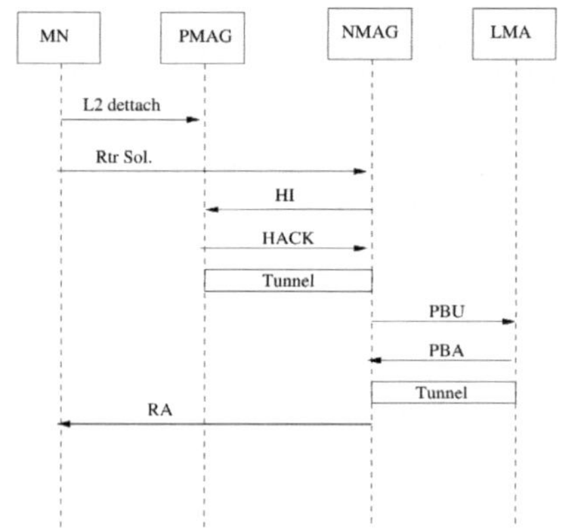

Figure 4. FPMIPv6 signaling flow in the reactive mode.

McNair, Akyildiz, and Bender [9][10] propose a framework to evaluate the performance of their proposal of two-path handover technique for MIPv6. The framework considers mathematical equations to calculate the specific operations of the proposed handover technique, bandwidth utilization and disruption time, that is, the time when the communication between nodes is interrupted because of the data path switch. These metrics are based on the latency measured between two network entities:

$$T = M + (T_w + M) \times \frac{q}{1-q}, \qquad (1)$$

where M is the time to deliver a message, including processing, transmission, and propagation delays; q is the probability of link failure, and T_w is the waiting time to determine if a message is lost. Hussien *et al.* [11] utilizes that modeling to evaluate the performance of a Quality of Service (QoS) extension for MIPv6 (*DiffServ-MIPv6*) developed by the authors.

Hussain, Bakar, and Salleh consider equations to model handover latency to evaluate an intra-domain PMIPv6-based handover technique for vehicular network using Media Independent Handover (MIH) [12]. The latency equivalent to the signaling exchanged between MN and MAG (T_{RS}) and between MAG and LMA (T_{LU}^{PMIPv6}) is as follows:

$$T_{RS} = \frac{1+P_f}{1-P_f}\left(\frac{M_S^{RS}}{B_{wl}} + T_{wl}\right), \qquad (2)$$

$$T_{LU}^{PMIPv6} = n_h\left(\frac{M_S^{PBU}}{B_{wd}} + T_{wd}\right), \qquad (3)$$

where P_f is the probability of link failure, M_S^{RS} and M_S^{PBU} are the size of the `Rtr Sol` and `PBU` messages, B_{wl} and B_{wd} are the wireless and wired bandwidths, T_{wl} and T_{wd} are the wireless and wired propagation delays, and n_h is the number of hops between the LMA and the MAG.

Makaya and Pierre [13] evolve the model in [9] considering the buffering aspects of FPMIPv6 and the queue delay in the handover latency equation. Thus, according to the authors, the latency of a signaling message exchanged between two nodes *x* and *y* (T_{x-y}) may be measured as follows:

$$T_{x-y} = \frac{1+q}{1-q}\left(\frac{M_{size}}{B_{wl}} + L_{wl}\right) + H_{x-y}\left(\frac{M_{size}}{B_w} + L_w + T_q\right). \quad (4)$$

The first part of the sum is the wireless overhead and it must be excluded if neither *x* nor *y* is a wireless device. The second part is the overhead in the wired medium. The $H_{(x-y)}$ is the distance in hops between the two entities x and y. The parameter q is the probability of failure of the wireless link, M_{size} is the average length of a message, and B_{wl} and B_w are the wireless and wired bandwidths, respectively. The propagation delay in wireless and wired media are L_{wl} and $L_w, respectively.$ The average queuing delay in each router is represented by T_q. Handover latency is the sum of the latency of all signaling messages exchanged during a handover. Taghizadeh *et al.* [14] apply the model in [13] to an analytical modeling framework for PMIPv6-based inter-domain protocols.

These contributions have in common the fact that the handover latency is calculated as the sum of all delays generated by each handover signaling message. This may seem appropriate for protocols like MIP and PMIPv6, where the signaling flow comprises synchronous messages. However, for PMIPv6-based protocols where there may be asynchronous messages, or messages that may be sent in parallel, these models may lead to incorrect assumptions. Thus, formal methods that are expressive enough to represent resource consumption and parallelism, like Petri Nets, may be the best suitable solution to model such protocols. Singh *et al.*[15] analyze several generations of mobile network systems, namely, GPRS, LTE and MANET using Petri Nets. The authors do not evaluate the performance of such technologies, however, they verify if they are robust and deadlock-free. Lakos [16] proposes to model MIPv4 networks in Mobile Petri Nets, a variation of Petri Nets that makes possible to represent the network divided into subsystems. Lakos does not present any performance evaluation, however, the author highlights the advantages of the graphical representation instead of a pure textual notation. Dutta *et al.* [17] use Timed Petri Nets to model the MIP binding update, including link-layer network association, CPU, memory, and bandwidth consumption. However, to the best of our knowledge, there are no studies about performance evaluation of PMIPv6-based protocols using Timed Petri Nets. It is important to fill that gap, since Petri Nets are a powerful mean to evaluate properties, resource management and synchronization in systems and, when associated to the cited mathematical models, it can help to predict systems performance.

IV. TIMED PETRI NET MODELING

In this section, the handover process in several PMIPv6-based protocols is represented as a Timed Petri Net. Each *place* in the Petri Net (represented by circles) reproduces a handover step achieved. Each *timed transition* of the Petri Net (represented by white rectangles) reproduces a signaling message exchanged between network entities with a delay calculated as in any latency modeling seen in Section III. The *token* (represented by a small circle inside a place) controls the state change. When there is a *token* in the first place of the Petri Net, it means that a new handover is about to start. The *arcs* in the Petri Net (represented by arrows) connect places to transitions and determine how many tokens a transition may produce to the subsequent place. Every time a *transition* is fired, it consumes a *token* from the previous *place* connected to it.

Figure 5 presents the Timed Petri Net for the PMIPv6 handover. This is equivalent to the signaling presented in Figure 2. At this time, the `T_L2Trigger` *transition* will fire after the link-layer handover time elapses. The `T_TxRtrSol` *transition* represents the ICMP message that the MN sends to its MAG. In that state, the `L3HOStart` *place* would have a *token* and the network layer handover could start. The `T_TxPBU` *transition* will fire after the delay equivalent to the delivery of the `PBU` message. The *token* would be removed from the `L3HOStart` *place* and a new *token* would appear in the `P1` *place*, representing that the LMA is in a state ready to send the `PBA` message. Then, the `T_TxPBA` *transition* waits the equivalent `PBA` signaling delay to fire. The Timed Petri Net is modeled as a directed circuit, that is, the last *transition* is connected to the first *place*. It may be helpful to simulate various iterations and, thus, to calculate average values.

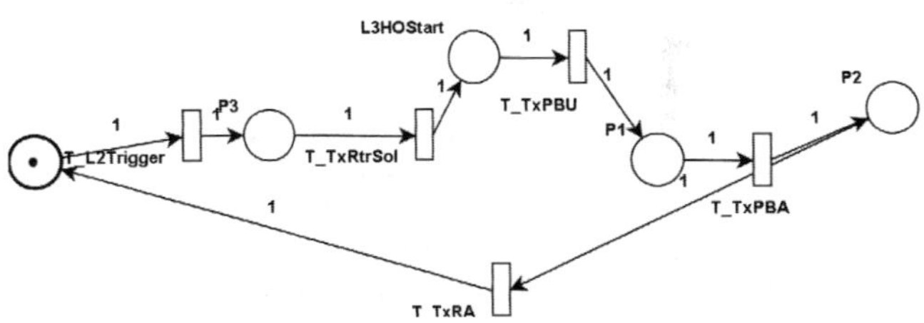

Figure 5. Timed Petri Net for PMIPv6 signaling.

Figure 6 presents the Timed Petri Net for the FPMIPv6 handover in the predictive mode. This is equivalent to the signaling presented in Figure 3. It is important to notice that the beginning of the tunnel setup depends only on the `T_L2Trigger` transition and the binding update may start only after the transition `T_TxRtrSol` fires. From this moment, the tunnel setup between MAGs and the binding update process may occur in parallel, as is expected in the FPMIPv6 predictive mode. That situation makes clear the advantage of using a Timed Petri Net model over modeling the handover latency as a sum of signaling delays. The parallelism is clearly expressed, which makes the model closer to the way the protocol is expected to work than with other modeling approaches.

Figure 7 presents the Timed Petri Net for the FPMIPv6 handover in the reactive mode. This is equivalent to the signaling presented in Figure 4. In that case, the tunnel setup

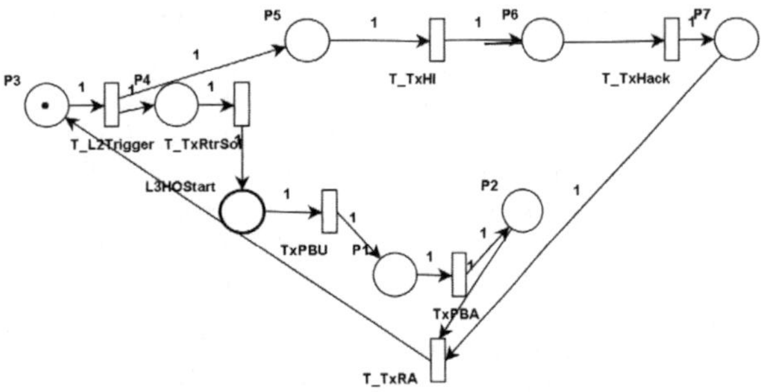

Figure 6. Timed Petri Net for FPMIPv6 signaling in the predictive mode.

between MAGs takes place after the `T_TxRtrSol` transition fires. In this model, the `T_TxPBU` transition may fire only after the `T_TxHI` fires, since it is sent by the same entity. This is represented by two arcs pointing to `T_TxPBU`. That dependency is not modeled in the predictive mode, since the tunnel setup occurs sooner, and, therefore, the `HI` message would always be sent before the `PBU` message.

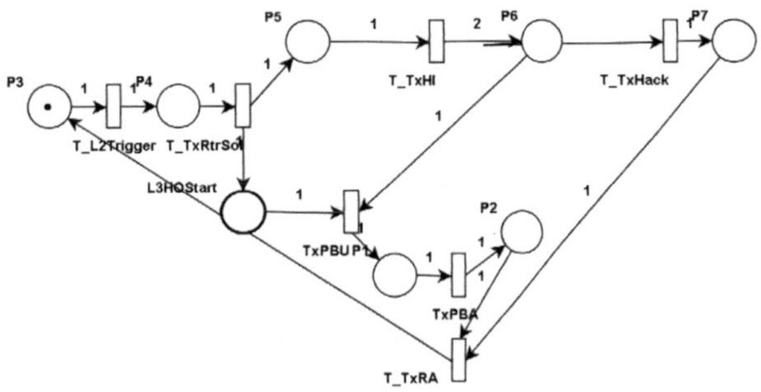

Figure 7. Timed Petri Net for FPMIPv6 signaling in the reactive mode.

It is important to notice that the use of Timed Petri Nets makes clear the main differences between PMIPv6 and FPMIPv6, and the FPMIPv6 proactive and reactive modes, due to its graphic features. It does not mean, though, that latency modeling as in related work may be discarded. Instead, the latency equations must be used to find a suitable value for each timed transition. With these two modeling techniques associated, one may obtain results that are closer to the ones that can be found in a real world environment.

V. Conclusions and Future Work

This paper proposed Timed Petri Nets as a tool for modeling PMIPv6-based protocols. Timed Petri Nets are a formal language capable of representing resource consumption, parallelism, synchronization, and time elapsing. This makes Timed Petri Nets helpful when studying the differences among protocols in a simple and clear way. Thus, protocol designers can raise design issues before investing in a deployment environment for testing.

This paper described a work in progress. Therefore, as future steps, a study on the characterization of signaling delays is expected. This will make possible to infer the corresponding probability distribution function and to model these protocols using Stochastic Petri Nets [18], where steady state results may be collected. Buffering mechanisms and data flow may be as well considered in future work. Modeling of O-PMIPv6 and T-PMIPv6 are further expected.

References

[1] S. Gundavelli, K. Leung, V. Devarapalli, K. Chowdhury, and B. Patil, "Proxy mobile IPv6," RFC 5213, aug 2008, retrieved: March 2017. [Online]. Available: http://tools.ietf.org/html/rfc5213

[2] H. Yokota, K. Chowdhury, R. Koodli, B. Patil, and F. Xia, "Fast handovers for proxy mobile IPv6," RFC 5949, september 2011, retrieved: March 2017. [Online]. Available: http://tools.ietf.org/html/rfc5949

[3] A. Rasem, C. Makaya, and M. St-Hilaire, "O-PMIPv6: efficient handover with route optimization in proxy mobile IPv6 domain," in Proc. IEEE 8th International Conference on Wireless and Mobile Computing, Networking and Communications, 2012, pp. 47–54.

[4] M. Liebsch, A. Muhanna, and O. Blume, "Transient binding for proxy mobile IPv6," RFC 6058, mar 2011, retrieved: March 2017. [Online]. Available: http://tools.ietf.org/html/rfc6058

[5] M. Bouhalouanea, S. Larbib, and H. Haffaf, "Combining bond graphs and petri nets formalism for modeling hybrid dynamic systems," in Proc. 10th International Conference on Future Networks and Communications, 2015, pp. 252–259.

[6] C. Chao and A. Thomaz, "Timed petri nets for fluent turn-taking over multimodal interaction resources in human-robot collaboration," The International Journal of Robotics Research, vol. 35, no. 11, 2016, pp. 2529–2538.

[7] E. R. Koodli, "Mobile IPv6 fast handovers," RFC 5568, july 2009, retrieved: March 2017. [Online]. Available: http://tools.ietf.org/html/rfc5568

[8] H. Soliman, C. Castelluccia, K. ElMalki, and L. Bellier, "Hierarchical mobile IPv6 (HMIPv6) mobility management," RFC 5380, october 2008, retrieved: March 2017. [Online]. Available: http://tools.ietf.org/html/rfc5380

[9] J. McNair, I. Akyildiz, and M. D. Bender, "Handoffs for real-time traffic in mobile IP version 6 networks ," in Proc. First Global Telecommunications Conference, 2001, pp. 3463–3467.

[10] ——, "An inter-system handoff technique for the IMT-2000 system," in Proc. IEEE INFOCOM, 2000, pp. 208–216.

[11] L. F. Hussien, A. Aisha-Hassan, M. H. Habaebi, O. O. Khalifa, and S. A. Hameed, "Development of analytical approach to evaluate (DiffServ-MIPv6) scheme," Research Journal of Applied Sciences, Engineering and Technology, vol. 7, no. 12, 2014, pp. 2529–2538.

[12] H. N. Hussain, K. A. Bakar, and S. Salleh, "A novel intra-domain continues handover solution for inter-domain pmipv6 based vehicular network," International Journal of Advanced Computer Science and Applications, vol. 2, no. 12, 2011, pp. 12–18.

[13] C. Makaya and S. Pierre, "An analytical framework for performance evaluation of ipv6-based mobility management protocols," IEEE Transactions on Wireless Communications, vol. 7, no. 3, 2008, p. 7.

[14] A. Taghizadeh, T.-C. Wan, R. Budiarto, F. T. Yap, and A. Osman, "A performance evaluation framework for network-based IP mobility solutions," International Journal of Innovative, Computing, Information and Control, vol. 8, no. 10, 2012, pp. 7263–7288.

[15] S. Singh, G. Singh, V. Narasimhan, and H. S. Pabla, "Petri net modelling and analysis of mobile communication protocols UMTS, LTE, GPRS and MANET," in Proc. International Conference on Computer Communication and Informatics, 2014, pp. 1–9.

[16] C. Lakos, "Modelling mobile IP with mobile petri nets," in Transactions on Petri Nets and Other Models of Concurrency III, K. Jensen, Ed. Berlim: Springer Berlin Heidelberg, 2009, vol. 5800, pp. 127–158.

[17] A. Dutta, B. Lyles, H. Schulzrinne, and J. Wang, "Systems modeling for IP-based handoff using timed petri nets," in Proc. 42nd Hawaii International Conference on System Sciences, 2009, pp. 1–10.

[18] M. A. Marsan, "Stochastic Petri nets: An elementary introduction," in Advances in Petri Nets 1989, G. Rozenberg, Ed. Berlin, Heidelberg: Springer Berlin Heidelberg, 1990, pp. 1–29.

CI-PMIPv6: An Approach for Inter-domain Network-based Mobility Management

Nivia Cruz Quental and Paulo André da S. Gonçalves
Department of Computer Science, Centro de Informática (CIn)
Universidade Federal de Pernambuco (UFPE)
Recife, Brazil
Email: ncq@cin.ufpe.br, pasg@cin.ufpe.br

Abstract—**This paper presents the Clustered Inter-domain Proxy Mobile Internet Protovol version 6 (CI-PMIPv6), an intra-domain and inter-domain Distributed Mobility Management solution for PMIPv6-based networks. It anticipates the exchange of mobile node information for future handovers using a Distributed Hash Table (DHT) structure. The main advantages of CI-PMIPv6 are: to avoid the introduction of a single point of failure; to allow a fast spread of information among network entities; to take advantage of the execution of inter-domain handover-related operations in parallel with the execution of intra-domain handover-related operations; and to avoid generating bottlenecks. Results show that, in the scenario studied, CI-PMIPv6 handover costs less and suffers less latency and packet loss in comparison with other schemes studied. Additionally, the values of goodput in CI-PMIPv6 are greater.**

Keywords–CI-PMIPv6; Distributed; Handover; Inter-domain.

I. INTRODUCTION

The evolution and widespread use of multimedia applications for mobile gadgets are the key factors for the rapid growth in the use of mobile networks. Mobile data traffic grew 60% between Q1 2015 and Q1 2016 [1]. Additionally, the emergence of mobile devices connected to vehicles expand the possibilities for use-case scenarios. Thus, efficient solutions for mobility management are a relevant and contemporary concern. Binding updates and tunneling setup are the main operations in IP mobility management and, therefore, the applicability of the related protocol may well be determined by how efficient these are. The Internet Engineering Task Force (IETF) Networking Working Group proposed the Proxy Mobile IPv6 (PMIPv6) protocol [2] mainly to resolve issues related to the energy saving and high latency found in Mobile IP (MIP). PMIPv6 introduces two types of entities: the Mobile Access Gateway (MAG), which tracks the location of the current Mobile Node (MN); and the Local Mobility Anchor (LMA), which plays a similar role as the MIP's Home Agent in a local domain. Signaling between MAG and LMA is responsible for updating the binding of the MN. Due to relying on a non-mobile entity to keep track of the MN, PMIPv6 has lost the MIPv6 inter-domain feature. Studies have been proposed on PMIPv6-based inter-domain solutions. However, they still face problems related to centered entities and the high cost of signaling.

In this paper, we propose CI-PMIPv6, a low cost and a low latency intra-domain and inter-domain solution. CI-PMIPv6 makes inter-domain handover possible by spreading information on MNs efficiently among LMAs from the different domains. Intra-domain handover is minimally changed to send useful updates for future inter-domain handovers to those LMAs. The main characteristics of CI-PMIPv6 are:

- **Distributed mobility management** - LMAs from each domain form a cluster, which runs a Kademlia-based DHT [3] so as to spread information efficiently; this avoids the use of global entities and, thus, avoids creating single points of failure and performance bottlenecks;
- **Network-based handover** - CI-PMIPv6 maintains the PMIPv6 advantage of reducing MNs' consumption of energy by avoiding host-based handover signaling and processing overheads;
- **Reuse of existing PMIPv6 entities to exchange inter-domain information** - the compatibility with PMIPv6 legacy systems is achieved; additionally, MAGs may remain unaware of inter-domain mobility, as in PMIPv6;
- **Anticipation of MN information for future handovers** - during the MN's ongoing handover, its current LMA proactively spreads the MN information to neighbor LMAs in the cluster; this information is needed for future inter-domain handovers and is rapidly available to neighbors LMAs, thereby avoiding time waste during such handovers due to the extra signaling needed to request and obtain such information.

By using CI-PMIPv6 it is expected that low inter-domain handover cost and latency will be achieved in comparison with other PMIPv6-based inter-domain approaches cited in the literature. The remainder of this paper is organized as follows: CI-PMIPv6 is detailed in Section II. Related work is presented in Section III. Section IV deals with evaluating the performance of CI-PMIPv6 and the results achieved. Finally, some conclusions are drawn and suggestions made for future research studies in Section V.

II. CI-PMIPV6

Figure 1 presents the CI-PMIPv6 architecture and shows that the LMAs form a cluster. Each LMA contains a Kademlia peer [3], and they are all connected to the same DHT. The choice of a Kademlia-based Peer to Peer (P2P) architecture for the cluster allows:

- LMAs to communicate without placing them in a hierarchy;
- Mobility management without centralized entities, thus avoiding bottlenecks and a single point of failure;

- MAGs to abstract the existence of the cluster, which is recognized only by the LMAs, thereby avoiding unnecessary signaling between the local domain and the core network;
- The MN information to be spread efficiently throughout the Kademlia STORE primitive.

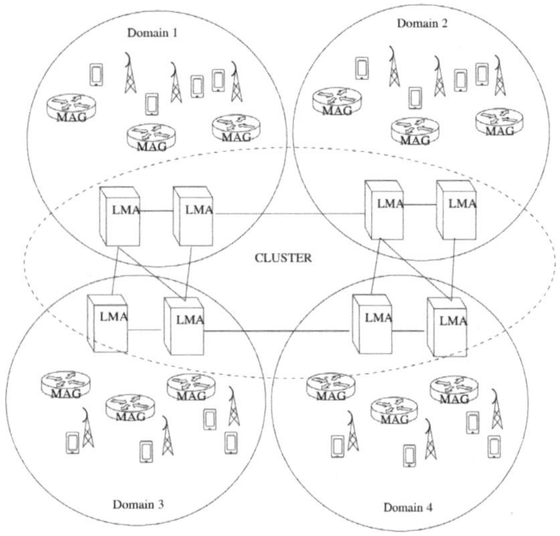

Figure 1. Domains in CI-PMIPv6.

The MN information is stored in its original LMA, which forwards it to its neighbors. Each piece of information in the cluster is represented in a <key, value> pair format, where:

- The key is the MN original IP address;
- The value is a triple of <MN current IP, MAG IP, LMA IP>.

The <key, value> pairs are stored in peers whose nodeIDs are the closest to the key. The nodeID, i.e., the identifier of the LMA as a Kademlia peer, is the LMA IP Address. Both keys and nodeIDs are in the 128-bit space, as in every IPv6 address, instead of in the 160-bit space as in the standard Kademlia proposal [3].

The PING, STORE, FIND_NODE, FIND_VALUE primitives, and the look-up procedures from Kademlia are valid for network refresh, information storage, location of peers, and information retrieval in the cluster. Selecting and registering LMAs in the same DHT is done according to agreements among engaged network operators. Likewise, CI-PMIPV6 introduces the new primitives UPDATE and DELETE. They are responsible for refreshing and removing <key, value> pairs in the cluster. These primitives follow the same logic as in the STORE primitive.

Figure 2 shows the signaling call flow for intra-domain handover. The flow is similar to that proposed by the PMIPv6 standard. After triggering the layer-2 event, the previous MAG (PMAG) exchanges deregistration signaling with the LMA. The LMA waits for a fixed interval before removing the binding definitively. When visiting the new network, the MN requests the new MAG (NMAG) for a route via the Internet Control Message Protocol (ICMP) Rtr Sol. message. Then, the NMAG must request the LMA to update its binding table with the messages *Proxy Binding Update* (PBU) and *Proxy Binding Acknowledgment* (PBA). A tunnel is set up between the LMA and NMAG to forward packets to the MN. The NMAG, then, may send the ICMP Rtr Adv. message to announce itself as the access router for that MN and then, the handover is finished. CI-PMIPv6 adds to that flow a call to the cluster UPDATE message. Thus, whenever the MN associates itself with a MAG, the cluster is updated. We assume that the LMA runs both the update operation and the rest of the intra-domain handover operation in parallel, e.g., the LMA runs both of the operations simultaneously on different cores. These two operations do not block each other. This is possible since the spread of binding information in the cluster is not useful for concluding the current intra-domain handover. MAGs do not need to interact with the cluster and may proceed with the handover normally. We further assume to be negligible the amount of time spent performing a system call for starting the update operation during intra-domain handovers. We also assume that traffic from the LMA to the cluster and traffic from the LMA to the MAGs can be kept isolated from each other. For instance, each LMA might have exclusive network interfaces and paths for communicating with MAGs. In this manner, update messages flowing from the LMA to the cluster during intra-domain handovers cannot block (e.g., head-of-the-line blocking in network interfaces) or affect (e.g., increasing queuing delay) messages flowing to the MAGs. The MN information is proactively spread in the cluster. The information will be necessary if there is ever an inter-domain handover executed by the MN. The MN information is rapidly available to neighbors LMAs in the cluster, thereby avoiding the need for the extra signaling to request and obtain such information during inter-domain handovers. Notice that CI-PMIPv6 takes advantage of the execution of inter-domain handover-related operations in parallel with the execution of intra-domain handover-related operations.

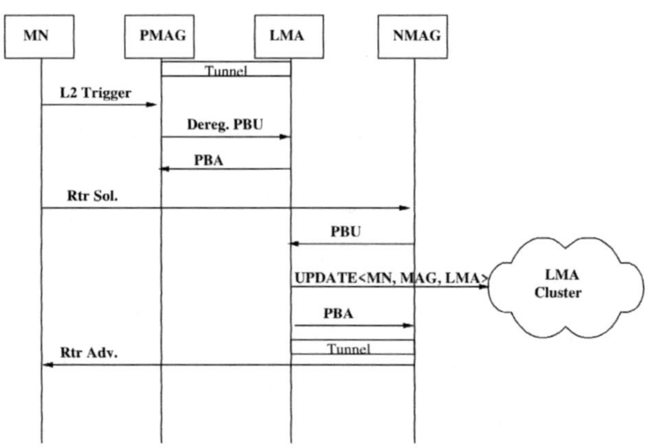

Figure 2. Intra-domain handover in CI-PMIPv6.

Figure 3 shows the signaling call flow for an inter-domain handover. The procedure is initially similar to the intra-domain handover. When detecting the link layer trigger, the PMAG sends the Dereg.PBU message to the previous LMA (PLMA). The PLMA sets a timer to wait for a period of time before removing the binding information in order to prevent a ping-pong effect. The MN enters the new domain and asks NMAG for a new route. The NMAG sends a PBUNoProf message to the LMA in its domain (new LMA - NLMA) to inform it that the MN was not originally registered in that domain. The NLMA searches for the MN IP in its cluster history and finds out that it originally belongs to the PLMA domain. Then, NLMA responds to NMAG with a `PBAProf` message containing the node information needed for registration. After that, the NLMA sends a `PBUInterdomain` message to the PLMA informing that the MN has entered a new domain. Thus, PLMA refrains from removing the node binding. This must happen before the timeout set aside for the removal in the PLMA. It updates its own cluster history instead and sends an `UPDATE` message to the cluster. In parallel, PLMA sends the `PBAInterdomain` message to the NLMA informing it that it is ready to redirect data traffic to the NMAG in the new domain. Thus, a tunnel is set up between PLMA and NMAG. It is important to notice that PLMA remains the anchor entity for the MN until the session ends. This simplifies the process of context switching.

The greatest CI-PMIPv6 opportunity for performance gains comes from the anticipated knowledge that LMAs get from cluster updates. The information obtained is useful in future inter-domain handovers. CI-PMIPv6 avoids the MAG, which is a local domain entity, to exchange handover signaling with the core network, where the cluster is and also where the network traffic is more intense. Additionally, the fact that the PLMA still manages communication after the inter-domain handover eliminates the need to create an additional tunnel, a tunnel between two LMAs. This avoids increasing the overhead of tunneling.

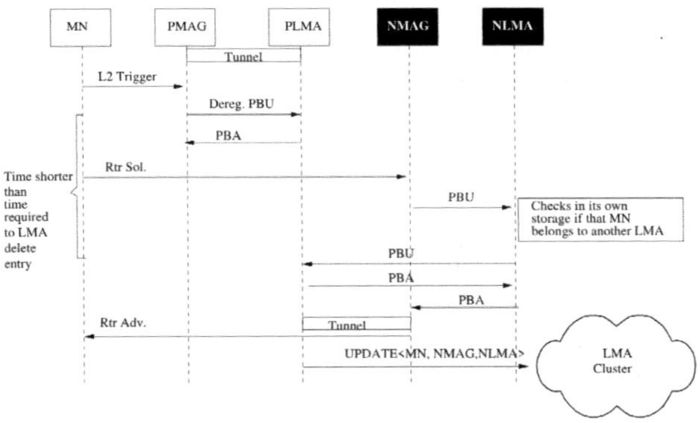

Figure 3. Inter-domain handover in CI-PMIPv6.

III. RELATED WORK

Park *et al.* [4] present a scheme where the LMA from a domain forwards the handover signaling to the LMA in another domain to achieve inter-domain handover. There are neither optimizations, nor additional entities. The consequence is the introduction of an extra tunnel between those LMAs and a duplicated number of signaling messages. Simulations with QualNET measures packet loss and latency in comparison with a scheme with PMIPv6/MIPv6 interworking. The authors state that the proposal is better suited for scenarios where handover is frequent. A similar proposal can be found in [5].

Zhong *et al.* propose the Enabling Inter PMIPv6 Domain Handover (EIPMH) [6]. The authors introduce the Traffic Distributor (TD), an entity that redirects data to the LMA while the MN is out of the original domain. The TDs are statically configured and have knowledge about other TDs, their IP prefixes, and mapping to the LMAs. In that proposal, the TD is responsible for assigning prefixes to its MNs instead of the LMA. The NLMA must send a query `PBU_Forwading` to the PLMA to find additional information about the MN and the TD responsible for communicating with the Internet. The TD also creates a tunnel to the NLMA. Also, there are tunnels between LMAs and between the NLMA and the MAG. The NS-2 simulation tool is used to evaluate performance. Latency and throughput are compared to those found in I-PMIP. However, the evaluation does not consider the extra overhead derived from the tunnel between the TD and the NLMA. The process of finding the PLMA, look-up for the NLMA, and the change of MAGs are not considered.

In the Newman *et al.* proposal [7], the original LMA keeps managing the node until the end of the session and exchanges signaling with the MAG in the new domain during inter-domain handover. That LMA is called the Session Mobility Anchor (SMA). It is assumed that LMAs from different domains already know each other and are physically close to each other. To locate the MAG in the new domain, the original LMA relies on a centralized entity called the Virtual Mobility Anchor (VMA), which undertakes location updates whenever a handover takes place. Hence, that solution faces the same single point of failure issue as in [6]. The authors state that I-PMIP sees to it that the policies of different domains remain transparent, since there is no direct connection between MAGs from different domains. Performance is evaluated by a theoretical analysis, which compares the I-PMIP latency to the latency found in MIP, and Hierarchical approaches for MIP and PMIP. According to [7], I-PMIP has proven to be more efficient in the scenarios studied. Nyguyen and Bonnet propose a similar solution in [8] focusing on routing optimizations.

Joe *et al.* [9] present an inter-domain approach based on an architecture that considers special types of MAG: the Boundary and Overlapping MAG (BMAG and OMAG, respectively). The BMAG is associated with only one LMA, while the OMAG is associated with more than one domain. Both are found in regions where a domain ends and another domain begins. Also, only one authentication entity for all domains is considered. The presence of a gateway guarantees maintenance of the IP address. The authors propose two solutions: Reactive and No-Gap. In the Reactive solution, a path is created between CN and PLMA and NLMA. The BMAG discovers a NLMA by geographical locating it. The authors do not specify how the look-up is done. The functionality of the BMAG is shared with edge routers. A tunnel must be created between the gateway and the NLMA, between LMAs, and between the PLMA and the NMAG. In the No-Gap approach, the OMAG has information from both domains and creates two simultaneous paths as the MN enters its area. Thus, the MN receives redundant information from both LMAs. Besides the PMIPv6 messages, extra signaling is exchanged between the NLMA and the gateway to confirm and obtain additional information about the MN. Additionally, the NLMA must authenticate the MN. A tunnel must be created between the gateway and the NLMA, and between the NLMA and the OMAG. The performance evaluation compares the solution with MIPv6, Fast Handovers for MIPv6, I.PMIPv6, and EIPMH by measuring handover latency. What may well be noticed is that the Reactive mode

TABLE I. CI-PMIPV6 AND RELATED WORK COMPARISON.

Solution	# extra messages in interdom. HO	# extra tunnels	Infrastructure maintenance	Compatibility with legacy systems
No-opt [4]	8	1	Yes	Yes
EIPMH [6]	6	2	No	No
I-PMIP [7]	6	1	No	No
No-Gap [9]	4	1	No	Yes
CI-PMIPv6	4	0	Yes	Yes

leads to greater overheads because of an additional tunnel in comparison to the No-Gap model. According to the authors, the No-Gap model is the most efficient model. This is why this paper gives more focus to the No-Gap solution, which has a counterpart in [10].

Table I summarizes the differences between CI-PMIPv6 and other inter-domain solutions. The non-optimized approach [4] has the greatest increase in extra signaling in comparison with the original implementation of PMIPv6. Additionally, there might be an overhead related to the addition of one more IP header caused by the extra tunnel. These factors may be responsible for a remarkable increase in latency during the inter-domain handover. The advantage is the absence of new entities and the compatibility with the PMIPv6 legacy system.

The EIPMH [6] introduces the TD - a centralized entity - to manage the transition between two LMAs. The authors acknowledge that there may be more than one distributor, each of which is responsible for a coverage area. Nevertheless, the handover between distributors is not covered by the authors. Furthermore, the solution adds two extra tunnels and requires changes in the infrastructure of the network.

I-PMIP [7] requires the existence of a centralized entity to maintain MNs information. It creates a single point of failure and causes changes in the network infrastructure. Additionally, the extra tunnel added may increase the packet delivery overhead.

The No-Gap solution [9] is one of the least expensive solutions in terms of signaling overhead. However, it requires changes in legacy border routers and generates redundant data packets in the same MAG, coming from different LMAs.

CI-PMIPv6 appears to be the least expensive solution, since the extra signaling necessary for inter-domain handover is one of the lowest, when compared with other solutions. It does not require extra tunnels and may interwork with PMIPv6 legacy systems. The cluster messages do not add extra signaling costs to the ongoing handover, since they are asynchronous and are necessary only in future inter-domain handovers. Thus, we expect that CI-PMIPv6 will have a smaller handover cost, lower latency - as a consequence, less packet loss - and a higher useful traffic rate than the other proposals.

IV. PERFORMANCE EVALUATION AND RESULTS

In this section, CI-PMIPv6 performance is compared to non-optimized, No-Gap, I-PMIP, and EIPMH solutions. The evaluation is based on the analytical modeling presented in [11] [12] [13]. This allows the cost of handover signaling in a session, latency and the packet loss of one handover, and the goodput in a session to be measured. We consider that mobile devices are attached to vehicles in a highway during a voice call (e.g., Skype). Inter-domain handover takes place as the MN arrives at a new domain. The mobility pattern follows the Fluid-Flow model [14]. That model considers average velocity (v), the subnet and domain coverage areas (A_M and A_D, respectively) and the subnet and domain perimeters (L_M and L_D, respectively) as parameters. The direction of movement is uniformly distributed in a range of 0 to 2π. Since this experiment is interested in a vehicular scenario, the choice of this model is very appropriate.

Two variables determine the dynamics of the MN: the domain crossing rate (μ_D) and the subnet crossing rate (μ_M). The former is the rate at which the node switches from one domain to another. It is equivalent to the inter-domain handover rate (Ng). The latter is the rate at which the node switches from one subnet to another. The intra-domain handover rate (Nl) considers a subnet crossing when this does not imply a domain crossing. That is, Nl is the difference between μ_M and μ_D. Their equations are as follows [11] [13]:

$$\mu_M = \frac{vL_M}{\pi A_M}, \tag{1}$$

$$Ng = \mu_D = \frac{vL_D}{\pi A_D}, \tag{2}$$

$$Nl = \mu_M - \mu_D. \tag{3}$$

Another important parameter to describe mobility of a node is the Session-to-Mobility Ratio (SMR), which relates session arrival rate and the subnet crossing rate as follows [11]:

$$SMR = \frac{\lambda_S}{\mu_M}. \tag{4}$$

If SMR is near zero, this means that the node has high mobility. The higher the SMR, the more static the node.

The signaling cost is the number of handover signaling messages, taking into consideration the distance in hops between two entities x and y, namely $H_{(x-y)}$, the underlying media, and the processing cost. For each protocol message sent, the signaling cost is (see [11])

$$C_{x-y} = \alpha(H_{(x-y)}) - \beta + PC_y, \tag{5}$$
$$PC_y = \varsigma \log N^y_{MN}, \tag{6}$$

where the parameters α and β represent the coefficients of unity transmission costs (in messages/hop) in wired and wireless links, respectively. The cost of processing at one end is represented by PC_y. It is measured based on a logarithmic search in a data structure with the size of the number of MN entries and a normalizing constant ς equivalent to the bandwidth allocation. If the reception of a message at one end does not imply the search in a local storage, PC_y is considered zero. Additionally, if the node that sends or receives the message is not an MN, the β factor is excluded. The handover signaling cost is the sum of the cost of all messages exchanged during a handover. The average cost is measured as a weighted sum of the intra-domain and inter-domain counterparts. It depends on Ng and Nl rates. The average cost [11] is presented as

$$cost = \frac{intraDHO\ cost \times Nl + interDHO\ cost \times Ng}{Nl + Ng}. \quad (7)$$

The inter-domain signaling cost for a session is the cost of one inter-domain handover multiplied by both Ng and the session duration:

$$cost\ in\ session = interDHO\ cost \times Ng \times session\ duration. \quad (8)$$

Handover latency is measured as the handover duration, i.e., the time a node spends without effective communication. The latency equation for a message exchanged between two nodes x and y is (see [13])

$$T_{x-y} = \frac{1+q}{1-q}\left(\frac{M_{size}}{B_{wl}} + L_{wl}\right) + H_{x-y}\left(\frac{M_{size}}{B_w} + L_w + T_q\right). \quad (9)$$

The first part of the sum is the wireless overhead and it must be excluded if neither x nor y is a wireless device. The second part is the overhead in the wired medium. The parameter q is the probability of failure of the wireless link, M_{size} is the average length of a message, and B_{wl} and B_w are the wireless and wired bandwidths, respectively. The propagation delay in wireless and wired media are L_{wl} and L_w, respectively. The average queuing delay in each router is represented by T_q. Handover latency is the sum of the latency of all signaling messages exchanged during a handover. As in the signaling cost, the average latency is measured as a weighted sum of the intra-domain and inter-domain counterparts as follows [11]:

$$latency = \frac{intraDHO\ lat \times Nl + interDHO\ lat \times Ng}{Nl + Ng}. \quad (10)$$

The average packet loss in a handover is the average number of packages not sent/received during handover. The packet loss (PL) is the product of the handover latency and the packet arrival rate (λ_p) [11], i.e.,

$$PL = T\lambda_p. \quad (11)$$

Finally, the goodput is a measure that relates the useful data traffic during a session and the total traffic (TOT), which is the total number of bytes transmitted during a session. The goodput is determined as follows (cf. [11]):

$$Goodput = \frac{TOT - (P_{size} \times PL_{session} + TOT \times PD)}{session\ duration}, \quad (12)$$

$$TOT = session\ duration \times \lambda_p \times P_{size}, \quad (13)$$

$$PD = \frac{40 \times H_{tunnel}}{(40 + P_{size}) \times H_{MN-CN}}. \quad (14)$$

Goodput additionally depends on the packet loss and the packet delivery (PD) overhead. PD overhead is the cost of tunneling the IP-in-IP extra 40-byte header along the path between an MN and its correspondent node (H_{MN-CN}).

TABLE II. EVALUATION PARAMETERS.

Parameter	Default value
Number of subnets per domain	7
Coverage area of each subnet (A_M)	1.87 km^2
Kademlia's constant (k)	10
MN velocity (v)	15 m/s
Prob. of failure of the wireless link (q)	0.5 (range 0-0.8)
Coefficient of cost in wired medium (α)	1 message/hop
Coefficient of cost in wireless medium (β)	10 messages/hop
Normalizing constant (ς)	0.01
Queuing time (T_q)	5 ms
Subnet residency time ($1/\mu_M$)	300 s
Prop. delay (wired link) (L_w)	0.75 μs
Prop. delay (wireless link) (L_{wl})	10 ms
Packet arrival rate (λ_p)	38 packets/s (100 kbps)
Session arrival rate (λ_S)	0.001 sessions/s
Average data packet size (P_{size})	300 bytes
Average signaling packet size (M_{size})	160 bytes

Packet size (P_{size}) and the PMIPv6 tunnel size in hops (H_{tunnel}) are parameters for the PD.

Now, we turn our attention to the perfomance evaluation of CI-PMIPv6. The signaling cost in a session is measured as a funcion of SMR. Latency and packet loss in one handover are measured as a function of the probability of failure of the link in the wireless network. The goodput in a session is measured as a function of SMR.

We consider in our evaluations that a domain has 7 subnets. Each subnet follows a hexagonal model and has one MAG. There is a central subnet that is managed by a single LMA. The other subnets surround the central subnet. The coverage area of each subnet is equal to 1.8 km^2 and the perimeter is equal to 5 km. Table II summarizes the values of the parameters used for performance evaluation. The Kademlia parameter k used in CI-PMIPv6, which represents the size of the neighborhood, is set to 10. This value is chosen based on a scenario where nodes have an average speed of 15 m/s (60 km/h) and may cross 10 domains during a session. The probability of failure of the wireless link ranges from 0 to 0.8 in experiments to consider the radio channel under different quality conditions during handover. The greater this probability is, the more link-layer retransmissions are necessary. We consider α to be equal to 1 message/hop and β to be equal to 10 messages/hop, since wireless links tend to cost more than wired links. The average queue time is a typical value of 5 ms. We consider that the average residency time of an MN is equal to 300 s, which corresponds to a mean speed of 15 m/s. The theoretical latency across a 4G LTE interface is in the order of 10 ms. We assume that the wireless link has a propagation delay of 10 ms in order to capture such behaviour. The propagation delay of wired links are assumed to be a typical value for Fast Ethernet. The arrival rate of packets corresponds to a voice call (e.g., Skype) and the session arrival rate allows consecutive voice calls that are 13 minutes long each. We consider that the average data packet size is 300 bytes long [15]. The average packet size used for handover signaling is 160 bytes long.

Figure 4 presents the influence of SMR on the overall cost during a session. If SMR is near zero, there is a high mobility scenario. If SMR is high, this means that the network mobility is low. Therefore, the cost tends to be lower with higher values of SMR for all proposals. When SMR tends to zero, there is a high number of handovers during a session. In this case, the number of messages exchanged during handover plays an important role in the overall cost. The scheme with no optimization has the worst performance and CI-PMIPv6 presents the lowest cost, since it requires fewer messages to accomplish handover. Additionally, the presence of a cluster that exchanges domains information proactively and in parallel with the current binding update simplifies the communication during future inter-domain handovers, which require less interaction between core network entities. The CI-PMIPv6 cost is always the lowest. In particular, it is 20% lower than the cost in No-Gap when the SMR is equal to 0.01.

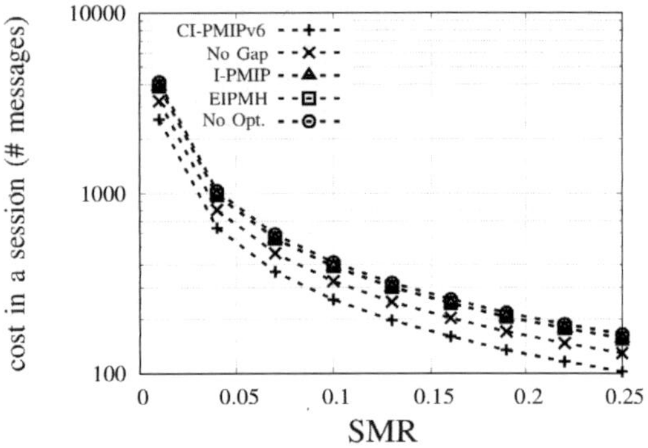

Figure 4. Overall cost *versus* SMR.

Figure 5 presents the average handover latency as a function of the probability of failure of the wireless link. This probability represents the reliability of the wireless channel and may degrade performance due to retransmissions. The EIPMH results are influenced by the high number of interactions in the core network. It has the highest latency until the probability of failure reaches 0.65. From this point on, the scheme without optimization has greater latency. This is due to the fact that it has more messages involving the MN, thus making the scheme more sensitive to the wireless media. I-PMIP presents slightly better results than No Gap. It is important to notice that CI-PMIPv6 presents the smallest results for latency. In particular, CI-PMIPv6 latency is 16% smaller than the latency in I-PMIP when the probability of failure is 0.8. In this case, CI-PMIPv6 still has a handover latency of 410 ms, which is 90 ms lower than the latency in I-PMIP. CI-PMIPv6 performs better because unnecessary interactions in both the core network and the wireless network were eliminated.

Figure 6 presents the number of lost packets as function of the probability of failure of the wireless link. The packet loss is directly related to the handover latency, since no buffering during handover is considered in the protocols. Considering that in this scenario the arrival rate is 38 packets/s, there is a significant loss of quality in the worst case even for the No-Gap scheme, which presents the second best result. The number of lost data packets for CI-PMIPv6 is the smallest in all cases studied. In particular, it is 16% smaller than the value observed for No-Gap when the failure probability is 0.8. The number of lost data packets for CI-PMIPv6 is always the smallest because CI-PMIPv6 has the lowest handover latency.

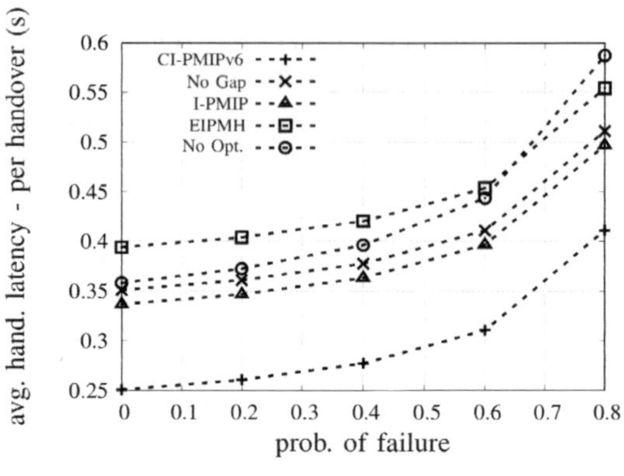

Figure 5. Overall latency *versus* prob. of failure of the wireless link.

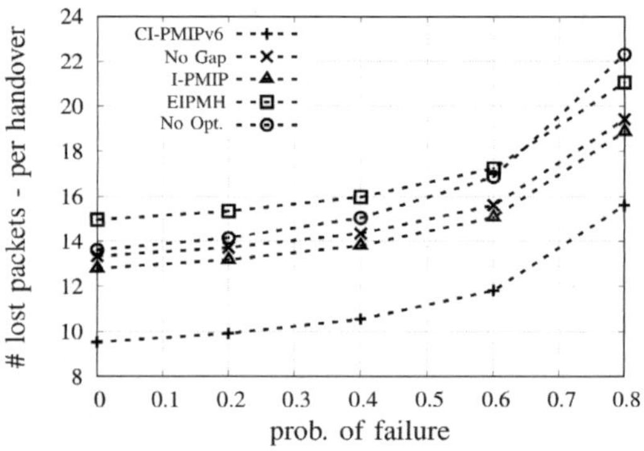

Figure 6. Packet loss *versus* prob. of failure of the wireless link.

Figure 7 presents the goodput *versus* the SMR. If SMR is high, it means that the network mobility is low. Thus, goodput tends to be more stable as SMR grows. CI-PMIPv6 has higher goodput for all SMR values. This means that the proposed scheme can send more useful data during a session. CI-PMIPv6 maintains the same number of tunnels created in PMIPv6. This avoids the PD overhead due to headers in IP-in-IP tunneling. EIPMH has the worst goodput because it requires the creation of two extra tunnels, besides the pre-existing PMIPv6 tunnel.

V. Conclusions and Future Work

This paper presented the CI-PMIPv6 as a distributed solution for inter-domain IP mobility. CI-PMIPv6 has a distributed design, which organizes LMAs from different domains in a cluster as Kademlia peers. In that cluster, information on MNs is spread proactively and in parallel with the current binding update, thereby simplifying future inter-domain handover processes.

CI-PMIPv6 was compared to several inter-domain approaches and results have shown that when CI-PMIPv6 is used, the cost, the latency, and the packet loss in the scenario studied are lower. Additionally, the goodput reaches higher values. In future work, it is intended to extend the solution to FPMIPv6. Further, the application of localized routing techniques may

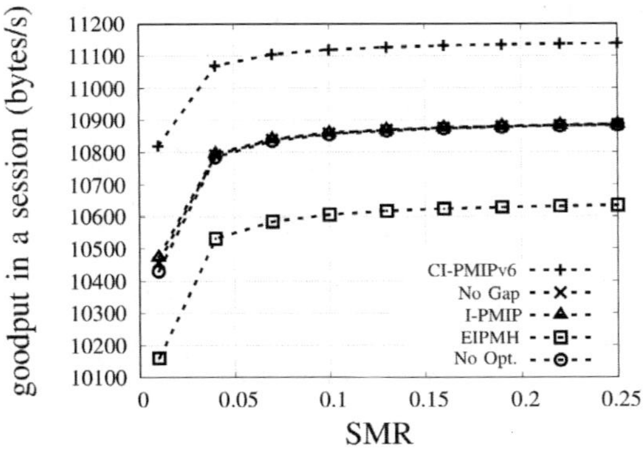

Figure 7. Goodput *versus* SMR.

be applied to optimize the CI-PMIPv6 performance in high mobility scenarios. Simulation experiments with CI-PMIPv6 is further expected. Future experiments with a variable number of domains will highlight the scalability of the cluster in comparison to other architectures.

REFERENCES

[1] Ericsson, "Ericsson mobility report," 2016, retrieved: March 2017. [Online]. Available: https://www.ericsson.com/mobility-report

[2] H. Modares, A. Moravejosharieh, J. Lloret, and R. B. Salleh, "A survey on proxy mobile IPv6 handover," IEEE Systems Journal, vol. 10, no. 1, mar 2016, pp. 208–217.

[3] N. Neumann, J. Lei, X. Fu, and G. Zhang, "Kademlia with consistency checks as a foundation of borderless collaboration in open science services," in Proc. of the 5th International Young Scientist Conference on Computational Science, Krakow, 2016, pp. 304–312.

[4] S. Park, E. Lee, F. Yu, S. Noh, and S.-H. Kim, "Inter-domain roaming mechanism transparent to IPv6-node among PMIPv6 networks," in Proc. of the IEEE 71st Vehicular Technology Conference, Taipei, 2010, pp. 1–5.

[5] H. Zhou, H. Zhang, Y. Qin, H. Wang, and H. Chao, "A Proxy Mobile IPv6 based global mobility management architecture and protocol," Mobile Networks and Applications, vol. 15, no. 4, 2010, pp. 530–542.

[6] F. Zhong, S. Yang, C. K. Yeo, and B. S. Lee, "Enabling inter-PMIPv6-domain handover with traffic distributors," in Proc. 7th IEEE CCNC, Las Vegas, 2010, pp. 1–5.

[7] N. Neumann, J. Lei, X. Fu, and G. Zhang, "I-PMIP: an inter-domain mobility extension for proxy-mobile IP," in Proc. International Conference on Wireless Communications and Mobile Computing: Connecting the World Wirelessly, Leipzig, 2009, pp. 994–999.

[8] T. T. Nguyen and C. Bonnet, "DMM-based inter-domain mobility support for proxy mobile IPv6." in Proc. IEEE WCNC, Shangai, 2013, pp. 1998–2003.

[9] I. Joe and H. Lee, "An efficient inter-domain handover scheme with minimized latency for PMIPv6," in Proc. International Conference on Computing, Networking and Communications, Maui, 2012, pp. 332 – 336.

[10] K.-W. L. et al., "Inter-domain handover scheme using an intermediate mobile access gateway for seamless service in vehicular networks," International Journal of Communication Systems, vol. 23, no. 9–10, 2009, pp. 1127–1144.

[11] A. Taghizadeh, T.-C. Wan, R. Budiarto, F. T. Yap, and A. Osman, "A performance evaluation framework for network-based IP mobility solutions," International Journal of Innovative, Computing, Information and Control, vol. 8, no. 10, 2012, pp. 7263–7288.

[12] J. McNair, I. Akyildiz, and M. D. Bender, "Handoffs for real-time traffic in mobile IP version 6 networks ," in Proc. First Global Telecommunications Conference, San Antonio, 2001, pp. 3463–3467.

[13] C. Makaya and S. Pierre, "An analytical framework for performance evaluation of IPv6-based mobility management protocols," IEEE Transactions on Wireless Communications, vol. 7, no. 3, 2008, p. 7.

[14] A. Salehan, M. Robatmili, M. Abrishami, and A. Movaghar, "A comparison of various routing protocols in mobile ad-hoc networks (MANETs) with the use of fluid flow simulation method," in Proc. 4th International Conference on Wireless and Mobile Communications, Athens, 2008, pp. 260–267.

[15] S. Molnár and M. Perényi, "On the identification and analysis of Skype traffic," International Journal of Communication Systems, vol. 24, no. 1, 2011, pp. 94–117.

SEED, A Server Platform for the Edge of the Network

Carlo Vitucci,
Technology management
Ericsson AB
Stockholm, Sweden
carlo.vitucci@ericsson.com

Alf Larsson
Senior Specialist
Ericsson AB
Stockholm, Sweden
alf.larsson@ericsson.com

***Abstract*—Software defined Network – Network Function Virtualization (SDN-NFV) has been the catalyst of most of the researches in the networking and telecommunication domain during the latest years and it is supposed to have important deployment in the early next ones. However, there is no common understanding why it is so important and why it is the winning solution for the next generation networks. This paper describes, from an infrastructure point of view, the challenges to understand what SDN-NFV deployment into the Radio Access Network (RAN) really means. Our approach identifies how the Server at the Edge (SEED) of the network should look like. The paper describes the meaning of moving SDN-NFV into the RAN (conceptually different than moving the RAN into the cloud) and identifies the key function enablers for meeting the operation agility request from Radio Access. Resources and meters handling as critical characterization to empower the Self Organizing Network (SON) concept without unacceptable performance cost are also described. The paper aims to emphasize the enablers of the new business model needed in the SEED more than being an exhaustive description of single components.**

Keywords-SDN-NFV; C-Mobile OS; operational agility, new business case.

I. INTRODUCTION

Today, the Telecom realm is facing an epic moment, a technology step that will drive the evolution of the networked system in the future and, at the end of the day, the End User services and life style. Although it has become common knowledge, it is important to recall what is behind the SDN-NFV fortune in order to clearly identify some design rules that should drive the design in the area.

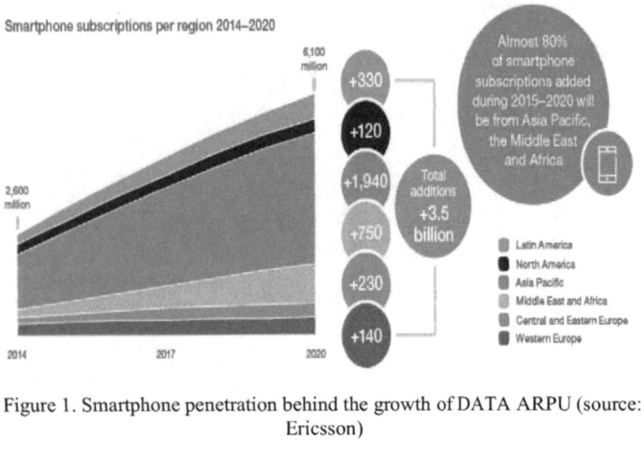

Figure 1. Smartphone penetration behind the growth of DATA ARPU (source: Ericsson)

Figure 2. The revenue from new subscription trend (source Chetan Sharma Consulting [2])

In the last years, Telecom operators have seen an exponential growth of data traffic and, at the same time, a significant income reduction from the "golden eggs goose" voice and Short Message Service (SMS). Concurrently, thesmartphone penetration is continuously increasing (see Figure 1), changing the user's usage style of connectivity [1] [3]. Today, it is a common condition for all operators to have most of their Average Revenue Per User (ARPU) coming from data traffic and indeed voice and SMS is often offered at a very cheap price in order to attract new customers and increase revenue from data traffic. The trend is not supposed to change in the next years: Ericsson prediction shows that, by 2021, there will be 28 billion connected devices around the world [1]. 5G technology is just the answer to such a tremendous demand of connectivity for data traffic [3].

Saying so, one could start thinking that the operators might have better income from increased network capability, but the picture is not complete: the majority of mobile users are not prepared to spend too much for using their smartphones and it is not a case that the revenue from new subscriber dropped down dramatically in the last years, as reported in Figure 2. Such a condition results in a significant reduction of operator margin in a way that some pessimistic vision [4] is predicting a possible "end of profitability" condition for their business. Even in a more optimistic prediction, it is however a fact that the current business model is not really sustainable and operators need a direction where their margins can start to increase again [5].

A common understanding is that SDN-NFV is a key to reduce Operating expenses (Opex) and Capital expenditures (Capex) and then increase operator's margin. But, it looks like that statement is without a strong background vision, or at least, not able to give the right clue of the operators' strategy. Just to avoid any misunderstanding, SDN-NFV architecture will reduce Opex and Capex, but it is not actually that huge of an incentive for the operators' business. In fact, Opex and Capex have been reduced during the latest years, mostly thanks to the cost reduction of technology, and the real truth is that today total cost and revenue are so close that one can hardly imagine a new golden era thanks only to Opex and Capex reduction. It seems enough for surviving in the Telecom market battlefield, but surely not enough to justify a new infrastructure investment by the operators. Eventually, let us consider the life cycle of a new Telecom technology: the delivery rate between a technology step (from 2G to 3G, from 3G to 4G and so on) has an aggressive pace, in most of the case "forcing" operators to make a new infrastructure investment. But reduced revenue and delivery interval is concurrently reducing the business case window, so operators are not actually too keen to join a new technology in such conditions and for sure they are looking at any new investment very carefully. So, what are the actual operators' needs then?

So far, their effort has been focused on a market where improvement of capacity and quality of the connectivity has been enough. But the richest market today is fully in the hands of the over-the-top content (OTT) media delivery companies (Google, Facebook, Netflix, etc.). A real shift of operators' business is the key to enter into such a rich market. Eventually, that will be a win-win condition, since OTT is perfectly aware that reducing the end-to-end (E2E) data contents latency will improve their business. They are also aware that accessing User Metadata (very well known by Telecom operators) will increase even more such a market thanks to new business cases. Those considerations are behind the successful story of the SDN-NFV. The architecture has been designed in order to feed that win- win condition. At the same time, reducing Opex and Capex creates a more green-power environment and allowing an easy deployment of a new technology in a shorter, safer and comfortable new way. The "core" promise of SDN-NFV is to guarantee a new "business environment" where Telecom operators are a stakeholder in the creation of new flexible services.

This paper explores how RAN is integrated into the SDN-NFV architecture in Section 2. Section 3 introduces the SEED as architecture element, which is further described in detail in Section 4. We end with conclusions in Section 5 and future works in Section 6.

II. SDN-NFV AND THE C-RAN

The European Telecommunications Standards Institute (ETSI) has set regulations and indications in order to design and define SDN-NFV architecture [7][8], but some parts are left for others to design. One of those parts is the so called Network Function Virtualization Infrastructure (NFVI), where the Radio Network vendors could play their significant role, in this way, both contributing to the SDN-NFV best deployment and improving their own business. The first discriminating condition to succeed in this challenge is their ability to integrate the traditional IT world with the Telecom one (as explicitly required by the new business case), that is, their ability to provide full SDN-NFV architecture up to the edge of the network: into the RAN. ETSI group defined the deployment of the SDN-NFV for the mobile network in their Use Cases study report [6]. According to that scenario, the current base station is actually split into two main objects: the Remote Radio Header (RRH), that is antenna and eventually the basic Layer 1, and the virtualized Baseband Unit (vBBU) as a service housed in a specific server implementing Layer 2 and Layer 3 of mobile protocols. Then, from an infrastructure point of view, the challenge is to understand what SDN-NFV deployment into the RAN really means, identifying how the server at the edge of the network should look like. The questions that initially need to be answered are: what are the characterizations and technologies that must be considered as key components of the server itself, which hardware characteristics are matching the requirements, which functions are clearly new components (services) of the platform housed into the server@edge (SEED) and which ones need more attention and effort to remove possible obstacles and limitations?

It is a long journey where the infrastructure designers must remember the real needs behind the SDN-NFV. Moreover, the operators' expectations have to be fulfilled and also a more complete understanding of other opportunities like footprint and energy consumption. For these reasons, it is worth to start considering the SDN-NFV deployment scenario from a system level view and then refer to it while defining services and functions. This paper wants to focus on the SEED concept, identifying its characterization to cope with the radio function requirements. In fact, the starting point of this paper is that it could be very difficult to move the RAN into the cloud and more suitable to port SDN-NFV into the RAN. This will give all the benefits of SDN-NFV described in the introduction and, concurrently, will answer the specific requirements needed at the edge of the network. The reference deployment model has

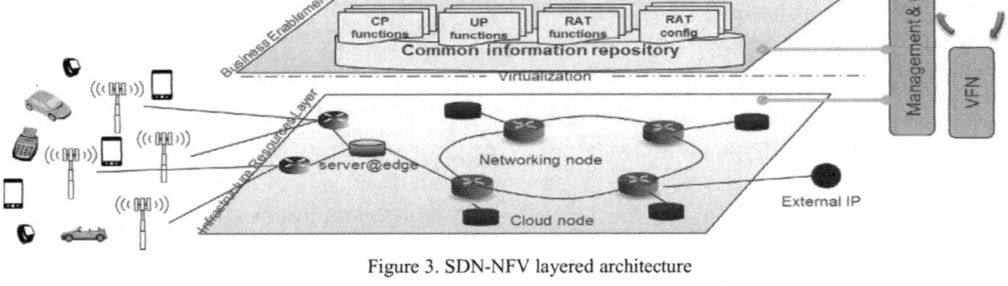

Figure 3. SDN-NFV layered architecture

been described [9][10] and ETSI made some progress in the same area [7] introducing the so called Mobile-Edge Computing (MEC) server. It offers application developers and content providers cloud-computing capabilities and an IT service environment at the edge of the mobile network.

In this paper, the MEC server is considered the starting point of any investigation of the SEED definition and characterization. Another aspect is to consider SDN-NFV as an overall system solution, an end-to-end solution from that perspective to avoid not fulfilling the fundamental requirements.

SDN-NFV architecture is built over three layers [11], as logically shown in Figure 3:

- Business Application Layer – where the enterprise business value model is defined
- Business Enablement Layer – where the enabling and capabilities value are defined
- Infrastructure Resources Layer – where the resources needed by the value are defined

In the next decades, enterprises will increasingly make their specific applications available on mobile devices. The next wave of mobile communication is to mobilize and automate industries and industry processes. This is widely referred to as machine-type communication (MTC) and the Internet of Things (IoT). OTT players will move to deliver more and more applications that require higher quality, lower latency, and other service enhancing capabilities). The SDN-NFV layered vision is the most useful to understand the service oriented approach supported by the architecture itself. Deployment over the network, functions blocks and their reference points have been the main focus of the ETSI group. There are also some concepts on the splitting of the current Base Station in RRH and vBBU and what it actually means for the current implementation of the Base Station Controller (BSC). As an example, one can refer to the LTE protocol deployment in order to figure out pros and cons while moving LTE function from RRH to the vBBU. The deployment of Radio Technology between RRH and BBU could be done in several ways, mostly deciding the point in the protocol chain where the split is done and so defining the interface typology between RRH and BBU. Depending on the decision taken, one can face different types of issues or constraints. An ETSI-based vBBU implementation, for example, is able to guarantee the highest service flexibility possible, so the highest level of operational agility (indeed very useful for Telecom Infrastructure providers as well, since deployment of a new technology could be handled in the same product handling shape of a new service deployment), but it is challenged by very aggressive latency time requirement. On the other hand, a "smooth" porting of the existing BSC solutions into the cloud could be attractive in term of legacy software or reduced latency time that would simply the first deployment, but it fails to answer the strong request of operation agility, because, in this case, the protocol splitting is done on the highest protocol layer only. In a similar way, splitting BSC between RRH and BBU could have important impacts by means of Fronthaul and Backhaul capacity demand [12]. The successful story of SDN-NFV deployment is passing by an infrastructure that matches all demands: there is nothing more important than the operational agility in the business behind the SDN-NFV and this simple consideration is driving the decision to where one should focus their effort: define and design an infrastructure for the SEED that cope with the latency time requirement. As already mentioned before, that is not a new concept indeed. It is in the ETSI studies while talking about the so called MEC Server [7]. What remains to be done is identifying the technical characterization of the C-mobile platform, the SEED, in order to handle the MEC server as needed. It is worth to mention that all network function should be handled as service, according to the layer architecture described in Figure 3. In SDN-NFV network, the deployment is based on Service Availability Concept: shortly, Radio Access must be a function deployed on the Business Enablement Layer and published in order to be used as component in a service chain at the Business Application Layer. The service chains capability [13] is considered a key accelerator of the SDN-NFV usage, since it is introducing a high level of operational agility, already mentioned as mandatory requirement. Note how the service chain is also a mindset in ETSI use case description of the BS [6] and it is at the very fundamental of SDN-NFV architecture description [14][15].

III. SEED, A SDN-NFV SYSTEM ELEMENT

SEED is the C-mobile platform for the MEC server, by definition the server at the edge of the network. It is designed to allow a unique and logical centralized network controller spread from end user to the data center. The characterization of the SEED could only be done with that picture in mind and the aim to never violate the operational agility. This concept is fully aligned with the ETSI group SDN-NFV use case about mobile network implementation [6]. From a high level functions point of view, the MEC server should be able to host: computing capability (for mobiles, as well as for generic services), connectivity (with external network, as well as with the radio interface), and storage, one of the value enabler resource for new business case. The above set of different capabilities is defining the SEED as described in Figure 4, duplicated by redundancy in order to have high reliability condition.

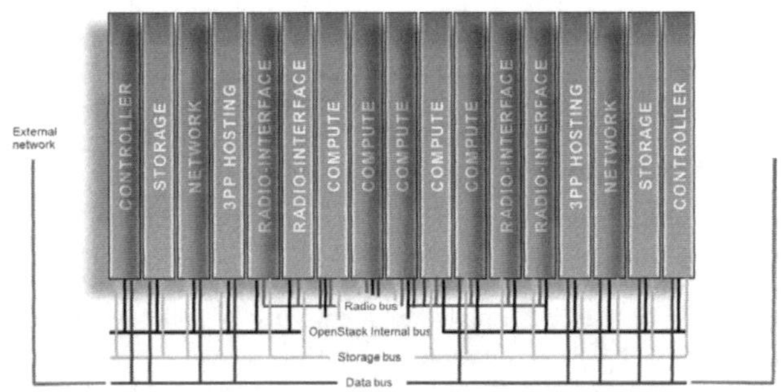

Figure 4. The SEED structured for function capabilities

The number of those capabilities for the SEED will define its size, which is a pure dimensioning calculation. The solution is fully aligned to the most common cloud platform (ref. User's Guide indication [16][17]). A bit more could be added about connectivity. In order to avoid unwanted disturbances in traffic bandwidth availability, Virtual Machine's (VMs) data, storage, network and radio buses should be kept independent from each other. To comply with the idea of SEED we need to look on a lower level than macro functions, try to figure out how the C-mobile platform looks like. Next, we will clarify some misunderstandings around some concepts that are normally pointed out while talking about SDN-NFV. The virtualization layer is not an option. Virtualization is the core of the SDN-NFV architecture and there is no alternative to conform to such architecture. All resources must be virtualized, with no exception. Functions are virtualized, and every single physical resource is virtualized as well. A downsize of the virtualization range is against the operational agility characterization that has been already mentioned previously as the key incitement for the business model behind the SDN-NFV [18]. Downsizing the virtualization means to downsize the operational agility, which affects the business capacity of the operators and eventually misses the expectation they have for the new business opportunity. Applications are services and handled as services into the new architecture. That means there is no software deployment as traditionally intended, but instances of service as VMs (or containers) deployed over the architecture and connected in a service chain to deploy a network value. One of the most common buzz words around SDN-NFV is Common Off The Shelf hardware (COTS), most of the time, used as an enabler to reduce Opex and Capex. Hardware evolution is always ongoing. Vendors are fighting their own war and they are fully aware of the needs/requirements coming from the next mobile generation world. So, why should we get stuck on COTS that most likely will be obsolete in a (short) while? Thinking about our main ideas of the implementation for the best SEED, we should identify the requirements of the hardware platform in order to achieve our optimal architecture. This means that the available COTS could not match our requirements. What hardware characteristics and performance will match our requirements is defining the next generation of COTS. What we actually need (and that is not only a design decision for software) is a suitable hardware in order to:

- Remove the latency obstacles to strengthen the operational agility, even thanks to ad hoc hardware assisted functions and accelerations;
- Improve connectivity;
- Design secure Quality of Service (QoS) resource usage for Service Level Agreement (SLA) handling;

IV. STRUCTURING THE SEED

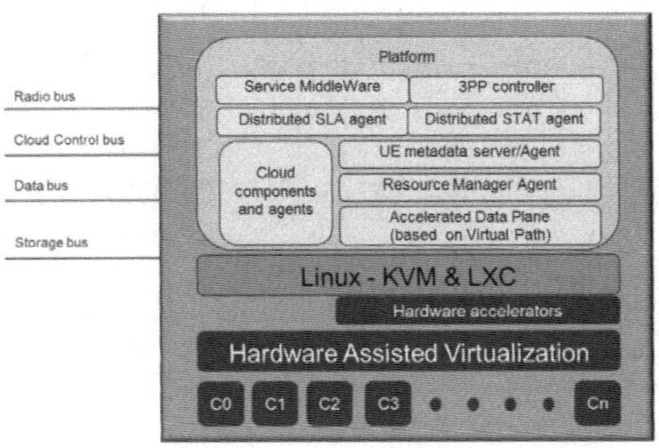

Figure 5. Main objects housed in SEED boards

Looking at the state of the art, Intel architecture seems to have better performance and virtualization features than other architectures: the management of virtualized objects requests less capability and introduce less latency in the system using Intel solution. Moreover, SDN-NFV implementation is strongly supported by the Open Software Community and by de facto a lot of functions and features in SDN-NFV are designed on Intel architecture first and then eventually ported on other targets. Though, power consumption needs to be considered, especially while referring to the edge of the network where power consumption is really a big issue and where other hardware architectures seem to be more efficient in the power consumption domain. Figure 5 is summarizing the main objects housed in SEED board, where differences are described in the next paragraphs.

A. Compute Platform for the Edge

The compute platform for the edge shall be based on 64-bits Linux Operating system (OS). Both hardware and software support the virtualization layer and this is pointing to a very specific set of needed features: reduce the cache pollution (e.g., Huge Page or Rapid Virtualization Indexing (RVI), depending on hardware architecture), support multi-core system, guarantee low power consumption, full set of hardware and software feature in order to speed up VM context switch, Virtual Interrupt Handling, hardware assisted trace & debug capability in a virtualized environment and virtual path. Both Kernel-based Virtual Machine (KVM) and Linux Containers (LXC) should be supported: for the reasons mentioned above, it seems a good choice to have a C-mobile platform able to handle both, but having VM's and container's concurrently in a service chain is introducing a level of complexity. The OpenSoftware Cloud components and agents are obviously there (OpenStack, OpenDayLight, ONOS, M-CORD and whatever is requested by the Management And Orchestration – MANO - of the system). Accelerated Data Plane in User Space (vSwitch, fastpath, direct interrupt delivery, etc.) is needed in order to design efficient connectivity solution. A Resource Manager Agent is needed and must be able to handle the resources reference point as described in the SDN-NFV architecture. Distributed SLA and STAT agents are needed and they shall interwork, not only to each other but to higher hierarchical SLA and STAT objects in the architecture. That is done in order to handle the available resources in a dynamic way and providing the support for Self Organizing Network (SON) capability. The hierarchical approach for meters and resources handling, as described in Figure 6, is crucial to avoid massive signaling. Moreover, the local resource-meters agents can apply the right taxonomy to create the resources relationship between different logical layers, from physical resources usage up to QoS. Important characteristic is the User Equipment (UE) metadata Server, as the service available in the SEED to publish the UE metadata and control the access/usage of them and the Third Party Product (3PP)-bridge controller. It will provide "close-to-UE" service capability to enterprises and other 'vertical' services. External connectivity to Radio bus, Cloud control internal bus (Management plane), data bus (data plane) and Storage bus (caching service) are available for the compute board.

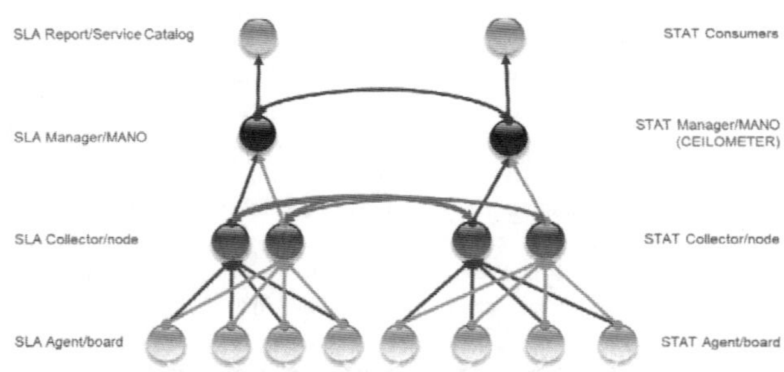

Figure 6. The hierarchical structure and co-relation of SLA and STAT

B. 3PP Hosting Platform for the edge

The hardware board is just the same as the compute one and likewise we can say about OS and virtualization layer. Platform components are the same or agents of the same functions in the compute board. For example, UE metadata client interworks with its server in order to provide the complete list of metadata info and 3PP bridge is the active component of its controller, devoted to provide connectivity channel between 3PP application and external internet/radio channels and, for that reason, responsible for security check, registration, authorization and encryption/decryption. The available connectivity channels are not the same: 3PP hosting - for security reason - shall not have a possibility to use the radio bus directly. This will allow resource control according to the SLA in the compute board, avoiding any possible malicious or faulty behavior of the 3PP applications themselves.

C. Radio-Interface Platform for the Edge

The board could be armed with dedicated hardware accelerators, needed to speed up the radio access protocols handling. It is not a limitation, as long as they are designed to be controlled as virtualized resource by the resource manager. With such differentiation, the board and the platform components/functions are not different from the components/functions mentioned so far for the SEED platform.

D. SEED Characterization

Connectivity and the efficient implementation of it is the critical key of the SEED. It is mandatory to avoid any bottleneck and additional overhead that will cost a lot for latency time. At the same time, the connectivity handling shall never be an obstacle for the service chain deployment concept (the operational agility is a mandatory requirement for the server at the edge of the network). Once one decides to share resources between different actors, it is fundamental that they can access them without creating disturbances to each other and according to the resource sharing agreement they have. It is like job scheduling where one wants threads continuously working and not starve them out. In case that happens, the thread may steal a job from someone else. Thereby maybe using another set of resources. The virtual path concept is trying to do the same with the connectivity access. Different VMs running should be able to access connectivity as they are running alone, based on the maximum available bandwidth defined in its SLA (the virtualized slice of connectivity assigned to it) and avoiding performance drawback due to system overhead (minimum or zero cost of virtualization layer, VM walkthrough data handling). The nature itself of SEED sets a specific requirement for the platform: provide a wide range of computing characterization and guarantee the agreed slice of computing resources won't be affected by other VMs running on board. This is quite clear once one starts thinking on a platform where there are strong time constrains application types, like radio services, relaxed time-constrains application types, like video or audio services, and no time-constrains application types, like general services. But that is not enough. If someone pays for a specific bandwidth and computing, platform shall protect those resources for it. Again, the macro effect should be that, no matter if the VM is working alone or not, it can always count on the resources slices assigned by SLA. For that reason, the platform shall schedule VM jobs according to the following rules: a) Provide strong isolation for VMs with strong time-constrains; b) Provide maximum CPU utilization for VMs with relaxed time constrains using SCHED_DEADLINE policy. SLA and Statistics are strictly correlated to each other and actually hierarchically spread all over the system (this concept is also emphasized in Figure 6). Indeed, STATs are far from being a passive snapshots recording, they are actively interworking with SLA and resource manager in order to deploy the best resource utilization of the network. The hierarchical implementation of resources and metrics handling is fully devoted to simplify the SON. SON brings a set of self-configuration and self-optimization use cases that allow a better control of the operational cost for the complex radio access technologies. Here, the role of the real-time data analysis, by all means, makes the difference. It involves all resources of the system, removing the over-allocation, which today is dominating the dimensioning of RAN and causes a huge wasting of money in most of the operational time [19] [20].

V. CONCLUSION

The opportunity to move SDN-NFV into the Radio Access Network is a crucial objective for the communication system in the next years. Fulfilling the customers' needs means to answer on the demand for the next generation mobile, create new business models for the operators and open new service market share for the infrastructure vendors. However, mobile cannot be handled as data center or networking nodes. Location, latency time, UE metadata are unique and added value for the radio access, which means an ad-hoc solution is the enabler for a successful and high performing product. A complete C-RAN solution is not considered suitable due to the fronthaul capacity explosion it meant and the more flexible approach of the Radio Access Network as a Service (RANaaS) looks more promising. The ad-hoc solution is based on the right implementation of the ETSI concept called MEC. This paper emphasizes the role of it as server@edge of the network, calling it SEED. SEED is a suitable set of heterogeneous hardware solution, designed to dramatically reduce the cost of virtualization. The engine of the SEED is the so called C-mobile platform, a horizontal, per sever distributed, platform able to support the main functions characterizing the SEED: SDN-NFV controller, UE Metadata access service, Radio Access as Service solution, 3PP hosting and granted SLA. To be fully dynamic, SDN applications need to be responsive to their environment, therefore, triggers for network changes need to be state-driven. This automated management will be based on real-time network data analysis. Hierarchical Resource Manager and big data handling in the meaning of SON support is a key enabler together with the needed support.

VI. FUTURE WORKS

All the concepts in the paper need investigation and future study. For example, the usage of sched_deadline in a virtualized environment needs c-groups extension for a complete control of container's thread. Moreover, a Greedy Reclamation of Unused Bandwidth (GRUB)-like mechanism implementation would decrease the Constant Bandwidth Server (CBS) effect of sched_deadline, providing a more performing latency time [21][22]. Usage of resources meters and statistics is a very interesting topic. One of the natural next steps is the evaluation of the taxonomy framework introduced in [23] for the characteristic resources of the Radio Access Network:

network slices, load balancing, resource abstraction and resource control as defined in [24].

REFERENCES

[1] http://www.ericsson.com/res/docs/2015/mobility-report/ericsson-mobility-report-nov-2015.pdf [retrieved: 03, 2017].

[2] Chetan Sharma Consulting, "US Mobile Market Update – Q1 2014, 2014.

[3] Ericsson Mobility Report, On the pulse of the networked society, June 2015.

[4] T. Kridel, "The End of Profitability", Tellabas Insight Q2, 2011, pp.14-15.

[5] K. Shatzkamer, "Applying Systems Thinking to Mobile Networking", Brocade Communications Webinar, 2015. Available from http://docplayer.net/8990528-Applying-systems-thinking-to-mobile-networking.html [retrieved: 03, 2017].

[6] ETSI paper, "Network Functions Virtualisation (NFV); Use Cases", ETSI GS NFV 001, v1.1.1, 2013, available from http://www.etsi.org/deliver/etsi_gs/NFV/001_099/001/01.01.01_60/gs_NFV001v010101p.pdf [retrivied: 03, 2017].

[7] Y. C. Hu, M. Patel, D. Sabella, N. Sprecher and V. Young, "Mobile Edge Computing - A Key Technology Towards 5G", Sept. 2015, availble from http://www.etsi.org/images/files/ETSIWhitePapers/etsi_wp11_mec_a_key_technology_towards_5g.pdf [retrieved: 03, 2017].

[8] ETSI paper, "Network Function Virtualisation (NFV); Network Operator Perspectives on Industry Progress", SDN & OpenFlow World Congress, Dusseldorf, 2014, available from https://portal.etsi.org/Portals/0/TBpages/NFV/Docs/NFV_White_Paper3.pdf [retrivied: 03, 2017].

[9] G. Karagiannis et al, "Mobile Cloud Networking: Virtualisation of Cellular Network", 21st International Conference on Telecommunications (ICT), 2014, pp. 410-415.

[10] C.Vitucci, J.Lelli, A.Pirri, and M.Marinoni, "A Linux-based Virtualized Solution Providing Computing Quality of Service to SDN-NFV Telecommunication Applications", In Proceeding of the 16th real time Linux workshop (RTLWS 2014), Dusseldorf, Germany, 2014, pp. 12-13.

[11] NGMN Alliance, "5G White Paper", NGMN, 2015 J.S. Harrison, M.M. Do, "Mobile Network Architecture for 5G Era – New C-RAN Architecture and distributed 5G Core", Netmanias, 2015, available from https://www.ngmn.org/uploads/media/NGMN_5G_White_Paper_V1_0.pdf [retrivied: 03, 2017].

[12] J.S. Harrison and M.M. Do, "Mobile Network Architecture for 5G Era – New C-RAN Architecture and distributed 5G Core", Netmanias, 2015, available from http://www.netmanias.com/en/post/blog/8153/5g-c-ran-fronthaul-kt-korea-sdn-nfv-sk-telecom/mobile-network-architecture-for-5g-era-new-c-ran-architecture-and-distributed-5g-core [retrivied: 03, 2017] .

[13] G. Brown, "Service Chaining in Carrier Networks", Heavy Reading, 2015, available from http://www.qosmos.com/wp-content/uploads/2015/02/Service-Chaining-in-Carrier-Networks_WP_Heavy-Reading_Qosmos_Feb2015.pdf [retrivied: 03, 2017].

[14] T.A. Satria, M. Karimzadeh, and G. Karagiannis, "Performance evaluation of ICN/CCN based service migration approach in virtualized LTE systems", IEEE 3rd International Conference on Cloud Networking (CloudNet), 2014, pp. 461-467.

[15] M.J. McGrath, "Network Functions as-a-Service over virtualized infrastructures", Ref. Ares(2015)3376865, 2015, available from http://cordis.europa.eu/docs/projects/cnect/0/619520/080/deliverables/001-TNOVAD32InfrastructureResourceRepositoryv10Ares20153376865.pdf [retrivied: 03, 2017].

[16] OpenStack, "OpenStack Operations Guide", OpenStack Foundation, 2014, avaiable from https://docs.openstack.org/ops-guide/ [retrivied: 03, 2017].

[17] C. Dixon, "OpenDayLight: Introduction, Lithium and Beyond", available from http://colindixon.com/wp-content/uploads/2014/05/brighttalk-odl-webinar.pdf [retrivied: 03, 2017].

[18] N. Nikaein et al, "Network Store: Exploring Slicing in Future 5G Network", in Proceeding of the 10th International Workshop on Mobility in the Evolving Internet Architecture, 2015, pp. 8-13.

[19] K.Trichias, R.Litjens, A. Tall, Z. Altman, and P. Ramachandra, "Self-Optimisation of Vertical Sectorisation in a Realistic LTE Network", Europen Conference on Networks and Communications, 2015, pp.149-153.

[20] S. Fortes, A. Aguilar-Garcia, R. Barco, F. Barba, J.A. Fernandez-Luque, and A. Fernandez-Duran, "Management Architecture for Location-Aware Self-Organizing LTE/LTE-A Small Cell Networks", IEEE 53(1) Communications Magazine, 2015, pp. 294-302.

[21] L. Abeni, J. Lelli, C. Scordino, and L. Palopoli, "Greedy CPU reclaiming for SCHED DEADLINE". In Proceedings of the Real-Time Linux Workshop (RTLWS), Dusseldorf, Germany, 2014.

[22] G.Lipari and S. Baruah, "Greedy reclaimation of unused bandwidth in constant bandwidth servers". In IEEE Proceedings of the 12th Euromicro Conference on Real-Time Systems, Stockholm, Sweden, 2000, pp.193-200.

[23] S. Cai, B. Gallina, D. Nyström, and C. Seceleanu, "A Taxonomy of Data Aggregation Processes", IEEE DAGGERS project paper, 2016, available from http://www.es.mdh.se/pdf_publications/4628.pdf [retrivied: 03, 2017].

[24] VG. Nguyen, TX. Do, and Y. Kim, "SDN and Virtualization-Based LTE Mobile Network architectures: A comprehensive Survey", Wireless Personal Communications, 2016, Volume 86, Number 3, pp. 1401-1438.

Distributed Control Plane Optimization in SDN-Fog VANET

Eugen Borcoci, Tudor Ambarus, Marius Vochin
University POLITEHNICA of Bucharest - UPB
Bucharest, Romania
Emails: eugen.borcoci@elcom.pub.ro, tudorambarus@yahoo.com, marius.vochin@upb.ro

***Abstract* — Vehicular Ad-hoc Networks (VANETs) migrate today towards emergent Internet of Vehicles (IoV), which promises advanced commercial and technical capabilities. IoV can be supported by other novel technologies like Cloud/Fog computing, Software Defined Networking (SDN) and Network Function Virtualization (NFV). However, a challenge in terms of cooperation is related to the distributed characteristic of IoV and logical centralization concept in SDN. A physically distributed SDN control plane could be a solution. This paper is a preliminary work proposing an IoV Fog-based architecture and a distributed SDN control plane. A specific problem is solved, to optimize the geographic placement of the SDN controllers based on multi-criteria optimization algorithms.**

Keywords — VANET; IoV; Software Defined Networking; Multi-criteria optimizations; Controller placement.

I. INTRODUCTION

The number of vehicles in the world has constantly increased, leading today to major traffic problems and associated events, including car accidents [1]. Specific technologies like *Dedicated Short-Range Communications* (DSRC) and architectural stacks like *Wireless Access in Vehicular Environments* (WAVE) have been developed for the emerging market of *Intelligent Transport System* (ITS) [1][2]. The specifications defined by IEEE802.11p and IEEE 1609 represent the most mature set of standards for DSRC/WAVE networks [2]. The traditional ITS has continuously evolved, including vehicular communication: vehicle to vehicle (V2V), vehicle to road (V2R), or more general vehicle to Infrastructure (V2I). These networks are denoted as *Vehicular Ad-hoc Networks* (VANETs). The basic components of a VANET are the *On-Board-Unit* (OBU) placed in the vehicle and *Road-Side–Unit* (RSU) placed on the roads. Naturally, VANETs have a distributed character both in data and control plane.

However, VANETs have limitations; despite their good potential to contribute in solving safety and traffic management problems with low operational cost, they did not attract a very high commercial interest [3]. The limitations are related to pure ad-hoc network architecture (in V2V case), unreliable Internet service, incompatibility with personal devices, non-cooperation with cloud computing, low accuracy of the services, and operational network dependency. Even for vehicular traffic management task, the current VANETs are not capable to meet the future needs. On the other hand, due to the high number of vehicles, the traffic congestion will increase significantly in coming years. It is estimated that a few minutes saved, experienced in the vehicular traffic, would globally produce revenues of tens of billions Euro per year by 2030 [4]. Therefore, extending the VANET architecture is indeed a must.

A novel and emergent solution to the above issues, is the *Internet of Vehicles* (IoV), which is seen as a global span network of a vehicle network [4][5]. At network edges, the IoV will be enabled by *Wireless/Radio Access Technologies* (WAT/RAT) interconnecting OBUs to RSUs, while traditional Internet and other heterogeneous networks will be used for wide area. The IoV can be considered as a special case of the *Internet of Things* [6], where the "things" are either vehicles or their subsystems. The IoV objectives include vehicles driving (this is a basic goal - in VANET), but also others - like vehicle traffic management in urban or country areas, automobile production, repair and vehicle insurance, road infrastructure construction and repair, logistics and transportation, etc. Generally, it is estimated that smart-cities systems will include a strong IoV component.

Several and recent strong technologies can contribute in a cooperating style to IoV development.

Cloud Computing (CC) offers services to large communities of users (processing power, storage, networking) Software/ Platform/ Infrastructure as-a-Service (SaaS/PaaS/IaaS/etc.) for a large variety of applications. However, CC relies on centralized computing resources grouped in large data centers, which is not fully suitable for some environments (e.g., mobile, vehicular, VANET, IoT), where real-time actions and fast system response are essential. Consequently, a new *Fog* or *Edge Computing* [7] has been recently proposed, to extend the CC paradigm, by bringing cloud-like services to the network edge, i.e., in the proximity of the users.

Software-defined networking (SDN) [8] separates the control plane (CPl) and data (forwarding) plane (DPl), thus enabling flexible and programmable external control of data flows through logical software entities, i.e., vendor-neutral controllers. This is a powerful approach, of high interest for operators and industry. The SDN centralized up-to-date logical view upon the network, facilitates a flexible network management, allowing on-the-fly modification of the network elements behavior.

The recently proposed *Network Function Virtualization* (NFV) [9], promises to highly increase the networks flexibility, by virtualizing many network functions and deploying them into software packages. Dedicated *Virtualized Network Functions* (VNF) can be defined, then dynamically created/destroyed, assembled and chained to implement legacy or novel services. NFV can cooperate with SDN in defining new flexible and powerful architectures. This approach is also attractive for IoV.

The large communities of users/terminal devices in IoT and IoV need powerful and scalable *Radio Access Technologies* (RAT). The 4G and the emergent 5G, based on cloud computing architectures (*Cloud Radio Access Network*- CRAN) are significant candidates for constructing the IoV access infrastructure [10][11].

While IoV is estimated to become a significant progress versus VANET, many IoV advanced features and integration with the above technologies (CC, SDN, NFV) can be seen, as well, as challenges and open research issues. In particular, applying SDN control in VANET/IoV has the challenge to harmonize centralization concept of the SDN control with the native distributed VANET character. A hierarchical control solution with several regional controllers can be considered.

This paper contains a preliminary effort, first, to define an SDN - distributed controlled IoV architecture. Then, an optimization is performed, by placing the SDN controllers in optimal locations, while following multiple criteria of interest in VANET. Such a multiple controller solution can also potentially solve the horizontal SDN scalability problems [12]. In the proposed architecture, the access points (RSUs or 3G/4G base stations) can be considered as SDN forwarder nodes. The SDN controllers can be co-located to some of these access points. The specific design problems are: *What is the optimal number and placement of the controllers? How to allocate the forwarder nodes to controllers?*

The controller placement problem is a NP-hard one [13]. Different solutions can be used, with specific optimization criteria, depending on the network context and scenarios. Frequently, several criteria are of interest, e.g.: (a) to maximize the *controller-forwarder* or *inter-controller communication* throughput, and/or reduce the latency of this communication; (b) limit the controller overload (load imbalance) by avoiding too many forwarders per controller; (c) find an optimum controllers' placement and forwarder-to-controller allocation, aiming to achieve a fast recovery after failures (controllers, links, nodes). Therefore, a multi-criteria algorithm should be naturally considered, capable to provide a global optimization.

The paper is organized as follows. Section II is an overview of related work. Section III introduces the SDN-based architecture of VANET. Section IV is dedicated to the SDN control plane optimization based on multi-criteria algorithms. Section V presents conclusions and future work.

II. SDN CONTROLLED VANET - RELATED WORK

This section shortly presents related work dedicated to VANET/IoV with SDN control.

Kaiwartya et. al. [4] presents an overview on IoV architectures, network model and challenges. The IoV includes an enriched set of vehicular communications in addition to V2V, V2R/V2I, i.e., *Vehicle-to-Personal* devices (V2P) and *Vehicle-to-Sensors* (V2S). Each IoV particular communication type can be enabled using a different WAT, e.g., IEEE WAVE for V2V and V2R, Wi-Fi and 4G/LTE for V2I, CarPlay/NCF (*Near Field Communications*) for V2P and Wi-Fi for V2S. The architecture can include vehicles and *Road Side Units* (RSU), but also other communication devices. Embedding such a large range of devices makes IoV more complex, (compared to VANET), but it has the important advantage to be strongly market oriented. The layered architectural stack includes a coordination layer at network level, where SDN/NFV technologies may be candidates. Horizontally, the architecture is a multiple-plane one in which a management plane can assure the overall management and orchestration of the assembly. The optimization of the control plane is not in the scope of this work.

Y. Lu et al. [14] shows that SDN, if applied to VANET, can provide flexibility, programmability and support for new services. An SDN-based VANET architecture and its operational mode to adapt SDN concepts to VANET environments are proposed. The architectural components are: SDN controller, SDN wireless nodes and SDN RSUs. The SDN controller is a single entity (logical central intelligence of the SDN based VANET) which performs the overall control of the system. The SDN wireless nodes are vehicles, seen as data plane elements (forwarders) under SDN control. The SDN RSUs are also treated as data plane elements, but stationary. Simulation is performed to demonstrate the benefits of the approach, while considering some specific use cases (e.g., routing). However, the variant of several SDN controllers is not considered.

A recent work [15] (K. Zeng et al.) proposes a general architecture comprising Cloud-RAN technology, to realize a soft-defined networking system, able to support the dynamic nature of future heterogeneous VANET functions and various applications. A multi-layer Cloud-RAN multi-domain architecture is introduced, where the resources can be exploited as needed for vehicle users. Virtualization (for flexibility) and hierarchical cloud computing (remote, local and micro clouds) are considered for structuring the system. The high-level design of a soft-defined HetVNET is presented in detail. A hierarchy (two levels) of SDN control is proposed (one primary controller and several secondary controllers exist; each of the latter controls a given service area). The problem of optimizing the placement of the secondary controller set is not treated.

Truong et al. [16] proposes a new promising VANET architecture called FSDN, which combines SDN and Fog computing; the latter additionally brings capabilities for delay-sensitive and location-awareness services. The solution covers V2V, V2I and Vehicle-to-Base Station communications. The SDN components are: *SDN Controller* (it controls the overall network behavior via *OpenFlow* – southbound interfaces; it also plays as Fog Orchestration and Resource Management for the Fog); *SDN Wireless Nodes* (vehicles acting as the end-users and forwarding elements, equipped with OBU); *SDN RSU* (controlled by the SDN Controller; it is also a Fog device); *SDN RSU Controller* (RSUC) (controlled by the SDN controller; at its turn it controls a cluster of RSUs connected to a RSUC through broadband connections before accessing to the SDN Controller). The RSUC can forward data, but also can store local road system information and perform emergency services. From Fog perspective RSUCs are fog devices); *Cellular Base Station* (BS) (these BSs perform traditional functions but they are SDN controlled via OpenFlow and are additionally capable to offer Fog services). The problem of distributed SDN control is not discussed in this paper.

Kai et al. [17] presents an overview of Fog – SDN computing for vehicular networks, considering several scenarios and issues. It is shown that a mixed architecture combining the SDN centralized control with edge cloud capabilities of Fog can be powerful and flexible enough to serve future needs of IoV. No optimization of the SDN control plane is treated.

In a recent study [18], the Fog idea is further extended by utilizing vehicles as infrastructures for communication and computation, named *Vehicular Fog Computing* (VFC). It uses a collaborative multitude of end-user clients or near-user edge devices, to carry out communication and computation, based on better utilization of individual communication and computational resources of each vehicle.

The problem of SDN controller placement is not quite new. It has been studied in various works [9][18-22], but only for fixed SDN-controlled networks, usually running single or multi-criteria optimization algorithms. The specific contribution in this paper is to apply such methodologies to the specific need and architecture of SDN-VANET networks where special optimization criteria can be defined.

III. SDN CONTROLLED VANET ARCHITECTURE

This section will introduce the architecture of an IoV heterogeneous network including SDN control and Fog capabilities. It is actually a modification and horizontal extension of the architecture proposed in [16].

The architectural elements considered are described below. The Data plane includes mobile units (vehicles) equipped with OBUs; advanced RSUs, which could have more resources (computing, storage) as to play also Fog role (F-RSU) and regular RSU like in traditional VANETs; base stations (BS) of WiMAX/3G/4G-LTE type.

Note that, given the Fog capabilities of some RSUs, it is useful to have a fixed network (it is a partial mesh) with broadband links interconnecting the RSUs. This will allow a cooperative RSUs functioning of the Fog infrastructure. From the SDN point of view, all the Data plane are (or could be seen as) forwarding nodes. The data plane can be geographically organized in several service areas, each one governed by a SDN controller.

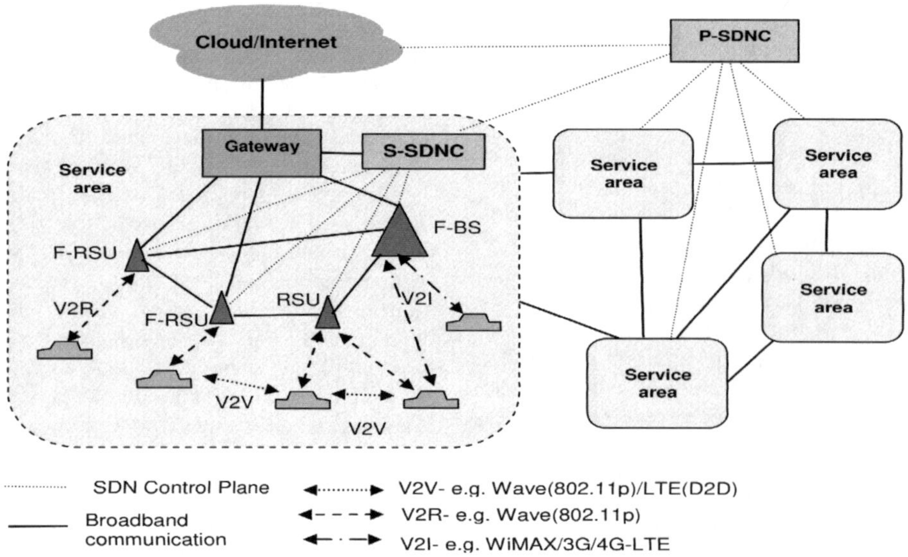

Figure 1. Generic IoV system architecture in study
F-BS - Fog-capable Base Station; F-RSU Fog-capable Remote Side Unit; P-SDNC- Primary SDN Controller; S-SDNC Secondary-SDN Controller; D2D- device to device communication

The SDN Control plane is organized on two levels. The primary SDN controller (P-SDNC) is the central element controlling the behavior of the network as a whole. Several service areas can exist and the Control plane should cover all these. In a simplified approach, it is assumed that a regional secondary SDN controller (S-SDNC) exists in each area and it is responsible of its functioning. The S-SDNC can also contain the resource management function of the Fog infrastructure (see RSUC entity in the previous section).

The P-SDNC is logically connected to each S-SDNC via the Control plane overlay or physical links. For the sake of simplicity, Figure 1 does not detail the physical infrastructure supporting the Control plane communications. The south SDN interfaces between the controllers and the lower level can be supported by the OpenFlow protocol or a similar one.

IV. IoV SDN Control Plane Optimization

This section develops a method to optimize the Control plane with regard of SDN controllers' placement.

A. Problem statement

The following assumptions are considered valid.

a. the whole access IoV geographic area is divided into several non-overlapping service areas.
b. each service area is covered by forwarders (RSUs and/or BSs) placed in fixed locations (the placement decision of the RSUs/BSs in some locations is out of scope of this study).
c. the network of forwarders in a service area can be represented by an abstract overlay graph whose properties are known by the optimization algorithm.
d. each service area can be controlled by one or, generally by several S-SDN controller(s) (the general case can provide a solution for a large service area with high number of RSUs).
e. the S-SDNCs will be co-located with some of the forwarders.
f. any SDNCs could be implemented as being 1-to-1 associated with a physical machine/node, or, several virtual controllers (based on NFV techniques) can exist in the same physical location. In the latter case the equivalent graph will have groups of nodes close together; however, the optimization solution would still work.

The optimization has two phases:

(1) given a set of criteria and a service area (region), what is the optimum placement of the S-SDNCs? This problem should be solved for each service area. The associated computation to run an algorithm can be performed in a centralized manner, e.g., in the P-SDNC.

(2) given the placement of the S-SDNCs and their equivalent higher level (overall) graph, what is the optimum placement of the unique P-SDNC, considering that it could be co-located to one node of this graph?

An early work of Heller et al. [13] has shown that the SDN controller placement problem is not new. If the metric is *latency,* then one gets the *facility or warehouse location problem* solved, e.g., by using *Mixed Integer Linear Program* (MILP) tools. Heller finds optimal solutions for realistic network instances, in failure-free scenarios, by analyzing the entire solution space, with off-line computations. Other studies [18–21] extended the approach, by considering several events like *controller* failures, *network links/paths/nodes* failures, controller *overload* (load imbalance), or *Inter-Controller Latency*, multi-path use cases, etc. The important thing is that the problem is a multi-criteria one, i.e., no unique solution is available satisfying all criteria.

Note that this work does not propose any new algorithms to optimize the controller placement for a given individual metric, but uses some previous multi-criteria overall optimization algorithm to obtain a trade-off solution in the novel IoV context.

B. Examples of metrics used for optimization

This sub-section is a very short presentation of a few typical metrics and optimization algorithms for controller placement. Several and more detailed examples are given in [23].

The network (of forwarders) in a service area is abstracted by an undirected graph G(V, E), where V,E are the sets of nodes and edges, respectively and n=|V| is the number of nodes. The edges weights represent an additive metric (e.g., *propagation latency*). The controllers will be co-located to some network nodes. Note that the number of controllers is much lower than the number of forwarders. After algorithm run, the controllers will be placed in some locations of forwarders. We denote a particular placement C_i of controllers, where $C_i \subseteq V$ and $|C_i| \leq |V|$. The number of controllers is limited to $|C_i| = k$ for any particular placement C_i. The set of all possible placements is denoted by $C = \{C_1, C_2 \ldots\}$

An example of a simple metric is d(v, c): *shortest path* distance from a forwarder node $v \in V$ to a controller $c \in V$. One can define, for a given placement C_i:

Worst_case_latency:

$$L_{wc} = \max_{v \in V} \min_{c \in C_i} d(v,c) \quad (1)$$

Average_latency:

$$L_{avg}(C_i) = \frac{1}{n} \sum_{v \in V} \min_{c \in Ci} d(v,c) \quad (2)$$

The algorithm should find a placement C_{opt}, where *either average latency* or *the worst case latency is minimized.*

Some comments are valuable to be given on this simple metric:

a. in IoV context, the latencies are dynamically changing, so the specific values used in (1) or (2) are actually some estimations (if static approach is applied) or otherwise they should be measured and averaged by a monitoring system and values delivered to the P-

SDNC. However, the process of obtaining the latency values is out of scope of this work.

b. the assignment of a RSU (seen as a SDN forwarder) to a given S-SDNC is based on selecting the closest S-SDNC to that RSU; so, there is no upper limit on the number of v nodes assigned to a controller; too many forwarders to be controlled by a given controller can exist, especially in large networks.

c. The placement solution does not consider any reliability features.

To solve the previous problem b., an additional criterion can be defined, i.e., to assure a good balance of the node-to-controller distribution. A metric *Ib(C$_i$)* will measure the degree of imbalance of a given placement C_i as the *difference between the maximum and minimum number of forwarders nodes assigned to a controller.*

$$Ib(C_i) = \{\max_{c \in C_i} n_c - \min_{c \in C_i} n_c\} \quad (3)$$

where n_c is the number of RSUs assigned to a controller c. An *optimization* should find that *placement which minimizes the expression (3).*

Another criterion useful could be the estimated capacity (max. bandwidth) between each pair of nodes in the graph (let it be B) and in the equation (1) or (2) the latency could be replaced bay the value 1/B for each overlay link.

In a multi-controller SDN environment, the inter-controller latency (Icl) has impact on the response time for the inter-controller mutual updating. Therefore, this is an important metric. For a given placement C_i, the *Icl* can be given by the maximum latency between two controllers:

$$Icl(C_i) = \max d(c_k, c_n) \quad (4)$$

Note that the attempt to minimize (4) will lead to a placement with controllers close to each other. However, this can increase the forwarder-to-controller distance (latency) given by (1) and (2). This is an example showing that a trade-off is necessary, *thus justifying the necessity to apply some multi-criteria optimization algorithms, e.g., like Pareto frontier - based ones* [22][23].

Various other metrics can be considered e.g., reliability-related, which consider node/link failures [20][21]. Other studies exploit the possible multiple paths between a forwarder node and a controller [22], hoping to reduce the frequency of controller-less events, in cases of failures of nodes/links. The goal in this case is to maximize connectivity between forwarding nodes and controller instances.

C. Overall optimization algorithm

Several optimization algorithms can be applied for the controller placement problem [13][19-22]. This paper uses a simple but powerful approach which is called multi-criteria decision algorithm (MCDA) [24] in a variant *reference level (RL) decision algorithm,* already used in [23] for a similar problem. The MCDA-RL selects the optimal solution based on normalized values of different criteria (metrics). Details on how to apply the MCDA-RL are given in the work [23]. Here, a similar approach is performed for the SDN controlled IoV.

The control plane optimization contains two phases, each composed of several steps which are described below.

Phase A. Optimization for S-SDNC controllers' placement.

a. The overall IoV geographic region (access part network) is conveniently divided in non-overlapping service areas, based on various criteria (commercial/ business, geographic, administrative, physical radio propagation criteria, vehicle traffic estimation data, etc.)

b. For each service area, the forwarder nodes (RSU, BS, gateway) placement is decided, based on criteria similar as in step a. An abstracted connectivity graph between RSUs should be derived. Note that not all RSUs should be considered as nodes in the abstract graph; usually the RSU-fog nodes or nodes having a minimum of resources (including electrical power) should be selected. Therefore, the branches of the graph might represent physical or overlay links. Some RSUs will be collocated with S-SDNCs.

c. The criteria of interest to be target of the MCDA-RL optimization are selected (e.g., controller-node latency, imbalance of a placement, inter-controller latency, etc.). These criteria will be mapped to the decision variables in MCDA-RL. If needed, the criteria can be assigned different priorities and the algorithm will consider them.

d. A reasonable number (heuristically decided) of S-SDNC controllers are supposed to be defined for each service area.

e. Repeat for each service area:

{e.1: For the parameters of interest, one should compute the *values of the metrics for all possible controller placements,* using specialized single-criterion algorithms and metrics like those defined in formulas like (1) - (4). This step will produce the set of candidate solutions (i.e., S-SDNC placement instances). This procedure could be time consuming (depending on network size) and therefore, could be performed off-line as suggested in [13].

e.2: Run the steps of the MCDA-RL (the details are shown in [23] and are not repeated here). The algorithm will provide as result the best trade-off solution (in Pareto [24] sense) for the S-SDNCs placement for this service area}.

Phase B. Optimization for P-SDNC controller placement.

Now the placement of the S-SDNCs is known; therefore, a connectivity graph linking the set of the S-SDNCs can be derived. Then the placement of the Primary SDNc should be computed in optimal sense by applying steps c. d. and e. of the Phase A.

D. Numerical example

A simple example illustrates the MCDA flexibility. Figure 2 shows a connectivity graph between RSUs, BS, etc., abstracted as vertices $v_1, ..v_6$. The numbers on the graph branches represent (generically) an additive metric (e.g., latency). Suppose that for this service area it is wanted to co-locate two S-SDNC controllers with some nodes v.

Suppose that for this network the metrics of interest and decision variables are on: d1: *Average latency* (1); d2: *worst latency (2)* (failure-free case); d3: *Inter-controller latency (4)*. We denote an S-SDNC controller with c_1 or c_2. The allocation of the forwarders to controller will be based in this example on shortest-path from forwarder to controller.

Several candidates for placement solutions can be considered, e.g.:

$C_1 = \{ [c_1\_in\_v_5 (v_5, v_2, v_4)], \quad [c_2\_in\_v_6(v_6, v_1, v_3)]\}$
$C_2 = \{ [c_1\_in\_v_4 (v_4, v_2, v_5)], \quad [c_2\_in\_v_6(v_6, v_1, v_3)]\}$
$C_3 = \{ [c_1\_in\_v_5 (v_5, v_1, v_2, v_4)], \quad [c_2\_in\_v_3(v_3, v_6)]\}$
$C_4 = \{ [c_1\_in\_v_3 (v_3, v_2)], \quad [c_2\_in\_v_6(v_6, v_1, v_4, v_5)]\}$

1. Case 1. The decision variables have equal priorities (p) i.e., p1=1, p2=1, p3=1. The values of the metrics are computed using equations (1), (2) and respectively (4) for each placement: C_1, ..C4. The final result after running MCDA is: *C_1 = the best placement.* In Figure 1, one can see that this placement is a good trade-off between node-controller latency and inter-controller latency.

2. Case 2. Different priorities are defined: p1=1, p2=0.5, p3=1, i.e., the worst case latency d2 has highest priority (lower value means higher priority). So, the solution minimizing the worst case controller-forwarder latency (this criterion has high priority) is searched by the MCDA. Finally, it is found after running MCDA, that *C_2= the best placement.* Figure 2 shows that worst case latency (node-controller) is minimized, however the inter-controller latency is in this case higher than in solution C_1.

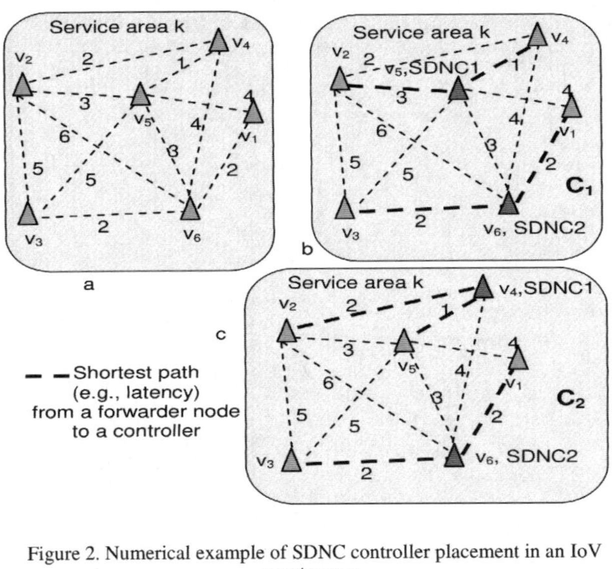

Figure 2. Numerical example of SDNC controller placement in an IoV service area

These examples prove how different network operator's policies can bias the algorithm results.

V. CONCLUSIONS AND FUTURE WORK

This paper presented a work in progress which proposed an IoV Fog-based architecture and a distributed SDN control plane. The architecture comprises RSUs, BS, geographically distributed in non-overlapping service areas which are interconnected. Some RSUs are advanced ones, having Fog capabilities. The whole infrastructure is controlled by a distributed SDN control plane.

The SDN control plane consists in several controllers organized on two hierarchical levels: a unique primary controller P-SDNC governing the assembly and several secondary S-SDNCs in the service areas. It is supposed that S-SDNCs could be collocated to some forwarder nodes (RSU, BS).

Then an optimization method is proposed for the geographic placement of the SDN controllers, by applying a multi-criteria optimization algorithms (MCDA). Some previously developed optimization algorithms have been used, but in a novel way adapted to IoV - SDN controlled context.

The optimization method proposed achieves an overall optimum (in Pareto frontier sense) and is very simple from implementation point of view. In particular, the MCDA-RL algorithm can produce a tradeoff (optimum) result, while considering several (weighted) criteria, part of them even being partially contradictory. The method is general and can be applied in various scenarios (including failure-free assumption ones or reliability – aware).

The computations could be performed offline, or even online (e.g., in the P-SDNC- which is naturally supposed in SDN technology to have knowledge upon its forwarding plane network). The S-SDNC placement algorithm could run in the P-SDNC, from time to time (or, event-triggered), especially if S-SDNCs are implemented as virtual machines in some forwarding network nodes, and the set of the active virtual machines should be re-defined. This approach will be for further study. Future work could deal with validation and simulation studies for large network environments (e.g., hundreds or more RSUs).

Future work will be done to apply the method proposed to other metrics, considering multi-path approach for forwarder-controller paths. Other area of investigation could consider the Fog node placement problem in the IoV access network, where similarity with the problem studied here can be found.

ACKNOWLEDGMENTS

This work has been partially funded by University Politehnica of Bucharest, through the "Excellence Research Grants" Program, UPB – GEX. Identifier: UPB–EXCELENȚĂ–2016 Research project Intelligent Navigation Assistance System, Contract number 101/26.09.2016 (acronym: SIAN).

REFERENCES

[1] S. Sultan, M. Moath Al-Doori, A.H. Al-Bayatti, and H.Zedan "A comprehensive survey on vehicular Ad Hoc Network", J.of Network and Computer Applications, Jan. 2014, https://www.researchgate.net/publication/259520963, [Retrieved: December, 2016].

[2] Yunxin (Jeff) Li, "An Overview of the DSRC/WAVE Technology", https://www.researchgate.net/publication/288643779_An_overview_of_the_DSRCWAVE_technology, 2012, [Retrieved: January, 2017].

[3] M. Saini, A. Aleleiwi, and A. Saddik, "How close are we to realizing a pragmatic VANET solution? A meta-survey" ACM Comput. Surv., vol. 48, no. 2, Art. no. 29, pp.1-36, 2015.

[4] O. Kaiwartya, A.H. Abdullah, Y. Cao, A. Altameem, M. Prasad, et.al., "Internet of Vehicles: Motivation, Layered Architecture, Network Model, Challenges, and Future Aspects" IEEE Access, Special Section on Future Networks, Architectures, Protocols and Applications, Vol. 4, pp.5536-5372, September 2016.

[5] Y. Fangchun, W.Shangguang, L. Jinglin, L. Zhihan, and S.Qibo, "An overview of Internet of Vehicles", China Commun., vol. 11, no. 10, pp. 115, October 2014.

[6] A. Al-Fuqaha, M.Guizani, M. Mohammadi,M. Aledhari, and M.Ayyash, "Internet of Things: A Survey on Enabling Technologies, Protocols, and Applications", IEEE Communications Surveys &Tutorials Vol. 17, No. 4, pp.2347-2376, 2015.

[7] F.Bonomi, R.Milito, J.Zhu, and Sateesh Addepalli, "Fog Computing and Its Role in the Internet of Things", August 2012, http://conferences.sigcomm.org/sigcomm/2012/paper/mcc/p13.pdf, [Retrieved: January, 2017].

[8] B. N. Astuto, M. Mendonca, X. N. Nguyen, K. Obraczka, and T. Turletti, "A Survey of Software-Defined Networking: Past, Present, and Future of Programmable Networks", Communications Surveys and Tutorials, IEEE Communications Society, (IEEE), 16 (3), pp. 1617 – 1634, 2014.

[9] B.Han, V. Gopalakrishnan, L. Ji, and S. Lee, "Network Function Virtualisation: Challenges and Opportunities for Innovations". IEEE Communications Magazine, pp. 90-97, February 2015.

[10] M. Peng, Y. Li, J. Jiang, J. Li, and C.Wang, "Heterogeneous cloud radio access networks: a new perspective for enhancing spectral and energy efficiencies", IEEE Wireless Communications, pp.126-135, December 2014.

[11] M. Peng, S.Yan, K.Zhang, and C.Wang, "Fog Computing based Radio Access Networks: Issues and Challenges", IEEE Network, vol. 30, pp.46-53, July/August 2016.

[12] Benamrane, F., Ben mamoun, M., & Benaini, R. (2015). Performances of OpenFlow-Based Software-Defined Networks: An overview. Journal of Networks, 10(6), 329–337. http://doi.org/10.4304/jnw.10.6.329-337

[13] B. Heller, R. Sherwood, and N. McKeown, "The controller placement problem," in Proc. HotSDN, pp. 7–12, 2012, , http://yuba.stanford.edu/~nickm/papers/hot21-heller.pdf, [Retrieved: February, 2017].

[14] Y.Lu, M.Gerla, R. Gomes, and E. Cerqueira, "Towards software-defined VANET: Architecture and services", MedHocNet.2014.6849111, https://www.researchgate.net/publication/271472780, [Retrieved: January, 2017].

[15] K. Zeng, L. Hou, H. Meng, Q. Zheng, N. Lu, et al., "Soft-Defined Heterogeneous Vehicular Network: Architecture and Challenges", IEEE Network, vol. 30, pp.72-79, July/August 2016.

[16] N. N. Truong, G.M.Lee, and Y.Ghamri-Doudane. "Software defined networking-based vehicular ad hoc network with fog Computing", Proceedings of the 2015 IFIP/IEEE International Symposium on Integrated Network Management (IM'15), May 2015, Ottawa, Canada. Piscataway, NJ, USA: IEEE, , pp. 1202–1207, 2015.

[17] K.Kai, W.Cong, and L.Tao, "Fog computing for vehicular Ad-hoc networks:paradigms, scenarios, and issues", The Journal of China Universities of Posts and Telecommunications, www.sciencedirect.com/science/journal/10058885, http://jcupt.bupt.edu.cn, 23(2), pp. 56–65, April 2016, [Retrieved: January, 2017].

[18] X. Hou, Y.Li, M. Chen, D. Wu, D. Jin, and S. Chen, "Vehicular Fog Computing: A Viewpoint of Vehicles as the Infrastructures", IEEE Transactions on Vehicular Technology, Vol. 65, No. 6, pp.3860-3873, June 2016.

[19] H. Yan-nan, W. Wen-dong, G. Xiang-yang, Q. Xi-rong, and C. Shi-duan, "On the placement of controllers in software-defined networks", ELSEVIER, Science Direct, vol. 19, Suppl.2, October 2012, pp. 92–97, http://www.sciencedirect.com/science/article/pii/S100588851160438X, [retrieved: November, 2016].

[20] D. Hock, M. Hartmann, S. Gebert, M. Jarschel, T. Zinner, and P. Tran-Gia, "Pareto-Optimal Resilient Controller Placement in SDN-based Core Networks," in ITC, Shanghai, China, 2013, http://ieeexplore.ieee.org/document/6662939/, [Retrieved: January, 2017].

[21] Y. Hu, W. Wendong, X. Gong, X. Que, and C. Shiduan, "Reliability aware controller placement for software-defined networks," in Proc. IM. IEEE, pp. 672–675, 2013.

[22] L. Muller, R. Oliveira, M. Luizelli, L. Gaspary, and M. Barcellos, "Survivor: an Enhanced Controller Placement Strategy for Improving SDN Survivability", IEEE Global Comm. Conference (GLOBECOM), December 2014.

[23] E.Borcoci, R.Badea, S.G.Obreja, and M.Vochin, "On Multi-controller Placement Optimization in Software Defined Networking -based WANs", The International Symposium on Advances in Software Defined Networks SOFTNETWORKING 2015, - Barcelona, Spain, http://www.iaria.org/conferences2015/SOFTNETWORKING.html, [Retrieved: January, 2017].

[24] A. P. Wierzbicki, "The use of reference objectives in multiobjective optimization". Lecture Notes in Economics and Mathematical Systems, vol. 177. Springer-Verlag, pp. 468–486, 1979.

An Application-Aware SDN Controller for Hybrid Optical-Electrical DC Networks

Giada Landi, Marco Capitani
Nextworks
Pisa, Italy
email: {g.landi, m.capitani}@nextworks.it

Domenico Gallico, Matteo Biancani
Interoute S.p.A.
Roma, Italy
email: {domenico.gallico, matteo.biancani}@interoute.com

Kostas Christodoulopoulos
Communication Networks Laboratory of the Computer Engineering and Informatics Department
University of Patras, Greece
email: kchristodou@ceid.upatras.gr

Muzzamil Aziz
Gesellschaft für wissenschaftliche Datenverarbeitung mbH
GWDG
Göttingen, Germany
email: muzzamil.aziz@gwdg.de

***Abstract* — The adoption of optical switching technologies in Data Centre Networks (DCNs) offers a solution for high speed traffic and energy efficiency in Data Centre (DC) operational management, enabling an easy scaling of DC infrastructures. Flexible, slotted allocation of optical resources is fundamental to efficiently support the dynamicity of DC traffic. In this context, the NEPHELE project proposes a Time Division Multiple Access approach for optical resource allocation, orchestrated through a Software Defined Networking controller which coordinates the DCN configuration based on real-time cloud application requests.**

Keywords - Software Defined Networking; Optical Data Centre Networks; TDMA.

I. INTRODUCTION

Data Centre (DC) traffic is increasing in volume and dynamicity, bringing new challenges in the design of DC Networks (DCNs) for guaranteeing high capacity, high scalability and energy efficiency together with the flexibility of adapting network configuration based on real-time traffic profiles and application needs. The NEPHELE project [1] proposes a novel DC architecture able to meet these requirements through a disaggregated DC architecture with a flattened DCN infrastructure at the data plane, based on optical switching and slotted resource allocation [2]. At the control plane, the Software Defined Networking (SDN) approach exploits the programmability of the optical data plane and integrates the allocation of the DCN resources in the global management of DC resources, including storage and servers. The open Application Programming Interfaces (APIs) at the SDN controller allow to efficiently coordinate cloud orchestration procedures for service lifecycle management with the provisioning of optical network connections, to transport the intra-DC traffic in isolated, multi-tenant virtual networks.

The interaction between cloud orchestrator and SDN controller is the key to bring application-awareness at the DCN level [3]. Rack-to-rack network connections are established on demand to serve traffic among the DC servers with guaranteed QoS, as driven by real-time application requirements. The automation introduced by the SDN controller reconfigures the DCN to automatically re-adapt the network resource allocation to the current traffic profile. The NEPHELE hybrid electrical-optical DCN data plane enables fine granularity exploiting the slotted resources of the Time Division Multiple Access (TDMA) technologies employed at the data plane. This guarantees the flexibility needed to efficiently accommodate different kinds of cloud applications, as well as high-load DC management traffic for Virtual Machine (VM) transfer and replication.

Previous works have presented NEPHELE architecture [3] and evaluated NEPHELE algorithms through simulation studies [4], while this paper introduces the software prototype of NEPHELE SDN controller for hybrid optical-electrical DCNs and its applicability in DC use cases. The paper is structured as follows. Section II presents use cases for dynamic network allocation in optical DCs, where NEPHELE control plane technologies improve current practices and overcome existing limitations. Section III describes the NEPHELE DC architecture, the hybrid opto-electric infrastructure and the SDN-based network control and cloud orchestration planes. The NEPHELE SDN controller and its software prototype is presented in Section IV. Section V provides conclusions, discussing future research directions in the area of optical DC networks.

II. USE CASES FOR OPTICAL DC NETWORKS

This section presents a set of use cases for DC services with challenges for DCN control, management and cloud orchestration. The use cases are based on current services that may benefit from NEPHELE technologies (Virtual DC), features enhancing existing cloud services (policy-based provisioning of cloud applications with QoS) or solve limitations in DC management (automated disaster recovery and autonomous cloud service upscaling).

A. *Virtual Data Centre*

The Virtual DC (VDC) use case focuses on the provisioning of highly scalable, customizable virtual instances of DC, delivered as isolated slices dedicated to different tenants but sharing the same physical DC infrastructure. VDC instances are requested by the cloud providers' customers using a web portal. Pre-defined templates define the main features of a VDC instance and the customer can choose different configuration settings (e.g., CPU, RAM, virtual network interfaces) selecting the flavor more suitable to run the desired cloud application. The cloud orchestrator automates the deployment and provisioning of the VDC instance, allocating the virtual resources and delivering the service in real-time to the customer.

The introduction of NEPHELE technologies in the DC architecture is essential to provide network performance guarantees for each VDC instance, exploiting the capabilities of the optical DCN. The integration between cloud orchestrator and SDN controller enables enhanced automation features. For example, scheduled backup or disaster recovery procedures may integrate mechanisms for automated DCN reconfiguration, reserving dedicated resources to the management traffic without affecting the QoS of other running services. Moreover, enhanced monitoring features can be defined on a per-service basis, with monitoring information made available through open APIs for DC administrators and VDC tenants as potential input for Service Level Agreement (SLA) validation tools.

B. *Policy-based Provisioning of Cloud Applications*

This use-case follows an application centric approach, while the previous one was based on an infrastructure perspective, where the customer required VDC instances replicating most of the features of real DCs. In this use-case, the customer is not interested in the capabilities of the assigned virtual infrastructure, but rather in the application that should run on top of it and in its requirements.

The cloud application platform handles packages that define the application business logic through metadata describing functional and non-functional requirements, like software components, their dependencies, interoperability, auto-scaling rules, etc. Based on these metadata, the cloud orchestrator is responsible to provision the middleware services according to user policies and SLAs, translating application-level requirements in a set of infrastructure-level characteristics and reserving the required virtual resources.

The level of automation in network configuration and resource allocation, enabled through the NEPHELE SDN approach, is an important aspect to reduce the cost of cloud application management. The virtualization of network services, provided by the SDN controller, introduces an abstraction layer that limits the complexity of describing the interconnectivity between middleware services, hiding the details of the DCN infrastructure through intent-based APIs exposed towards the cloud orchestrator.

C. *Disaster recovery*

The recovery of data and internal states of applications running in the cloud is one of the most critical aspects of cloud services. Cloud providers usually offer several options for management of backups. For example, backup copies of VMs or volumes can be created manually by the customer, following an on-demand approach, in order to save the contents before performing critical operations. Alternatively, they can be triggered periodically as part of the DC management operations. The cloud provider may implement profile-based strategies for storage protection or mirroring, with storage snapshots collected periodically, saved within the same or different DC location. The restoration is triggered by the customer and it is automated through orchestration procedures at the cloud platform.

The traffic generated to move snapshots among servers in the same or in distributed DCs requires large bandwidth, but is delay-tolerant. Its huge load must not impact the traffic generated by the cloud applications running in the cloud, so it would need dedicated connections. In this context the NEPHELE system can efficiently handle the orchestration of the network configuration, reserving intra- or inter-DC connections with the capacity required to enable fast data transfers. These reservations are integrated in the snapshot procedures: they can be performed on-demand in case of customer-driven backups or scheduled with advance reservations and calendar-based mechanisms for periodical snapshots.

D. *SLA Monitoring and Automated Upscaling*

Elasticity is one of the main benefits of cloud services: cloud applications can scale up and down, on-demand or automatically, based on their load and their compliance with SLAs agreed between service consumer and provider. The NEPHELE system extends this capability to network resources. Open APIs integrate monitoring and dynamic modification of network connections in scaling procedures.

In particular, NEPHELE SDN controller can implement mechanisms to monitor the network performance for each single VDC instance and to evaluate the compliance with the SLA established with the customer. In case of data plane failures or other kinds of SLA breaches related to network performance, the NEPHELE controller can automatically react reconfiguring the virtual infrastructure and establishing alternative paths. These actions may be also triggered in response to failures on computing/storage resources, under the coordination of the cloud orchestrator.

The capability to expose per-tenant network monitoring information through open APIs is an additional feature that can be useful for customers who want to maintain deep control on their virtual infrastructure. For example, these data can be used to detect the need of additional resources in specific VDC instances (e.g., triggering VMs replication to handle variable traffic loads, upgrading of capacity for existing network connections). This option is particularly interesting for VDC tenants who act as service providers and would like to increase and decrease application loads dynamically, reducing costs when resource needs are lower. The cloud orchestrator itself may implement an auto-scaler service, enabling the automated upscaling or downscaling of VDC instances based on customer-driven auto-scaling policies configured at the deployment stage.

III. NEPHELE DATA CENTRE ARCHITECTURE

NEPHELE DC architecture is based on the SDN concept, with decoupling between network data and control plane and their interaction via open interfaces and protocols at the South Bound Interface (SBI) of the SDN controller. This approach allows to customize the network programmability using dedicated SDN applications that interacts with the controller using its North Bound Interfaces (NBI). In DC scenarios, the controller is typically responsible for network virtualization and provisioning of underlying connectivity. On top of that, a cloud management platform orchestrates the whole set of DC resources (computing, storage, networking) interacting with the related controllers and it is responsible to deliver end-to-end cloud services for upper layer applications. NEPHELE architecture is compliant with this trend and proposes a three layer architecture, as follows:

- The DCN data plane employs hybrid optical-electrical technologies to support high capacity and energy efficiency. The TDMA enables high flexibility and fine granularity in resource reservation, to efficiently host different types of traffic flows reducing the overprovisioning.
- The network control framework is based on an SDN controller extended to operate over TDMA-based optical infrastructures. It is responsible for the efficient and flexible configuration of the DCN, in compliance with the requirements of the cloud applications running in the DC.
- The cloud orchestration framework operates the DC infrastructure; it jointly coordinates and orchestrates the resource allocation in the servers and in the DCN, delegating the actual DCN configuration to the network control framework.

A. *Data Plane Architecture*

The data plane architecture of the NEPHELE DCN is represented in Figure 1 and it is based on a flat topology with a two-tier network that can be easily scaled in the east-west direction without increasing traffic latency and congestion. The key of the NEPHELE data plane scalability is given by the definition of I parallel planes, each of them including R unidirectional rings connecting P pods. A pod is made of I POD switches and W hybrid electrical/optical (Top Of the Rack) TOR switches. Each TOR switch is connected to all the I POD switches of the pod, where each port of the TOR switch is connected to a different POD switch.

At the rack level, there are Z innovation zones, where an innovation zone is a collection of hosts, storage, memory and other devices. The innovation zones in a rack are connected to a TOR switch with L_E conventional Ethernet links to TOR electrical ports and L_O all-optical links to TOR optical ports. Consequently, each TOR switch has $Z(L_E+L_O)$ ports interconnecting Z innovation zones and I ports interconnecting to the POD switches.

NEPHELE optical network adopts Wavelength Division Multiplexing (WDM) technology and each of the R fiber rings carries WDM unidirectional traffic with W wavelengths. The optical links from TOR to POD switches carries a single wavelength at a time, with traffic multiplexed in the time domain using TDMA slots. In the upstream direction wavelength assignment is performed dynamically, per TDMA slot, identifying uniquely the position of the destination TOR switch within the target POD switch. On the other hand, in downstream wavelength assignment is static.

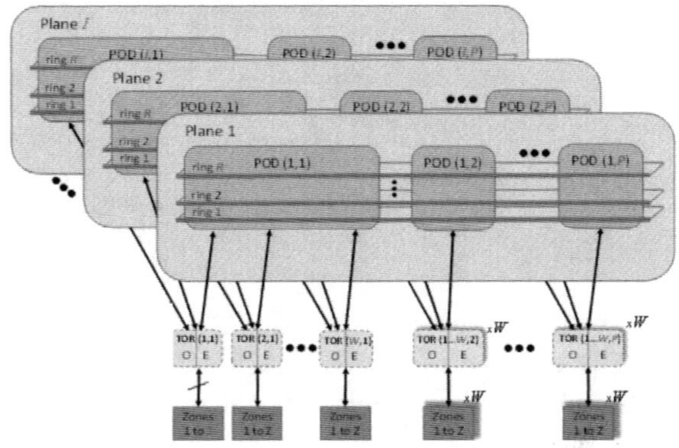

Figure 1. NEPHELE data plane architecture.

B. *SDN-based Control and Orchestration Architecture*

The peculiarity of the NEPHELE network control framework is inherent in its procedures, protocol extensions and algorithms to operate the DCN hybrid data plane applying TDMA concepts in order to obtain a finer granularity and dynamicity in the assignment of network resources. The final objective is the provisioning of intra-DC connections that optimize the usage of the DCN physical infrastructure, while guaranteeing the desired level of QoS for the applications running in the virtual environments.

In NEPHELE, DCN resource allocation is driven from the dynamicity of the traffic demands. These dynamics are captured in a traffic matrix built in real time, based on cloud service requests for new application profiles. Some application awareness is thus transferred from the cloud platform to the network control plane, with extended controller's NBI to enable a more tight cooperation between network controller and cloud orchestrator. This also implies the capability to manage enriched cloud service models at the orchestrator level, with service templates describing network requirements and traffic patterns, as expected by the cloud applications. These parameters constitute the input for the decision engines at the network controller and feed advanced algorithms for application-aware network allocation [4].

The architecture of the NEPHELE control and orchestration infrastructure is depicted in Figure 2. The Cloud Management Platform (e.g., OpenStack) orchestrates the resource of the entire DC and delivers virtual infrastructures to different tenants. All the different devices of the DCN are controlled through a centralized SDN controller which implements the network logic. For scalability reasons, the controller logic can be split across several entities following a hierarchical approach, with child controllers dedicated to single planes or pods and an upper layer parent controller responsible for coordinating the whole DCN configuration [3].

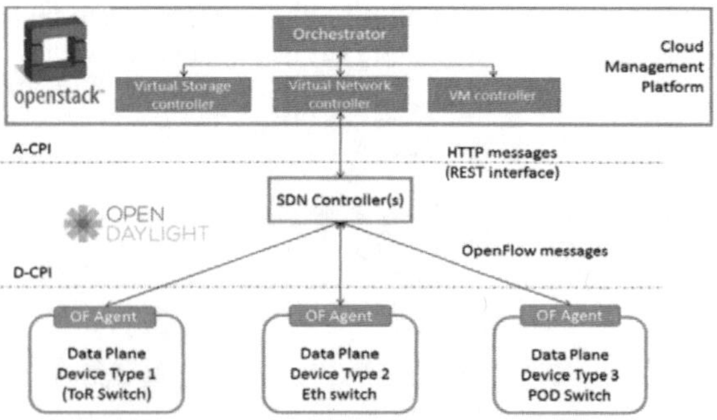

Figure 2. NEPHELE control and orchestration frameworks.

In NEPHELE, the SDN controller prototype has been developed in the OpenDaylight [5] framework. It offers a Representational State Transfer (REST) based interface at its northbound side to receive requests for application traffic profiles, driving the creation of new network connections. Traffic requirements are translated into dynamic network configurations applied to the DCN elements. The interaction with the data plane is based on extended OpenFlow (OF) [6] messages, enhanced to support advertisement, operational configuration and monitoring of optical and hybrid nodes.

IV. NEPHELE SDN CONTROLLER

A. *SDN Controller Functional Architecture*

The NEPHELE SDN controller adopts a twofold strategy for network resource allocation, with real-time reactions for short-term decisions and periodical reconfiguration of the entire DCN for medium-/long-term decisions.

The short-term strategy is applicable to service requests that requires fast activation, to upscaling or downscaling requests of already active services and to react to data plane failures with fast recovery. These cases require high dynamicity and automation of control procedures, so the SDN controller adopts faster "online" algorithms to react quickly to single events, even if leading to suboptimal solutions. The short-term strategy, takes into account single requests instead of the global traffic matrix: it allocates additional resources to serve the new request, given the previous DCN allocation for existing service. This option is well suited for on-demand provisioning and fast recovery of network connections. However, in order to maximize the DCN usage, medium and long-term strategies provide better performance. In this case Application traffic profiles are used as input to build periodically an application-aware traffic matrix. Offline scheduling algorithms elaborates the traffic matrix and re-plan the NEPHELE DCN, computing optimal resource allocation solutions.

Figure 3 shows the functional architecture of the NEPHELE SDN controller, identifying its main components and interactions for short- and medium/long-term resource allocation. The south-bound drivers enable the interaction between SDN controller and data plane; they implement the extended OF protocol for configuring TOR and POD switches and the OVSDB [7] protocol for configuring the OpenVSwitch instances on the servers.

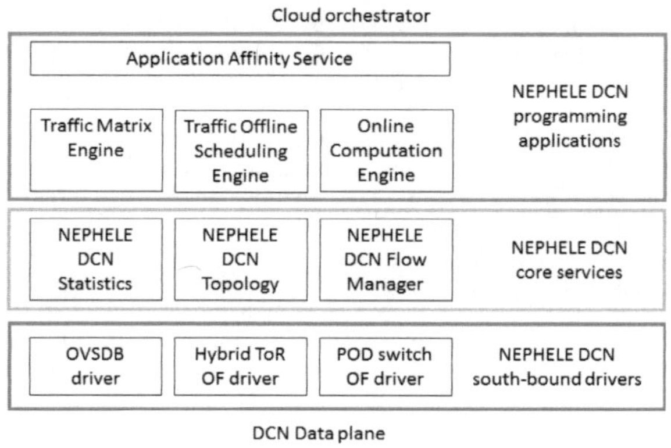

Figure 3. NEPHELE SDN controller: functional architecture.

The core services provide basic functions, abstracting details of the physical resources with unified information models. Core services are invoked by upper layer SDN applications to collect network topology or monitoring information or issue configuration commands through protocol-independent and technology-agnostic interfaces. In compliance with the OpenDaylight architecture, all the services define their interfaces using YANG models [8] and can be invoked by other OpenDaylight components or by external entities via REST APIs.

The NEPHELE network logic is implemented in the DCN programming applications. They employ dedicated algorithms for short- and medium-/long-term decisions at the *Online Computation Engine* and at the *Traffic Offline Scheduling Engine* respectively. The *Application Affinity Service* coordinates the workflows for the DCN allocation, based on applications' traffic profiles. As in core services, all the DCN programming applications expose REST APIs to enable the interaction with the cloud platform.

B. *DCN Configuration Workflows*

This section describes the workflows to allocate network resources in the NEPHELE DCN following the approach based on the periodical reconfiguration of the whole infrastructure, with the optimal allocation solution computed by the offline scheduling engine.

The workflow initiates from the Application Affinity Service, when it receives a request to initiate a network connection for a particular application profile. The details of the requested connections are forwarded to the Traffic Matrix Engine, which updates the current traffic matrix with the new data and returns it. Then, the Application Affinity Service sends the resulting traffic matrix to the Offline Engine, which starts to re-compute the allocation of the network resources for the entire DCN (see Figure 4).

Two strategies for ToR resource allocation are supported. In the *quasi distributed* strategy, the controller takes decisions about slot allocations on output ports, while each ToR decides the source ports to empty. In this case, the traffic matrix is a Kx3 matrix. Each row includes 3 elements *(s,d,t)*, where *s* is the source ToR, *d* is the destination ToR and *t* is the number of slots required between *s* and *d*. In the *fully centralized* strategy, all scheduling decisions are taken at the controller. In this case, the *s* element of each row in the traffic matrix represents the source southbound port of the ToR. Details about the engine algorithms and their performance are available in [4].

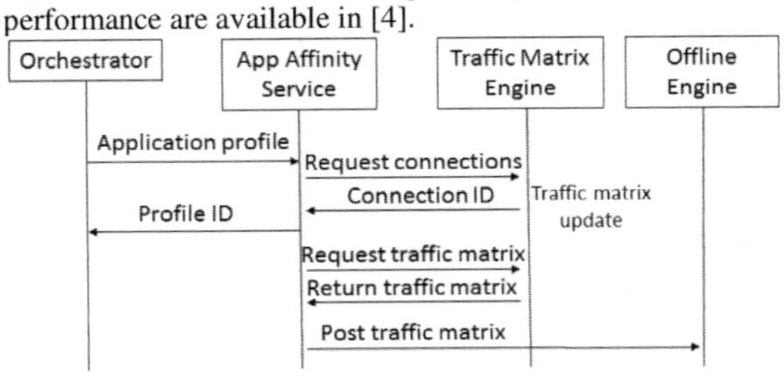

Figure 4. Workflow for creation of a new application profile.

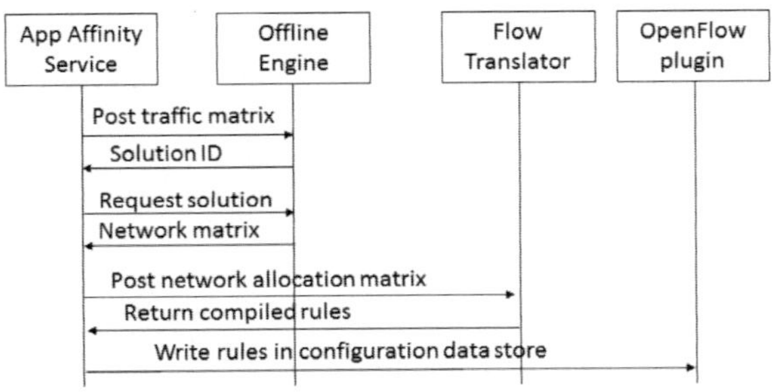

Figure 5. Workflow for updating DCN resource allocation.

Depending on the dimension of the DCN, the engine computation may take time, so the Application Affinity Service requests the network allocation solution with periodical polling queries to the engine until the result is available (see Figure 5). The network allocation provides the details of the time slots and wavelengths to be used for the different connections, taking into account the constraints of continuity along the entire paths (no wavelength or time slot conversion is supported at the data plane). As soon as the computation terminates, the Application Affinity Service forwards the solution to the Flow Manager which de-aggregates the data contained in the matrix and returns the list of flow rules to be installed on the physical devices.

The flow rules defined in NEPHELE extend the traditional rules of the OF protocol. In particular, the flow match structure defines a wavelength and a bitmap of time slots to properly classify the incoming traffic on optical ports, while the same parameters are defined in the flow action structure to specify a cross-connection between two WDM ports for a given set of time slots. The extended YANG model of the OpenDaylight OF plugin is reported in Figure 6, highlighting the extended parameters.

The flow rules resulting from Flow Manager elaboration are then written in the OpenDaylight configuration data store, triggering the procedures at the OF plugin to send the associated Flow Mod messages. At the data plane level, the OF messages are intercepted by device-specific agents, which handle the translation to configuration commands towards the FPGA controlling the hardware.

```
module opendaylight-action-types {
    namespace "urn:opendaylight:action:types";
    prefix action;
    grouping action {
        choice action {
            case output-action-case {
                container output-action {
                    leaf output-node-connector {
                        type inet:uri;
                    }
                    leaf max-length {
                        type uint16;
                    }
                    leaf wavelength {
                        type uint16;
                    }
                    leaf timeslot {
                        type string {
                            pattern '[01]{80}';
                        }
                    }
                }
            }
        }
```

```
module opendaylight-match-types {
    namespace "urn:opendaylight:model:match:types";
    prefix "match";
    grouping match {
        leaf in-port {
            type inv:node-connector-id;
        }
        leaf in-phy-port {
            type inv:node-connector-id;
        }
        leaf wavelength {
            type uint16;
        }
        leaf timeslot {
            type string {
                pattern '[01]{80}';
            }
        }
```

Figure 6. YANG model extensions for encoding of wavelength and time slots in OpenFlow match and action structures.

C. *NEPHELE Controller Prototype*

The proof-of-concept prototype of the SDN controller developed in the NEPHELE project is based on the OpenDaylight controller, Lithium version, with extended internal components and a set of SDN applications developed from scratch. In particular, for what regards the controller internal modules, the OF OpenDaylight plugin has been enhanced to support the concepts of wavelengths and timeslots in OF rules at the SBI. On the other hand, the software components for the coordination of traffic matrix computation and application-aware resource allocation are developed as external SDN applications which make use of the controller REST APIs. In particular, the scheduling engine is a standalone application written in C and the algorithm implementation is a translation of MATLAB code converted using MATLAB coder. The other SDN applications are Java applications based on the Spring MVC framework. The controller code is released as open source software and it is available on github [9].

The current implementation provides mechanisms for: (i) accepting requests that specify application requirements in terms of connections between innovation zones with a given reserved bandwidth; (ii) aggregating these requests into a global DCN traffic matrix; (iii) computing a network-wide resource allocation strategy for the current DCN traffic load; (iv) translating the allocation strategy in the set of extended OF rules for the configuration of the NEPHELE data plane; and (v) request the OF plugin to install these rules on the POD and ToR switches.

The NEPHELE controller offers a unified service access point through the REST-based NBI of the Application Affinity Service, enabling its integration with cloud management platforms, like OpenStack. The Northbound API is documented using the Swagger 2.0 tool, which also produces an interactive web-based graphical interface embedded in the application itself.

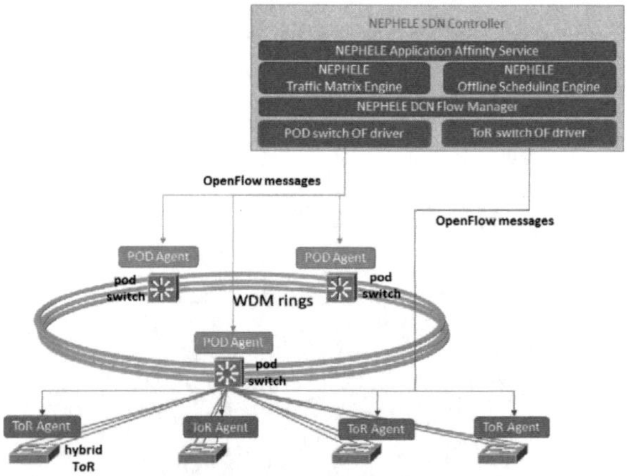

Figure 7. Prototype of NEPHELE controller

Beyond the REST APIs, the OpenDaylight DLUX GUI has been extended to allow requests for provisioning of DCN connections, visualize traffic matrix and flows installed as a result of the Offline Engine computation. The GUI provides a monitoring and diagnostic tool for the DCN administration.

The NEPHELE SDN controller prototype has been demonstrated in a simple environment with a mix of emulated and physical devices at the OFC 2017 conference. The demonstration [10] (Figure 7) shows the entire DCN configuration workflow, from the specification of new application-based connections via GUI, to the elaboration of the optimal resource allocation solution, up to the OF-based interaction with the optical data plane through the OF agents.

V. CONCLUSIONS

This paper has presented an SDN-based control plane for a scalable DCN based on hybrid opto-electrical devices with TDMA technologies, designed in the NEPHELE project. An architecture for the intra-DC infrastructure has been proposed, together with solutions for efficient network resource allocation, based on the global DCN traffic as declared in applications' traffic profiles. Finally, the paper has introduced the proof-of-concept prototype of the NEPHELE controller.

The next steps in the NEPHELE research involve the integration of the SDN controller in a wider environment for the provisioning of inter-DC services. The project will build a hierarchy of controllers, where child controllers will be responsible for resource allocation in single DCNs and in inter-DC network domains (e.g., based on flex-grid optical technologies), while a parent controller will coordinate the end-to-end service provisioning.

ACKNOWLEDGEMENT

This work has received funding from the European Union's Horizon 2020 research and innovation programme under grant agreement No 645212 (NEPHELE).

REFERENCES

[1] NEPHELE project web-site: http://www.nepheleproject.eu/ [retrieved: March, 2017].

[2] K. Christodoulopoulos, K. Kontodimas, K. Yiannopoulos, E.Varvarigos, "Bandwidth Allocation in the NEPHELE Hybrid Optical Interconnect", 18th International Conference on Transparent Optical Networks (ICTON), Trento, 2016, pp. 1-4.

[3] M. Aziz et al. "SDN-Enabled Application-Aware Networking for Datacenter Networks", 2016 IEEE International Conference on Electronics, Circuits, and Systems (ICECS), Monte Carlo, 2016, pp. 372-375.

[4] K. Christodoulopoulos, K. Kontodimas, A. Siokis, K. Yiannopoulos, E.Varvarigos, "Collisions Free Scheduling in the NEPHELE Hybrid Electrical/Optical Datacenter Interconnect", 2016 IEEE International Conference on Electronics, Circuits, and Systems (ICECS), Monte Carlo, 2016, pp. 368-371.

[5] OpenDaylight web page https://www.opendaylight.org/ [retrieved: March, 2017].

[6] Open Networking Foundation, "OpenFlow Switch Specification" version 1.3.1, ONF TS-007, September 2012.

[7] B.Pfaff and B. Davie, "The Open vSwitch Database Management Protocol", IETF RFC 7047, December 2013.

[8] M. Bjorklund, "YANG – A Data Modeling Language for the Network Configuration Protocol (NETCONF)", October 2010.

[9] NEPHELE SDN controller code: https://github.com/nextworks-it/oceania-dcn-controller [retrieved: March, 2017].

[10] P. Bakopoulos, "SDN Control Framework with Dynamic Resource Assignment for Slotted Optical Datacenter Networks", Optical Networking and Communication Conference & Exhibition, OFC 2017, Los Angeles, US, March 2017.

NFV Information Model Extensions for Improved Reliability and Lifecycle Management

Giovanni Fausto Andreotti, Paolo Secondo Crosta, Emanuele Miucci, Giuseppe Monteleone
ITALTEL S.p.A.
Milan, Italy
e-mail: {fausto.andreotti, paolosecondo.crosta, emanuele.miucci, giuseppe.monteleone} @italtel.com

Abstract—**This paper focuses on improvements in Management and Orchestration within the Network Function Virtualization (NFV) domain. The key benefits are related to automation in the Virtual Network Function (VNF) lifecycle, adaptation to different network traffic loads and new models for improving network resilience. These could be achieved by introducing some extensions of the NFV Information Model. Firstly, we propose the introduction in the VNF Descriptor (VNFD) of an Information Element providing the dependencies between Virtual Deployment Units (VDUs) that allows managing the VDUs' instantiation process in a more efficient way. Secondly, we suggest an extension related to the execution of script(s) - including the possibility to pass parameters - in response to particular events detected by the VNF Manager (VNFM). Finally, we propose a new Information Element for describing high availability features, thus defining possible redundancy schemes that allow the execution of specific operations tailored for each single instance of the VNF. In order to support the validity of the proposed approach, we provide some practical examples based on a real implementation of a VNF Session Border Controller.**

Keywords - Network Function Virtualization, Orchestration, Information Model, VNF Descriptor, Lifecycle Management.

I. INTRODUCTION

Network Function Virtualization (NFV), in addition to Software Defined Networking (SDN), is a rapidly emerging approach in the telecommunication field. By adopting NFV, Communication Services Providers (CSP) expect to achieve consistent cost reductions with respect to the current situation in which network equipment consists of proprietary black boxes, containing a bundle of proprietary Software (SW) and customized Hardware (HW) provided by a single Telecom Equipment Manufacturer. The adoption of the NFV concept is just the starting point to introduce in the Telco world the benefits that virtualization has brought in the Information Technology (IT) sector. Besides significant cost reductions, NFV also raises great expectations on the possibility (a) to achieve a never experienced network flexibility and service agility, (b) to introduce automation in all lifecycle of Network Functions (NFs) from deployment, installation and commissioning to operational phases, (c) to adapt the network to different traffic loads thanks to a novel cloud elasticity model, and (d) to develop new models for improving network resilience [10].

In fact, the objective of NFV is to allow Service Operators to achieve a high reduction in capital investments along with greater operational agility by implementing challenging architectural updates and deep changes in service models and operating procedures.

Virtualization is not a new technology. What is new is the way to use virtualization in Telco environments. Thanks to NFV, it is possible a paradigm shift moving from manual, complex and error prone configuration processes to deployment automation. Automation means flexibility, agility and the possibility to minimize complexity and errors. After the deployment, when the function is in operation it is possible to perform monitoring, scaling, healing, failover, continuous delivery and infrastructure upgrades.

In the NFV architecture, specified by the European Telecommunications Standards Institute (ETSI) NFV Industry Specification Group (ISG) [8], three main domains are identified [3]:

- Virtualized Network Function (VNF), as the software implementation of a network function which is capable of running over the Network Functions Virtualization Infrastructure (NFVI)
- NFVI, including hardware resources (Compute, Storage, Networking) and the virtualization layer that provides Virtual resources (Virtual Compute, Virtual Storage, Virtual Networking) supporting the execution of the VNFs
- NFV Management and Orchestration (MANO), which covers the lifecycle management of VNFs and Network Services (NS), managing the resources of NFVI and focusing on all virtualization-specific management tasks necessary in the NFV framework.

In this paper, we will focus on the Management and Orchestration domain. In particular, we propose some extensions of the NFV Information Model that can be used to increase efficiency in the lifecycle management of Network Functions and to improve the overall system reliability. Our experience as VNF provider conducted us to identify some flaws in the NFV Information Model and corresponding specific enhancements that future implementations could benefit from. In order to achieve this goal, we introduce some additional Information Elements (IEs) in the VNF Descriptors (VNFDs) that allow a deeper control of VNFs.

The paper is organized as follows: Section II gives an overview of the ETSI standard model for NFV, with regard to the MANO architecture, including the lifecycle management of Virtual Network Functions and a general description of the NFV Information Model. Section III, the main part of the paper, provides a rationale for the extensions to VNF Descriptors, as well as some practical examples to support the validity of the proposed approach. Finally, Section IV will draw the conclusions.

II. ETSI NFV ARCHITECTURAL MODEL

The ETSI NFV architectural framework [1] [2] is shown in Figure 1.

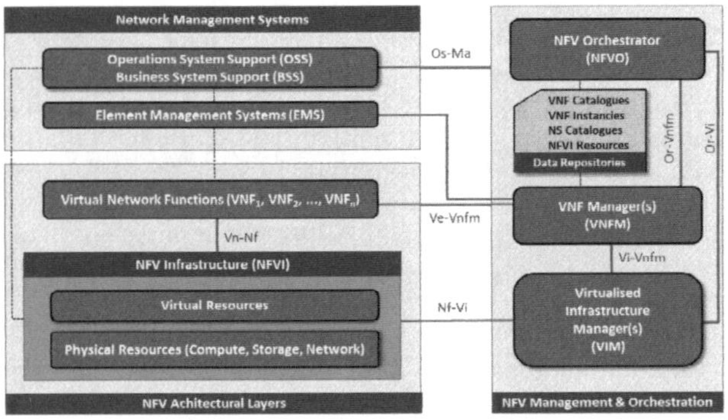

Figure 1. ETSI NFV architectural model.

The functional blocks in the framework can be grouped into three main entities: (1) NFV Architectural Layers, (2) NFV Management and Orchestration, and (3) Network Management Systems. These entities, as well their constituent functional blocks, are connected together using a set of defined reference points. The NFV architectural layers include the NFVI and VNFs. NFVI is the combination of both hardware and software resources, which make up the environment in which VNFs are deployed, while VNFs are implementations of NFs that are deployed on those virtual resources.

A. *NFV-MANO Framework*

The NFV MANO [3] consists of three functional blocks, the Virtualized Infrastructure Manager (VIM), the VNF Manager (VNFM) and the NFV Orchestrator (NFVO), and four data repositories (NS Catalogues, VNF Catalogues, VNF Instances and NFVI Resources).

1) VIM - It manages and controls NFVI physical and virtual resources in a single infrastructure domain. This implies that an NFV architecture may contain more than one VIM, with each of them managing or controlling NFVI resources from a given infrastructure provider. In principle, a VIM may be specialized in handling a certain type of NFVI resource (e.g., compute-only or storage only), or could manage multiple types of NFVI resources (e.g., nodes in the NFVI).

2) VNFM - Each VNF instance is assumed to have an associated VNFM. The VNFM is responsible for the management of the lifecycle of VNFs. A VNFM may manage a single or multiple VNF instances of the same or different types. It is also possible that a single VNFM handles all the active VNF instances for a certain domain.

3) NFVO - It is aimed at combining more than one function so as to create end-to-end services. To this end, the NFVO functionality can be divided into two broad categories: (a) resource orchestration, and (b) service orchestration. Resource orchestration is used to provide services that support accessing NFVI resources in an abstract manner regardless of the type of VIMs, as well as governance of VNF instances sharing resources of the NFVI infrastructure. Service orchestration deals with the creation of end-to-end services by composing different VNFs, and the topology management of the network services instances.

4) Data Repositories - These are databases that keep different types of information in the NFV MANO. Four types of repositories can be considered: (a) the NS Catalogue is a set of pre-defined templates, which define how network services may be created and deployed, as well as the functions needed for the service and their connectivity, (b) the VNF Catalogue is a set of templates which describe the deployment and operational characteristics of available VNFs, (c) the NFVI Resources repository holds information about available/allocated NFVI resources, and (d) the VNF Instances repository holds information about all function and service instances throughout their lifetime.

B. *VNF Lifecycle Management*

NFV is based on the principle of separating network functions from the hardware where they run on by using virtual hardware abstraction. The virtualization of network functions will change their lifecycle management by introducing automation and flexibility. Lifecycle management of VNFs is possible after a preliminary operation, the so-called VNF package on-boarding. After that, by accessing to a VNF catalogue it is possible to create one or more VNF instances of a VNF. A VNF instance corresponds to a run-time instance of the VNF software, i.e., all the VNF components are instantiated and the internal and external network connectivity configured.

During its lifecycle a VNF instance can be in one of the following states:

- instantiable, i.e., the on-boarded process for the VNF has been correctly performed
- instantiated, i.e., not configured, configured & not in service, configured & in service
- terminated.

The lifecycle is controlled by a set of operations, described in the following list:

- VNF Instantiation
- VNF instance Scaling (horizontal/vertical)
- VNF instance Update or Upgrade
- VNF instance Healing
- VNF instance Termination.

It is worth mentioning that a subset of lifecycle management (LCM) operations, as VNF Instantiation and Termination, are always available for every single VNF instance.

Some other operations, such as VNF Scaling, are performed if required by the deployment flavor of the VNF instance. Some procedures related to VNF lifecycle management provide both manual and automatic mechanisms. Scaling, for instance, can be manually requested or automatically performed when triggered upon the occurrence of specific events defined as criteria for matching rules and actions for scaling. All the operations during the lifecycle are handled by specific workflows that are built on the basis of the tasks to perform and the associated parameters (i.e., in case of instantiation, the VNF ID, the deployment flavor, etc.). A workflow has a starting point and different tasks that can be performed sequentially or in parallel, in order to perform all the necessary activities.

A VNFD is used for defining workflows for the automation of specific phases. For instance, by modelling the VNFD using a description language it is possible to describe the VNF with a service template in terms of components (e.g., Virtual Deployment Units or VDUs), relationships (dependencies, connections) and management processes. The management processes can be defined as plans describing how a VNF instance is instantiated and/or terminated considering that the VNF is a complex application composed by different nodes.

C. *NFV Information Model*

In this subsection, we provide a brief description of the IEs used to carry the necessary information about a VNF. In fact, one of the ways the IEs can be used is as part of descriptors in a catalogue or template context.

The IEs to be handled by the NFV MANO, including the ones contained in the VNFD, need to guarantee the flexible deployment and portability of VNF instances on multi-vendor and diverse NFVI environments, e.g., with diverse computing resource generations, diverse virtual network technologies, etc. To achieve this goal, hardware resources need to be properly abstracted and VNF requirements must be described in terms of such abstractions.

With reference to Figure 1, the Vi-Vnfm interface [4] enables the interaction between the VNFM and the VIM, providing the methods to operate cloud resources on the NFVI, in particular computing, storage and networking resources. After the upload of the VNF package, the VNFM under operator's request or by a request coming from the Or-Vnfm interface [5] can start to perform the lifecycle management of a VNF via the Ve-Vnfm interface [6].

The VNF package contains all artifacts needed to perform the lifecycle management for the associated VNF:

- descriptors (VNFDs)
- metadata, scripts and other proprietary artifacts
- optionally, SW images of the VNF Components (VNFCs).

The VNFD is a template which describes a VNF in terms of its deployment and operational behaviour requirements. It is primarily used by the VNFM in the process of VNF instantiation and lifecycle management of a VNF instance. The information provided in the VNFD is also used by the NFVO to manage and orchestrate network services and virtualised resources on the NFVI. The VNFD also contains connectivity, interface and KPIs requirements that may be used by NFV MANO functional blocks to establish appropriate virtual links within the NFVI between its VNFC instances, or between a VNF instance and the endpoint interface to the other NFs. The VNFD contains all the information needed for the lifecycle management, such as:

- basic information for VNF identification
- internal networks description
- VDUs description: for each VNFC (corresponding to a VM type) it is defined the flavor of the VM, the SW image for the VM and the number of VMs to activate. Configuration scripts are also provided for the lifecycle management phases and triggered during the instantiation or by specific events
- meters or measurements associated to VNF scaling. In fact, when the VNF is in operation, measurements can be collected from the VNF itself and/or from the infrastructure, e.g., the number of session attempts per second; the contemporary active sessions; CPU, RAM, disk usage; etc.
- alarms and associated actions. Criteria may be defined in terms of rules to check on the measurements, e.g., the value of a meter is greater than a specific threshold for a specified period of time; etc. When a rule is matched, specific actions can be performed, such as the activation of a scaling policy, etc.
- scaling policies, e.g., to add an instance of a VNFC when specific conditions are matched.

III. ETSI NFV Information Model Extensions

The aim of this section is to provide a detailed description, the rationales, the relationships and the benefits of each proposed extension of the Information Model.

The ETSI GS NFV-IFA 011 [7] is the reference specification that provides requirements for the structure and the format of a VNF Package to describe the VNF properties and associated resource requirements in an interoperable template.

In the following, we describe the extensions – in terms of newly added IEs – of this specification, and related use cases to show the benefits introduced in the lifecycle management of VNFs.

An overview of the Information Model extensions is summarized in Table I. Generally, a VNF is composed by one or more VNFCs that are described by means of deployment templates, i.e., VNFD and related VDUs, respectively. In the table we have listed the proposed attribute extensions - *dependencies*, *MetadataScript* and *highAvailability* IEs - and their relationships with descriptors at the VNFD (vnfd) or VDU (vnfd:vdu) level.

TABLE I. OVERVIEW OF INFORMATION MODEL EXTENSIONS

ETSI GS NFV-IFA 011 Specification Extensions		
Entity relationship	VNF	VNFC1, ..., VNFCn
Deployment template	VNFD	VDU
Descriptor	vnfd	vnfd:vdu
proposed attribute extensions (new IEs)	dependencies	MetadataScript, highAvailability

All the use cases are based on a real implementation of a Session Border Controller (SBC). This VNF provides its functionalities thanks to the interworking of 5 VNFCs, as depicted in Figure 2: a front-end load balancer (FELB), an Operation and Maintenance module (OAM), a component managing the SIP signalling traffic (SIG) working with a database (DB) for storing the information of the active calls and a Border Gateway (BGW) function engaged when audio or media transcoding is required for the incoming traffic.

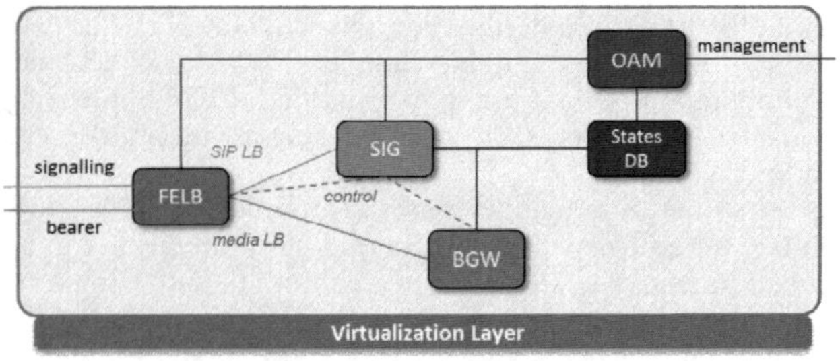

Figure 2. SBC logical components.

These components can be organized and managed to implement protection mechanisms in order to guarantee redundancy and to support high availability requirements.

A. Dependencies

In this subsection, we provide the description of the *dependencies* and *VduDependencies* attributes that could be added to indicate the dependencies among the VDUs during the instantiation process. In fact, sometimes it is necessary to coordinate the process of instantiation with information that is available - at platform level (e.g., IP addresses) or application level - at specific times. As originally proposed in the ETSI MANO specification [3], we believe it is necessary to include in the VNFD an IE providing the dependencies between VDUs since it describes constraints that affect the structure of a VNF.

Table II shows the structure of the *dependencies* IE that has to be added to the VNFD standard description [7].

TABLE II. *DEPENDENCIES* INFORMATION ELEMENT

Attribute(s) of the *dependencies* VNFD IE	
Attribute	dependencies
Qualifier	M
Cardinality	0..N
Content	VduDependencies
Description	Describes dependencies between VDUs. Defined in terms of source and target VDU, i.e., target VDU "depends on" source VDU. In other words, sources VDU shall exist before target VDU can be instantiated/deployed.

The *VduDependencies* IE provides indications on the order in which VDUs associated to the same VNFD have to be instantiated. The contents of a *VduDependencies* type shall comply with the format provided in Table III.

TABLE III. *VDUDEPENDENCIES* INFORMATION ELEMENT

Attribute(s) of the *VduDependencies* IE		
Attribute	source	target
Qualifier	M	M
Cardinality	1..N	1..N
Content	Identifier	Identifier
Description	The listed VDUs shall be instantiated before the VDUs listed in the target parameter.	The listed VDUs shall be instantiated after the VDUs listed in the source parameter have been instantiated completely.

In Figure 3, it is shown a sequence diagram based on a real implementation of a VNF SBC. It is worth to mention that in this case, all the VNFCs should be instantiated after the OAM component, since this component has a central role coordinating the communications with the VNF Manager on behalf of all the other VNFCs.

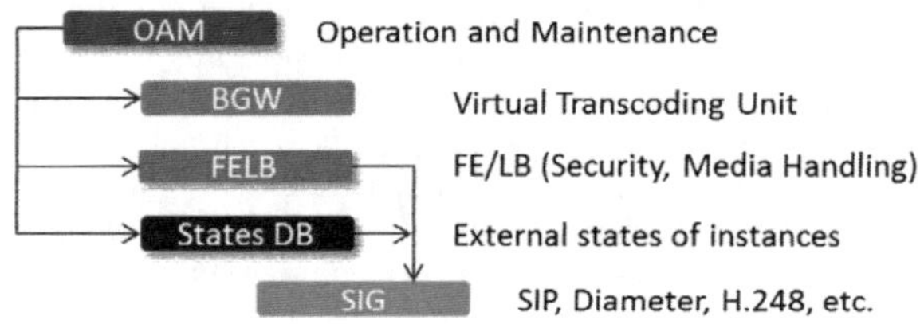

Figure 3. SBC components sequence diagram.

As shown in Figure 4, the dependencies explained above have been expressed by using the JavaScript Object Notation (JSON) [9].

```
"dependency": [{
        "vdu-id": "felb",
        "depends-on": "oam"
        }, {
        "vdu-id": "sig",
        "depends-on": "oam"
        }, {
        "vdu-id": "states",
        "depends-on": "oam"
        }, {
        "vdu-id": "bgw",
        "depends-on": "oam"
        }, {
        "vdu-id": "sig",
        "depends-on": "felb"
        }, {
        "vdu-id": "sig",
        "depends-on": "states"
    }].
```

Figure 4. *Dependencies* script example.

Alternatively, ETSI envisages the use of a scripting language to express dependencies on virtual resources, but at the time of this writing, no consensus has been reached yet about the format to be used and the standardization process of a Domain Specific Language is still underway.

B. MetadataScript

In this subsection, we provide the description of the *MetadataScript* and *LifeCycleMetadataScript* attributes. These extensions are related to the execution of script(s) in response to particular events detected on a VNFM reference point. The ETSI GS NFV-IFA 011 specification [7] already supports the execution of scripts – but only at the VNF level

- with the *LifeCycleManagementScript* IE that can be launched in response to lifecycle events or external stimulus detected by the VNFM. These LCM scripts should be embedded in the VNF Package and used in the LCM execution environments provided by generic VNF Managers. In par.6.2.6, the specification provides a list of requirements (VNF_PACK.LCM.001) for the scripting Domain Specific Language (DSL).

Table IV shows the structure of the *MetadataScript* IE that has to be added to the VDU standard description [7].

TABLE IV. *METADATASCRIPT* INFORMATION ELEMENT

Attribute(s) of the *MetadataScript* VDU IE	
Attribute	MetadataScript
Qualifier	M
Cardinality	0..N
Content	LifeCycleMetadataScript
Description	Includes a list of events and corresponding scripts producing metadata required during the VDU instantiation.

A *LifeCycleMetadataScript* IE, instead of the *LifeCycleManagementScript* formerly defined in the original specification, has been defined and extended to comply with specific needs originated from practical use cases.

The attributes of the *LifeCycleMetadataScript* IE shall follow the indications provided in Table V. The advantages of this extension, compared with the existing standard specification, are (a) the possibility to execute script(s) at the VDU level, and (b) the possibility to pass parameter(s) to the script(s).

TABLE V. LIFECYCLEMETADATASCRIPT INFORMATION ELEMENT

Attribute(s) of the *LifeCycleMetadataScript* IE				
Attribute	event	script	role	parameter
Qualifier	M	M	M	M
Cardinality	1	1	1	0..N
Content	String	Not specified	String	Not specified
Description	Describes a VNF lifecycle event or an external stimulus detected on a VNFM reference point.	Includes metadata template.	Describes the role of the VDU in redundancy scheme(s). Possible values are "Active" or "Passive".	VDU specific parameters passed to the script. Each of them represents the run-time value of a NFVI resource (e.g., IP address, VNFC instance name, etc.).

In Figure 5, we provide an example based on a real implementation of the Session Border Controller VNF.

It is worth noting that this IE allows the VNFM a complete flexibility in the lifecycle management process of different VNFs/VNFCs: in this example, the script for the instantiation of the OAM component needs information from the infrastructure (i.e., the IP address of the connection point cp_oam_int, the hostname of the VNFC and the related domain_name) which will be available only at runtime.

```
"lifeCycleMetadataScript": [{
            "event": "CREATION",
            "script": "instantiate_oam",
            "role":"active",
            "parameters": [
            "$$param.cp_oam_int.ipaddress",
            "$$param.hostname",
            "$$param.domain_name"
            ]
    }].
```

Figure 5. *LifeCycleMetadataScript* script example.

According to our experience, the proposed syntax is general and can be easily adapted in order to suit different VNFM providers.

C. *HighAvailability*

In this subsection, we provide the description of the *highAvailability* attribute. Availability is defined as the state to perform a required function at a given instant of time or at any instant of time within a given time interval, assuming that the external resources, if required, are provided. This attribute is important for telecom operators that want to offer their customers services that perform as expected whenever the service is requested.

Comparing the VDU IE originally proposed in the ETSI MANO specification [3] with the one described in ETSI GS NFV-IFA 011 [7], the *high_availability* IE is no longer specified. The reason provided by ETSI is based on the assumption that the VNFM alone can hardly manage the multitude of redundancy schemes: high availability policies should be performed by each single VNFC at the application level.

Instead, in our opinion, an attribute specified at the VDU level allows the VNFM to execute specific operations tailored for each single instance, thus simplifying the implementation of the VNF itself.

Table VI shows the structure of the *highAvailability* IE that has to be added to the VDU standard description [7].

TABLE VI. *HIGHAVAILABILITY* INFORMATION ELEMENT

Attribute(s) of the *highAvailability* VDU IE	
Attribute	highAvailability
Qualifier	M
Cardinality	0..1
Content	Enum
Description	Defines redundancy model to ensure high availability. Possible values are "ActiveActive" or "ActivePassive". • ActiveActive: implies that two instance of the same VDU will co-exists with continuous data synchronization. • ActivePassive: implies that two instance of the same VDU will co-exists without any data synchronization.

For example, the statement *"highAvailability":"ActivePassive"* implies the active part to request a set of parameters which can be different from the configuration set which is needed by the passive part.

Furthermore, the active and passive counterparts would require a different set of instantiation/configuration scripts. As shown in Figure 5, this condition could be easily enforced by using an additional attribute defined in the *LifeCycleMetadataScript* IE, i.e., the *role* attribute, which can assume "*active*" (or "*passive*") values, as described in Table V.

IV. CONCLUSIONS

In this paper, some improvements have been proposed in Management and Orchestration of Virtual Network Functions, based on extensions of the Information Model specified by ETSI. The need for these additional IEs in the VNFD/VDU descriptor(s) has been originated from a real implementation of a novel NFV-compliant Session Border Controller solution. The key points addressed have been more flexibility in the management of network functions and increased reliability of virtualized systems. As a result of this work, we provided a detailed description, rationales, relationships and possible benefits coming from the new attributes, as well as practical examples to support the validity of the proposed approach. The extensions have been applied and successfully validated on a SBC solution, thus demonstrating very useful and easy to fit into the ETSI specification framework.

REFERENCES

[1] ETSI Industry Specification Group (ISG) NFV, "ETSI GS NFV 002 V1.1.1: Network Functions Virtualization (NFV); Architectural Framework," http://www.etsi.org/deliver/etsi_gs/nfv/001_099/002/01.01.01_60/gs_nfv002v010101p.pdf, [retrieved: March, 2017].

[2] ETSI Industry Specification Group (ISG) NFV, "ETSI GS NFV 003 V1.1.1: Network Functions Virtualization (NFV); Terminology for Main Concepts in NFV," http://www.etsi.org/deliver/etsi_gs/NFV/001_099/003/01.01.01_60/gs_nfv003v010101p.pdf, [retrieved: March, 2017].

[3] ETSI Industry Specification Group (ISG) NFV, "ETSI GS NFV-MAN 001 V1.1.1: Network Functions Virtualization (NFV); Network Functions Virtualization Management and Orchestration", December 2014.

[4] ETSI Industry Specification Group (ISG) NFV, "ETSI GS NFV-IFA 006 V2.1.1: Network Functions Virtualization (NFV); Management and Orchestration; Vi-Vnfm reference point – Interface and Information Model Specification", April 2016.

[5] ETSI Industry Specification Group (ISG) NFV, "ETSI GS NFV-IFA 007 V2.1.1: "Network Functions Virtualization (NFV); Management and Orchestration; Or-Vnfm reference point – Interface and Information Model Specification", October 2016.

[6] ETSI Industry Specification Group (ISG) NFV, "ETSI GS NFV-IFA 008 V2.1.1: "Network Functions Virtualization (NFV); Management and Orchestration; Ve-Vnfm reference point – Interface and Information Model Specification", October 2016.

[7] ETSI Industry Specification Group (ISG) NFV, "ETSI GS NFV-IFA 011 V2.1.1: "Network Functions Virtualization (NFV); Management and Orchestration; VNF Packaging Specification", October 2016.

[8] ETSI - NETWORK FUNCTIONS VIRTUALISATION http://www.etsi.org/technologies-clusters/technologies/nfv.

[9] The JSON Data Interchange Format. http://www.ecma-international.org/publications/files/ECMA-ST/ECMA-404.pdf.

[10] V. Eramo, E. Miucci, M. Ammar; and F. G. Lavacca, "An Approach for Service Function Chain Routing and Virtual Function Network Instance Migration in Network Function Virtualization Architectures," in IEEE/ACM Transactions on Networking, vol.PP, no.99, pp.1-18.

GPU-accelerated Video Transcoding Unit for Multi-access Edge Computing Scenarios

Antonino Albanese, Paolo Secondo Crosta, Claudio Meani, Pietro Paglierani,
ITALTEL,
Castelletto, Milan, Italy

e-mail: {antonino.albanese, paolosecondo.crosta, claudio.meani, pietro.paglierani}@italtel.com

Abstract—**The exponential growth of video traffic and the outburst of novel video-based services is revealing the inadequacy of the traditional mobile network infrastructure. To respond to this and to many other demands coming from today's society, the 5G and the Multi-access Edge Computing (MEC) initiatives are proposing novel network architectures. In this context, this paper proposes the Video Transcoding Unit (VTU) application, which, leveraging on MEC principles, brings several functionalities to the edge of networks, greatly improving User Experience with mobile terminals. The VTU can be implemented as a SW (Software)-only Virtual Network Function, or be accelerated by a Graphics Processing Unit (GPU). Specific tests are described and discussed, showing the clear superiority of the HW (Hardware)-accelerated implementation in terms of computing performance and efficiency. A possible use case is presented, in which the VTU is used in a Stadium or in large public venues during crowded events like a sporting match or concerts. The work presented in this paper was undertaken under the EU Horizon2020 Sesame Project.**

Keywords-NFV; MEC; 5G; HW-acceleration; GPU; Video transcoding.

I. INTRODUCTION

The recent worldwide explosion of mobile data traffic has been impressive, and it is clear that this trend will continue in the coming years.

The fast spreading of smart terminals together with new services based on high-definition video have been the main triggers of this explosion, revealing the inadequacy of the architectural and technological approach adopted so far in the design of the traditional mobile network infrastructure. The telecommunication market, previously dominated by voice traffic and text messages, is rapidly shifting to a completely different and far more complicated scenario, made of millions of connected applications where even different actors have made their appearance, like machines and "things" (smart home gadgets, vehicles, drones, robots, also including sensors and actuators).

This way, Internet and communication networks have become crucial for any evolutionary process of modern societies and economies. This fact led to the definition of a new kind of infrastructure based on the "fifth generation" - 5G - architecture as a response to the requirements coming from the more diverse fields of the future world [1].

5G aims at assuming a fundamental role in the new society; it is not only a simple evolution of previous mobile networks – as was the passage from 3G to 4G - but it stands as a real revolution, able to create the appropriate ecosystem for technical and business innovation [2].

From the technological point of view 5G will take advantage of the last years' experience coming from the convergence of the telecom world with Information Technology. This strong movement addressed the necessity coming from Network Operators of reducing general costs, achieving better scalability and reducing the deployment time of new services and resulted in a new architectural vision based on Software-Defined Networking (SDN) and Network Function Virtualization (NFV) [3].

5G will bring the SDN and NFV concepts in the radio communications environments and will use them in a new architectural framework where Multi-access Edge Computing (MEC) will play a major role.

MEC Technology and Architecture concepts are a way to improve both Efficiency and User Experience for a certain number of services. MEC is an ETSI initiative that uses virtualization, small cells, SDN and NFV principles to push network functions, services and content to the edge of the mobile network [4][5].

The MEC servers are typically directly attached to the base station, but this is not a strict rule because, in this regard, the MEC guidelines are widely open. They provide computing, storage and networking resources that are virtualized and shared by multiple virtual machines.

Traditionally, all data traffic originating in data centres is forwarded to the mobile core network. The traffic is then routed to a base station that delivers the content to the mobile devices. In the mobile edge scenario, MEC servers take over some or even all of the tasks originally performed in a data centre. Being located at the mobile edge, this eliminates the need of routing data through the core network, lowering communication latency. As such, the MEC paradigm helps to reach the severe requirements posed by 5G in terms of throughput, latency, scalability and automation. It's important to note that many of the concepts that are at the basis of MEC and the advantages they bring to a broad range of services are valid regardless of 5G technology (in fact MEC concepts can be similarly applied to fixed networks) and can be demonstrated prior to the coming 5G.

There are many services that could benefit from being hosted at the edge of the network. Several use cases have been defined in the specification of MEC architecture to demonstrate the advantages of the introduced concepts. One of these use cases regards video traffic in stadiums and/or large public venues where the video created during a sport event or a concert is routed to a MEC server that is responsible for its local distribution, without involving backhaul connection to the core network. The video contents are then stored in this edge platform and can be locally elaborated with applications running on the same MEC server to create new services and improve User Experience.

This paper presents the Italtel VTU application, which, leveraging on MEC principles, brings several functionalities to the edge of networks, greatly improving User Experience with mobile terminals. VTU speeds up upload and download of Video contents, reduces latency and contribute to increasing the battery life of connected devices offloading them from heavy transcoding operations.

This paper shows how an application such as the VTU could fit in a real use case foreseen by 5G and MEC and what are the limitations of a SW-only implementation with respect to a GPU-accelerated one.

The paper is organized as follows. Section II provides a brief functional description of the VTU. Section III briefly discusses why HW acceleration should be considered in developing a VNF such as the VTU. Section IV presents the performance characterization of VTU with and without GPU. Section V shows a possible use case for VTU during localized crowded events. Finally, Section VI summarizes the main results of this work.

II. VTU Description

The VTU can convert video streams from one video format to another. It can either run on bare metal environments, or it can be implemented as a VNF providing optimized video transcoding function, for the benefit of many other VNFs, to create enhanced services.

Depending on the type of application that should be provided, the source video stream could originate from a file within a storage facility, as well as coming in form of packetized network stream from another VNF. Moreover, the requested transcoding service could be mono-directional, as in video stream distribution-like applications, or bi-directional, like in videoconferencing (see Figure 1).

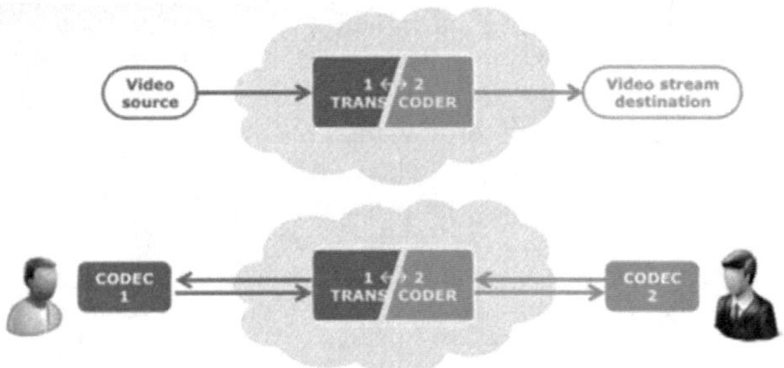

Figure 1. Simplified VTU model .

In the VTU, the audio and video transcoding capabilities are provided by the Libav library [6], a very popular open source library, which can perform encoding and decoding according to a wide set of coding standards. The AVConv tool from Libav is used for performing the conversion between audio and video formats and containers; while it already supports a wide variety of hardware accelerations, native GPU support in encoding tasks is quite limited, experimental and restricted only to H.264 and H.265 standards, exploiting the NVidia NVENC hardware encoder of medium and high level NVidia GPUs [7]. The AVConv tool running in the VTU has been modified so that VP8 encoding tasks can also greatly benefit from the virtualization of GPUs.

The VTU VNF is implemented as SW module running on a virtual machine and can be installed in one or multiple physical servers clustered together through a local communication fabric. The VTU can support a large set of video codecs, and in particular the most recent and popular ones, such as H.264, H.265 and VP8/VP9 [8][9].

III. VTU and HW Acceleration

Although software-only functions can give acceptable performance in many applications, when compute-intensive workloads running at the data plane are of interest, such as those based on video data processing, quite poor results can be obtained. In these cases, to reach the expected performance, it is often necessary to consider a slightly different approach that involves the use of Hardware accelerators. In general, managing HW accelerators and making them transparently available to every VNF goes against the assumption of every virtualized environment, of having a uniform HW platform made of CPU-only computing elements. The presence of HW accelerators bound to a virtual function implies the use of a SW layer that must be HW-aware, thus significantly complicating system management operations and scalability [3][9]. Though, the advantages of HW acceleration can be so preponderant, in particular when performance, latency or Service Level Agreement (SLA) requirements are challenging, that not considering them can push a commercial product out of the market. In fact, acceleration is not just related to performance, but also to the reduction of the number of physical servers, footprint, network appliances and power consumption. In short, it can make the difference in the commercial proposition of a product.

A distinctive feature of VTU is the possibility not only to run on general purpose CPUs but also to exploit the Hardware acceleration provided by a GPU, to improve the compute performance of video codecs. To this end, two different architectural approaches can be used. The first one, also known as "cooperative CPU- GPU" makes use of a GPU to offload the most compute-intensive functions of the video codec (usually, the Motion Estimation block), while the main algorithm is kept running on the CPU. The second approach, conversely, uses full HW implementation of video codecs. Today, various HW versions of the most popular encoding schemes, such as H.264, HEVC, VP8 and VP9, are available [7][10]. The fully HW approach can provide higher compute performance than cooperative CPU-GPU algorithms. Though, the HW approach very often lacks the flexibility in service management needed by service operators, thus the cooperative approach is still preferred in many real-life implementations. The VTU can adopt both GPU-accelerated approaches. In fact, it can use the Nvidia NVEnc encoder for the H.264 and H.265 encoding schemes [7]. Also, the CPU-GPU cooperative approach described in [11][12] can be used for the Google open Source VP8 encoder.

IV. VTU PERFORMANCE

We carried out many tests in Italtel laboratories to achieve a full performance characterization of the VTU, both for the SW-only version, and the GPU-accelerated one. For the sake of brevity, in the following, a few meaningful results are presented and discussed. In particular, Figure 2 and Figure 3 show the results obtained with the VTU featuring the H.264 and H.265 transcoding, (expressed in frames per second) without HW acceleration (SW-only) and with HW acceleration (using a GPU). The processing implies decoding from the input format to the one required as output.

In all tests, the same H.264 Full HD video file (1080x1920 resolution) was used as input. The VTU provided four different video resolutions as output, in four different transcoding tests: VGA (480x640 pixel), HD480 (480x852 pixel), HD720 (720x1280 pixel), HD1080 (1080x1920 pixel).

The horizontal axis in Figure 2 and Figure 3 represents output resolution, while the vertical axis indicates the achieved output frame-rate in frames per seconds (fps).

The SW-only VTU was running on a server with a single socket Intel Xeon E5-2630v3 2.4GHz, 8 Core CPU, with 64 GB DDR4 RAM. The Encoder used in this case for H.264 and H.265 is X264 and X265, respectively.

The GPU-accelerated VTU was running on the same server with the addition of a NVIDIA® QUADRO® M4000 GPU in a x16 PCIe Slot. The Encoder used by the GPU for H.264 and H.265 is NVIDIA NVENC.

Figure 2 and Figure 3 collect the results of the tests achieved with H.264 and H.265 encoders respectively. In both cases only one session was launched for each test.

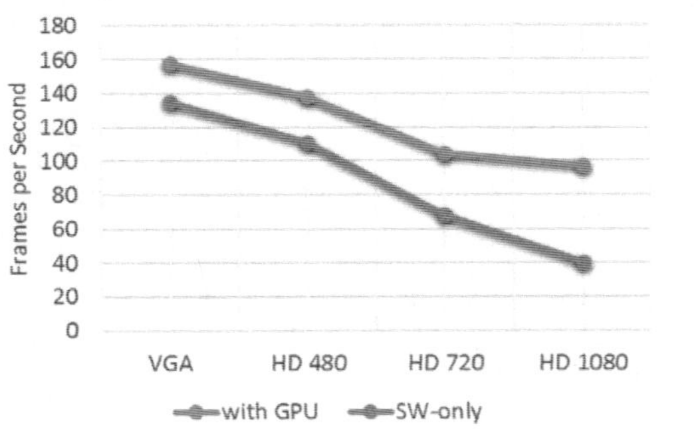

Figure 2. H.264 single session encoding performance (higher is better).

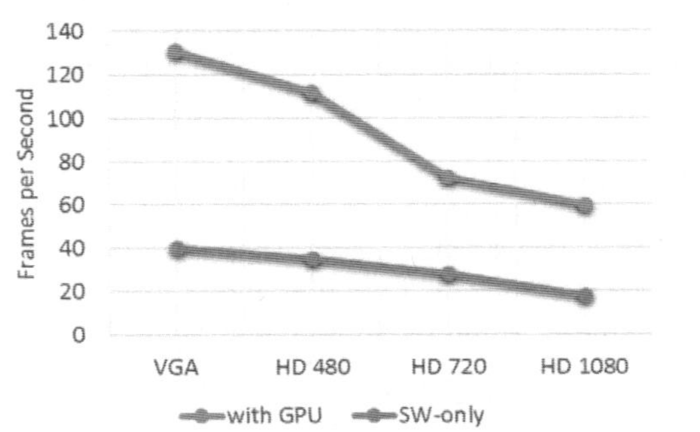

Figure 3. H.265 single session encoding performance (higher is better).

As one can easily see, the performance improvement using the GPU compared to a SW-only solution is remarkable in all cases. This confirms the need of GPU acceleration especially in modern and future scenarios where 4K or even higher video resolutions are going to be used.

Another important aspect to emphasize is related to the occupation of compute resources during transcoding. Although in SW-only mode CPU resources were completely occupied (all the CPU cores were running at 100%), using the GPU both CPU and GPU resources were only partially used. For example, during the H.264-HD1080 test reported before, in which only one encoding session was launched, the VTU was using only 20% of available GPU resources. This fact led us to a second set of tests in which multi-session performance was analyzed. In this new set of tests, the focus was on a single case, i.e., H.264 HD1080, launching 2, 4, 8, and 16 concurrent transcoding sessions.

The results are reported in Figure 4 and Figure 5.

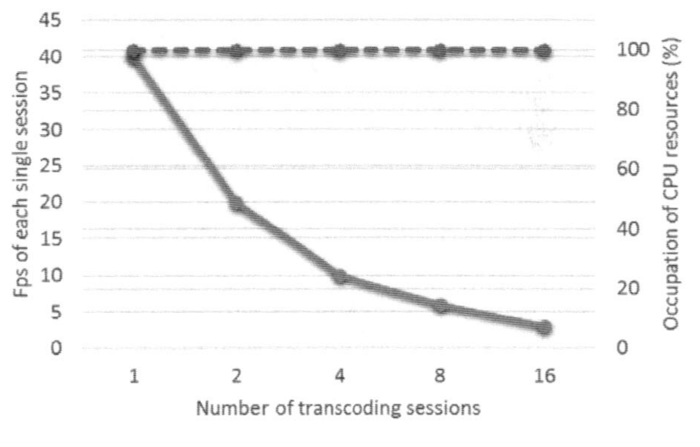

Figure 4. H.264 HD1080 encoding SW-only in multi-session transcoding tests (performance are related to each single session) with percentage of CPU resources utilization.

Considering the SW-only implementation (Figure 4) the performance of each single session decreases with the total number of executing sessions. Comparing the performance of 1 session to that with 16 concurrent sessions the result is the same. In fact, aggregating the fps of all the 16 sessions we obtain 16x2.5= 40fps (in case of 16 concurrent sessions the single session fps is 2.5). This can be easily justified considering that the CPU occupation during the processing is always around 100% also running a single session.

The same is not true using the GPU (Figure 5). In this case the CPU is only partially used because the workload is mainly offloaded to the GPU whose resources are, in turn not fully used (as the dotted lines show). Using the GPU with 16 concurrent sessions we reach 24 fps for each session, for a total of 16x24=384fps. The 384/40 ratio brings to a 9.6x gain in performance using the GPU respect to a SW-only solution. During the GPU test with 16 transcoding sessions the CPU was running at 70% giving it the possibility to run other tasks. This was not possible with SW-only solution, because in such a case the CPU was always 100% occupied.

Comparing the efficiency of the two solutions in term of performance/watt we see another important advantage of using the GPU. In fact, in case of 16 sessions (H.264-HD1080), the power consumption of the server running the SW-only VTU is around 200W while with GPU is around 300W. The gain in efficiency for GPU-accelerated VTU is then 6.4 ((384/300) / (40/200)).

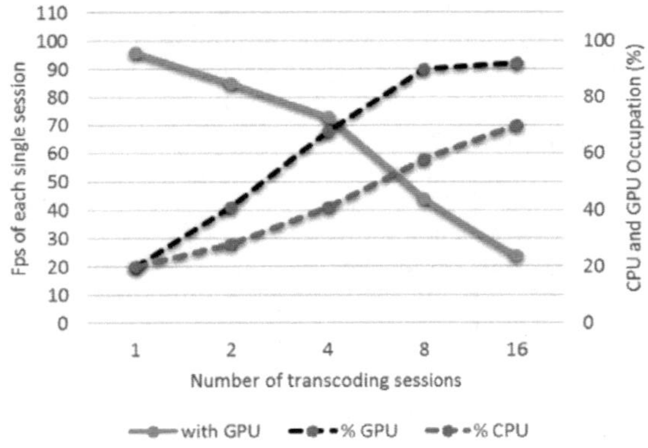

Figure 5. H.264 HD1080 encoding with GPU in multi-session transcoding tests (performance are related to each single session) with percentage of CPU and GPU resources utilization.

Similar considerations could be made regarding costs (the GPU used costs only around 70% the price of the server) and physical space (the space occupied by the server with or without GPU is the same, the latter being hosted inside the server).

V. A USE CASE FOR VTU

A possible use case for the VTU can be described by the following two scenarios.

"Imagine being at a stadium, where a football match takes place. Your team scores a goal but you are not in the best position to appreciate it or the action was confusing and you did not realize who scored the goal and how. You would like to have the possibility to watch on your smartphone the most relevant actions from different points of views"

Or:

"You are attending a crowded concert in the front row close to the stage and you want to show to other friends attending the concert far from the stage some video in real time, picturing the performance in progress. Also, the concert organizers could decide to show on the gigantic main screen a collage of real time videos coming from spectators to give them a more immersive and engaging experience."

In this type of contexts, there is an overwhelming demand for services that give the possibility to the users to have videos on their smartphones or tablets on demand, as services provided, for instance, by the Stadium.

From the technological perspective, what is needed to implement such type of services is a networking infrastructure featuring a very rapid upload and download of large files, such as HD videos. In addition to that, the possibility to process in a highly effective way video streams is a mandatory function to provide enhanced services. VTU, implemented in a MEC environment, represents a possible answer to that demand coming from the market. The HW-accelerated transcoding of video streams can help in reducing the computational workload of mobile terminals converting video streams from the uploaded format to one more suitable for the receiving terminal, increasing its battery life.

The whole process of upload, transcoding and download takes place locally in the MEC server (Figure 6) offloading the backhaul connection towards the core network. This reduces latency and avoids backhaul traffic congestion.

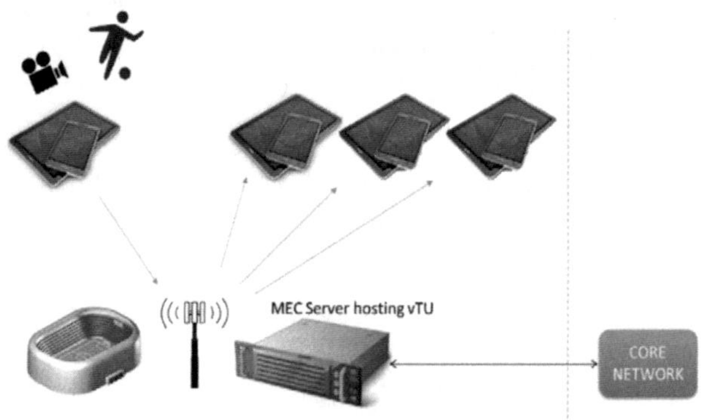

Figure 6. VTU use case: providing low lantency video sevices during localized crowded events leveraging MEC architecture

To this end, the MEC server must be equipped with its own high performance storage where all the videos uploaded from the users are kept for a certain amount of time, for instance a week. During this period a suitable application can make them available on demand outside the perimeter of the stadium, e.g., at home. The spectators during a sporting event can then upload many videos and delete them immediately to preserve memory space on their mobile devices, having the possibility to choose at a later time which one to download.

To provide these services, the Stadium or the event organization will make available an App to download on spectators' smartphones.

VI. CONCLUSION

This paper has presented the Video Transcoding Unit (VTU) application, which, leveraging on MEC principles, brings several video data processing functionalities to the edge of networks, greatly improving User Experience with mobile terminals. The VTU can be implemented as a SW-only VNF, or be accelerated by a GPU. Specific tests have been reported showing the clear superiority of the HW-accelerated implementation. A possible use case has been presented in which the VTU is used in a Stadium or in large public venues during crowded events like a sporting match or a concert. This work was undertaken under the EU Horizon2020 Sesame Project.

ACKNOWLEDGMENT

This research received funding from the European Union H2020 Research and Innovation Action under Grant Agreement No.671596 (SESAME project).

The authors are grateful to Mr. Marco Beccari and Mr. Luca Di Muzio who carried out the laboratory tests described in this paper.

REFERENCES

[1] 5G Infrastructure Public Private Partnership (PPP): The next generation of communication networks will be Made in EU. Digital agenda for Europe. Technical Report, European Commission. February 2014.

[2] NGMN: 5G White paper (2015).

[3] ETSI: ETSI GS NFV-MAN 001 v1.1.1: Network Functions Virtualisation (NFV); Management and Orchestration (2014)

[4] ETSI: Mobile-Edge Computing - Introductory Technical White Paper (2014)

[5] B. Blanco et al., "Technology pillars in the architecture of future 5G mobile networks: NFV, MEC and SDN", Computer Standards & Interfaces, Available online 4 January 2017, ISSN 0920-5489.

[6] Libav. [Online]. Available from: http://libav.org/documentation/ 2017.03.27

[7] NVIDIA NVENC Programming Guide [Online]. Available from: https://developer.nvidia.com/nvenc-programming-guide 2017.03.27.

[8] N. M. Cheung, X. Fan, O. C. Au, and M. C. Kung, "Video Coding on Multicore Graphics Processors," in IEEE Signal Processing Magazine, vol. 27, no. 2, pp. 79-89, March 2010.

[9] P. Paglierani, "High Performance Computing and Network Function Virtualization: A major challenge towards network programmability," 2015 IEEE International Black Sea Conference on Communications and Networking (BlackSeaCom), Constanta, 2015, pp. 137-141.

[10] WebM Video Hardware RTLs [Online]. Available from: https://www.webmproject.org/hardware/ 2017.03.27.

[11] P. Comi et al., "Hardware-accelerated high-resolution video coding in Virtual Network Functions," 2016 European Conference on Networks and Communications (EuCNC), Athens, 2016, pp. 32-36.

[12] P. Paglierani, G. Grossi, F. Pedersini, and A. Petrini, "GPU-based VP8 encoding: Performance in native and virtualized environments," 2016 International Conference on Telecommunications and Multimedia (TEMU), Heraklion, 2016, pp. 1-5.

Combined NFV and SDN Applications for Mitigation of Cyber-Attacks Conducted by Botnets in 5G Mobile Networks

Giacomo Bernini*, Pietro G. Giardina*, Gino Carrozzo*, Alberto Huertas Celdrán†, Manuel Gil Pérez†,
Jose M. Alcaraz Calero, Qi Wang‡, Konstantinos Koutsopoulos§, and Pedro Neves¶
* Nextworks, 56122 Pisa, Italy
Email: g.bernini@nextworks.it; p.giardina@nextworks.it; g.carrozzo@nextworks.it
† Dept. Ingeniería de la Información y las Comunicaciones, University of Murcia, 30071 Murcia, Spain
Email: alberto.huertas@um.es; mgilperez@um.es
‡ University of the West of Scotland, Paisley PA1 2BE, UK
Email: jose.alcaraz-calero@uws.ac.uk; qi.wang@uws.ac.uk
§ Creative Systems Engineering, 28is Oktovriou (Patision) 119, 11251 Athens, Greece
Email: k.koutsopoulos@creativese.eu
¶ Altice Labs, 3810-106 Aveiro, Portugal
Email: pedro-m-neves@alticelabs.com

***Abstract*—5G networks are envisioned to support substantially more users than the current 4G does as a direct consequence of the anticipated large diffusion of Machine-2-Machine (M2M) and Internet of Things (IoT) interconnected devices, often with significantly higher committed data rates than general bandwidth currently available into Long Term Evolution (LTE) and broadband networks. The expected large number of 5G subscribers will offer new opportunities to compromise devices and user services, which will allow attackers to trigger much larger and effective cyber-attacks. Significant advances in network management automation are therefore needed to manage 5G networks and services in an efficient, scalable, and effective way while protecting users and infrastructures from a wide plethora of advanced security threats. This paper presents a novel self-organized network management approach for 5G mobile networks where autonomic capabilities are tightly combined with Network Functions Virtualization (NFV) and Software-Defined Networking (SDN) technologies so as to provide an effective detection and mitigation of cyber-attacks.**

***Keywords*–SDN; NFV; 5G; cyber-protection.**

I. Introduction

5G aims to provide a scalable network infrastructure to meet the exponentially-increasing demands on mobile broadband access, both in terms of the number of connected users and required bandwidth. In this context, cyber-security widely recognized as a well-known challenge is already targeting all the layers of any ICT system, and it is becoming even more crucial to protect infrastructures due to the potential size and effects of cyber-attacks. Increased availability, service continuity, resilience, and delivery assurance for a broad spectrum of 5G services and applications are some of the security keywords that when combined with the anticipated levels of 5G mobility are required for the evolution of current security infrastructures towards more flexible, dynamic, and adaptive solutions.

Deep and extensive cloudification of services, with integration of edge and centralized clouds is another 5G key aspect that is accelerating the adoption of Network Functions Virtualization (NFV) and Software-Defined Networking (SDN) technologies as key enablers of truly dynamic and automated service management in 5G networks, including multiple recurrent provisioning, maintenance, and service resilience [1].

The combination of NFV and SDN capabilities is the base for a required paradigm shift in the way 5G networks will be planned, deployed, and operated, i.e., to truly achieve autonomic management of 5G networks. The main target is to achieve a highly intelligent management platform for smart self-management of complex networking scenarios where proactive and reactive actions are automated in order to resolve and mitigate a wide plethora of networking problems (from performance issues to network failures and cyber-attacks), thus minimizing the intensive manual maintenance and troubleshooting tasks for network operators, leading to significant decrease in operational costs.

Such a novel paradigm for fully-automated and highly intelligent self-organized network (SON) management must provide four key functionalities in a continuous loop for automated detection and reaction to cyber-attacks, following the well-known MAPE approach: Monitor, Analyze, Plan, and Execute, as depicted in Figure 1. In *Monitor* phase, dedicated SDN-enabled sensors are deployed in the network infrastructure to facilitate system-wide distributed monitoring. These sensors are basically not only traditional monitoring sensors deployed in physical infrastructures, but also NFV and SDN applications spread across edge and core ETSI-compliant NFV Infrastructures (NFVI) Points of Presence (PoPs) that enable end-to-end user, network, and service awareness by means of specialized security-related metrics. At *Analyze* phase, the heterogeneous and specialized metrics collected during monitor feed data analysis processes encompassing scalable data analytics and machine learning techniques to produce key indicators and symptoms in the form of high-level metrics for particular 5G service affecting conditions, such as security threats, intrusions, denials of service, etc. At *Plan* phase indicators and symptoms generated by the data analysis processes are then combined and further analyzed to produce high-level tactical actions with the aim of reacting (possibly in a proactive mode) to the diagnosed conditions. The goal of the Plan task is to take decisions upon heterogeneous network security issues, which translate into actions to be enforced for network and service re-configuration. Finally, at *Execute* phase, the action plan is enforced over the heterogeneous physical and virtualized 5G network infrastructure. Either deployment of new SDN-enabled virtualized actuators, or re-configuration of

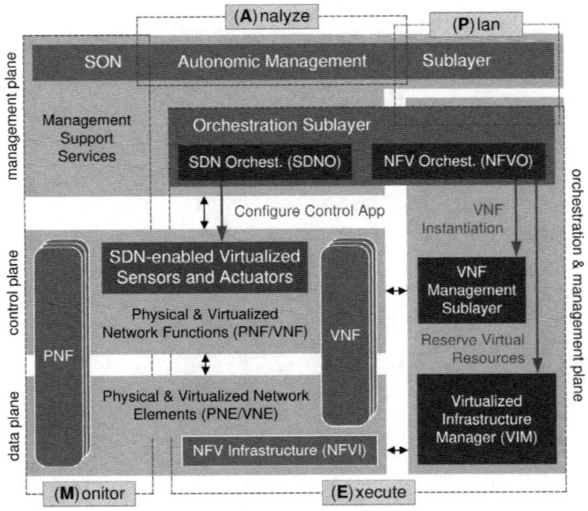

Figure 1. Autonomic network management architecture with NFV & SDN.

existing NFV and SDN applications may be included in action plans. End-to-end service orchestration is needed to coordinate lifecycle management of end-to-end 5G services composed by NFV and SDN applications.

The above concepts are the building blocks in the reference architecture depicted in Figure 1 where the self-organized management platform suitable for 5G networks and services is addressed under the SELFNET research project, funded by the EC under the Phase 1 of the 5G Public Private Partnership (5G-PPP) within the H2020 Framework Programme. SELFNET specifically addresses these network management challenges of 5G networks by closing the control loop while leveraging and enhancing standard NFV management and orchestration approaches currently targeted by ETSI NFV [2].

This paper presents a self-organized management approach, compliant with the MAPE approach, which aims at detecting and mitigating cyber-attacks in 5G mobile networks. Dedicated NFV and SDN applications for the purpose of cyber-attacks conducted by botnets are described (Section II), as well as orchestration (Section III) and lifecycle (Section IV) management principles and workflows for their effective operation in 5G scenarios. Conclusions are finally drawn in Section V.

II. Detection and Mitigation of Botnets in 5G Mobile Networks

5G networks, like any other radio communication systems, are prone to being compromised by attackers who use elements connected to the 5G antennas (the users equipments –UEs), to serve as a stepping stone for launching cyber-attacks, such as Distributed Denial of Service (DDoS) attacks, among others. In 5G, the detection and mitigation of botnets will present an even greater challenge due to the massive number of connected devices as well as a higher data rate. To this end, we propose decoupling traditional botnet detection procedures into two phases at two complementary levels of abstraction; namely:

1) Detection at *high-level* to proactively identify suspect Command & Control (C&C) channels, by monitoring and analyzing network traffic flows exclusively.
2) Fine-granularity detection at *low-level* through Deep Packet Inspection (DPI) to confirm the real existence of the C&C channels detected in the previous phase.

Monitoring network flows during the first high-level detection phase allows us to analyze big volumes of data quickly and in near real-time. A deep analysis of network packets is not feasible in a first step due to the massive amount of traffic in the network. For this reason, the deep analysis is conducted in a second step between the peers identified as suspects during the first step, but carrying it out for a much smaller number of peers. The *sensor* in charge of gathering the traffic network flows to be subsequently analyzed, from a high-level detection perspective, is called *Flow-Based Monitoring* (FBM), while the deep analysis is performed by a DPI tool, such as Snort [3]. The latter also acts as a sensor, although at lower granularity than the other. Both phases make reference to the two detection control loops defined in the Self-Protection use case within the 5G-PPP SELFNET project [4], which is augmented in this paper by the full integration of end-to-end orchestration and application management components so as to proactively detect potential botnets in 5G mobile networks.

Once the second detection phase confirms the actual existence of the botnet, our approach is based on the deployment of a reaction based on the so-called deception approach to counter the botnet and, consequently, the potential cyber-attacks that it could produce. This reaction consists of deploying and enforcing a virtualized and personalized honeynet as an *actuator* (HNet) by using honeytoken techniques [5] to isolate the UEs shaping the botnet. It aims at cloning the botnet zombies –UEs known as *bots*– to emulate their behaviors. As a result, the real attacker (i.e., the botnet's owner) will not be aware that part of the attack actions have been disabled by the HNet. Sensors and actuators, as detailed earlier and summarized in Table I, are dynamically deployed and operated as NFV applications (see Section IV).

For their operation, i) the DPI sensor needs access to the raw network packets exchanged between the suspicious peers to be inspected and ii) the HNet actuator requires the network flows of the C&C channels detected by the DPI to be redirected to the emulated bots while blocking the real ones. To this end, an actuator listed in Table I as FlowT has been implemented as an SDN application to reconfigure the flow tables of the virtual switches providing the following two features:

- *Network Flow Mirroring* to send copy of the network packets of given peers to the DPI for their inspection, thereby starting the second detection control loop.
- *Network Flow Diversion* to redirect the network flows of given peers to the HNet, where they are isolated to avoid cyber-attacks (*mitigation phase*) and learn new knowledge when changing botnet behavioral patterns.

The whole set of detection and mitigation actions for these two control loops mostly matches the bottom layers in Figure 1. The *SON Autonomic Management Layer* sitting on top provides those autonomic features needed to have an intelligence-driven 5G management platform. It is in charge of analyzing the metrics and events gathered from the sensors and deciding *when*, *where*, and *how* to deploy and configure sensors and actuators in a coordinated way.

Figure 2 shows the overall workflow aimed at detecting and mitigating botnets in 5G networks, expanding the previous SON Autonomic Management Layer in a pool of modules addressing the MAPE capabilities, as detailed in Section III.

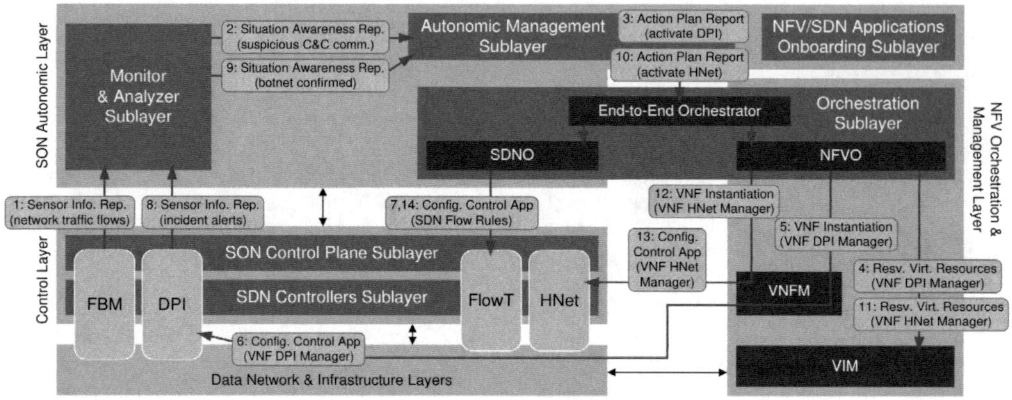

Figure 2. Overall workflow for detecting and mitigating botnets in 5G mobile networks.

TABLE I. SET OF NFV- AND SDN-APPS DEFINED FOR THE SELF-PROTECTION USE CASE.

Name	Type	Short description	Input data	Output data
FBM	NFV-App (sensor)	Flow-based monitoring for high-level detection of suspect C&C channels	Raw network packets	Metrics on the network status: Number of packets, size, frequency between peers, etc.
DPI	NFV-App (sensor)	Deep packet inspection for detecting distributed threats (e.g., bots) at low level	Raw network packets	Alerts or events that report incidents on a cyber-attack or the confirmation of existence of bots
HNet	NFV-App (actuator)	Build a virtualized and personalized honeynet by creating fake bots	List of new threat targets (incl. the attackers' IP addresses to be diverted) and configuration	Network traffic sent to the C&C server emulating the real bots' behavior
FlowT	SDN-App (actuator)	Reconfigure the flow tables of the vSwitches to enable DPI and HNet	New flow tables for the affected/under attack virtual network	New traffic steering policies to be routed to the OpenDaylight controller(s)

Specifically, pattern recognition techniques are being used in SELFNET for the first high-level detection phase, so as to identify similar patterns in behavior between peers, while DPI tools with 5G support, such as Snort, provide the expected deep analysis in raw network packets depending on the botnet type (identified as suspected by the first autonomic loop). These detection phases are encompassed by the *Monitor & Analyzer Sublayer*, which feeds the *Autonomic Management Sublayer* with potential *symptoms* about a security-related problem. This latter examines the detected symptom, searching the *causes* that produced it and deciding certain actions (*tactics*) through machine learning techniques to be enforced. Reinforcement learning techniques are also used to further refine the previous decision-making process, by making use of reward (and punishment) mechanisms in case the tactical actions help to detect other bots.

With a pool of sensors and actuators already deployed in the network, 5G mobile users can move from one location to another, implying that deployed detection or mitigation functions will need to be adapted accordingly. They should be moved following users' mobility, in order to continue monitoring and analyzing those UEs under inspection (detection phase) or even emulating their behaviors (mitigation phase) as was previously done. As an example, consider the 5G mobile scenario shown in Figure 3.

In this figure, one or more UEs served from RAN1 move and are served by RAN2. In the case that they were being analyzed (by a DPI) or emulated (by a HNet) in RAN1, the corresponding sensors and/or actuators capabilities will be dynamically migrated to RAN2 to keep their detection and mitigation processes up and running (either with new deployments or re-using existing applications in RAN2).

For scalability purposes, multiple distributed SDN controllers may be deployed to control specific segments of the network, all managed by the *Orchestration Sublayer* acting as a centralized coordination point.

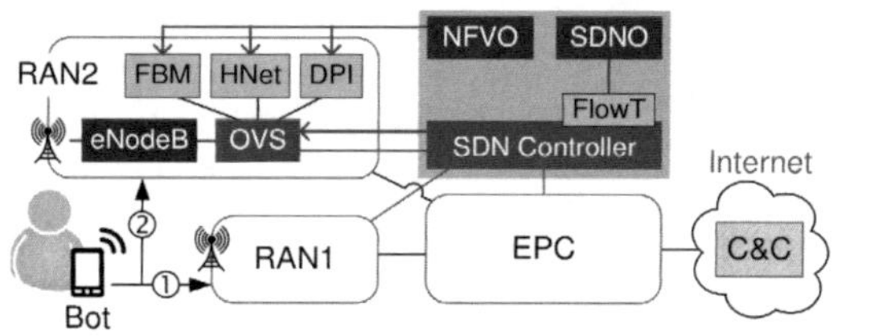

Figure 3. 5G mobile scenario where combining NFV- and SDN-Apps.

III. END-TO-END ORCHESTRATION OF COMBINED NFV AND SDN APPLICATIONS

The evolution towards a 5G enabled service architecture will lead to the creation of a new service environment, built over a mesh of micro data centers (also known as PoPs) coordinated by advanced service management platforms. These platforms, including advanced virtual infrastructure management platforms, will provide enhanced agility for new services creation and operation, being also a contributor for costs reduction due to use of common purpose hardware.

At present time, the creation of a new service requires the setup of an engineering project to coordinate and govern the configuration of several distinct network elements and the creation of specific service logic in proprietary delivery and control platforms. Additionally, the management of this distributed service intelligence over several network appliances (also known as Physical Network Functions –PNFs) requires the setup of complex management processes. All this together compromises the agility to launch new services. The migration of service logic to virtualized (VNFs) and software-defined functions (SDN-Apps), allows the service provider to reduce significantly the operational impact of launching new services.

A complete autonomic management loop opens the possibility to explore a wide set of new use-cases for service providers, usually known as self-* (e.g., self-healing, self-protection, self-optimization). Nevertheless, the challenges to orchestrate NFV and SDN applications are much more complex when compared with physical functions. Virtual and software-defined functions can be dynamically on-boarded, provisioned, started, paused, and stopped, whereas the management procedures over physical functions are much more limited and static. The instantiation of a virtual and/or software-defined network service is expected to be a fully automated procedure, without human intervention, while the instantiation of a physical service sometimes requires the explicit intervention of human resources on the field.

In this context, Operational Support Systems (OSS) are naturally evolving to deal with such a wide and differentiated pool of resource types (VNFs, PNFs, and SDN-Apps) in order to provide end-to-end services composed by any combination of virtual, legacy, or SDN-based function. In particular, the need for a holistic orchestration component, which combines all the required logical resources management to deliver a service, must be provided. This component, known as End-to-End Service Orchestrator (E2E-SO) and its main interactions is briefly depicted in Figure 4.

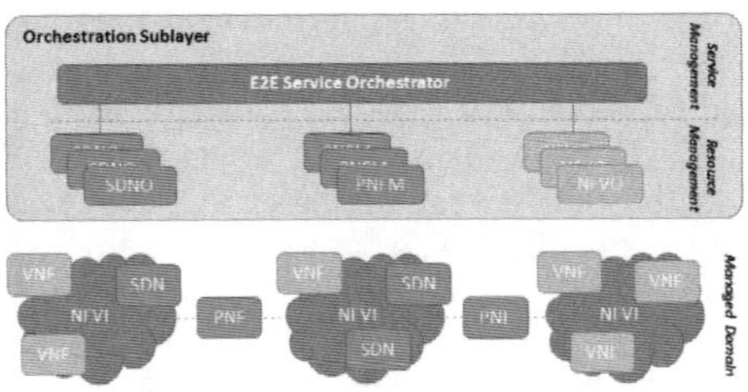

Figure 4. 5G End-to-End Service Orchestrator high-level concept.

According to the E2E-SO concept, software components (SDN-Apps and VNFs) are dynamically managed and configured for provisioning E2E services through the utilization of Resource and Application Management modules. The displayed PNFM concept regards the need for on-the-fly reconfiguration of PNFs and delivery of an E2E service that spans beyond the borders of a single PoP. This need is addressed in the context of the Application Management abstraction that is realized by the instantiation of a pool of adaptation objects per resource instance (PNF, SDN-App, VNF), which enable a scalable orchestration approach spanning multiple domains and PoPs. This pool of objects provides a common interface to be utilized by the E2E-SO during instantiation, configuration, and reconfiguration of the three resources types. In the case of PNFs, the adaptation objects are generated by manual registration of the PNFs available in each PoP, whereas for the SDN-Apps and VNFs the lifecycle management triggers the automated provisioning of the related configuration objects.

Applying the E2E orchestration concept to the concrete case of cyber-attacks, the E2E-SO will have a key role in both autonomic loops of the scenario, being the entity responsible for orchestrating all the required elements to deliver the action required by the autonomic manager, as depicted in Figure 2.

Before the first control loop, the E2E-SO is key to deploy and configure the FBM VNF sensor, which will be responsible to provide the flows monitoring and therefore trigger the first control loop. Thereafter, during the first autonomic loop, based on the monitored flows (step 1) through the FBM VNF, a suspicious botnet symptom is detected (step 2). As a result of this symptom, in order to ensure that a cyber-attack is happening, the autonomic manager requests the E2E-SO to activate a DPI to analyze the suspicious botnet network traffic (step 3). The E2E-SO instantiates (if not yet instantiated for other tenants) and configures a DPI VNF sensor (in this case Snort) according to the information (e.g., location, botnet signature, etc.) provided by the autonomic manager (steps 4, 5, and 6). The E2E-SO interacts with the NFVO to deploy and configure the DPI VNF. Additionally, still as a result of the first autonomic loop, the E2E-SO is also responsible for requesting the SDNO to activate and configure the FlowT SDN-App to apply, through the SDN Controller, the mirroring of the potential zombie network traffic towards the deployed DPI VNF (step 7).

At this stage the second autonomic loop is started and, as a result, when a potential zombie is confirmed as an attack, an event is triggered by Snort (step 8). This event is processed, filtered, enriched, and provided to the autonomic manager (step 9) confirming that a cyber-attack is taking place. Consequently, the autonomic manager requests the E2E-SO the isolation of the attack (step 10). As a result, the E2E-SO requests the NFVO the deployment and configuration of a HNet VNF in order to create emulated zombies (steps 11-13). Finally, the E2E-SO has to coordinate the diversion of the attacker network traffic towards the HNet by requesting the SDNO to configure (step 14) the FlowT SDN-App for this action. In the end, zombies being attacked are isolated.

IV. Automated Management of Sensors and Actuators Lifecycle

5G networks pose challenging requirements in terms of automation and performance for deployment of new services. The aspect of network management is being critical for the efficient provisioning and maintenance of new services in 5G networks. In accordance to the 5G KPIs [6], the reduction of services provisioning time from 90 days to 90 minutes is possible if the whole lifecycle of network functions and applications to be deployed and combined as services in the 5G network infrastructure is managed by means of coordinated and automated procedures.

Common and homogeneous mechanisms and procedures are needed to manage the whole lifecycle of individual NFV- and SDN-Apps (i.e., instantiation, configuration, start, stop, scale, termination, etc.) irrespectively of their specific logic or function. This means that sensors and actuators listed in Section II need to be properly encapsulated to be coordinated by the E2E-SO and achieve a high degree of automation in the detection and mitigation of cyber-attacks.

A. NFV and SDN Applications Onboarding

The very first aspect of lifecycle management of NFV- and SDN-Apps refers to their onboarding in the management platform. With reference to Figure 2, this is provided by the *NFV/SDN Application Onboarding Sublayer*. When an application is onboarded it becomes available to be instantiated, configured, and composed with other applications and network functions in support of specific E2E 5G services. However, the onboarding sublayer is more than a simple catalogue listing applications and network functions. It is a full onboarding service, managing a set of operations including applications onboard, enable, disable, update, and offboard, with management of software images for VNFs and SDN bundles upload for SDN-Apps. Moreover, the onboarding service is responsible for notifying all these operations within the management platform to all those components involved in the applications lifecycle management and operation (mostly E2E-SO, SDNO, and NFVO).

Starting from the VNF Package definitions in the ETSI MANO specifications [2], we defined the concept of App Package to support the one-click automated onboarding of both NFV- and SDN-Apps with a common approach valid for all kinds of sensors and actuators. An App Package is a single entity (in the form of a software archive), which encapsulates a given sensor or actuator. It is the container of all the information needed to operate a given application, including a set of information organized in folders and JSON files. In particular, the full structure of an App Package is shown in Figure 5.

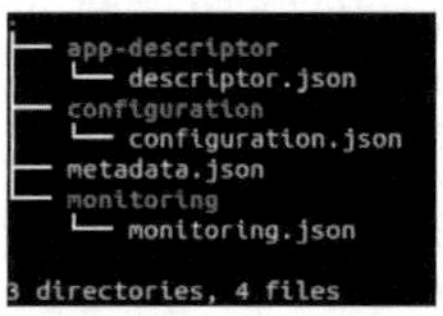

Figure 5. App Package structure.

In this context, the structure of an App Package includes a set of JSON files organized as follows:

- *metadata.json*: includes generic onboarding information for the application, like application family (sensor or actuator), class (VNF or SDN-App), and type, augmented with specific software image and bundles registration data. For VNFs, it also includes information of specific lifecycle scripts to be used to apply actions on the VNF.
- *app-descriptor/*: it is the folder containing the app descriptor file *app-d.json*, which provides information related to requirements for instantiation and management, in terms of resources to be allocated and configured for proper app operation. For VNFs, it follows the standard VNF Descriptor (VNFD) format defined by ETSI [2]
- *configuration/*: it is the folder containing the app configuration information file *configuration.json*, which provides information related to the configuration primitives actions exposed by the App. It models parameters and actions to be applied for proper management and control of the specific app operational behaviors
- *monitoring/*: it is the folder containing the app monitoring information file *monitoring.json*, which provides information related to the monitoring metrics exposed by the app when it is a sensor. It models both metric parameters and operations to collect them.

B. Lifecycle Management of NFV Applications: VNFM

The reference baseline for the NFV applications encapsulation is the ETSI MANO framework [2], with the VNFM as key component responsible for the lifecycle management of all the sensor and actuator VNFs listed in Section II. The VNFM aims to provide a unified and common approach for the lifecycle management of sensor and actuator VNFs, thus exposing primitives towards Orchestration Sublayer components (e.g., the NFVO) to instantiate and control the VNFs in the NFV Infrastructure. The VNFM functions as defined by ETSI can be considered as generic and common functions applicable to any type of VNF. The VNFM depicted in Figure 2 implements the following VNF lifecycle management operations specified by ETSI: 1) VNF instantiation, including VNF configuration according to the VNFD included in the correspondent App Package, which describes attributes and requirements to realize such VNF and provision it; 2) VNF instance modification, that basically consists into an update of the VNF configuration; 3) VNF instance scale out/in (i.e., allocate or terminate Virtual Machines in support of a given VNF) and up/down (i.e., increase or decrease virtual resources for a given VNF); and 4) VNF instance termination.

We implemented the VNFM as a stand-alone prototype [7] on top of the OpenBaton open source project, and enhanced it for this work to integrate the DPI and HNet VNFs. OpenBaton [8] is an ETSI MANO compliant tool, which can be easily integrated with existing cloud platforms like OpenStack [9] and adapted to different types of VNFs. For each VNF, a lifecycle management agent is embedded in the correspondent Virtual Machine to enable the communication with the VNFM and implement specific actions on the VNF according to the lifecycle scripts included in the App Package. The agent enables the containerization of VNFs into encapsulated VNFs and provide a common lifecycle management message bus interface based on RabbitMQ [10] towards the VNFM, i.e., in support of the four operations described above. In particular, with reference to the VNFs listed in Section II (i.e., the DPI and the HNet), and the workflow in Figure 2, this message bus interface is used in steps 6 and 13 for taking care of VNFs configurations during the two control loops.

For the DPI VNF, the configuration operation allows the Snort application to start inspecting those network flows identified by the Monitor and Analyzer components as suspected to belong to a potential botnet. The Snort VNF is indeed configured with the following parameters: i) IP addresses and ports identifying the suspected network flow involving the potential bot and C&C server and ii) the detection rule, specifying the pattern or payload content to be identified by the DPI engine. For the HNet VNF, the configuration operation enables the emulation of a bot identified by the second loop of Monitor and Analyzer detections. In practice, the HNet is configured by the VNFM with: i) type of botnet to be emulated; ii) frequency of the requests to be sent to C&C server; iii) identifier of the bot to be emulated; and iv) IP address of the C&C server.

C. Lifecycle Management of SDN Applications: SDNO

The concept of the SDN Application Management, as realized by SDNO foresees two types of applications: i) SDN-Apps, which regard software components that are deployed and executed in a runtime environment outside the SDN Controller and utilize its NorthBound Interface (NBI), this being, in practical terms, an SDN-App implementing a network application logic that is carried out through a number of transactions with the Northbound interfaces of the SDN Controller focusing on specific high level tasks, such as extracting topology information or network metrics, applying any forwarding rules, etc.; and ii) SDN-Controller-Apps, which are software packages deployed directly in the SDN Controller runtime environment utilizing directly the services provided by other components of the controller or by southbound protocol plug-ins.

In essence, SDN-Apps intent to abstract the details of the Northbound Interface of the SDN Controller, as offered by the various features and bundles activated in the Controller, and while they are handling internally the complexity required to apply a particular forwarding rule or isolate and expose a view of the information that is available in the Controller, at the same time they are providing a uniform interface to be invoked in the context of an end to end service orchestration. This interface streamlines the way information has to be structured and contextualized so that the applications can be catalogued in terms of what is offering and what high level (abstracting SDN Controller NBI model) parameters are required in order to offer it. On the other hand, SDN-Controller-Apps are structured and developed according to the SDN Controller's principles and they are exporting their application model via the controller's NBI. Typically, the SDNO based approach focuses on the development of a number of SDN-Apps that enable a more effective and targeted use of what is offered by SDN-Controller-Apps.

An SDN-App may be included in various service compositions, which in turn may require that a separate instance of the app implementation is launched per service. Thus, contrary to the shared nature of SDN-Controller-Apps, SDN-Apps may be instantiated multiple times with each instance being associated with a particular tenant. Instantiation of an SDN-App can occur only after proper insertion of the app in the onboarding catalogue, which is reflected on the SDNO in terms of registration of the app implementation under the particular app type REST endpoint. The SDNO assigns to the newly registered app an implementation order identifier that is thereafter used by the SDNO to export the implementation for management purposes towards the E2E-SO. The supported management functions include app removal, which is triggered by the onboarding catalogue and instance management requested by the E2E-SO. For every app registered with the SDNO, the configuration extract from its descriptor (as presented in Section IV-A above) is collected from the notification generated by the onboarding catalogue through the message bus. This piece of information is processed by an adaptation object, which the SDNO is generating when an instance of the SDN-App is requested by the E2E-SO. The object analyses the configuration descriptor and provides a unique REST endpoint for every action the SDN-App is offering, to be invoked by the E2E-SP whenever the configuration of the SDN-App has to be updated. The configuration for all the apps is based on a key-value format. The adaptation object is also launching a Docker container [11] from a Docker image where the SDN-App binaries are installed. Those binaries are thereafter configured via execution commands through the Docker API according to the communication (remote execution, REST, environment variable settings) protocol indicated in the onboarding descriptor.

For the FlowT SDN-App, the SDNO prepares a Docker image with Python support and installs the FlowT implementation therein. For any instance of the app that is requested by the Orchestrator a separate Docker container based on the previous image is instantiated and an adaptor object is started. The adaptor object exports a number of action endpoints relating to the FlowT configuration actions (*"mirror"*, *"divert"*, *"mirror-del"*, *"divert-del"*, *"remove-all"*). The E2E-SO may post thereafter, to the proper REST endpoint identified by the FlowT instance ID, the required JSON formatted configuration sets as {*"key": "key name","value": "requested value for key"*} arrays, that communicate the specific parameters required for activating the related action. In the case of *"mirror"*, action the following parameters have to be defined: source and destination IP addresses of the flow, the IP address of Snort, and the identifier of the OVS instance to be configured. Similarly, for *"divert"* action the parameters are the same but instead of the Snort IP the HNet IP address has to be provided.

V. CONCLUSIONS

5G networks will need to be managed in a very flexible, dynamic, and scalable way, targeting a high degree of automation in the deployment of new services on top of virtualized and distributed infrastructures. This paper presented a self-organized network management approach where autonomic functions are combined with NFV- and SDN-Apps for detection and mitigation of cyber-attacks conducted by botnets. While NFV- and SDN-Apps, together with VNFM and SDNO lifecycle management functions, have been developed and integrated into virtualized testbed infrastructures, future work will involve implementation of E2E-SO and autonomic components.

ACKNOWLEDGMENT

This work was partially funded by the EC H2020 5G-PPP Programme under Grant Agreement number 671672 - SELFNET (*Framework for Self-Organized Network Management in Virtualized and Software Defined Networks*), and by a Séneca Foundation grant within the Human Resources Researching Training Program 2014 (FEDER/ERDF).

REFERENCES

[1] C. Cleder Machado, L. Zambenedetti Granville, and A. Schaeffer-Filho, "ANSwer: Combining NFV and SDN features for network resilience strategies," Proceedings of the 2016 IEEE Symposium on Computers and Communication, pp. 391-396, June 2016.

[2] ETSI NFV ISG, "Network Functions Virtualisation (NFV); Management and Orchestration," ETSI GS NFV-MAN 001 V1.1.1, Dec. 2014.

[3] Sourcefire, Inc., "Snort: An open source network intrusion detection and prevention system," https://www.snort.org [retrieved: March, 2017]

[4] M. Gil Pérez and G. Bernini, "Self-protection against botnet attacks - Solutions by 5G PPP project SELFNET," Eurescom Message, pp. 13-14, Winter 2016.

[5] W. Fan, D. Fernández, and Z. Du, "Versatile virtual honeynet management framework," IET Information Security, vol. 11, no. 1, pp. 38-45, Jan. 2017.

[6] The 5G Infraestructure Public Private Partnership, "Key Performance Indicators (KPI)," https://5g-ppp.eu/kpis [retrieved: March, 2017]

[7] G. Bernini, E. Kraja, G. Carrozzo, G. Landi, and N. Ciulli, "SELFNET Virtual Network Functions Manager: A common approach for lifecycle management of NFV applications," Proceedings of 2016 5th IEEE International Conference on Cloud Networking, pp. 150-153, Oct. 2016.

[8] The OpenBaton project, "A ETSI NFV compliant MANO framework," http://openbaton.github.io [retrieved: March, 2017]

[9] The OpenStack project, http://openstack.org [retrieved: March, 2017]

[10] Pivotal Software, Inc., "RabbitMQ message queue service," https://www.rabbitmq.com [retrieved: March, 2017]

[11] Docker, "The world's leading software container platform," https://www.docker.com [retrieved: March, 2017]

AUTHOR INDEX

International Academy, Research,
and Industry Association (IARIA)
412 Derby Way
Wilmington, DE 19810

ISBN 978-1-5108-4316-5

9 781510 843165

Ninth International Conference on eHealth, Telemedicine, and Social Medicine (eTELEMED 2017)

Held at DigitalWorld 2017

Nice, France
19 - 23 March 2017

IARIA